On Deaths and Endings

On Deaths and Endings brings together the work of psychoanalytic scholars and practitioners grappling with the manifold issues evoked by loss and finality.

The book covers the impact of endings throughout the life cycle, including effects on children, adolescents, adults, those near death and entire societies. New psycho-analytic perspectives on bereavement are offered based on clinical work, scholarly research and the authors' own, deeply personal experiences. The contributors present compelling, often moving, inquiries into subjects such as the reconfiguration of self-states subsequent to mourning, the role of ritual and memorials, the tragic impact of unmourned loss, modern conceptualizations of the death instinct, and terror-based losses.

In that much psychotherapy is conducted with people who have suffered some form of loss, this book will be an invaluable resource for all mental health professionals. The emphasis on the potential of working through the vicissitudes of these experiences will provide inspiration and hope both to those who have endured personal loss and to anyone working with grieving patients.

Brent Willock is President of the Toronto Institute for Contemporary Psycho-analysis and a member of the faculty of the Toronto Child Psychoanalytic Program and the Institute for the Advancement of Self Psychology.

Lori C. Bohm is a member of the faculty and Supervising Analyst at the William Alanson White Institute, New York, and Supervisor of Psychotherapy at City College of New York and St Luke's/Roosevelt Hospital Center.

Rebecca C. Curtis is a member of the faculty and Supervisor at William Alanson White Institute, New York, Supervisor at the National Institute for the Psycho-therapies and Professor of Psychology at Adelphi University.

Contributors: Anna Aragno, Lori C. Bohm, Mark B. Borg, Olga Cox Cameron, Rebecca C. Curtis, Veronica Fiske, Rita V. Frankiel, Bruce Herzog, Sharron W. Kaplan, Yuko Katsuta, Anita Weinreb Katz, David Kirschner, Glenys Lobban, Karen Lombardi, Stephen W. Long, Michael O'Loughlin, Judith Lingle Ryan, Ionas Sapountzis, Ross M. Skelton. Joyce Slochower, Vamik D. Volkan, Sara Weber, J. Gail White,

D1145406

Contents

On Deaths and Endings

Psychoanalysts' reflections on finality,
transformations and new beginnings

Edited by Brent Willock, Lori C. Bohm
and Rebecca C. Curtis

Routledge
Taylor & Francis Group

LONDON AND NEW YORK

Rebecca C. Curtis; individual chapters, the contributors

Typeset in Times by Garfield Morgan, Swansea, West Glamorgan
Printed and bound in Great Britain by TJ International Ltd, Padstow, Cornwall
Cover design by Lisa Dynan

British Library Cataloguing in Publication Data
A catalogue record for this book is available from the British Library

Library of Congress Cataloging in Publication Data
On deaths and endings : psychoanalysts' reflections on finality,
transformations and new beginnings / editors Brent Willock, Lori C. Bohm,
Rebecca C. Curtis.
      p. cm.
   Includes bibliographical references and index.
   ISBN 0-415-39662-X (hbk) – ISBN 0-415-39663-8 (pbk) 1. Death–
Psychological aspects. 2. Bereavement–Psychological aspects. 3. Loss
(Psychology) 4. Psychoanalysis. I. Willock, Brent. II. Bohm, Lori C. III. Curtis,
Rebecca C.

   BF789.D4O5 2007
   155.9'3–dc22
                                                  2006017655

ISBN 978-0-415-39662-2 (hbk)
ISBN 978-0-415-39663-9 (pbk)

PART IX
Conclusion

Contributors

Anna Aragno, PhD Psychoanalyst and author; previously faculty and supervisor, Post Graduate Center for Mental Health and Washington Square Institute, New York City.

Lori C. Bohm, PhD Supervising analyst and faculty, William Alanson White Institute; supervisor of psychotherapy, Clinical Psychology Doctoral Program, City College of New York and St. Luke's/Roosevelt Hospital Center; private practice in New York City and Hastings-on-Hudson.

Mark B. Borg, Jr, PhD Community/clinical psychologist and interpersonal psychoanalyst; graduate, Psychoanalytic Certification Program, William Alanson White Institute; cofounder and principal partner, Community Consulting Group, a community revitalization organization; lives and practices in New York City.

Olga Cox Cameron, PhD Psychoanalyst, private practice; lecturer, postgraduate courses in psychoanalytic theory, psychoanalysis and literature, St. Vincent's University Hospital and Trinity College, Dublin.

Rebecca C. Curtis, PhD Faculty and supervisor, William Alanson White Institute; supervisor, National Institute for the Psychotherapies; professor of psychology, Adelphi University.

Veronica Fiske, PhD Supervisor and senior psychologist, Queens Hospital; candidate, Postdoctoral Program in Psychoanalysis and Psychotherapy, Adelphi University; private practice, Manhattan.

Rita V. Frankiel, PhD Training and supervising analyst, New York Freudian Society; associate clinical professor, Postdoctoral Program in Psychoanalysis and Psychotherapy, New York University; fellow, International Psychoanalytic Association; lecturer, child psychoanalysis, Center for Psychoanalytic Training and Research, Columbia University.

Bruce Herzog, MD Psychoanalyst; faculty, Toronto Institute of Psychoanalysis, Toronto Institute for Contemporary Psychoanalysis and the Institute for Advancement of Self Psychology; private practice, Toronto.

Sharron W. Kaplan, DSW Graduate, Postdoctoral Program in Psychoanalysis and Psychotherapy, Adelphi University; faculty, Mt. Sinai Medical School; private practice, Manhattan.

Yuko Katsuta, MD Practitioner learning psychoanalysis and psychotherapy at William Alanson White Institute and National Psychological Association for Psychoanalysis, New York City.

Anita Weinreb Katz, PhD Clinical psychologist; faculty, Postdoctoral Program in Psychoanalysis and Psychotherapy, New York University, the Object Relations Institute and the Metropolitan Institute for Psychoanalytic Psychotherapy; member, Institute for Psychoanalytic Training and Research; fellow, International Psychoanalytic Association; private practice, individuals and couples, Manhattan.

David Kirschner, PhD Graduate, Postdoctoral Program in Psychoanalysis and Psychotherapy, Adelphi University; founding director, Nassau Center for Psychotherapy and South Shore Institute for Advanced Studies; private practice, Merrick and Woodbury, NY.

Glenys Lobban, PhD Clinical psychologist and psychoanalyst; graduate, Postdoctoral Program in Psychoanalysis and Psychotherapy, New York University; supervisor, Clinical Psychology Doctoral Program, City University of New York; lives and practices in New York City.

Karen Lombardi, PhD Professor, Derner Institute of Advanced Psychological Studies, Garden City, NY; faculty, Postdoctoral Program in Psychoanalysis and Psychotherapy, Adelphi University; faculty, Northwest Center of Psychoanalysis, Portland, Oregon and Seattle, Washington; private practice, Sea Cliff, NY.

Stephen W. Long, PhD Clinical psychologist/psychoanalyst; adjunct professor, psychology of aging, Derner Institute of Advanced Psychological Studies, Garden City, NY; clinical supervisor, predoctoral internship, geropsychology rotation, Department of Veterans' Affairs Medical Center, Northport, NY; private practice, Huntington, NY.

Michael O'Loughlin, PhD Faculty member and supervisor, Derner Institute of Advanced Psychological Studies, Garden City, NY; faculty member, School of Education, Adelphi University; private practice, New Hyde Park, NY.

Judith Lingle Ryan, MSW Graduate, Westchester Center for Psychoanalysis and Psychotherapy; recently retired from private practice, Nyack, NY; now a writer.

Ionas Sapountzis, PhD Professor, School Psychology Program, Long Island University; faculty and supervisor, Postdoctoral Program in Psychoanalysis and Psychotherapy, Derner Institute, of Advanced Psychological Studies, Garden City, NY.

Ross M. Skelton, MSc Senior lecturer, philosophy and logic, Trinity College, Dublin; founder, MSc Program in Clinical Psychotherapy and MPhil Program in Psychoanalytic Studies, Trinity College; editor in chief, *International Encyclopaedia of Psychoanalysis*; private practice, psychoanalytic psychotherapy, Dublin.

Joyce Slochower, PhD, APBB Professor of psychology, Hunter College; faculty, Postdoctoral Program in Psychoanalysis and Psychotherapy, New York University, the Object Relations Institute, the National Training Program, and the Psychoanalytic Institute of Northern California.

Vamik D. Volkan, MD Professor emeritus of psychiatry and founder, Center for the Study of Mind and Human Interaction, University of Virginia, Charlottesville, VA; training and supervising analyst emeritus, Washington Psychoanalytic Institute, Washington, DC; Senior Erik Erikson Scholar, Austen Riggs Center, Stockbridge, MA.

Sara Weber, PhD Faculty, Child and Adolescent Training Program, William Alanson White Institute; graduate, Postdoctoral Program in Psychoanalysis and Psychotherapy, New York University; supervisor, Derner Institute of Advanced Psychological Studies, Garden City, NY; practitioner of Buddhism; private practice, Brooklyn, NY.

J. Gail White, PhD Supervising analyst and faculty, Toronto Institute for Contemporary Psychoanalysis; private practice, Toronto.

Brent Willock, PhD President, Toronto Institute for Contemporary Psychoanalysis, Ontario Society for Contemporary Psychoanalysis; faculty, Toronto Child Psychoanalytic Program, Institute for the Advancement of Self Psychology; advisory board, International Association for Relational Psychoanalysis and Psychotherapy.

Acknowledgments

The editors wish to thank the Joint International Conference planning committee: Drs. Mary Anne Geskie, Cynthia Heller, Rebecca C. Curtis, Frances Newman, Ross Skelton, Lori C. Bohm, Brent Willock. Their labor laid firm foundations for the stimulating discussions that eventually evolved into this book. For special mention, we would like to single out Dr. Michael Stern, who chaired the committee with common sense, calmness, and good humor. For their crucial support, we would also like to thank the members of the psychoanalytic societies of New York University's Postdoctoral Program in Psychoanalysis and Psychotherapy, Adelphi University's Postdoctoral Program in Psychoanalysis and Psychotherapy, the William Alanson White Institute, the Irish Forum for Psychoanalytic Psychotherapy, and the Toronto Institute for Contemporary Psychoanalysis. Ms. Kate Hawes and her staff at Routledge, including the anonymous reviewers, have been extremely supportive from the beginning of our contacts with them. Our authors, too, have blessed us with their unwavering commitment. It has been delightful to work with them through all phases of this collective enterprise. Finally, our families deserve special gratitude for accepting, with grace, significant periods of time in which we were otherwise preoccupied. For everyone's support, including many not mentioned, a heartfelt thank you.

Part I

Overture to finality

Chapter 1

Thoughts for our times on transience and transformation

Brent Willock

> To know death better is to put it back in its rightful place.
> (Louis-Vincent Thomas, *Anthropologie de la mort*)

Prelude

Freud (1915) was writing in his finest form in the concluding portion of "Thoughts for the times on war and death." Having discussed the depths of degradation that can be activated during international conflagration, he launched his penetrating, final section, "Our attitude towards death," with an arresting remark: "The second factor to which I attribute our present sense of estrangement in this once lovely and congenial world is the disturbance that has taken place in the attitude which we have hitherto adopted towards death" (p. 289). Deficiencies in our capacity to fully face finality, he believed, had serious, negative repercussions with respect to the overall quality of our lives.

Conventional cultural attitudes toward mortality were characterized by the founder of psychoanalysis as "the denial of death" (p. 295). (Years later, that phrase became the title of Ernest Becker's (1973) Pulitzer Prize winning book.) While we routinely espouse the sensible view that death is natural, undeniable, unavoidable, we behave as if it were otherwise, Freud (1915) cogently observed. We prefer to marginalize the topic, "to eliminate it from life" (p. 289). Consequently, when cherished, unconscious illusions of immortality are confronted with actual death, we are deeply affected, "as though we were badly shaken in our expectations" (p. 290). At these uncomfortable moments, unwelcome reality has succeeded in painfully perforating our protective shield of denial. The resulting, disequilibrating experiences range from difficult to traumatic.

Before Freud put his mind to this problem, philosophers had contributed their insights to elucidating the phenomenon of finality. They believed that the intellectual enigma death presented to primeval man forced him to reflection, thereby serving as the starting point for all speculative thought.

While Freud (1915) agreed with these philosophers with respect to the monumental significance of finality, he nonetheless chided them for thinking too philosophically. What released the human spirit of inquiry was not the intellectual enigma, and not every death, he asserted. The essential impetus emanated, rather, from conflictual feelings evoked or exacerbated by the decease of loved ones who are, at least sometimes, perhaps unconsciously, also experienced as alien and hated. His emphasis was on the conflagration of ambivalence precipitated by such loss. "Of this conflict of feeling psychology was the first offspring" (p. 293), he averred. If we lend some credence to both the philosophers and Freud, then we are in a position of pondering the imposing possibility that both philosophy and psychology arose out of early human beings' confrontation with the ashes and bones of the departed.

Projecting himself far back in the cultural evolution of our species, Freud imagined our ancestors tasting the bitter pain of loss of (ambivalently) loved ones. Unable to keep personal death at a safe distance, our forebears were, nonetheless, unwilling to fully acknowledge its power and significance. It was impossible for them (and us) to conceive of themselves as nonexistent, Freud believed. In these stressful circumstances, humans crafted a cunning compromise.

Bowing once more to the imperious actuality of the reality principle, our predecessors conceded that they, too, would die. Nonetheless, they denied this inevitability the significance of annihilation. Beside the deceased body of the beloved, they invented spirits; not the kind to drown our sorrows but, rather, phantoms to elevate élan vital, that is, spirits to raise spirits.

Postmortem physical changes in the dead gave rise to the conception of an individual composed of a body and a separable soul (originally several souls, prefiguring contemporary interest in multiple selves). The persisting memory of the deceased provided a basis for assuming other forms of existence, specifically the powerful notion of life continuing after apparent cessation.

Over time, religions succeeded in representing this afterlife as the more desirable, valid, important one. They managed to reduce the finite existence that had transpired to a mere preparatory phase for the truly significant, eternal, life hereafter. From there, it was relatively easy to extend conceptions of life in the opposite direction, yielding ideas of earlier existences, transmigration of souls, and reincarnation. These potent concepts were skillfully designed and promoted to deprive death of its more incomprehensible, frightening meaning as the total termination of life.

The far-reaching success of this vital human project to rob death of its significance led to unfortunate, unanticipated side-effects. One particularly disturbing sequella was that life became "impoverished, it loses interest . . . It becomes shallow and empty" (p. 290), Freud believed. This affective barrenness consequent to eliminating the full meaning and impact of death from life provided fertile soil for various remedies for our alienation to spring up. One of the more dangerous of these antidotes, Freud thought, was the exhilaration furnished by international conflagration. "War is bound to sweep away this conventional treatment of death" (p. 291). With the outbreak of hostilities, mortality returns to center stage. Marginalization is reversed. Denial is undone. "Life has, indeed, become interesting again; it has recovered its full content" (p. 291). Assuming Freud's perturbing analysis to have some validity, one can only conclude that we pay a high price, often the supreme one, for underestimating finality.

Nearly a century after Freud shared his disquieting thoughts, Jed Sekoff (1999) noted that psychoanalysis, itself, has a history of beckoning death into its reach, only to push it away. (This ambivalence illustrates what Lewy (1941) referred to as the "return of the repression," that is, defensive disciplinary inattention and regression subsequent to the achievement of insight.) Death hardly sits with sex, attachment, or self at the centre of recent analytic discourse, Sekoff observed. Attempts to think about the subject, such as Green's (1986) or Ogden's (1995) descriptions of deadness as a fundamental psychic entity, have drawn criticism for manifesting an unnecessarily grim vocabulary.

With the advent of the modern era, Sekoff (1999) noted, death receded from the front parlor or bedroom to the funeral home or hospital suite. So, too, has death disappeared from psychoanalytic discourse, abandoned excessively to new age prophets and self-help programs, he observed. The thoughtful contributions in the book you are holding may help bring death back toward the center of the analytic, and broader cultural dialogue.

Sekoff's perspective, like that of so many of our authors, proved personally evocative. It prompted me to recall my own grandfather, who had been a blacksmith in Glengarry County, Canada. His innate strength, reinforced by his daily labor, made him a natural athlete. His prowess at the caber (beam) toss was renowned as far away as Montreal and New York. I, however, remember him more as lying paralyzed for several years in a bed beside his wooden, roll-top desk, a few feet away from the huge, woodburning stove in the kitchen, the warm heart of the home he had built so many years before. Right to the end he was close by the people who meant the most to him. This was a different dying compared to how his daughter, my mother, expired in the company of strangers in a modern, long-term care facility during the time I was editing this book.

Given our tendency to shun this morbid topic or, as Freud put it, "to hush it up" (p. 289), some might question the wisdom of creating a whole book devoted to this theme. Wouldn't a single article suffice? Could such a dreary or terrifying volume ever be an attractive object to its intended audience? Would its very title spell the death of desire? When our colleague, Dr. Art Caspary, proposed a symposium on this subject, some feared it would not fly. It might, instead, go over like the proverbial lead balloon, taking on the dead weight of inanimacy inherent in the topic, rather than providing a more buoyant vehicle suitable for soaring, imaginative, intellectual/clinical adventure. Despite some initial concerns of this nature, it proved fairly easy to achieve unanimity about the importance of promoting scholarly exploration in this area. Consequently, colleagues from the psychoanalytic societies of the William Alanson White Psychoanalytic Institute, New York University's Postdoctoral Program in Psychotherapy and Psychoanalysis, Adelphi University's Postdoctoral Program in Psychoanalysis and Psychotherapy, the Toronto Institute for Contemporary Psychoanalysis, and the Irish Forum for Psychoanalytic Psychotherapy assembled at Trinity College Dublin for a conference on Deaths and Endings in the summer of 2002.

Death, we learned, can be a most engaging, lively topic. War is by no means the only way to transcend the stultifying limitations of traditional attitudes toward this difficult topic. Indeed, the Trinity discussions proved remarkably congenial despite the diverse psychoanalytic viewpoints in attendance that, in some other situations, might have been more inclined to make war rather than love(ly discourse). Nonetheless, war may have played some role in the vitality of this assembly. Our call for papers was circulated shortly before Al Qaeda's attack on Manhattan's World Trade Center. That assault had a powerful impact on the subject matter chosen by several authors and, indeed, on the sense of importance and timeliness many perceived in responding to the call.

Quite apart from the unanticipated influence of September 11, there was something inherently special about a symposium devoted to finality. I was reminded of this unique quality at a meeting of the Toronto Society for Contemporary Psychoanalysis where Dr. Gary Rodin, head of psychosocial oncology and palliative care at the University of Toronto, presented his paper, "Psychoanalytic reflections on mortality." During the discussion, analysts not only engaged with the theoretical points he was making, but also shared their own, very personal experiences pertaining to the death of loved ones. Others, I am sure, were thinking similar thoughts, even if they did not express them. An unusual degree of closeness was established.

This awesome topic seems to promote a certain intimacy. We crave both the theoretical insights our discipline affords and the personal stories we are moved to share when we engage this topic. There is a particular wisdom contained in the stories we exchange at these moments. No doubt from time immemorial, we have sensed the importance of such sharing. When these narratives are integrated with the treasures of theoretical formulation we have been forging during the past century, a powerful, moving literature results. The ensuing chapters provide a rich immersion in this special place, the confluence of personal and theoretical wisdom.

So moving and stimulating were the discussions in Dublin that the spirit propelled us to create this volume. We viewed our mandate as updating and extending an already noble tradition in this area of psychoanalytic investigation. The literature to which we would be contributing includes such classics as Eissler's (1955) *The Psychiatrist and the Dying Patient*. That book, over fifty years old, fruitfully combined theoretical perspectives on thanatology, extensive case illustrations, and thoughtful consideration of the arts. Our work draws on a similarly diverse, but even broader range of viewpoints. We are the beneficiaries of numerous advances in theoretical formulation and clinical practice. The impact of these new ideas is richly reflected throughout the following chapters.

Our authors' chapters cover an impressive array of interrelated topics. Building upon one another, their contributions combine to create a comprehensive view of our complex subject. Immersing oneself in this rich flow of ideas will, I believe, eventuate in a sense that one has not only encountered, but also come to grips with many, if not all, facets of this crucial, challenging topic.

Bereavement

Following this "Overture to finality," the second part of this book (Grief and mourning) commences where all philosophy and psychology may have begun, namely with the emotional tasks, challenges, and opportunities presented by the death of a loved one. In the first of that group of chapters, Dr. Anna Aragno, an accomplished psychoanalytic writer, surveys the vast psychoanalytic literature on mourning. Her division of the relevant research according to themes focused on during various epochs helps organize what can otherwise seem like an overwhelmingly large field of inquiry. Through her work, Dr. Aragno reveals important transformations that have occurred, and continue to evolve in our understanding of bereavement. Like several of our authors, she is unusually self-revelatory, adding authenticity and vitality to her delineation of theory.

In Chapter 3, Dr. Vamik D. Volkan, an eminent contributor to this field, discusses his belief that not only individuals, but also large groups, even entire societies, can have significant problems with bereavement. Nations, like persons, can become stuck in a problematic position of perennial mourning. Differentiating creative from pathological mourning, Dr. Volkan emphasizes the importance of what he calls linking objects and linking phenomena. His interest and expertise in both bereavement and international conflict is strikingly congruent with Freud's seminal thoughts on these conjoined topics.

In Chapter 4, Dr. Judith Lingle Ryan reflects on the sudden, tragic loss of her son as she delves into important theoretical matters pertaining to bereavement. Like Dr. Aragno, she is sensitive to the limitations of our earliest models of mourning. She does, however, find herself resonating with Melanie Klein's ideas about the potentially supportive role of internal object relations. (Klein, herself, lost her own son in strikingly similar circumstances. That tragic event no doubt impacted her own writing on this topic.) Dr. Ryan also found the ring of truth in some contemporary contributions. Philip Bromberg's beliefs about the protective value of dissociative mechanisms and Stuart Pizer's cogitations concerning the importance of living with paradox were especially helpful to her.

In Chapter 5, Dr. J. Gail White shares moving work with a patient struggling with feelings of absence and aloneness. This case concerns psychic loss of a parent, even though there was no "actual" loss. Failure to mourn such absences can leave one encapsulated in early dynamics, with little or no room for future, intimate, adult relationships. The troubled, driven condition of her analysand strongly supports Freud's view, cited earlier, that failure to face finality impoverishes our lives, making them "shallow and empty." On a hopeful note, Dr. White's analysis reveals the reverse to also be true. Finding a way to work through such matters – giving up illusions and defensive denial – enriches one's life enormously.

In the final chapter of this part, the well-known psychoanalytic author, Joyce Slochower, voyages beyond the consulting room to explore the importance of sociocultural support, ritual, and memorialization in facilitating mourning. Like some other authors in Part II, she stresses processes of internalization and integration that do not end a year or two after loss, but continue throughout the lifetime of the mourner in an ongoing, transformative process. While keenly aware of the importance of psychoanalytic treatment for some patients suffering from arrested, pathological mourning, she is equally attuned to the fact that for many people, including our patients, much of the crucial therapeutic action occurs with other people, in other places, by other means.

Childhood and adolescence

The third part of this book deals with issues pertaining primarily to losses experienced early in life. In the first chapter of this group – a courageously personal one – Dr. Michael O'Loughlin struggles to understand the reverberating impact of very early developmental loss and trauma throughout the life cycle. In particular, he is interested in the origins and manifestations of unsymbolized, free-floating forms of primitive dread and emptiness. In his investigation of disquieting experiences likely deriving from the presymbolic period of development, he found the work of Searles, Klein, Kristeva, and Green especially informative. He illustrates the importance of analysts being willing and able to connect their own split-off states of deadness and associated agonies in order to effectively empathize, connect to, and help patients.

In Chapter 8, Dr. Anita Weinreb Katz examines the film *American Beauty* in a penetrating, sometimes harrowing exploration of the impact of the trying transition from childhood to adolescence not only on youth but also on their parents. Adolescents' struggles with physical maturation, separation, and sexuality typically stir up parallel conflicts in parents. These reawakened issues can precipitate regressive processes as parents re-engage with unfinished business from their own youth. Encountering these conflicts often contributes significantly to mid-life crisis. Each new beginning for the child is potentially an ending for the parents, Dr. Katz notes. Likewise, each ending is potentially a new beginning.

In Chapter 9, Dr. Glenys Lobban usefully explores the impact of the analyst's assumptions about normal or successful mourning on both analytic and mourning processes. Her focus is on patients who lost a parent during adolescence. The inability of these patients to truly mourn leads to significant blockages in crucial areas, such as relationships and career. When the surviving parent is unable to tolerate their own and/or their child's grief, it can be difficult or impossible for the adolescent to experience and complete necessary grief work. These children seem, instead, to resort to dissociative mechanisms in order to keep on functioning. In treatment, these adults reconnected with their pain, sadness, rage, and denial that had been so long split off. Frequently, it is the analyst's experience of troubling, dissociated feelings that enables these affects and defenses to be brought into the therapeutic process. In keeping with and extending the transformative processes emphasized by Dr. Aragno in Chapter 2, Dr. Lobban found that her patients were able to accept the finality of the death once they found a way to bring some aspect of their relationship and connection with the deceased parent into the present and future. This act of transportation enabled them to tolerate and eventually transcend that finality. Transforming the primal relationship on the internal plane enabled them to move on with their lives.

In Chapter 10, Dr. Sara Weber examines excruciating endings, and potential endings that arise for some children when troubled marriages are terminated, but never-ending conflict, legal and otherwise, continues. Such children struggle with degrees of object loss, often without significant support from preoccupied, troubled caretakers. These children worry that partial losses may become total. Having at least one severely disturbed parent, they must often make terrible choices. They can accept one caretaker's distorted view of the other, thereby losing some of their relation to reality. Alternatively, they can stick with what's real and risk losing their accusing parent. Child analysts and others will readily resonate with the dilemma Dr. Weber portrays. They likely will derive sustenance from her sharing her experience and thoughts on these matters.

Violence and terror

What came into existence beside the dead body of the ambivalently loved one was not only the doctrine of the soul, belief in immortality, and a powerful source of guilt. Additionally, Freud believed, the earliest ethical commandments arose in these circumstances. The primal prohibition established by the emerging conscience was "Thou shalt not kill." This law constituted a reaction against the satisfaction of the hatred hidden behind the more obvious grief, he thought. This prohibition was gradually extended to strangers who were not loved and, finally, even to enemies. This core taboo "makes it certain that we spring from an endless series of generations of murderers, who had lust for killing in their blood, as, perhaps, we ourselves have today" (p. 296). In modern times, unconscious death wishes and ambivalence no longer lead to the doctrine of the soul and to ethics, but rather to neurosis, he stated.

In keeping with the founder of psychoanalysis' creative linking of war, hatred, death, and neurosis, our fourth part is devoted to the relationship between loss, on the one hand, and violence and terror on the other. In Chapter 11, Dr. David Kirschner offers a disturbing, enlightening portrayal of the role unmourned loss associated with adoption can play in the epigenesis of some killers. From his extensive clinical and forensic experience, he provides hair-raising illustrations of how inability to deal with loss has played major, tragic roles in cases of parricide and serial killing.

Adoption involves significant loss for all members of the adoption triad. Birth parents lose children; adoptive parents experience the death of the dream of the child they longed to conceive; adoptees lose birth parents and their sense of origins. Dr. Kirschner points out that adoptees' need to grieve is often not understood, even by therapists. Only when such losses are addressed can the potential gains of the new beginning with the adoptive family be fully realized. By examining extreme, but regrettably far too frequent cases, Dr. Kirschner sheds light on a much wider spectrum of less violent situations that pertain not only to adoption but also to other forms of loss.

In Chapter 12, Dr. Veronica Fiske examines clinical conundrums that emerged for her in relation to the September 11 assaults on the World Trade Center. This event marked the beginning of the end of normality in her experience of her work, her patients, and her self. She felt a loss of safety in the world in general and, particularly, in the therapeutic setting. Herself an immigrant, she became acutely sensitive to the new, widespread wariness of "foreigners" in her adopted country. One might regard this change as a culture-wide retreat from the depressive position as much of society, feeling threatened and under attack, shifted to a more aggressive, paranoid-schizoid position. Dr. Fiske demonstrates various ways she and her patients struggled in their efforts to regain their previously healthier state of being and relating.

In Chapter 13, Dr. Mark B. Borg tackles a psychoanalytically unusual, but socially important topic. He explores "necessary ruthlessness" in relation to problems of homelessness and severe mental illness. Like Dr. Fiske in Chapter 12, he attends to problematic aspects of the larger social context in which we dwell, and practice our profession. In the midst of daunting problems that exceed our collective capacities to solve, he suggests we have developed a culture of ruthlessness. Such hardening may be necessary for survival. "Civil society" nonetheless pays a considerable price for dividing our collective identity into the secure and the hopeless, much as Freud said we impoverished our lives by marginalizing death. The distinction between the fortunate and the doomed is partly based on projection of frightening self-states. Dr. Borg believes our need to dissociate ourselves from those whom we might anxiously wish nonexistent reflects our underlying fears of being invalidated, precipitating our fall from grace, plummeting us through the social safety net. Ultimately, he believes, this anxiety reflects fear of death. From this perspective, deadening our empathy for unfortunate others simultaneously alienates us from and destroys our compassion for aspects of ourselves.

Death drive

Freud's (1920) most controversial concept, the death instinct, has been rejected, ignored, or transcribed into more ordinary, acceptable notions of destructiveness by most analysts. Some Kleinians continue to maintain faith in this battered construct. Despite widespread repudiation, Freud's provocative idea will not simply rest in peace. It continues to intrigue many scholars concerned about ultimate issues.

In our fifth part, Dr. Karen Lombardi reflects on the phenomenon of negativity in relation to Freud's grave concept. Refusal, negation, denial, and disavowal are all part of Freud's death instinct, she notes. After considering Klein's rather different death instinct, Dr. Lombardi considers more recent views, such as those of Green and Matte Blanco. Negativity is crucial to the birth of the subject, she emphasizes. Separating me from not-me, that birth simultaneously implies death to a more encompassing sense of self. (In some respects, Dr. Lombardi explores processes similar to those that concerned Dr. Borg in Chapter 13 related to constricting the social self. Borg was, however, concerned with a developmentally later time in identity formation.)

In Chapter 15, Professor Ross M. Skelton also differentiates the death drives of Freud and Klein, then considers these concepts in relation to Matte Blanco's intriguing ideas. In Klein's view, we all live unconsciously in anxious dread of internal annihilation related to the death instinct. Matte Blanco moved away from this view toward Freud's. From the viewpoint of Matte Blanco's bi-logic, Freud's death drive provides fresh insights into the nature of life. Like the pre-Socratic philosopher, Parmenides, Matte Blanco had a deep feeling for the human desire to return to the earliest, indivisible stillness of what he calls the symmetric mode of being. As Grotstein emphasized, however, this longing can also be felt as a dangerous retreat from the logic and structural supports of everyday living. This yearning can, therefore, loom as a threatening, implosive journey, tantamount to dying. Rather than promising restoration or transformation, this wish can precipitate panic.

Dying patients

While Sekoff lamented modern society's attempt to banish death from familiar hearth to sterile institution, analysts in our sixth part ventured boldly into those newer domains to help and learn. In Chapter 16, Dr. Sharron W. Kaplan shares her unique experience working on a home care hospice team with patients close to death's door. That emotionally demanding work affected her profoundly, including her approach to subsequent analytic practice and theory. She strives to integrate her previous social work self and her current psychoanalytic self. In this endeavor, she leans toward authors favoring an integrated "bodymind." She is also interested in the interconnectedness of bodyminds, something she believes can happen on the level of subtle sense perceptions and memories. Reflecting on compassion in analysis and elsewhere, she notes that this sentiment involves fluid boundaries between subjectivities. Her thinking about compassion complements Borg's ideas (Chapter 13) on problems encountered in a culture of ruthlessness.

In Chapter 17, Dr. Stephen W. Long describes sensitively attuned, highly effective work with elderly patients approaching their end in a nursing home. He found three contemporary, relational concepts particularly helpful: mirroring, mutuality, and the holding environment. He shares three cases in each of which a different one of these ideas figured prominently. One has the privilege of witnessing difficult patients struggling with loss transforming from unhappy, nasty, grumpy states to rather wonderful ones. Dr. Long convincingly demonstrates how the experience of being understood, held, and related to in appropriate ways can have a profoundly positive impact on the final developmental transition, from life to death.

In Chapter 18, Dr. Bruce Herzog discusses the importance of affect sharing throughout the life cycle. His moving work with two dying patients demonstrates the power of the human need to experience authentic connection and have someone hear our story. These principles, simultaneously simple and profound, can transform a tragic, lonely event into one that is both bearable and meaningful.

Aesthetics

Due to conventional culture's propensity to peripheralize death, we eagerly seek in literature and the theatre "compensation for what has been lost in life," Freud (1915, p. 291) contended. "There we still find people who know how to die." Our seventh part explores the mutually enriching relationship between psychoanalysis and literature. In Chapter 19, Dr. Olga Cox Cameron explores the importance of futurity. Skillfully, yet concisely, she weaves ideas from philosophy, linguistics, literature, and psychoanalysis to create a compelling vision of the anticipatory sense as an essential dimension of human subjectivity. In its absence, space, time, and subjectivity dissolve. Helplessly trapped in the stasis of the present, nothing different or new can emerge. In trauma, this endless present is governed by the repetition compulsion. Similar stasis is encountered in psychosis and in relation to death. These states lie outside the usual protective barrier furnished by ordinary ego functioning grounded in a sense of possible futures.

Dr. Cameron's delineation of the problematic nature of the loss of futurity stands in stimulating counterpoint to Dr. Volkan's emphasis on the need, through mourning, to render object representations of lost loved ones (including things) futureless. We need to achieve an internal burial of them, he notes, even though the representation of the well-buried object will continue forever, as some of our other authors have underscored. In this transformative process, our ghosts become ancestors, as Loewald (1980) so famously phrased it.

In Chapter 20, drawing from the treasure chest of her Japanese background, Dr. Yuko Katsuta shares an enchanting, ancient folktale, enriching us with her culture's creative perspective on mortality. She considers Nature as a bridge between Human Nature and the Supranatural. Pondering the connection between life and death, finite and infinite, she leads one to wonder whether mortality makes any sense without some notion of immortality. One is reminded of Irwin Z. Hoffman's (1998) important ideas concerning the essential dialectic between life and death. There is much to meditate on in Dr. Katsuta's seemingly simple, yet profound, transcultural contribution.

Termination

One way psychoanalysis has approached finality is through the topic of ending treatment. It has been said that termination is one of the least taught, least supervised, least written about subjects in our field. Our last major part focuses on this important subject.

In Chapter 21, Dr. Rita V. Frankiel draws on her extensive clinical and theoretical expertise to share ideas about a group of patients who have especial difficulty ending treatment. They usually come from backgrounds containing considerable emotional deprivation and abuse. They turn to their inner worlds, their imagination, seeking compensation for the shortcomings of difficult, endangering realities. These factors, combined with defenses like omnipotent control, make it difficult for them to understand psychoanalysis as transferential reliving, rather than being completely real. Change and termination can be excruciatingly difficult for these analysands. These events can feel out of control and, literally, terminal.

To explore such issues, Dr. Frankiel presents a patient with morbid attachment to a cruel, possessive, internal object. She understands this pathological adhesion as arrested, distorted mourning. To become free, the patient must acquire the capacity to tolerate separation. As part of this process, supplementing Freudian with Kleinian analysis, Dr. Frankiel considers the idea that such patients often have a very concrete fantasy wish that they feel must be gratified. Otherwise, the analysis will be terribly incomplete, if not a total failure. Treatment involves the death of the absolute need for this wish to be fulfilled.

In Chapter 22, Professor Rebecca C. Curtis reflects poetically on her personal analysis with Dr. Stephen Mitchell, and its ending. She shares thoughts that arose after the analysis, consequent to the unexpected death of this important, much loved figure. She believes patients do not usually have sufficient opportunity to mourn with others when their analyst dies. Writing this chapter helped her come to grips with this loss, much as had been the case when she publicly acknowledged feelings about her parents at their funerals. In the course of her narrative, she conveys memories of how Dr. Mitchell worked, jogged, and decorated his office. These details help us to know a little bit more about this revered analyst, even as we all continue to mourn his loss.

In Chapter 23, Dr. Ionas Sapountzis creates a rich tapestry of thoughts arising from work with children whose treatments ended suddenly. He skillfully ties these experiences in with others related to troubling, multi-generational experiences in his family of origin. All these events involved wrenching experiences pertaining to a felt need for self-silencing. Bravely, Dr. Sapountzis shares bone-chilling horrors in the history of his family. He articulates how these events profoundly affected him. Reflecting on those experiences has fueled his resolve to see, feel, think and, above all, speak, in order to transform the pain of such sudden endings and self-silencings into meaningful events that can enliven the present and future, in the consulting room, and in all other places in life.

In our concluding part, Dr. Lori C. Bohm completes our compilation with her reflections on this entire volume. Reflecting the spirit of this book, her piece is appropriately titled "The transformative potential in the work-ing through of deaths and endings."

Coda

Known for his seemingly dour view that the purpose of psychoanalysis is to transform neurotic suffering into normal misery, Freud had similarly tough-minded things to say with respect to death. We would be well advised to give it the place in our thoughts which is its due and to give more prominence to unconscious attitudes toward this topic, he advised. Taking truth more into account would, he believed, make life more bearable. Stoically, he averred that: "To tolerate life remains, after all, the first duty of all living beings" (1915, p. 299). Our illusions are valueless if they make it harder to endure life, he remarked. In his characteristically blunt manner, he signed off his profound essay with the parting advice, "If you want to endure life, prepare yourself for death" (1915, p. 299).

Despite the hard-edged tone of Freud's sentiments on life and death, his outlook was in line with other philosophers who grappled with such matters in the past. For example, as he prepared to drink the hemlock juice and meet his death, Socrates is said to have opined that, "The aim of those who practice philosophy in the proper manner is to practice for dying and death" (Plato, 1981). In a somewhat less somber tone, Epicurus (1964) counseled that, "The art of living well and the art of dying well are one."

In a less harsh manner than Freud, nearly a century later, Sekoff (1999, p. 121) suggested we all need to take the full measure of death, if only to face the question, "What is it to be alive?" We cannot hope to approach an answer to this essential query, he believed, unless we are prepared to encounter transience, that is, the fading and passing of ourselves and our objects. One might regard this reference to impermanence as an allusion to the next essay Freud (1916) published after his "Thoughts for the times on war and death," namely, "On transience."

The Canadian poet Alden Nowlan (Pedersen, 1984) opined that there are only two subjects one can write about, love and death. (To the extent that he is right, he is in accord with Freud's belief that Eros and Thanatos are the two fundamental drives underlying all our activities.) Musing that if he were a guru, instead of advising people to meditate, he would counsel them to sit down and think about their own death for several minutes each day. "They'd be much happier during the rest of the day and probably kinder to the people around them," he suggested. Nowlan no doubt knew a great deal about what he was speaking. At the time of the impressive interview in which he made these remarks, he had already had three operations for cancer. Three months later, he was no longer with us, except in what he left behind.

Another Canadian poet, Jaime Jenkinson, might concur with Nowlan's view on the overriding importance to those of the pen of the subjects of love and death. Speaking to the intricate intertwining of both these themes that infuse the human condition with so much meaning, joy, and pain, she shared the following insights about mortality and transience in her lovely poem, evocatively entitled, *The Death of Dying*:

People die sometimes
But longer no more
You can remember them in your mind
You can still remember them in your heart
But if you want to see them again
Close your eyes and hug your heart
Then you will be able to see them again

Jaime was eight years old when she dictated this poem to her father. She was struggling to come to grips with her grandmother's death. When her father shared this sensitive verse with me, Jaime was nine. She had just lost another grandparent. Her enigmatic title and the lines that followed flowed from her young soul, speaking volumes about the nature of transience and transformation. Her touching poem has much to communicate and teach. (I am grateful to Jaime and her parents, Jim and Nancy, for permission to publish this beautiful verse.)

"We are unable to maintain our former attitude towards death, and have not yet found a new one," Freud (1915, p. 292) declared. His observation can be construed as a challenge to us all. The fine chapters in this volume will surely assist us in progressing toward that much needed, deeper understanding of transience. Freud, Sekoff, Nowlan, Plato, Epicurus, and others are undoubtedly correct in their conviction that facing finality is essential for wellbeing and progress, not only for individuals, but also for nations and the world. The penetrating, intriguing, illuminating, often courageous thoughts of our authorial collective provide many valuable tools for coming to grips with this essential dimension of life.

References

Becker, E. (1973) *The Denial of Death*. New York: Free Press.

Eissler, K.R. (1955) *The Psychiatrist and the Dying Patient*. New York: International Universities Press.

Epicurus (1964) *Letters, Principal Doctrines, and Vatican Sayings*. Trans. R.M. Geer. New York: Macmillan.

Freud, S. (1915) Thoughts for the times on war and death. *Standard Edition*, 14: 273–300. London: Hogarth Press, 1957.

—— (1916) On transience. *Standard Edition*, 14: 305–307. London: Hogarth Press, 1957.

—— (1920) *Beyond the Pleasure Principle*. *Standard Edition*, 18: 3–64. London: Hogarth Press, 1955.

Green, A. (1986) The dead mother. In A. Green, *On Private Madness*, pp. 142–173. London: Hogarth Press.

Hoffman, I.Z. (1998) *Ritual and Spontaneity in the Psychoanalytic Process: A Dialectical-constructivist View*. Hillsdale, NJ: Analytic Press.

Lewy, E. (1941) The return of the repression. *Bulletin of the Menninger Clinic*, 5: 47–55.

Loewald, H. (1980) *Papers on Psychoanalysis*. New Haven, CT: Yale University Press.

Pedersen, J. (1984) *Alden Nowlan* (videocassette). National Film Board of Canada, Atlantic Regional Production Centre.

Plato (1981) *"Phaedo," Five Dialogues*. Trans. G.M.A. Grube. Indianapolis, IN: Hackett.

Ogden, T.H. (1995) Aliveness and deadness of the transference-countertransference. *International Journal of Psychoanalysis*, 76: 695–710.

Sekoff, J. (1999) The undead: necromancy and the inner world. In G. Kohon (ed.) *The Dead Mother: The Work of André Green*, pp. 109–127. London: Routledge.

Thomas, L-V. (1975) *Anthropologie de la mort*. Paris: Payot.

Part II

Grief and mourning

Chapter 2

Transforming mourning

A new psychoanalytic perspective

Anna Aragno

"Death will no longer be denied; we are forced to believe it. People really die; and no longer one by one, but many, often tens of thousands in a single day" (p. 29). Freud wrote these stark words in 1915 in "Thoughts for the times on war and death," yet they might just as well have been written today. For many, the year 2001 suddenly brought danger and death into their collective reality. For some, this new awareness transformed complacency into new consciousness. Without the cognized backdrop of the randomness of this final curtain, living lacks the chiseled contours that mute omnipotence and help juxtapose each precious moment against an inevitable end.

It is, however, the personal encounter with death and its severance of a cherished relationship that hurtles us into an adaptive crisis from which we cannot emerge but transformed. The irrevocability of death makes this a loss like no other. Though we summon prior coping mechanisms, *nothing* adequately prepares for this final separation. The intensity of pain and degree of psychosocial upheaval is such that we fear we will not survive. Yet we do. How we adjust, the subject of this chapter, is by laboring through a painful, lengthy process in a disorganized state, gradually modulating affect, habituating to change, and memorializing a relationship. Slowly, over time, we accomplish the internal and external tasks of mourning.

As psychoanalysts we are in a unique position to trace our inner experiences, rendering us prime subjects for our own research. Virtually all authors of seminal works on mourning have suffered early, profound losses. Freud's (1917) spearheading paper differentiating normal mourning from melancholia appeared after he had experienced familial losses. Like all psychobiological crisis points, the shifting course of bereavement has to have been experienced and *known* for its transformative potential to be meaningfully understood. This chapter, also, is born of a grief experienced and observed, and was undertaken as a study of the anatomy of grieving in adult bereavement during the first year.

Initially, as I searched for maps and models, paths and paradigms, for my chaotic anguish, I realized that unless we are drawn by personal interest to the literature on object loss and mourning, many of us remain conceptually arrested at Freud's (1917) model, proposed at the height of his thermodynamic metapsychology. Based on the idea that "mental" activity moves from unbound to bound energy, and that interpersonal bonds are made and unmade through the investment and retraction of "libidinal cathexes," there is here only the faintest prefiguration of structural ideas to be consolidated later on.

Studies of bereavement have come a long way since "decathexis" was viewed as its central achievement moving toward quite different ideas regarding its resolution. The metatheoretical thread that has received little attention and is of most interest to me (symbolization) on close scrutiny accounts for much of the transformative potential inherent in loss. In 1997, I proposed a non-energic, semiotic, developmental model of mind founded on stages of symbolization. In ontogenesis, the developmental stages in the evolution of semiotic mediation appear serially; these same semiotic progressions are recapitulated whenever experience is modulated and mediated verbally. This model provided explanatory principles for the modulation of drive, affect and experience in early life, as well as for the transforming effects of the talking cure. With this modern conception of the "mind's work" in place, Freud's "grief work," clinical "working-through," and symbolization all look much alike, and can be understood as situation-specific aspects of the same processes, a point noted by others (Shane and Shane, 1990; Hagman, 1995). Knowledge of semiotic forms and progressions proves important in studying mourning, particularly when distinguishing between defensive, or partial resolutions, and differentiating between childhood and adult forms.

Age and stage of development, availability of support, ability to express and process affect, intrapsychic structure, and individual capacities for symbolization all play key roles in determining the course of bereavement. Given the complexity and multidetermination of this process, its psychoanalytic study necessitates a multiperspectival approach with close scrutiny of all its various dimensions. "Normal" adjustment will differ in different sociocultural situations and for different types of losses, varying according to temperament and circumstance and, above all, depth and quality of the object tie, the *significance* of the deceased to the survivor.

Mature mourning is the expression of organismic efforts to absorb, metabolize and integrate a profound biopsychosocial and often spiritual crisis, challenging deep strata of intrapsychic and physiological equilibrium. Its analytic study requires an examination of the shifting ratios and concomitant working and reworking, in different ways at different stages, of all its dimensions. The multiperspectival-developmental underpinnings of this approach imply that mature bereavement is predicated on a fully differentiated psychic structure, a capacity for symbolization, and ego strength sufficient to endure the potentially disintegrative effects of acute grief. Immature and/or aberrant form of mourning, i.e., avoided, denied, somatoform, obsessional, displaced, incomplete or unending, are determined by age, nature of object tie, and the existing defenses and psychic structure at the time of loss.

This chapter discusses specific processes involved in the intrapsychic transformation that, ideally, unfolds as a result of a fully elaborated bereavement. Its central thesis is that the "labor" of mourning is a fluid, multidimensional process reviving prior losses and separations, calling for revisiting and reworking the deepest recesses of intrapsychic organization. Far from severance, detachment, or "decathecting" of the bond with the deceased, its *constructive* travail consists in reorganizing the core-ego and self-with-other identity, reconfiguring both on an inner plane. This deepens and strengthens the self while transmuting the relationship through a "re-membering" that preserves the cherished dialogue within.

If, as Freud determined, part of the ego is a "precipitate of abandoned object cathexes," mourning ought to strengthen and enrich the survivor. Yet given the physicalistic and often pessimistic coloring of Freud's writings, this transformative, even transcendent, aspect of his theories – the idea that nothing is ever wholly lost without some substantial internal gain – is not always in evidence. Current bereavement studies are unearthing precisely these restitutional and creative potentials accompanying loss.

This chapter examines factors called into play through separation and loss, features and forms of highly interrelated processes of representation, recollection, reconstruction, internalization, symbolization and narratization. These self-propelled, meaning-making tendencies yield lasting internal restructuring. Supplementing description with careful scrutiny of these processes results in a deeper understanding of the transformative functions of mourning. What is required is an analytic breakdown of the challenges that confront grievers with multiple, interrelated tasks of a transitional process that has its own timetable. Ultimately, it is to the tides of a contemporary, constructivist paradigm that emphasizes the restorative, regenerative resources harnessed at this time of crisis that we will turn, albeit not before looking back and surveying the literature.

II

Mourning has a quite specific psychical task to perform: its function is to detach the survivor's memories and hopes from the dead. When this has been achieved, the pain grows less.

(S. Freud, 1913–1914, p. 65)

Each single one of the memories and expectations in which the libido is bound to the object is brought and hypercathected and detachment of the libido is accomplished in respect of it.

(S. Freud, 1917, p. 245)

From its very beginnings, psychoanalysis has been interested in separation and loss, mindful of their extraordinary impact and potentially lethal sequelae throughout the lifespan. A number of the famous "Frauleins" of *Studies on Hysteria* (Breuer and Freud, 1893–1895) fell ill as a consequence of caring for terminally ill, loved ones. For these ladies, the throttling of emotional response during these stressful circumstances was sufficiently pathogenic to precipitate mental breakdown. The "work of remembering" or verbalized recall with emotional release through which these women subsequently labored might, today, be recognized as an expression of the acute stage of early bereavement when the cathartic function of "giving sorrow words" is so important. This "work of remembering" had, by 1914, become the pivotal clinical process of "working through" and, by 1917, the "grief work" in Freud's landmark "Mourning and melancholia" which definitively oriented the psychoanalytic study of bereavement toward intrapsychic dynamics.

Even a brief overview of the considerable literature that has burgeoned since reveals three broad stages in a trajectory that moves away from the "decathexis" model toward ideas more in line with a contemporary, constructivist *Zeitgeist*. Transcendence of loss through "meaning reconstruction" (Neimeyer, 1988, 2001), continuity of self-experience (Gaines, 1997) and internalization of relationship (Baker, 2001) are major new themes. What follows does not pretend to be a complete review of the literature (for which interested readers can turn to Siggins, 1966; Jacobs, 1993; Hagman, 1995). I am more interested in tracing subtle changes in approach resulting from paradigm shifts that gradually alter the nature of our observations and understanding.

From roughly the early 1920s, three overlapping stages in the evolution of psychoanalytic thinking on mourning are discernible orienting toward the prevailing cultural and psychological attitude toward death, emotions and object loss. Each was marked by certain dominant figures who opened the way toward changing attitudes. Through seminal contributions, they steered focus toward the enormous implications of attachment and loss, expanding our knowledge and advancing our understanding.

The *"decathexis era"* (roughly from 1917 to the late 1950s) was dominated by Freud's metapsychological concepts regarding energic investment and retraction from objects. The "work" of mourning undoes ties that bind. Disengagement of libido, resolution of ambivalence, identification and renunciation, became cornerstones of what has been handed down as *the* standard psychoanalytic model of bereavement, although it is questionable whether Freud intended this.

In his only work specifically on the subject, Freud (1917) was concerned with differentiating between the intrapsychic dynamics of normal grief and its pathological, depressive version. The predominance of ambivalence and hostile reproach turned against the self in the latter precludes the smooth transition from object cathexis to identification. Similarly, in Addendum C of *Inhibitions, Symptoms and Anxiety*, Freud (1926) was attempting to pinpoint different structural conditions producing anxiety and pain, or uncomplicated mourning, in the wake of object loss. Although not stated in such terms, Freud (1923, 1926) was pointing to the vicissitudes of attachment and loss in relation to degrees of intrapsychic differentiation, to *kinds* of object-relationship and *qualities* of object ties. Focus on intrapsychic structure inevitably leads to a developmental approach that examines degrees of self-object differentiation as well as the more advanced, intrasystemic differentiations within the ego itself. This presages what is later elaborated as the difference between self-object versus object loss, or pre-structural versus post-structural loss, the former producing lesions to the core-self, the latter different forms of mourning. Intrapsychic structure and the degree of self–other differentiation at the time of loss generates different kinds of unconscious fantasies and narrative beliefs in relation to the deceased and plays a considerable role in the capacity to complete intrapsychic separation from the deceased rather than falling back on regressive or defensive solutions such as merger with an idealized imago.

Other significant works of the time colored by the idea that mourning evaporates into renunciation are Deutsch's (1937) study of unexpressed grief and Klein's (1940) exploration of the relationship of mourning to manic-depressive states. Deutsch's (1937) article yielded a famous citation that summarized certain key assumptions of the era:

> The process of mourning as a reaction to the real loss of a loved person *must be carried to completion*. As long as the early libidinal or aggressive attachment persists, the painful affect continues to flourish, and vice versa the attachments are unresolved as long as the affective process of mourning has not been accomplished.
>
> (Deutsch, 1937, p. 230, original emphasis)

As a consequence of psychological casualties in survivors of World War II, alongside the psychoanalytic model, there sprang two subsidiary branches in the study of bereavement. Heralded by Lindeman's (1944) classic survey of the typology and management of the "symptoms" of acute grief, the first, "psychiatric branch" evolved into important medical research into the potentially devastating organic repercussions of profound grief. It is now well documented that physiological sequelae of the stress of bereavement affect the cardiovascular, neurohormonal, immunological and central nervous systems. In addition to a broad range of psychological problems, due to immuno-suppression, grievers are at risk for a variety of stress related diseases. Suicide and other forms of sudden death at anniversaries have also been documented.

The second branch, initiated by Spitz's (1945, 1946) famous studies of infant hospitalism, established a line of observational research on the mother–infant dyad and the effects of early object loss that has become a major psychoanalytic tradition. Spitz's uncovering and naming the syndrome of anaclitic depression – which may sometimes end in marasmus and death – confirmed that mothering functions nourish far more than the baby's body. In order to thrive, humans require interpersonal interactions from the start. Spitz's observations of maternal deprivation in orphaned war babies were taken up and vastly expanded by an Englishman, John Bowlby (1969, 1973, 1980), whose work, spanning several decades, culminated in three seminal volumes on childhood attachment, separation, and loss.

Aside from the enormous value of drawing attention to the consequences of making and breaking human bonds, there are pros and cons in both these lines of research. Problematic aspects of the psychiatric branch are the standardization and pathologizing of a natural, highly individualized process and the medicalization of sadness, rendering various cognitive and emotional expressions of this difficult passage into "symptoms" to be "managed" or "treated." Engel's (1961) classic article, "Is grief a disease?" responded to this trend by delineating three predictable stages in the "healing" of the emotional wound of object loss. The most problematic tendency evolving out of the second line of research has been a pervasive propensity to draw simplistic parallels between real childhood experiences and their transferential recapitulations in the clinical situation.

Deepening interest flowered into a second era between the mid 1950s and late 1970s that might be defined as the "heyday" of systematic research into childhood loss and adult bereavement. Given the ubiquity of separation and object loss, and their relevance to psychoanalysis, once mourning was generalized to include intrapsychic processes of oedipal object renunciation, many major analysts contributed to the topic. Clinical papers appeared on: the persistence of unconscious reunion fantasies in adults with early parental loss (Jacobson, 1965); activation of grieving and growth in treatment (Fleming and Altschul, 1963); mourning accomplished through the transference (McCain, 1974); and, more theoretically, intrapsychic structuring of ego and superego as a consequence of separation and loss (Loewald, 1962). Analysts examined types of defenses summoned to diminish the pain and mitigate the full impact of the irrevocability of death. They investigated affect blunting, timetables for normal versus abnormal reactions to loss, and internal conditions predisposing toward healthy, neurotic or psychotic manifestations of pathological grief. In an atmosphere in which the concept of mourning was extended to include many forms of loss, including termination in analysis, analysts studied adult and childhood bereavement in relation to restitution, sublimation, creativity and genius (Segal, 1952; Eisenstadt, 1978; Pollock, 1989).

The rich yields of this period are best illustrated by the seminal works of Bowlby (1961, 1963, 1969), Pollock (1961, 1989), and Parkes (1972). Bowlby's specialized research of childhood attachment and loss, and Pollock's studies of all aspects of adult bereavement, epitomize the exhaustive scope and lasting advances on the subject that emerged from this period. The magnitude of the topic lends itself to interdisciplinarity; Bowlby leaned heavily on ethological studies, Parkes documented medical research, and Pollock expanded the scope of investigation to cross-cultural, familial, phylogenetic, comparative primate studies, historical, religious and social dimensions.

Inevitably, controversy arose regarding when and if the young psyche is capable of genuine mourning. Wolfenstein's (1966) "How is mourning possible?" precipitated a debate leading to important papers from the developmental camp (Nagera, 1970; Solnit, 1970; R. Furman, 1973; E. Furman, 1974a, 1974b). Discussions centered around the capacity for object constancy, firmness of attachment, availability of support, degree of ego development and strength of ego endowments.

With his universal, biologistic views of mourning, Bowlby was, in no small part, responsible for instigating this debate. Ultimately, he was criticized within psychoanalytic circles for blurring distinctions between childhood reactions to separation and the more complex, intrapsychic elaboration of the adult mourning response. Bowlby believed the human response to object loss, at all ages, to be a biologically based amalgam of anxiety, anger, longing, and sadness that begins with shock and numbness, moves to protest, appeals for help, increasingly anguished efforts at recovery, and continues through disorganization and despair, resolving in a more or less stable reorganization and the return of hope. Because Bowlby considered this cascade of emotional behaviors as manifestations of psychological underpinnings, he saw no reason to differentiate between earlier and later forms of what he understood as a cohesive, instinctual system. Descriptively, evidence indicated that responses were similar in both groups, hence it would be wiser to assume underlying similarities (Bowlby, 1963).

Bowlby isolated four main pathological variants of mourning, concluding that many features suffusing each were found in normal childhood grief responses. Yet as Brenner (1974) would stress, relationships between overt behaviors and unconscious meanings are complex, highly varied, individualized, and not easily apparent. Condensation and multidetermination preclude simple correlations between manifest productions and latent signifiers.

While most analysts concur that pathological forms of mourning arise primarily as a result of quality of object tie, intrapsychic structure, and defenses in use, Bowlby emphasized the pathogenic effects of the suppression of full emotional expression and consequent splitting of the ego through repression. A normal outcome necessitates expression of the whole panoply of affects pertaining to the instinctual system, including reproach-ful yearning and angry despair, accompanied by sadness and weeping. Expression of all components of ambivalence, for Bowlby, is the mark of healthy mourning. The inability to accept these strivings promotes repres-sion, rendering them less amenable to working-through and change.

Pollock's (1989) work on adult mourning is so encompassing and multi-dimensional that it is virtually impossible to do it justice. His contributions to the "mourning-liberation process," begun in the mid 1950s after his mother's sudden death, are unprecedented in scope and depth. The range of subjects in his collected papers includes: sociohistorical accounts of funeral suicides and killing rites; studies correlating immunological weakness to certain forms of grief; manifestations of abnormal mourning; transgenera-tional anniversary reactions; biographies of famous writers, artists and leaders who suffered childhood parental loss.

Pollock's research methodology follows the best of psychoanalytic traditions, his reports an amalgam of introspection (as he moved through his own bereavement), observations of relatives, cases, and contemporary writings. His ability to objectify his own evolving experiences yielded insights not only into himself but also to his understanding of mourning theory as he collaborated "with my past investigative self, my present investigative self, and with my forebearers who set the stage for me" (Pollock, 1989, p. ix). Anchored in an evolutionary perspective, his inter-disciplinary scholarship spread to scientific, philosophical, artistic, epistemo-logical and even metaphysical queries, his writings strewn with intellectual challenges that take the reader and the subject to new heights.

Pollock viewed mourning as a phylogenetic, universal adaptive process (of which the stages of bereavement are a subclass) that can result in: successful completion with creative outcome; arrests at various stages; or a pathological, deviant process leading to depressive, potentially lethal dis-orders. With origins in "separating experiences" of early childhood, mourning has its own developmental progression, with an optimal outcome of increased individuation and creativity. Intrapsychic processes underlying stages of shock and acute and chronic grief are designed to accommodate the loss and generate "internal rearrangements" facilitating active mastery of a trauma experienced passively. Pollock vastly expanded the meaning of "mourning" to include all types of major life transitions. All change involving "loss" of something and "gain" of the new entails mourning. None more than he better understood or more thoroughly investigated the complex interaction between behavioral, sociohistorical, emotional, cognitive, and physiological factors underlying bereavement.

By the mid 1980s, in its twilight and with new ideas beckoning, this immensely productive era had contributed a number of phase and stage models of mourning, organizing an otherwise turbulent, chaotic passage into a predictable course of steps leading to resolution. Mourning was now understood as a painful, natural process designed to restore equilibrium. Despite even Pollock's transformational ideas, however, the biologistic phase-stage paradigm remained firmly planted in homeostatic, rather than transformational, principles. Only Loewald (1962) carefully examined interrelationships between separation, object-renunciation, mourning and the creation of psychic structure, providing theoretical underpinnings that could yield truly transformational principles. Otherwise, the idea that "identification" plays an important role in the resolution of mourning was widely accepted, with the exception of Bowlby.

Understanding that degrees of self-object differentiation underlie a continuum that begins with wholesale incorporation, moves through partial, unconscious identifications to selective internalizations, Loewald correctly pointed to *internalization* as the intrapsychic mechanism pursuant to object loss. The psychological sequelae of mourning, for Loewald, are to be viewed as boundary-creating experiences, promoting increased differentiation between self and object, as well as within the ego system itself, between ego and superego. He drew parallels between structuralizations occurring through renunciation, loss, and the phases of mourning in terminating an analysis. By focusing on internalization and identification – the structural modifications occurring as a result of object loss – he returned the study of mourning to intrapsychic dynamics, where Freud had begun in 1917, picking up, more or less, where Freud left off, concluding: "The work of mourning is not confined to a gradual relinquishment of the lost object but also encompasses processes of internalizing elements of the relationship with the object to be relinquished" (Loewald, 1962, p. 139).

By the end of the second era, most analysts concurred that: (1) mourning is a natural process to be fully experienced and expressed; (2) ideally, its compound emotions and conflicts of ambivalence ought to be acknowledged and worked-through; (3) as much as possible ought to be brought to consciousness; (4) the process must be carried to completion or it will be expressed through alternate channels.

By the 1970s, there had appeared a number of popular publications promoting new awareness regarding death, caring for the dying, and bereavement. Kubler-Ross's (1969) best-selling paperback, *On Death and Dying*, offered a five-stage program for the dying and those attending their final passage. There followed Becker's (1973) Pulitzer prize winning *The Denial of Death* and other poignant, literary accounts such as C.S. Lewis' (1976) portrait of his own profound bereavement. A number of important compendia in the professional literature of the 1980s (Wortman and Silver, 1987; Dietrich and Shabad, 1989; Tedeschi *et al.*, 1998) expanded the growing literature.

By the 1990s, unmistakable signs of a "new wave" approach to understanding loss can be detected, based on ideas more commensurate with a constructivist paradigm. Contemporary trends focus on how human faculties themselves can shape and create adaptive processes that accomplish the central tasks of "meaning reconstruction" (Neimeyer, 2001) and continuity of self-experience, while promoting internal preservation of a past relationship. Anything but "detachment" guides the theoretical thrust of this new vision of mourning that points, rather, to the determinant role that bonding and qualities of relationship – whether internal or external – play in psychological life and wellbeing. Interpersonal factors come to the fore and are viewed as feeding psychological processes which depend on the availability of a supportive milieu. New themes in the literature revolve around: the central role of the "other" (Hagman, 1996); differential effects on narcissistic and psychological integrity of self-object versus object loss (Shane and Shane, 1990); implications for unconscious repetition in the intergenerational transmission of traumatic themes through the inability to mourn one's childhood (Shabad, 1993); regressive, potentially devastating consequences of identification with the aggressor in incomplete mourning (Shabad, 1993, 2001); the value of enduring dialogue (Kaplan, 1995); the role of continuity and change in self–other representations in fostering inner transformation (Horowitz, 1990).

While recognizing the importance of *being able to mourn* – now a vastly expanded concept implying the capacity to yield to change as prerequisite for psychological maturation – there is a concomitant appreciation for the preservation of internal continuity through processes of internalization that sustain and transform the inner world of the bereaved. "Emphasis on the need to detach," writes Gaines (1997, p. 549), "has obscured another part of the work of mourning, which is to repair the disruption to the inner self-other relationship." "Grief is resolved through the creation of a loving, growing relationship with the dead that recognizes the new psychological or spiritual . . . dimensions of the relationship" (Shapiro, 1996, p. 552). There is greater recognition of unconscious, reparative processes set in motion immediately, alongside the first catabolic stages of shock and acute grief, and of bereavement as a psychosocial transition.

"Mourning alone," as Furman (1974a, p. 114) stressed, is "an almost impossible task." For a hopeful outcome, the real needs of the newly bereaved must, in some part, be met. These are for others to provisionally serve key functions, such as: helping to contain and modulate overwhelming emotions; listening empathically and encouraging verbalization; helping stabilize a disrupting collapse in self-continuity and narcissistic equilibrium by providing a responsive, temporary, holding space.

Among the prominent voices of the "new wave," Hagman's (1995, 1996, 2001) stands out. In his 1995 critical review of mourning theory, he summarized key assumptions underlying the standard model, offering a "more accurate way of viewing mourning" (Hagman, 1995, p. 919) that turns much of what came before upside down. The repropositioning of central points of the standard model is reiterated in "Beyond decathexis"

(Hagman, 2001), a point by point revision that is virtually a manifesto for a new view of mourning. Key changes are: a shift from phase/stage models to a task-oriented view of mourning as a varied, personalized transition in which crisis of meaning and identity are central; viewing mourning as a psychosocial process in which the communicative function of grieving and qualities of responsiveness are emphasized; problems arising are seen as often caused by the failure of others to engage with the bereaved; understanding the importance of preserving dialogue and the value of an internally transforming relationship with the deceased.

Contemporary approaches acknowledge that the labor of grieving entails no less than "relearning the world of our experience" (Attig, 2001, p. 33). They point to the potentially invigorating thrust toward growth and individuation that lurks in the shadow of loss, an idea intimated in Pollock's evocative hyphenation, "the Mourning-*Liberation* Process." Under a constructivist banner, new wave voices highlight the active role of the human mind in gathering the threads of personal continuity in the face of change and refinding meaning in the aftermath of loss and despair.

III

Earth, isn't this what you want: to arise within us,
invisible? Isn't this your dream
to be wholly invisible someday? O Earth: invisible!
What, if not transformation, is your urgent command?
(Rainer Maria Rilke, 1922)

Due to the complex interaction of many variables, the mourning process is ill suited to standardized formats or timetables. People grieve in individualized ways, with no clearly marked end point. From the solitary mourner of the turn of the century, we have come to see the griever embedded in a significantly impacting social milieu, the primary task of internal detachment supplanted by self-reorganization, transcendence, and "meaning-reconstruction" (Neimeyer, 1998, 2001). We grieve differently at different ages and for different kinds of loss. Bereavement for a terminally ill friend, an elderly parent, a distant relative, the sudden death of a child or soulmate, differs in depth, intensity and duration. Personal response is influenced by intrapsychic, situational, and sociocultural factors, the ability to tolerate and contain turbulent emotional states, and individual capacities for symbolization. Nothing is predictable when overall functioning is dramatically disrupted by internal demands and many real adaptive changes. The form and course bereavement takes is complex and can be understood dynamically only through careful exploration of the contextual and intrapsychic particulars of each case.

Because mourning is such a personal process, only experiential knowledge seems to do it justice. The mourning analyst carries both the burdens and benefits of a professional instrument and psychological insight. Trained to enter living experience while simultaneously observing it, I will use my own bereavement as a singular example. My approach through the shifting phases of mourning was to understand its manifestations as efforts to metabolize, organize, process and master a profound biopsychosocial, transpersonal, spiritual crisis that challenges the deepest recesses of organic and intrapsychic stability. Precisely because of its highly disorganizing qualities, it offers extraordinary opportunities for deep self-examination, transformation and maturation. Those who have allowed themselves to be suffused by chaotic affects and the upheaval of such introspection encounter age-old existential questions of meaning. Their stark answers point to the power of the human mind to come to grips with tragedy, despair, the loss of all that one was or cherished and, through creative integration of new purpose and meaning, to survive. Analytic breakdown of the above-mentioned dimensions provides a fluid framework for the exploration of bereavement at any age. Such a multitask approach simultaneously yields a phenomenological description of shifting phases in the process over time and helps focus on the psychological and adaptive tasks in each.

Early humans introduced rituals at precisely these life junctures, creating a communal holding that helped cushion, contain and structure personal crisis. Funeral and burial traditions provide for rapid disposal of the body and serve important psychosocial needs. Their proscribed, formalized actions externalize and organize what is otherwise excruciating to experience and integrate alone. The triphasic *schema* of the ritual passage van Gennep (1909) described, with clearly marked phases of entrance, liminal disintegration and reaggregation, underscores the psychosocial underpinnings of identity shifts, providing a template for crisis as a paradigm for growth. What rites compress and traditional codes program, the contemporary griever must often articulate alone. However, the more an individual relies on communal help to structure personal experience, the less likely he/she is to reach higher levels of consciousness and individuation by working it through autonomously.

A close look at shifts during the first year of adult mourning reveals four overlapping stages within a broad, triphasic design. Traversing these successfully establishes habitual ways of coping, accomplishing various crucial, biopsychosocial tasks that continue to increase integration and restructuring. This is neither a simple nor linear process. Precisely because it is so multidetermined, like working-through, it spirals around repeatedly, highlighting now one issue, now another, with oscillations, temporary regressions and new emotions and cognitions appearing all the time.

Mourning is draining. One is consumed by preoccupation with the deceased, exhausted by persistent, intense grief that affects every system.

Core stabilities are severely tested and taxed over time. Only slowly do we yield to painful, transformational processes that germinate unconsciously long before we can implement them consciously.

Mourning a beloved partner has been likened to the slow healing of a severe wound. Regardless of how smooth or stormy the relationship, loss of the soulmate is like an amputation. One feels the phantom limb as a great gash in the soul that cannot stop bleeding. Interpersonal ligaments that bind such infinite intimacy are woven through the deep tissue of daily habit, crystallizing into a self-with-other identity rooted in shared hopes and memories, unspoken understanding, comforting conversations, common interests and the sheer joy of mutual presence. Their sudden absence, like a massive volcanic eruption, produces seismic reverberations that penetrate every sphere and crevice of internal and external experience.

After the initial numbing shock-reaction wears off, acute grief bursts in. The subjective feeling is of having a sharp knife lodged permanently in the middle of one's chest. Periodically, physical pain gives way to outbursts of a sorrow so overwhelming it cannot find adequate outlet. The classic picture of early bereavement is acute organic distress; weeping, moaning, restless longing, searching, irritability, anger, blame, anxiety, loss of appetite, body weight, sleep, and a need to share memories and grief. Attempts to integrate the reality of the loss lag far behind the sheer force of instinctual reaction. This cluster of intensely painful, mixed emotions, producing cognitions that range from obsessive accusations to morbid guilt, is understandable as an attempt to mitigate the impact of an irrevocable abandonment, and to undo the loss by preserving a close, internal connection with the deceased that grows deeper with time.

Although psychological aspects remain pervasive in adult bereavement, undoubtedly the *biological*, instinctual reaction is at the forefront during the first few months. We are assisted in understanding this group of mixed emotions by the work of Bowlby on the phenomenology of separation and loss in early childhood. His research provides a template for the typical cascade of behavioral-affects underlying instinctual responses to loss. All genuine mourning reaches archaic layers of the personality, but for those with lesions from early loss or separation, current loss reopens embedded scars, reawakening early traumatic-affects, generally encoded organically. Their reliving obliges a reworking of symptomatic sequelae, often with serious physiological repercussions. The present loss revives the specter of underlying lesions to a core self, with self-esteem and motivational issues reappearing. The triadic sequence of yearning, despair, acceptance, under-lying instinctual adaptation, continues to work itself out at deep biological levels throughout mourning, with increased acceptance and a concomitant decrease of painful affects predominant at the beginning.

The principal tasks of this first trimester are metabolization of shock and modulation of raw emotions (particularly if the loss was unexpected) through talking, weeping, and sharing the events in a way that begins to accommodate the experience. It is here that the role of others can be of inestimable value. By their empathic support and availability to listen and share the grieving, family and friends are doing far more than being helpful. They are serving crucial functions such as cushioning shock, holding unmanageable affects, maintaining daily routines that facilitate continuity of experience, offering hope, creating coagulants of practical and psychological organization in a sea of chaotic despair. These modulating interactions are internalized, providing a platform from which to continue the more private, lonely course of mourning. Where this support is lacking, the bereaved are doubly burdened. Curiously, many widows and widowers are subtly ostracized, even by family and friends. Social life undergoes radical revising during and after the mourning period.

By the second trimester, there appear short gaps of respite between the relentless intensity of grieving. The subsiding of overwhelming affects leaves room for the work of the mind. Accommodation lags behind assimilation, yet the restructuring of mourning is already going on unconsciously and dreams of this time reveal the vicissitudes of this trajectory.

We have become acutely aware of the sensory deprivation created by absence. So many habitual stimuli were associated with the beloved. Their voice and laughter, the contour of their frame, their expressions and conversation are what we long for. In so many ways, the other was our point of reference. C.S. Lewis (1976) portrayed this thwarted connection perfectly:

> Thought after thought, feeling after feeling, action after action, had H. for their object. Now their target is gone. I keep on through habit fitting an arrow to the string: then I remember and have to lay the bow down.
>
> (Lewis, 1976, p. 55)

Surrounded by reminders – the empty chair, the unused spectacles and pillow, the vacuum of silence – *absence* now defines us. The more we are able to give time to remembering, to generating our own, new, internal "targets" that signify what *was* and no longer is, carving these sensory longings into mental images, the more are we able to relinquish what is gone. This is the beginning of the work of "symbolization." What is lost to the senses becomes mind.

The pervasive states of this phase are sadness, loneliness and intense missing. In an attempt to organize the grief, calendric markers became important to me. For the entire first year, I honored the anniversary day and hour, each week. Simple acts like walking to familiar places, maintaining familiar habits through seasonal change, helped cultivate remembrance. Time stops for the grief-stricken. To look back is, initially, too painful. Forward lies a void. We are disorganized, dislodged, dismembered. Ritual markers, temporal or ceremonial, help organize experience.

Identity, also, is in disarray, the self depleted and deprived of familiar narcissistic comforts and sustenance. Suddenly, the self-with-other identity has been supplanted by a self that is without. Initially, and for a long time, we are defined by what we have lost, our social role demoted from wife to widow, our inner selves withered like parched roots. Neither what we were, nor yet what we will become, we hover uncomfortably, in the disintegrative space of liminality. But identity is made and remade. Of all life's crisis points, mourning is a time of potentially powerful, personal reinvention. In order to maintain continuity of self-experience, one has to look back and refind an earlier self that existed before the relationship, while also creating a new self, alone, but not abandoned. The libidinal membrane that had been extended to encompass and include the beloved in sensory reality must be folded inward and reconfigured around a core self that is as yet too enfeebled to fill the gap. Slowly, internalization transfigures this core. Where love was preponderant, the new self is strengthened and enriched by the love one bore for and received from the deceased. Integration of the loss, self-soothing, continuity of self experience, restructuring our inner and outer life, the ongoing tasks of this phase, all go hand in hand. Together they help habituate to change and move toward new self-definition.

While grief pangs and dark moments continue to erupt, by the third trimester it is the *psychological dimension* of mourning that predominates, consciously and unconsciously. From a psychoanalytic perspective, the intrapsychic (including structural, dynamic and relational components) determines the course bereavement will take. These dynamics can complicate, even impede, the mourning process when there is residual ambivalence or conflictual resentment toward the deceased, or when avoidance, reaction formation, or splitting are major defenses. Insufficient differentiation between self and other, and within the ego system, between a strict superego and the ego-core, can lead to severe survivor guilt and/or self-punishing depressions. Conversely, where there is adequate self-object differentiation within the ego – essentially a post-adolescent structure – the transition to internalization takes place through selective identifications with valued characteristics of the beloved. Internalization parallels processes of intrapsychic restructuring.

Traditionally, psychoanalysis has focused on the superego–ego dynamics of mourning. I would like to revive the neglected but important role of the ego-ideal in this scenario and suggest that, for some, major structural enrichment comes from direct introjection into the ego-ideal of selective traits and admired attitudes of the deceased. Aspects of their qualities and manner are paid enduring tribute by becoming the better parts of ourselves. The internal reorganizations resulting from the labor of mourning do not just "come about." They are *brought* about, through personal articulation.

It is important to appreciate that the ego is struggling to master actively what has been experienced helplessly. The accomplishment of major tasks of mourning, such as working through acute grief, reconfiguring the libidinal membrane, reliving, remembering, and integrating the loss, gradually generate resilience and self-reliance that fortify the ego.

By the beginning of the fourth trimester, preoccupation with the deceased has developed into an all-consuming *relationship review*. Every aspect, from the first meeting through myriad moments, scenarios and scenes, is summoned to recall, relived, remembered, again and again, and finally cast to memory. The earlier, raw emotions have mellowed and the quality of grieving and weeping changes over time. Remorse, regrets, renewed appreciation and ever increasing love feed this process, strengthening the sense of a gentle, inner presence. Gratitude is a great antidote to despair.

It is apt here to mention the *transpersonal* and *spiritual* dimensions of mourning. Not everyone finds solace for private pain by stretching their thoughts to encompass the suffering of others. For some, this empathic expansion provides a deep sense of universal kinship with other grievers and with the vulnerability and pathos of the human condition. We contemplate generations that lived before us, all of which suffered loss and the inevitable meeting with death, and feel comforted by the universality of the human experience. Perhaps this is the font of Agape, the seat of universal compassion that makes our lot in life more bearable.

Even those who do not subscribe to organized religion, who are not buoyed by their faith, find themselves looking skyward, pallidly, with primordial longings, yearning for a benevolent deity to bestow some solace. Winged creatures captured my gaze. Their soaring represented the human spirit, free, so alien to the psyche is the finality of biological life. Flight embodies the universal fantasy of a higher realm, the immortality of the soul. Continuing to work-through such longings leads to an enduring love that transcends death, transfiguring what was a real relationship into a *sacred union within*.

In the fourth trimester, the disorganizing impact of the loss gives way to social and psychological adjustments governed more and more by conscious awareness. A will beyond the will, perhaps a biological lifeline, carries a good part of the weight as, unexpectedly, traces of letting go and acceptance weave a scab over raw wounds. Transcending grief and longing, identity reorganization, and the conscious, reflective, relationship review, are eased by the experience of an enduring, gentle inner presence. The ego-ideal, for me, was a benevolent, guiding force, as I deliberately turned grief-pangs into growth-spurts by disciplining my attention toward sublimatory, creative pursuits. Sadness in this tentative phase of restructuring is mitigated by internal dialogue, particularly approaching the first anniversary.

The ending of the first year is important for its propensity to ignite powerful, unconscious, anniversary reactions. By this time, key habits of coping will have been established, even though reviewing and internal restructuring of the relationship extends well beyond this time. Several interrelated tasks must have been at least partially begun for pathological fixation points, somatizations, or other deviant expressions of mourning not to set in. In addition to having experienced the full cycle of seasonal changes, the first year closure demarcates a point in time that many traditions wisely ritualize, as though mourning may not end until a rite of closure has been completed. In the Jewish tradition, the anniversary is marked by "unveiling" the gravestone, a symbolic act that underscores the finality of passing while casting their memory into the permanence of stone. Certain American Indian tribes convene a ceremony at this time to "wipe away the tears" of the grieving.

Honoring the anniversary day with a particularized commemoration simultaneously signals the closing of concentrated grieving and the commencement of a new stage of reflection and acceptance. For me, this was marked by a conscious commitment toward healing and personal transformation. Not until I entered this phase could I grasp or even see the potential in the hidden seeds spread throughout the soil of loss. It is only after the closure of this anniversary that we can begin to look back from the event forward, and organize a narrative yielded out of the mourning process itself. This important new step contributes to the integration and restructuring of the lost relationship as part of the biographical past.

Significant loss disrupts the cohesion of the life-narrative. The changed reality must be made sense of, integrated into dominant life themes, a strand of continuity written into the framework of the overall life. Narrative orients backward from a point in time. Only retrospectively can we give meaningful shape to a sequence of events. Authoring one's first year of bereavement in the context of inner restructuring of the relationship becomes a starting point for a new life-narrative with the self-after-the-loss as protagonist. Now, looking forward must supersede longing backward. If this does not occur, the inner presence grows into an undifferentiated introject rather than a distinctive aspect of the inner world. A core thus merged cannot attain the psychic autonomy requisite for life pursuits.

Signifying and symbolizing activities are accompanied by linguistic commentaries that lay down traces of verbal reference gradually modifying the *form* of the loss experience. These can be thought of as differentiating and boundary-creating processes. Along this semiotic continuum, *signification* is not enough to engender deep structural transformation, for which only true *symbolization* suffices. If we would have something live eternally, it must first die completely to the senses, and this requires a deeper, broader articulation of the loss. Gradations in the semiotic mediations of mourning have widespread implications. At the most primitive levels, where little or no signification has taken place, there may be rapid restitutions and equivalencies hurried in to substitute for the functions served by the deceased.

Some degree of signification will result in a more mature resolution, but one still prone to seeking duplications, hence repetitions that allay the prolonged labor of articulating the far-reaching considerations of loss and finality. Only a complete symbolization of the experience carries through the deep transformation indicative of profound, intrapsychic change.

Language helps organize, contain, and mediate life experience. Conversely, it constrains, defines and influences how experiences are lived. Discourse semantics and the paradigms in which they are embedded are so important in the study of mind because they create our worldviews. We draw from them in highly subliminal ways. The paradigm shift that brought us to constructivism changed the dominant parables of loss, and hence our experience of mourning. From the nineteenth-century romantic griever, the Victorian eternal-mourner, and the Freudian renunciation and repression paradigms, we arrived at an acceptance and transcendence model containing a new faith in the reparative, regenerative nature of the mind as part of the natural world. The storylines and imagery that serve this paradigm are of reconstruction, rebirth – the phoenix rising from its ashes, shoots swiftly sprouting from charred forests, the kindling of lights at the darkest point of the winter solstice, the transfiguration of landscapes, reborn each spring. This greening paradigm weaves nature's laws through human lores to understand the human spirit through the creative workings of the human mind.

This is why, in my opinion, the Christ story – and the stories Christ tells – interpreted psychologically are among the greatest stories ever told. They are designed to lead us away from the concrete, corporeal, "thing" itself, toward transcendence of loss through acceptance. Lasting love results from total loss. The Christ story is a parable for the human mind, teaching that in loss is transformation. Whether we speak of symbolization and sublimation, or transfiguration and resurrection, we are referring to faculties of the mind, its ability to rise above our biological plight. In this sense, mourning is transforming. The transfiguration is within.

Acknowledgments

An earlier version of this chapter was published in 2003 in *Psychoanalysis and Contemporary Thought*, 26(4): 427–462. The current version is published here by kind permission of Dr. Leo Goldberger, head of Psychoanalysis and Contemporary Science, Inc., and editor of *Psychoanalysis and Contemporary Thought*.

References

Attig, T. (2001) Relearning the world: making and finding meanings. In R.A. Neimeyer (ed.) *Meaning Reconstruction and the Experience of Loss*, pp. 33–53. Washington, DC: American Psychological Association.

Baker, J.E. (2001) Mourning and the transformation of object relationships: evidence of the persistence of internal attachments. *Psychoanalytic Psychology*, 18(1): 55–73.

Becker, E. (1973) *The Denial of Death*. New York: The Free Press.

Bowlby, J. (1961) Processes of mourning. *International Journal of Psychoanalysis*, 42: 317–340.

—— (1963) Pathological mourning and childhood mourning. In R.V. Frankiel (ed.) *Essential Papers on Object Loss*, pp. 185–221. New York: New York University Press, 1984.

—— (1969, 1973, 1980) *Attachment, Separation and Loss*, Volumes 1, 2 and 3. New York: Basic Books.

Brenner, C. (1974) Some observations on depression, on nosology, on affects and on mourning. *Journal of Geriatric Psychiatry*, 7: 6–20.

Breuer, J. and Freud, S. (1893–1895) *Studies on Hysteria. Standard Edition*, 2: 1–309. London: Hogarth Press, 1955.

Deutsch, H. (1937) Absence of grief. *Psychoanalytic Quarterly*, 6: 12–22.

Dietrich, D. and Shabad, P. (eds) (1989) *The Problem of Loss and Mourning Psychoanalytic Perspectives*. Madison, CT: International Universities Press.

Eisenstadt, M. (1978) Parental loss and genius. In R.V. Frankiel (ed.) *Essential Papers on Object Loss*, pp. 273–296. New York: New York University Press, 1994.

Engels, G. (1961) Is grief a disease? *Psychosomatic Medicine*, 23: 18–22.

Fleming, J. and Altschul, B. (1963) Activation of mourning and growth by psychoanalysis. *International Journal of Psychoanalysis*, 44: 419–431.

Freud, S. (1913–1914) *Totem & Taboo. Standard Edition*, 13: 1–161. London: Hogarth Press, 1955.

—— (1915) Thoughts for the times on war and death. *Standard Edition*, 14: 273–300. London: Hogarth Press, 1957.

—— (1916) On transience. *Standard Edition*, 14: 305–307. London: Hogarth Press, 1957.

—— (1917) Mourning and melancholia. *Standard Edition*, 14: 237–258. London: Hogarth Press, 1957.

—— (1923) *The Ego and the Id. Standard Edition*, 19: 12–66. London: Hogarth Press, 1961.

—— (1926) *Inhibitions, Symptoms and Anxiety. Standard Edition*, 20: 87–172. London: Hogarth Press, 1959.

Furman, E. (1974a) *A Child's Parent Dies: Studies in Childhood Bereavement*. New Haven, CT: Yale University Press.

—— (1974b) Some of the effects of the parent's death on the child's personality development. In R.V. Frankiel (ed.) *Essential Papers on Object Loss*, pp. 382–402. New York: New York University Press, 1994.

Furman, R.A. (1973) A child's capacity for mourning. In R.V. Frankiel (ed.) *Essential Papers on Object Loss*, pp. 376–381. New York: New York University Press, 1994.

Gaines, R. (1997) Detachment and continuity: the two tasks of mourning. *Contemporary Psychoanalysis*, 33: 549–571.

Gennep, A. van (1909) *The Rites of Passage*. London: Routledge & Kegan Paul, 1960.

Hagman, G. (1995) Mourning: a review and reconsideration. *International Journal of Psychoanalysis*, 76: 909–925.

—— (1996) The role of the other in mourning. *Psychoanalytic Quarterly*, 65: 327–352.

—— (2001) Beyond decathexis: toward a new psychoanalytic understanding and treatment of mourning. In R.A. Neimeyer (ed.) *Meaning Reconstruction and the Experience of Loss*, pp. 13–31. Washington, DC: American Psychological Association.

Horowitz, A.J. (1990) A model of mourning: change in schemas of self and other. *Journal of the American Psychoanalytic Association*, 38: 297–324.

Jacobs, S. (1993) *Pathological Grief: Maladaptation to Loss*. Washington, DC: American Psychiatric Press.

Jacobson, E. (1965) The return of the lost parent. In R.V. Frankiel (ed.) *Essential Papers on Object Loss*, pp. 233–290. New York: New York University Press, 1984.

Kaplan, L.J. (1995) *No Voice is Ever Wholly Lost*. New York: Simon & Schuster.

Klein, M. (1940) Mourning and its relation to manic-depressive states. *International Journal of Psychoanalysis*, 21: 125–153. In R.V. Frankiel (ed.) *Essential Papers on Object Loss*, pp. 95–122. New York: New York University Press, 1984.

Kubler-Ross, E. (1969) *On Death and Dying*. New York: Macmillan.

Lewis, C.S. (1976) *A Grief Observed*. New York: Bantam.

Lindemann, E. (1944) Symptomatology and management of acute grief. In R.V. Frankiel (ed.) *Essential Papers on Object Loss*, pp. 18–31. New York: New York University Press, 1984.

Loewald, H. (1962) Internalization, separation, mourning, and the superego. In R.V. Frankiel (ed.) *Essential Papers on Object Loss*, pp. 124–140. New York: New York University Press, 1994.

McCann, M.E. (1974) Mourning accomplished by way of the transference. In R.V. Frankiel (ed.) *Essential Papers on Object Loss*, pp. 449–467. New York: New York University Press, 1984.

Nagera, H. (1970) Children's reactions to the death of important objects: a developmental approach. *The Psychoanalytic Study of the Child*, 25: 360–400.

Neimeyer, R.A. (1998) *Lessons of Loss: A Guide to Coping*. New York: McGraw-Hill.

—— (2001) The language of loss: grief therapy as a process of meaning construction. In R.A. Neimeyer (ed.) *Meaning Reconstruction and the Experience of Loss*, pp. 261–392. Washington, DC: American Psychological Association.

Parkes, C.M. (1972) *Bereavement: Studies of Grief in Adult Life*. New York: International Universities Press.

Pollock, G.H. (1961) Mourning and adaptation. In R.V. Frankiel (ed.) *Essential Papers on Object Loss*, pp. 162–179. New York: New York University Press, 1984.

—— (1989) *The Mourning-Liberation Process*, Volume 1. Madison, CT: International Universities Press.

Rilke, R.M. (1922) Sonnets to Orpheus II, 29. In W. Lepman (ed.) *Rilke: A Life*. Trans. R. Exner. New York: Fromm International, 1987.

Segal, H. (1952) A psychoanalytical approach to aesthetics. *International Journal of Psychoanalysis*, 33: 196–207.

Shabad, P. (1993) Repetition and incomplete mourning: the intergenerational transmission of traumatic themes. *Psychoanalytic Psychology*, 10(1): 61–75.

—— (2001) *Despair and the Return of Hope: Echoes of Mourning in Psychotherapy*. Northvale, NJ: Jason Aronson.

Shane, M. and Shane, E. (1990) Object loss and selfobject loss: A consideration of self psychology's contribution to understanding mourning and the failure to mourn. *Annual of Psychoanalysis*, 18: 115–131.

Shapiro, E. (1996) Grief in Freud's life: reconceptualizing bereavement in psychoanalytic theory. *Psychoanalytic Psychology*, 13: 547–566.

Siggins, S.L. (1966) Mourning: a critical review of the literature. *International Journal of Psychoanalysis*, 47: 14–25.

Solnit, A.J. (1970) A study of object loss in infancy. *Psychoanalytic Study of the Child*, 25: 257–272.

Spitz, R. (1945) Hospitalism: an inquiry into the genesis of psychiatric conditions in early childhood. *The Psychoanalytic Study of the Child*, 1: 53–74.

—— (1946) Hospitalism: a follow-up report on investigation described in volume I, 1945. *The Psychoanalytic Study of the Child*, 2: 113–117.

Tedeschi, R.G., Park, C.L. and Calhoun, L.G. (eds) (1998) *Posttraumatic Growth: Positive Changes in the Aftermath of Crisis*. Mahwah, NJ: Lawrence Erlbaum.

Wolfenstein, M. (1966) How is mourning possible? *Psychoanalytic Study of the Child*, 21: 93–123.

Wortman, C.B. and Silver, R.C. (1987) Coping with irrevocable loss. In G.R. Vandenbos and B.K. Bryant (eds) *Cataclysms, Crises and Catastrophes: Psychology in Action*, pp. 185–235. Washington, DC: American Psychological Association.

Chapter 3

Individuals and societies as "perennial mourners"

Their linking objects and public memorials

Vamik D. Volkan

The loss of an important person or thing initiates grief and mourning. In psychological literature a *grief reaction* and a *mourning process* are often not differentiated. Norman Itzkowitz (2001) wrote:

> Although dictionaries give grieving and mourning as synonymous, for me they are not the same emotionally. To grieve and experience sorrow that accompanies it is a much more transitory matter than mourning. Mourning is a process, and you have to go through the entire process and emerge at the other end before you can let go of the deceased. As such, it takes time. Dictionaries neither grieve nor mourn, otherwise they would know the difference.
>
> (Itzkowitz, 2001, pp. 173–174)

I refer to the initial reactions to a loss as "grief." It includes a sense of *shock* if the mourner was not prepared to lose a psychologically significant person or thing. The sense of shock alternates or is accompanied by some *physical reactions* such as shortness of breath, tightness in the throat, a need to sigh, muscular limpness, and a loss of appetite. As shock and its physical symptoms abate, the mourner experiences a wish to have the loss reversed. He or she may *deny*, at least for a while, that the loss actually took place. A more common phenomenon is the mourner's utilization of *splitting* (Freud, 1940). This splitting is not the same as that of borderline individuals. Borderline individuals typically split their self-images and/or object images. The mourner splits an ego function so that opposing perceptions and experiences can take place simultaneously. For example, a woman knows that her dead husband is lying in a coffin at a funeral home. But this same grieving widow "hears" her husband's car as it crunches the gravel in the driveway.

Grief also includes the mourner's *bargaining* with "God," "Fate," oneself or others in order to reverse the death of someone or to undo the burning of his or her beloved house, as if such reversals were possible: "If I were not stuck in traffic and home earlier, I would have prevented the accident that caused the death of my wife or the burning of my house." The mourner, in his/her mind, may become preoccupied with the idea of taking a different route when driving home that day and avoiding the heavy traffic, or may dream of reversing the tragedy in other ways.

In reality the lost person or thing never reappears and the mourner feels *guilty*, to one degree or another, for not reversing the outcome of the tragedy and/or for continuing to live while someone else is gone or something is destroyed. The mourner's own guilt is complicated because – again to one degree or another – the mourner is also angry that, by being lost, someone or something induced in him or her a narcissistic wound. The lost person or thing will no longer satisfy the mourner's wishes. For example, the mourner will no longer go to bed with his dead wife or take shelter in a burned house, but such wishes still exist. The mourner's feelings of guilt and anger may be conscious. Most often, however, such feelings are repressed. We know these feelings exist if the grieving mourner seeks psychological treatment or is already undergoing treatment. The therapist then can "hear" a great deal about the mourner's guilt and anger. Often the mourner displaces his or her anger onto someone else or something else. A mourner may feel anger towards a physician who had taken care of his dead wife for example, or he may become irritated with the manufacturer of the gas stove that originated the fire that burned his house.

Most importantly and obviously, a mourner's grieving is accompanied by pain and sorrow. A mourner, in a sense, keeps hitting his or her head on a wall, a wall that never opens up to allow the dead person or lost thing to come back! This itself induces some anger, but this type of anger is a healthy indication that the mourner is beginning to accept the facts.

A typical grief reaction takes some months to disappear. In truth, there is no typical grief reaction because the circumstances of a loss are varied and each individual has his or her own degree of internal preparedness to face significant losses. Grief reactions may reappear for a time at the anniversary of the event when the loss took place.

A grief reaction itself can be complicated. There are adults who spontaneously cry and feel pain and anger whenever something in their environment reminds them of their original loss. Once I had an analysand who spent the first two and half years on my couch crying and exhibiting a grief reaction at each session. After a while, she would become interested in other topics that had nothing to do with her loss. During her next session, she would grieve again. She was *fixated* in grief.

Mourning is a more silent and internal phenomenon. It begins when the individual still exhibits a grief reaction and typically continues for years. Sigmund Freud's (1917) paper on "Mourning and melancholia" contains what is still one of the best descriptions of the mourning process. What Freud wrote can be restated using today's psychoanalytic terminologies including some additions. I will now do that.

The physical loss of a person or thing does not parallel the mental "burial" of the object representation of the lost person or thing. In fact, the physical loss (or even a threat of a physical loss) turns the adult mourner's attention to the object representation of what was lost. (In this chapter I will focus on adult mourning and will deal with children's reactions to loss only briefly.) The adult's mourning process refers to the sum of mental activities the mourner performs in reviewing and dealing with the object representation of the lost person or thing. As long as we live, we never lose the object representation of significant others or things even when they are lost in the physical world.

If a mourning process is completed, for practical purposes, we make the object representation of the lost person or thing "futureless" (Tähkä, 1984). The object representation of the lost item is no longer utilized to respond to our wishes; it has no future. A young man stops fantasizing that a wife who had been dead for some time will give him sexual pleasure, for example, or a woman stops wishing to boss her underlings at a job from which she had been fired years before. It can be said that we "bury" the object representation of a lost person or thing when we manage to make them futureless.

During the mourning process, the mourner reviews, in a piecemeal fashion, the object representation of what has been lost and, in so doing, he or she is able to *keep* aspects of the lost person or thing's images within his or her own self representation. This is possible due to a mourner's *identification* with the aspects of the object representation of the lost item.

When such identifications are *selective* and "healthy," the mourning process is considered "normal." The mourner, after going through the pain of grief and spending considerable energy reviewing the object representation of the lost person or thing, "gains" something from these experiences. For example, by assimilating the functions of a deceased person, the mourner can now perform such functions himself or herself. A year or so after his father's death, a philandering young man becomes a serious industrialist like his dead father used to be. A woman who depended on her husband to reinforce her sense of femininity may emerge from a healthy mourning feeling confident and womanly. An immigrant who had lost his country may create a symbolic representation of his country in a painting or song. Most identifications take place unconsciously.

Freud (1917) was also aware of *unhealthy identifications*. If a mourner related to the lost person or thing with excessive ambivalence while this person still lived or the thing still existed, the mourner may end up identifying with the object representation of the lost item in an unhealthy manner. Such people are unable to create a selective and enriching identification. Instead, they assimilate the object representation "in toto" (Smith, 1975, p. 20) into their self-representation. Accordingly, the love and the hate (ambivalence) that originally connected the mourner to the lost person or thing now turn the mourner's self-representation into a battleground. The struggle between love and hate is now felt within the mourner's self-representation that assimilated the ambivalently related object representation through a total identification. Freud called this condition "melancholia."

When hate toward the assimilated object representation becomes dominant, mourners may even attempt to kill themselves in order to "kill" the assimilated object representation. They may want to shoot, psychologically speaking, the object representation assimilated within their self-representation and, accordingly, shoot themselves. Melancholia (depression) after a loss can be fatal.

My clinical studies of various types of grief reactions and mourning processes of individuals began in the late 1960s and lasted for two decades or so. I described my findings in dozens of papers and two books (Volkan, 1981; Volkan and Zintl, 1993) and as editor of a book (Volkan, 1985). Since the mid 1980s, I spent more time studying societal mourning (Volkan, 1988, 1997, 2004a; Volkan et al., 2002). I have not made many references to other scholars' works in this summary of the psychodynamics of grief and mourning; such references are available in my previous publications.

While studying complicated mourning among individuals, I described a rather brief, but intense, psychotherapy for those suffering from it. I named this technique "re-grief therapy" (Volkan and Showalter, 1968; Volkan, 1972; Volkan et al., 1975; Volkan and Josephthal, 1980). Later, others used this technique in less intense and modified ways. I hold, however, that to successfully use this technique, one should not modify it.

In studying complications encountered in mourning, my coworkers and I also focused on a specific type of complication that we called "established pathological mourning." We referred to individuals suffering from this specific complication as "perennial mourners." The rest of this chapter will review and update my findings on individuals who are perennial mourners. I will also refer to societies as perennial mourners.

Perennial mourners

Mourning can be divided into two categories: developmental mourning and mourning over concrete losses. (In this chapter, I am mainly focusing on the concrete losses of adults.) *Developmental losses* refer to "losses" individuals experience as they move up the developmental ladder from babyhood through adolescence. At this latter time, people go through a "second individuation" (Blos, 1979) and firmly establish their identity as well as their personality organization. Development can be conceptualized as a series of "losses and gains." A baby "loses" his or her mother's breast in order to gain the potential of physically separating from the mother. A young child "loses" his or her transitional object in order to gain the ability to create further, beyond the creation of a transitional object (Winnicott, 1953). An oedipal child "loses" his or her parent of the same sex in order to gain experiences in triangular and then multiple person relationships. An adolescent "loses" (modifies) many of his or her existing self and object images in order to crystallize a "new" self-representation and "new" object representations. Wolfenstein (1966, 1969), I believe correctly, saw a parallel between a youngster's going through an adolescence passage and an adult's normal mourning process. The former becomes a model for the latter.

If someone experiences difficulties in going through developmental losses and thus cannot "learn" how to separate internally from significant others or things, this person, as an adult, will be prone to complications when facing *concrete losses* (or even threats of concrete losses) such as losing a loved one, a job, or prestige. Clinicians treating adults suspected of having complicated grief or mourning can learn a great deal by examining these patients' reactions to developmental losses and learning how they experienced the adolescence passage.

When a mourner had been extremely dependent on or highly ambivalent toward the one who died (or thing which was lost) and had "unfinished psychological business" with the deceased, complications in mourning can be expected. Such ambivalent or even hostile dependency usually stems from unfinished psychological business originating from earlier developmental levels. Accordingly, the patient cannot permit the dead person (or the lost thing) to disappear. He, she (or the lost thing) is needed to resolve previous unfinished conflicts and/or gratify previously ungratified wishes.

Another major factor that complicates mourning comes from the contamination of the mourning process with reactions to a trauma. When a loss is associated with experiences of helplessness, passivity, shame and humiliation, mourning is accompanied by other psychological tasks such as turning helplessness and passivity into assertion and activity and reversing shame and humiliation. A loss may be traumatic in its own right, especially when it is sudden and unexpected, but above and beyond the loss itself, the combination of a loss with actual *trauma* complicates mourning in a serious way. Often, unless a person deals with the trauma first, the mourning process cannot be put in its "normal" tract. Losses occurring during wars and war-like situations, accompanied by terror or terrorism, would most likely complicate mourning. When a loss occurs due to a murder, suicide or other such devastating tragedy, the rage expressed through such events unconsciously becomes connected with the mourner's "normal" level of anger while grieving. The mourner does not wish to "know" his or her anger if this anger means an unconscious connection with a murderer or other rage-filled people that cause destruction.

Complications in mourning do not always lead to "melancholia" (depression), but may result in another outcome, called "established pathological mourning." Adults suffering from it become "perennial mourners," doomed to remain preoccupied with aspects of their mourning for decades to come and even until the end of their lives. Perennial mourners experience their mourning without bringing it to a practical conclusion. There are various degrees of severity of such a condition. Some perennial mourners live miserable lives. Others express their unending mourning in more creative ways, but even most of these people, when not obsessed with their creativity, feel uncomfortable.

The following is a description of the internal world of a perennial mourner. To a large degree, the mourner cannot identify with the selected, enriching aspects of the object representation of the lost one. On the other hand, the mourner does not end up identifying totally with the object representation. In other words, the mourner cannot go through "normal" mourning and cannot develop depression. Instead, the mourner keeps the object representation of the lost person or thing within his or her self-representation as a specific, *unassimilated* "foreign body." In the past, we called such an unassimilated object representation an *introject*. The ambivalent relationship of the past continues in the mourner's involvement with the introject. The mourner is torn between a strong yearning for the restored presence of the lost person or thing and an equally deep dread that the lost item might be confronted. The presence of the introject provides an illusion of choice. In this way, it reduces anxiety, but having an introject also means the continuation of an internal struggle with it.

The term "introject" does not appear in contemporary literature. I think we should keep it. It fully describes the situation as it appeared in the following perennial mourner.

A man came to see me, complaining that his younger brother had been disturbing him daily. He did not know how to deal with the situation. He sought treatment in order to free himself from his brother's influence. He explained that while driving to work in his car his brother constantly talked with him, even when my patient wanted some time for himself or when he wanted to listen to the car radio. His brother gave him advice about everything. For example, he made suggestions as to how my patient should behave when meeting his boss or when talking to a particular secretary at work. My patient did not like his brother's advice. Sometimes he told his brother to shut up, but the younger man continued to talk and irritate him. When both men were young, my patient experienced considerable sibling rivalry.

I pictured my patient in his car with his brother sitting next to him. I even imagined that my patient and his brother lived together in the same house or at least nearby, which would explain their riding together each workday to the downtown business area. Therefore, I was really surprised when my patient, in his sixth session, informed me that his brother had died six years before in an accident. The "brother" with whom he had conversations while driving to work was actually his brother's unassimilated object representation.

My patient felt it to be lodged in his chest. Sometimes he experienced this object representation as a puppet-sized younger brother sitting on one of his shoulders, literally a symbolized burden, but most of the time the "brother" was inside my patient's body image.

An introject is a special object representation with which an individual wishes to identify, but the identification does not take place and the object representation, with its own "boundaries," remains in the individual's self-representation as an unassimilated mental construct. Such an introject excessively influences the person who has it.

Having an "introject" of the lost person or thing and having an interaction with it does not make the mourner a psychotic individual. Outside his special "relationship" with his younger brother's object representation, my patient was simply a neurotic. He did not experience any break with reality except when communicating with his introject. An established pathological mourning may *imitate* a psychotic condition, so a clinician needs to be alert and not confuse it with schizophrenia or related, excessively regressed conditions.

A perennial mourner daily expends energy to "kill" or to "bring back to life" the lost person or thing. The severity of this preoccupation varies from individual to individual. In severe cases, this struggle renders the mourner's adaptation to daily life very difficult. Perennial mourners are compulsive about reading obituary notices. This betrays not only anxiety over their own death, but also an attempt to deny that of the one they mourn because they find no current mention of it. Some such mourners fancy they recognize their lost ones in someone whom they encounter at a distance. They make daily references to death, tombs, or graveyards in a ritualistic way, and talk about the dead in the present tense. The listener gets the impression that the speaker's daily life includes some actual relationship with the deceased who continues to watch over him or her. If the lost item is a thing, the perennial mourner thinks about scenarios that involve finding and losing this thing again and again. Sometimes this "losing and finding" becomes generalized. For example, friends might know the perennial mourner as an individual who very often loses car keys, then finds them in unexpected places.

Perennial mourners have "typical dreams." They can be classified as follows:

- "Frozen" dreams: Many perennial mourners spontaneously use the term *frozen* to describe the fixation of their mourning and also to describe some of their dreams, which are often like slide shows, composed of still, frozen images. The term "frozen" also reflects lifelessness.
- Dreams of life-and-death struggle in which the dreamer sees the one who has died or is lost as still engaged in a life-and-death struggle. The

dreamer tries to rescue the person or thing – or to finish him, her, or it off. The outcome remains uncertain because the dreamer invariably awakens before the situation can be resolved.

- Dreams of loss as an illusion. For example, the perennial mourner dreams of seeing the dead body but noticing something about it, like sweat, that denies the reality of death.

Linking objects and linking phenomena

Returning to my patient who had conversations with his dead brother while driving to work, it will be recalled that sometimes he felt a little "figure" had been sitting on his shoulder. This imagined figure was an *externalized* version of his brother's introject. In 1972, after studying fifty-five individuals suffering from complicated grief reactions and/or mourning processes, I coined the terms "linking object" and "linking phenomenon." Briefly, these terms describe some mourners' externalized versions of introjects of lost persons or things. My patient "created" this imaginary figure and it was his *linking phenomenon*, connecting him with his dead brother. For some perennial mourners, a song, a hand gesture, even a certain type of weather condition may function as a linking phenomenon.

Most individuals with established pathological mourning utilize *concrete inanimate objects* such as a special photograph (and also, but seldom, an animate object such as a pet) that symbolize a meeting ground between the object representation of a lost person or thing and the mourner's corresponding self-image. I call such objects *linking objects*. Mourners "choose" a linking object from various items available. A linking object may be a personal possession of the deceased, often something the deceased wore or used routinely, like a watch. A gift the deceased made to the mourner before death, or a letter written by a soldier on a battlefield before being killed, may evolve into a linking object. A realistic representation of the lost person, such as a painting, can also function as a linking object. There are also what I call "last minute objects," something at hand when a mourner first learned of the death or saw the dead body. They relate to the last moment in which the deceased was regarded as a living person.

Sometimes linking objects are "selected" soon after an individual loses someone. Such items become crystallized as linking objects when the individual develops an established pathological mourning. Becoming a perennial mourner, he experiences the linking object as "magical." The mourner may hide it, but needs to know the object's whereabouts; it must be protected and controlled. Since a person can control an inanimate thing more easily than an animate one, most linking objects are inanimate. If a linking object is lost, the mourner will experience anxiety, often severe.

Through the creation of a linking object or phenomenon, the perennial mourner makes an "adjustment" to the complication within the mourning process, making the mourning "unending" so as not to face the conflict pertaining to the relationship with the object representation of the deceased. By *controlling* the linking object, perennial mourners control their wish to "bring back" (love) or "kill" (hate) the lost person, thus avoiding the psychological consequences if any of these two wishes are gratified. (If the dead person were to come back to life, the mourner would depend on him or her forever. If the dead person were "killed," the mourner's existing anger would cause feelings of guilt.)

Since the linking object or phenomenon is "out there," the mourning process is *externalized*. Mourners do not feel the struggle with the introject within themselves. The linking object contains the tension of ambivalence and anger pertaining to the narcissistic hurt inflicted by the death. When mourners "lock up" a photograph that has become a linking object in a drawer, they "hide" their complicated mourning in the same drawer. All such a person needs is to know where the photograph is safely tucked away. Such people may unlock the drawer during an anniversary of the loss and look at the photograph or touch it, but as soon as they feel anxious, the photograph is locked up again.

There are linking phenomena and objects that connect a person with complicated mourning, not to a deceased, but to a significant lost *thing*. The Austrian painter Wolff Werdigier provided a moving illustration of this recently. His father, a Jew, lost his wife and son during the Holocaust. Later, he married Werdigier's German mother. Werdigier, due to his background I suspect, has been very interested in human nature, group violence, psychoanalysis and the Middle East conflict. During the 1990s as well as in the 2000s, he painted dozens of psychoanalytic concepts. One of his paintings is titled *Attachment to Ground*. The painting shows the agonized face of a person whose body disappears in yellow sand. There are old-fashioned door keys stuck in the sand that surrounds the head of this individual. The keys symbolize the linking objects of many Palestinians. I learned from Werdigier that when the Israelis bulldoze their homes, most Palestinians keep the keys to their front doors and become perennial mourners over losing their homes. They control the keys in order to "freeze" their mourning. The hope that they might rebuild their homes and the expectation for revenge are locked up in the keys.

Linking objects and phenomena should not be confused with childhood transitional objects and phenomena that are reactivated in adulthood. Certainly there are some severely regressed adults, such as some schizophrenics, who reactivate the transitional relatedness of their babyhoods and "recreate" transitional objects. A transitional object represents the first not-me, but it is never totally not-me. It links not-me with mother-me and is a temporary construction toward a sense of reality (Winnicott, 1953; Greenacre, 1969). Linking objects contain high-level symbolism. They must be thought of as tightly packed symbols whose significance is bound up in the conscious and unconscious nuances of the relationship that preceded the loss. Therefore, not every keepsake or memento cherished by a mourner should be considered as a linking object possessing a significant investment of symbolism and magic. A linking object or phenomenon is an external bridge between the representations of the mourner and that of the lost person or thing, just as the introject serves as an internal bridge.

Positive functions of linking objects: the AWON story

Initially in my decades-long study on grief and mourning, I focused on the pathological aspects of linking objects and linking phenomena. I considered their existence *only* as a sign of a mourner's "freezing" his or her mourning. I later wrote about the linking object or phenomenon as a source of inspiration that gave direction to creativity in some individuals (Volkan and Zintl, 1993). Complicated mourning still remains in such individuals, but now is expressed in art. It is not proper to refer to someone who created such a thing as the Taj Mahal as "pathological."

Furthermore, when my colleagues and I developed the technique of "re-grief therapy," we learned that a linking object or phenomenon can often produce a positive outcome. Having a linking object or phenomenon helps adults maintain hope and a potential to open their psychological wounds, then heal them. The technique of "re-grief therapy" centers on mourners bringing linking objects to therapeutic sessions. The aim is to help the mourner reinternalize what had been externalized onto the linking object. This reinternalization will reactivate the mourning process. The therapist's task is to help the mourner to complete the mourning instead of keeping it "frozen."

I learned more about the positive psychological importance of having linking objects when, in the early 1990s, I began to interview and/or get to know well over one hundred persons whom the US government officially recognized as "World War II Orphans." For the next dozen years, until the opening of the World War II Memorial in Washington, DC in 2004, I followed their lives closely. These men and women, in their fifties or sixties when first I got to know them, had lost their fathers during World War II. Their fathers were killed when these individuals were very young. Many of them, in fact, were born after their fathers were no longer around. Most of them had no, or very little, memory of their fathers. In 1991, during the fiftieth anniversary of Pearl Harbor, they organized themselves under the umbrella of "The World War II Orphans Network" (or AWON – American War Orphans Network) and played a role in adding gold stars to one wall of the World War II Memorial. Each of these 4000 stars represents 100 American war dead. By the time the Memorial opened on Memorial Day in 2004, there were more than 800 members of AWON, which itself functioned as a shared linking phenomenon for the members. I tried to understand why they waited so long to organize themselves. I came to the conclusion that when the orphans' own children reached the ages of their fathers when they were killed, the orphans had a new external stimulus, besides the anniversary of Pearl Harbor, to deal with their mourning.

When I refer to the members of AWON, I am describing the consequences of childhood losses. The psychology of these losses is different from adult mourning. Prior to age 2 or even 3, a child has little of what psychoanalysts call "object constancy," that is, they do not yet have the ability to fully form and maintain the mental representations of other people or things. The World War II orphans who lost their fathers before age 3 created a total fantasy of their biological fathers. Those who became fatherless between ages 3 and 10 also, to one extent or other, developed fantasized father representations. The older ones, close to age 10, would have some realistic father images, but their fathers were stationed in faraway places and these children were not able to have concrete interactions with them during some crucial developmental years.

The AWON members illustrate how losing their fathers became intertwined with the difficulties of dealing with their "developmental losses" described earlier. Even those who were provided with father substitutes, such as stepfathers, created and maintained fantasized biological father figures and, psychologically, interacted with them significantly. Furthermore, they were "special" because of the title given to them by the government: World War II Orphans. Governmental funds that provided for their education added to their "specialness." Their psychology was different in significant ways from that of children who, in their childhood, lost their fathers due to illness, accidents, murder or suicide. Their being "special" supported their self-esteem, but often being "special" and, especially, "hiding" it from others, such as step-siblings, is a psychological burden.

Societal expectations and pressures that existed in the early or mid 1940s, even to the extent that widows were sometimes considered "available" or "loose women," "forced" many war widows to "erase" any concrete links to their dead husbands. If they remarried, they brought no items to their new homes that had belonged to or connected them with their first husbands, except, of course, their children. Often they remained silent and did not share with the war orphans their "memories" of their first marriages and the trauma they experienced as war widows. Thus a great number of World War II orphans whom I got to know as adults did not have any concrete linking objects connecting them with their biological fathers. Those who had concrete linking objects, such as their fathers' photographs, letters, medals or graves, fared better in creating more realistic father images and in adjusting to life. All of the World War II orphans were involved in an obligatory "father search" (Hadler et al., 1998). They needed to find "him" in their lives, in their spouses, for example. This created psychological difficulties. As adults, AWON members had become perennial mourners.

They clung to their linking objects or began spending considerable time and energy trying to find new, concrete linking objects. For some, finding such a concrete linking object would be the first "miracle." Some traveled very long distances to jungles where their fathers' planes had crashed, with the hope of finding a dog tag or piece of bone. The main function of such linking objects was to help the war orphans "know" that their fathers, once upon a time, really existed. Through the utilization of these linking objects, some of them were able to modify their fantasized father representations and make such representations more realistic. After this, many such individuals were able to restart their grieving and mourning and begin to honor their fathers' mental representations' as "futureless" representations. Grieving included the typical reactions and lots of tears, which other AWON members could share. Their mourning process became more silent and personal. As one of them who is completing her mourning told me, she "misses" her grieving reactions. With insight, she added that "losing" her grieving allowed her to "gain" her mourning.

Societal mourning and public memorials as shared linking objects

Public memorials are built not only for memorializing the dead, or a lost land, but also for the living, or a regained land. During the official and unofficial ceremonies connected with the opening of the World War II Memorial, I accompanied hundreds of AWON members and observed how they experienced the Memorial as their shared linking object connecting them to their dead fathers. They reactivated their grief and mourning and "reburied" their fathers at this location. For those orphans whose lost fathers had no graves, the World War II Memorial became the first symbolic burial place of the dead. The orphans, as well as hundreds and hundreds of other Americans, began leaving pictures, letters, medals, and flowers at the memorial site, psychologically communicating with their lost ones.

Keeping in mind the focus of this chapter, I will concentrate only on public memorials that evolve as *shared linking objects* for societal or large-group – such as ethnic, national or religious group – mourning. Like an individual perennial mourner's linking object, a monument associated with a group's mourning may have a "negative" aspect associated with the wish to keep the mourning process active in the hope of recovering what was lost. Such a wish fuels feelings of revenge. On the other hand, it may have a "positive" function connected with a wish to "lock up" the unfinished aspects of the mourning process in marble or metal and help the group adjust to its current situation without re-experiencing the impact of past shared trauma and loss, along with associated disturbing feelings. One wish can be dominant in relation to one monument, while the other is dominant in relation to another monument. Both shared wishes toward a public monument may coexist until years, decades, or centuries pass and the monument, for future generations, loses its emotional impact and becomes simply a work of art.

Ethnic, national or religious groups mourn after their members share a massive trauma and experience losses (Volkan, 1988, 2004a; Volkan *et al.*, 2002). A large-group mourning does not refer to all or many members crying openly and talking about their losses. Large-group mourning manifests itself mostly by modifying existing societal processes, initiating new ones, or developing modified or new political ideologies (Volkan, 2004b).

One such societal mourning process has been studied by Williams and Parkes (1975). In the Welsh village of Aberfan, an avalanche of coal slurry in 1966 caused the deaths of 116 children and 28 adults. Within five years of the tragedy there was a significant increase in the birth rate among women in the village who had not themselves lost a child. This tragedy was regarded as an act of "God." There was no humiliation and wish for revenge. The societal response to such a tragedy was a "positive" regeneration.

When actual and fantasized trauma is due to "others" and is accompanied by helplessness, shame and humiliation, the group's mourning may include the evolution of a new political ideology. For example, since the birth of modern Greece in the 1830s, after the struggle for independence and separation from the Ottoman Empire, the Greeks evolved an ideology called the "Megali (Great) Idea," which was a response to their experiencing many types of losses while they were Ottoman subjects. The Megali Idea refers to regaining all the lands that Greeks considered "lost" to others. These losses were symbolized by the loss of Constantinople (present-day Istanbul) in 1453 to the Turks. The shared mental representation of this loss became the Greeks' *chosen trauma* (Volkan, 1991) and was transmitted from generation to generation. A "chosen trauma" is the shared mental representation of ancestors' tragedy and the heroes and losses connected with it. Decades or centuries later, when the descendants face new challenges, a chosen trauma can be reactivated, mainly through political propaganda that inflames feelings about ancestors' losses. Thus, new societal and political attitudes or activities are initiated (for details, see Volkan, 1988; Volkan and Itzkowitz, 1994).

Let me return to public memorials connected with losses at the hand of "others," starting with Yad Vashem in Jerusalem. It is a shared linking object connecting Jews – and anyone who is horrified with the idea of the Holocaust – to incredible losses. When I first visited Yad Vashem many years ago, I was accompanied by an Israeli friend. We went through the memorial in silence. As we were leaving, my friend asked how I felt. I recall feeling very angry with him because I experienced his question as asking whether I was a human being or not. A memorial like Yad Vashem is a place where mourning is "stored" and affects pertaining to it are experienced. Since there are many other places like it, such as the former concentration and death camps, and countless other ways to recall and express feelings of grief and mourning regarding the Holocaust (in religious and political ceremonies, books, poems, songs, art, movies, conferences), Yad Vashem is not associated with keeping the wounds caused by the Holocaust alive in the hope of recovering what has been lost in the past. It is associated with keeping the State of Israel safe, not with a deep sense of revenge. It is one of the significant locations of a *still active* mourning process.

Until recently, the Crying Father Monument in Tskhinvali, South Ossetia, as a shared linking object, not only served in an attempt to keep South Ossetians' shared mourning process firmly externalized, but also reinternalized and re-externalized it again and again, fueling feelings of revenge. The following is a brief story of this monument.

After the Republic of Georgia seceded from the Soviet Union in 1990, major ethnic conflicts erupted in Georgia. One of them, which was bloody, was between Georgians and South Ossetians. South Ossetia, like Abkhazia, declared its independence from the Republic of Georgia. Even now, South Ossetia maintains its own "borders" and "government," even though it is not an internationally recognized political state. During the 1991–1992 siege of the South Ossetian capital city Tskhinvali by the Georgian forces, Georgians occupied the city's cemetery. When three young South Ossetian combatants died simultaneously, they were buried in the yard of School #5 on the city's Lenin Avenue. During subsequent weeks, more and more dead defenders were buried there. (There are about one hundred graves there now.) Later, South Ossetians built a small chapel and erected the Crying Father Monument in this schoolyard. In South Ossetian culture, men are not supposed to cry, so the *crying* male represents extreme grief. The monument evolved as a shared linking object and became a "sacred" site where the society's grief reaction and mourning process were externalized. When my colleagues and I visited it for the first time without permission from authorities, we were perceived as intruders rather than visitors coming there to feel empathy for South Ossetians. Some South Ossetian patriots carrying revolvers quickly surrounded us. My colleagues and I survived this incident. I report it here to illustrate how much aggressive affect this monument was able to inflame.

Following the siege, there were repeated ceremonies at the schoolyard, leading to the reinternalization and re-externalization of grief and mourning. Authorities would use every possible excuse to hold such ceremonies; they were held at various anniversaries and during religious holidays. School children were encouraged to write and read poetry about victimization and remember lost persons and land. Utilizing this shared linking object reinforced the image of the enemy. Every school day, children and teachers passed the Crying Father Monument. This continued to "poison" their emotions. As a decade passed after the siege of Tskhinvali, fewer ceremonies were held at this location. Some influential South Ossetians who kept contact with my colleagues and me began to speak of their dilemma: They must either remove the graves and the monument to another location or build a new school. The first option was unthinkable because their religious beliefs forbade them to disturb the dead. On the other hand, the South Ossetians, because of their extreme economic difficulties, could not afford to build a new school. I have not been to this part of the world for several years, and do not know what their solution has been. However, I believe that the Crying Father Monument as a shared linking object still has the potential to open the South Ossetians' wounds without leading to a completion of their societal mourning. In late summer 2004, Georgians and South Ossetians began fighting again and some people were killed. I suspect that South Ossetians went to the Crying Father Monument to inflame their aggressive feelings against the Georgians.

In the United States, the Vietnam Veterans Memorial also evolved as a shared linking object that reactivated many Americans' grief and mourning. Unlike the Crying Father Monument, it helped Americans accept that their losses were real and that life will go on without recovering them. Architect Jeffrey Karl Ochsner (1997), who studied the influence of the Vietnam Veterans Memorial on the nation, wrote: "We choose to erect grave markers and monuments to commemorate the lives of the dead; we usually do not intend to build linking objects, although objects we do make clearly can serve us this way" (p. 166). Ochsner added that when the Vietnam War came to an end, "The most common response was, in effect, denial" (p. 159). The dead, of course, were mourned by family members and friends and were buried quietly. "However, the construction of the Vietnam Veterans Memorial, with the inscribed names of the dead and missing, seemed to change all this" (p. 159).

Maya Yin Lin, the memorial's young designer, wanted to take a knife and cut open the earth, and "with time the grass would heal it" (Campbell, 1983, p. 150). Visitors to the Vietnam Veterans Memorial see their reflections on the black polished stone where the names of the dead and the missing are carved. Visitors' reflections link their own images with the object representations of the lost ones. Kurt Volkan (1992) states: "By touching the stone and etching the names, the living bonded with dead – after all, a name is a symbolic term that embodies everything about one's existence" (p. 76). He added: "Thus, this Wall [the monument] can be as personal as a mother crying for her lost son, or as public as a nation weeping a past history that has yet to be resolved" (p. 76). The Vietnam Veterans Memorial not only opened a wound, but also helped Americans to heal it.

The building of the World War II Memorial sixty years after the ending of that war, I believe, will help not only the members of AWON, but also Americans in general, to complete the group mourning process in a more adaptive way. Meanwhile, after the terrible events on September 11, 2001, losses of persons and things are increasing daily due to terrorism, and

America and its allies' response to it. In the long run, the idea of not publicly showing dead American combatants and their coffins and making wars rather "sterile," will, I think, make American *societal* mourning over those lost in Afghanistan, Iraq and elsewhere difficult. Meanwhile, affected Muslim groups' shared complicated mourning over the loss of thousands of individuals who have been killed and will be killed by Americans and others, including their own rival groups, since September 11, will initiate new societal and political processes that will drastically influence international relations for decades and perhaps centuries to come.

Last remarks

I have studied various types of grief and mourning over four decades. This chapter reviews and updates some of my findings. I especially focus on two concepts that I coined many years ago: "perennial mourning" and "linking objects." I illustrate how many life situations that individuals and societies experience can be explained, to a great extent, by these concepts.

In the early days of my studies, I examined individual mourners and their pathologic, as well as creative responses to losses. During the last decades, I focused more and more on large (i.e., ethnic) group mourning as I traveled through many troubled spots of the world, involved in unofficial diplomacy that brought together representatives of enemy groups for negotiations. I came to the conclusion that international relations, besides utilizing primitive defenses such as massive projections and introjections, are heavily connected with the psychology of losses and gains, in other words, with shared mourning processes.

References

Blos, P. (1979) *The Adolescence Passage*. New York: International Universities Press.

Campbell, R. (1983) An emotive apart. *Art in America*, May: 150–151.

Freud, S. (1917) Mourning and melancholia. *Standard Edition*, 14: 237–258. London: Hogarth Press, 1957.

—— (1940) Splitting of the ego in the process of defense. *Standard Edition*, 23: 271–278. London: Hogarth Press, 1964.

Greenacre, P. (1969) The fetish and the transitional object. In P. Greenacre, *Emotional Growth, Volume 1*, pp. 315–334. New York: International Universities Press.

Hadler, S.J., Mix, A. and Christman, C.L. (1998) *Lost in Victory: Reflections of American War Orphans of World War II*. Denton, TX: University of North Texas Press.

Itzkowitz, N. (2001) Unity out of diversity. *Mind and Human Interaction*, 12: 173–175.

Ochsner, J.K. (1997) A space of loss: the Vietnam Veterans Memorial. *Journal of Architectural Education*, 50: 156–171.

Smith, J.H. (1975) On the work of mourning. In B. Schoenberg, I. Gerber, A. Wiener, A.H. Kutscher, D. Peretz and A.C. Carr (eds) *Bereavement: Its Psychological Aspects*, pp. 18–25. New York: Columbia University Press.

Tähkä, V. (1984) Dealing with object loss. *Scandinavian Psychoanalytic Review*, 7: 13–33.

Volkan, K. (1992) The Vietnam Memorial. *Mind and Human Interaction*, 3: 73–77.

Volkan, V.D. (1972) The "linking objects" of pathological mourners. *Archives of General Psychiatry*, 27: 215–222.

—— (1981) *Linking Objects and Linking Phenomena: A Study of the Forms, Symptoms, Metapsychology, and Therapy of Complicated Mourning*. New York: International Universities Press.

—— (ed.) (1985) *Depressive States and their Treatment*. Northvale, NJ: Jason Aronson.

—— (1988) *The Need to Have Enemies and Allies: From Clinical Practice to International Relationships*. Northvale, NJ: Jason Aronson.

—— (1991) On "chosen trauma." *Mind and Human Interaction*, 3: 13.

—— (1997) *Bloodlines: From Ethnic Pride to Ethnic Terrorism*. New York: Farrar, Straus and Giroux.

—— (2004a) *Blind Trust: Large Groups and their Leaders in Times of Crisis and Terror*. Charlottesville, VA: Pitchstone.

—— (2004b) Chosen trauma, the ideology of entitlement and violence. Paper read at the "Violence or Dialogue: Between Collective Fantasy and Collective Denial" meeting. Federal Office of Foreign Affairs, Berlin, Germany, June 10–12.

Volkan, V.D. and Itzkowitz, N. (1994) *Turks and Greeks: Neighbours in Conflict*. Huntingdon, UK: Eothen Press.

Volkan, V.D. and Josephthal, D. (1980) The treatment of established pathological mourners. In T.B. Karasu and L. Bellak (eds) *Specialized Techniques in Individual Psychotherapy*, pp. 118–142. New York: Brunner/Mazel.

Volkan, V.D. and Showalter, R.C. (1968) Known object loss, disturbance in reality testing and "re-grief work" as a method of psychotherapy. *Psychiatric Quarterly*, 42: 358–374.

Volkan, V.D. and Zintl, E. (1993) *Life after Loss: The Lessons of Grief*. New York: Charles Scribner's Sons.

Volkan, V.D., Cilluffo, A.F., and Sarvay, T.L. (1975) Re-grief therapy and the function of the linking object as a key to stimulate emotionality. In P. Olsen (ed.) *Emotional Flooding*, pp. 179–224. New York: Behavioral Publications.

Volkan, V.D., Ast, G., and Greer, W. (2002) *The Third Reich in the Unconscious: Transgenerational Transmission and its Consequences*. New York: Brunner-Routledge.

Williams, R.M. and Parkes, C.M. (1975) Psychosocial effects of disaster: birth rate in Aberfan. *British Medical Journal*, 2: 303–304.

Winnicott, D.W. (1953) Transitional objects and transitional phenomena. *International Journal of Psychoanalysis*, 3: 89–97.

Wolfenstein, M. (1966) How mourning is possible. *Psychoanalytic Study of the Child*, 21: 93–123.

—— (1969) Loss, rage and repetition. *Psychoanalytic Study of the Child*, 24: 432–460.

Chapter 4

Affects, reconfiguration of the self and self-states in mourning the loss of a son

Judith Lingle Ryan

The changes

made that day are with us still, they change
us even now. I couldn't tell how bare
that day has laid me. Such a blankness
should come to all who think they know what
happens next, and next, and, that after October,
comes November. Unplanned events can leave

us detached, cut off, untreed, like leaves
blown here and there. I won't tell of changes.

These words, from a poem entitled "Something I Couldn't Tell You," were written by Susan Pliner more than ten years after the sudden death of her little boy.

On August 12, 1995, our 23-year-old son, Sean, died on Mount Rainier. He and a fellow park ranger, roped together for safety, fell 1200 feet down an icy glacier while carrying supplies to an injured climber. A tall, strawberry blond with an infectious grin, Sean was an earth science major in college, a passionate outdoorsman and musician. He was the youngest of our three children, and our only son.

A sudden, premature death unleashes a river within. Initially it is experienced as a life-threatening flood, requiring mobilization of psychic resources. Over time, its waters recede, but waves and even floods recur, and always there are myriad streams meandering within us, and in our lives.

In spite of an increasing literature on mourning, the psychoanalytic world, in my experience, often operates from outdated notions: that mourning is a linear event, easing steadily over time; that mourning can and should be worked through; that as clinicians we are the arbiters of pathological or nonpathological grief. That the loss of a loved one is just that: the loss of a person, rather than an event that permanently alters the survivors' internal and external worlds.

In this chapter I will try to do what the poet does not do: I will try to tell of changes. I am writing from my own experience, not because I believe it is universal, but because I hope it will contribute to an ongoing psycho-analytic dialogue about mourning. I will focus first on the initial, acute, affective changes, which I tried to protect myself from with the blankness of dissociation; and then turn to the evolving changes over time in the configuration of myself and myself within my family, as well as the ongoing complexity of shifting affective states.

My instantaneous response to the news of Sean's death was profound dissociation. It was as if I stepped behind glass, into a room of white noise from which I could observe, even as I continued to participate in all that needed to be done. My thinking became fragmented; I could not always hold onto an entire thought. My body ached. I sometimes cried, but I couldn't sob. Mostly I was agitated and disconnected – from myself, from Sean, and to some extent from everyone I loved. One day I experienced for the first and only time in my life an impulse to cut myself. I understand this now as a wish to break through the white noise and feel some kind of pain. I had a fantasy of breaking plates on the rocky beach of the Hudson River, on which we live, but I couldn't allow myself that release.

At other times I felt a manic sense of wellbeing. This was made up no doubt of denial, but also of relief that somehow I was still alive, and so were my husband and our daughters.

I found that sometimes a taste or smell could soothe me, momentarily breaking through my dissociation. I wrote in an essay describing the first weeks after Sean's death:

> I am learning that the soft coral pink of a rose, or the heavy scent of a lily, or the taste of a ripe homegrown tomato can pierce just for a moment the cotton batting of my mind . . . And in that moment I will feel calm, almost peaceful, free from my pervasive restlessness.

I was unable, because of the depth of my dissociation, to conjure up Sean's features, his voice, or the feel of him. I believe now that I was trying to ward off an intolerable dilemma: to hold onto him when he is forever missing creates unbearable yearning; not to be able to hold him internally is equally unbearable. I abruptly stopped remembering my dreams (and would not recover them for months), so my nights were literally blank. I was terrified that I had lost Sean altogether. I grasped at photographs and stories, I read his journal, I looked for his face in his sisters' faces. I was hungry for others' stories about him, and I felt reassured by their memories that they were holding onto him, even as I feared that he might slip from my grasp.

In spite of my dissociation, I did feel comforted by my husband's arms around me at night, and by the presence and love of our daughters, even though I could not take them in as I wished. Others' tears reassured me when I could not cry. Over time – at least a year – I experienced a palpable sense of my friends as not only containing, but also holding onto my feelings, until I could gradually take them in. I was frightened not only of losing Sean, but also of losing an essential part of myself: my grieving, heartbroken self.

Within a few months I found a therapist whose capacity to be moved by my experience, undaunted by my sorrow, sustained me for a long time. With her I could weep more freely than anywhere else, unburdened by fears of upsetting others, and reassured by the boundary of the forty-five-minute hour. In addition, she held onto Sean, and to my relationship with him. I felt this concretely, and to some extent I still do – she knows Sean as I knew him, at least to the degree that anyone is capable of that kind of knowing, and she knows him only through me. Although I am now much less afraid of losing him internally, I still feel reassured that she carries my relationship with him, and in that way she holds us both.

The work of mourning is exhausting. For months a debilitating fatigue would overcome me suddenly, and I would have to stop and lie down. As much as I needed to feel and express my sorrow, I needed dissociation as well. Without it I could not have rested, or rebuilt my strength for the next wave.

What *is* the work of mourning? As I attempted to ride the waves of my grief, I relied on my intellectual capacity to self-reflect with an urgency born of a desperate need for control. I tried to grasp the pieces of what was happening to me, and to understand the nuances of my fears.

The work of mourning is not just to accept that a loved one is never coming home – but to learn to tolerate the meanings of his death to one's sense of self. These meanings are not static, but continue to evolve. For instance, Sean's death has new meaning in our family now that we have grandsons who are old enough to ask questions about him.

How do I understand what dissociation was protecting me from, as the conscious and unconscious work of mourning proceeded? First, dissociation protected me from an onslaught of sadness that I feared would never stop. Second, it protected me from a fear that my world of internal objects had become too impoverished by Sean's death to sustain me. Third, it protected me from a sense of shattering internal disruption, including an overturning of my familiar sense of self. And finally it protected me – and often still does – from the despair of impossible longing for Sean.

As the blankness and white noise began to dissipate, waves of sorrow and mania became stronger. I reread Melanie Klein's "Mourning and its relation to manic-depressive states," and was astonished by my recognition of her description of the bipolar nature of grief. Klein (1940) understands this as reflecting the fact that when an adult grieves, the mourning of the child in the depressive position is revived. I was moved by her understanding of mania as a defense against pining for the lost object, as well as its power to deny what the ego feels to be a "perilous dependence upon its loved objects" (p. 131).

Klein understands the feelings of triumph in mania as triumph over the person who has died. I would argue that those feelings may be better understood as triumph over the power of that death to destroy the survivors. Anne Alvarez (1992, p. 131) posed the question, in a discussion of Winnicott's (1935) paper, "The manic defence": "Certainly this is a defence against deadness, but why is it not also an assertion of . . . aliveness?" However defensive it may be, it contains essential energy, temporary relief from sorrow, and seeds of genuine hope.

Klein elaborates the mourner's "unconscious phantasies of having lost his *internal* 'good objects' as well . . . These too are felt to have gone under, to be destroyed, whenever the loss of a loved person is experienced" (p. 135). The agitation I felt for at least a year after Sean's death contained a fear that my good objects would not be sufficient to carry me through the assault of his loss. In March, seven months after his death, I wrote: "Sean's absence is relentless, daily, depleting, somehow eroding the possibilities of all my other attachments."

Klein's patient (possibly Klein herself) is also a mother who has lost her son. Klein suggests, "Along with sorrow and pain her early dread of being robbed by a 'bad' retaliating mother is reactivated and confirmed." She understands the mourner's internalized good objects to represent "ultimately [her] beloved parents" (p. 135). Any fear of being punished that I experienced was deeply unconscious; closer to consciousness, perhaps, was a sense that my internal parents had let me down. Although I have not always been happy, I have tended to feel lucky, likely to be safe from disaster. I have been nurtured well enough to carry a good storehouse of internal objects.

It occurs to me that my fear of having lost those objects is akin to the fear of a small child in a loving and protective family who nonetheless is faced with a devastating loss, which her parents could not prevent. My internal good objects, who were responsible for my sense of safety in the world, had failed me – fooled me, even – and I was frightened to rely on them again.

I did not experience the distrust of others that Klein describes. I spent time every week with friends and colleagues, even when I was too tired to participate. I spoke regularly with my sister and my daughters. My husband and I continued to receive condolence letters from people across different times and places in our lives. I hungered for those letters. I wrote in my journal that, "In some way the larger the circle of people who know and care, the safer I feel." I wonder if I felt safer not only because they were carrying Sean, but also because I was trying desperately to replenish my internal world.

Phil Bromberg (1994) has written, "Dissociation is not fragmentation. In fact, it may be reasonably seen as a defense against fragmentation" (p. 521). In the summer of 1998, as the third anniversary of Sean's death approached, I was beset by a series of nightmares. I worked to make sense of the way they seemed to express something I could not afford to feel when Sean died – in fact, not until three years later. I looked back to the month of his death, and I wrote in an essay entitled "Sudden death":

> The news that Sean had been killed assaulted my identity, and it felt like an attack on my mind. I was stunned and frightened . . . I felt panicked by my experience of standing face to face with irreconcilable truths, fearful that I could go crazy. My belief that I had a healthy, vibrant son was starkly contradicted by news that his body was grievously broken, and that he was dead.
>
> I held these two truths side by side like two snapshots, frantically looking from one to the other; I couldn't grasp my own reality.

My daughter, Ashley Ryan Gaddis, has written in a similar vein in her memoir:

> I have always been Sarah's younger sister, [and] Sean's older one . . . I am the middle child . . . That's me . . . We are the Ryan children, and there are three of us . . .
>
> [When] I received that early morning phone call, my identity, my sense of self, and my notion of who I am were thrown into an upheaval. My family was no longer five, or was it? Was I still the middle child?

According to Bromberg (1994), dissociation may be called into play when "drastically incompatible emotions or perceptions are required to be cognitively processed within the same relationship and such processing is . . . beyond the capacity of the individual to contain . . . within a unitary self-experience" (p. 520).

Dissociation is a container, and it buys time. I needed time to absorb the unbelievable – the not yet believable – news that the son I had cherished for twenty-three years was dead; that my family had suffered what felt like an amputation; that I had become a bereaved mother; that there was a before and after in our lives that might not ever be bridged.

Later in my essay, "Sudden death," I refer to the "harsh task of recreating in my mind our family map." "Slowly contradiction evolved into paradox," I wrote.

> We are still a nuclear family of five, even though we are only four. I am still the mother of a son, even though he is not alive. "How many

children do you have?" If I choose to say "two" to the hapless and unsuspecting questioner, the answer is also "three."

Stuart Pizer (1996) has written about paradox. He speaks of the necessity of tolerating "paradox that we cannot resolve or eliminate; otherwise we could not enjoy the continuity of consciousness" (p. 501). He writes further: "Paradox requires bridging; and bridging is just that – a passage back and forth, an 'interstate' commerce, and not an integration in the sense of a cumulative, progressive knitting together into one ultimately whole cloth" (p. 502).

"Interstate commerce" – what a brilliant phrase, which can cover attempts to juggle experiences and selves across moments and across years. I travel back and forth regularly across the deep crevasse in my time line that opened up when Sean was killed. Other changes – the deaths of my elderly parents, my daughters' marriages, the births of their children – have evolved in my consciousness in what I think of as an organic way. But Sean's death created a gap, and I leap across "before" and "after" internally almost every day.

When my tow-headed grandson lies on the floor lining up Sean's old toy cars in a precise row, I can experience a breathtaking moment of familiarity, love, amusement, sadness, anger, continuity and – again, that gap – disruption. Poignant, yes, but that word doesn't do justice to the complexity of affective and self-experience that is possible in that moment.

Of course not every such moment is so emotionally nuanced. Daily life is full of demands and distractions. But grieving doesn't stop, and it can catch me unaware. I am having breakfast in Italy where I am vacationing with my sister. I never traveled here with my children, so I am neither enriched nor burdened by memories of when we were five and breakfasted together in this place. But as I sip my cappuccino I hear someone at another table, an American mother, say, "My son lives about an hour from here." For whatever reason, that comment, which I might barely have noticed on another day, stabs me. My son lives – where? I feel an ache for Sean, but I shake it away.

My husband has said, "It's like Monopoly. We keep being sent back to Go." There are moments of yearning, there are hours and days of renewed sorrow. The waves of grief are not so powerful any more, but there are still waves – sometimes catching us off guard, at other times more predictable. Summer includes Sean's birthday in early June and his death date in August. Navigating the months from May to September is always difficult, although our sadness can be tempered by the pleasures of summer: the soothing of a sail on the river, the physical stretch of a long hike, or the stimulation of traveling in a new place.

The well of sorrow that I carry is as deep as ever. I don't drink as fully from it as I did early on, but it is always there. Sometimes I dip into it and weep, but sometimes I deliberately turn away from sadness into mild mania, or I soothe or distract myself. I am reluctant to privilege one response as healthier than another. I need that repertoire.

Stuart Pizer (1996) has said, "Perhaps any multiplicity of self-structure must entail at least minidissociations" (p. 504). It seems to me that a healthy re-engagement in life after traumatic loss requires an ongoing capacity to dissociate. Is every moment of turning away from sadness a moment of dissociation? I don't think so. But exploring the distinctions is beyond the scope of this chapter.

I have sufficiently broken through my initial blankness that I am no longer afraid of losing Sean internally. The conundrum is that when I ache for him – as I did unexpectedly in Florence – I taste his presence most acutely. Or turn that around: when I look at the photo in our home of him on the mountain, the red stubble of his beard glistening in the sunlight, and I imagine stroking his face, my longing for him is too powerful to sustain, and I have to look away.

Seven years later I have recovered my capacity for both love and work. I have became a writer, which I think of as Sean's legacy to me. What began as a way to express and contain my grief has become a vehicle for finding possibilities in myself that years of analysis could not unearth. The commerce among my affective states when I write is busy – I move back and forth among sorrow, relief, joy, pride, frustration, fear, ambition, sometimes satisfaction.

"The changes made that day, are with us still, they change us even now." The poet is right. The changes, the meanings of Sean's absence – and his ongoing presence – in my sense of who I am, in my life in the world and in my family continue to evolve. I anticipate that they always will.

Acknowledgments

Susan Pliner's poem "Something I Couldn't Tell You" is reproduced by kind permission of the poet. It was first published in 1983 in *The American Poetry Review*, 12(6), and republished in M. Stever and P. Farewell (eds) (1990) *Voices from the River*. Sleepy Hollow, NY: Slapering Hol Press.

References

Alvarez, A. (1992) *Live Company*. London: Routledge.

Bromberg, P. (1994) "Speak! That I may see you": some reflections on dissociation, reality, and psychoanalytic listening. *Psychoanalytic Dialogues*, 4: 517–547.

Gaddis, A.R. (unpublished manuscript) *Remembering Sean*.

Klein, M. (1940) Mourning and its relation to manic-depressive states. *International Journal of Psychoanalysis*, 21: 125–153.

Pizer, S. (1996) The distributed self: introduction to the symposium on "The Multiplicity of Self and Analytic Technique." *Contemporary Psychoanalysis*, 32: 499–507.

Pliner, S. (1990) Something I Couldn't Tell You. In M. Stever and P. Farewell (eds) *Voices from the River*. Sleepy Hollow, NY: Slapering Hol Press. First published in *The American Poetry Review*, 1983, 12(6).

Ryan, J. (2006) *Journey from Mount Rainier: A Mother's Chronicle of Grief and Hope*. Nashville, TN: Westview.

Winnicott, D.W. (1935) The manic defence. In D.W. Winnicott, *Through Pediatrics to Psychoanalysis: Collected Papers*, pp. 129–144. New York: Brunner/Mazel, 1992.

Chapter 5

Failure to mourn

The brutal bargain

J. Gail White

In his celebrated poem "The Dead Woman," Pablo Neruda wrote: "My feet will want to march toward where you are sleeping. But I shall go on living." This poem points to the difficulty giving up old, lost objects and ways. If the poets discovered the unconscious (as Freud believed) and have always known its power, it is perhaps because they intuitively sense that the unconscious has its reasons which are often blind to rational thought.[1]

The fragment of analysis that forms the basis for this case discussion recounts the analytic story of an encapsulated child within a man, a man suspended between the living and the dead, struggling to go on living as a man, a man who made a brutal bargain in the face of unbearable psychic maternal loss. His failure to mourn this loss has left him unable to commit to an adult, intimate relationship. To help such a man re-engage with the world necessitates significant mourning, a process that allows him to find meaning in the world once again.

The first encounter (three years ago)

Matthew, a tall, handsome, physically fit man who appeared very boyish walked into my consulting room with resolve. He asked which chair I preferred. I sat down and he sat directly opposite me. He looked at me with a studied, serious expression. After a brief silence, he began talking in a beseeching manner.

M: Life is a series of acting roles for me. I don't know who I am. I'm a blank slate. I work hard to have opinions, to define myself. I feel I become what I imagine the person I am with would like me to be. I think of myself as Woody Allen's character Zelig. And serious relationships, not one has lasted beyond three months. And that's pushing it! I've about given up.

In the anguished silence that followed, he stared imploringly at me. I was overwhelmed by the depth of his despair, but also surprised by how scripted his opening statement had seemed. I made a painfully obvious remark:

G: So, you want to feel real, and move beyond temporary relationships.

M: That's why I'm here. I heard you are good with "almost lost causes" (he laughed self-consciously).

Flattered, but daunted by his expectations of myself, I encouraged him to tell me about his life. As his story unfolded, I gathered the following information. Matthew, it seems, was on an endless quest, a frantic search for the "right one." "Someday" (*someday I will meet the right one*), and "if only" (*if only she were two inches taller*) fantasies had so far allowed him to retain some hope, but avoid the deeper loss anxiety. He had developed techniques to narcissistically reassure himself about being libidinally vital when he felt blank and/or deadened. He told me about compulsive masturbation and detailed the life of a "lady-killer." I steadied myself for the rough rhythms of seduction and betrayal: one broken heart after another (women abandoned in the depth of love, wives of friends ravished, hearts broken everywhere but, interestingly, never his heart, it seemed). I learned much later that his heart was packed away for safekeeping. Yet he seemed no rogue, but a desperate soul looking for connection. I was struck by his genuinely sad existence.

M: I'm totally out of control in my quest to meet women. I am giving up hope that the right one is out there. But I'm like an addict. I can't stop frantically dating. I don't really enjoy things. I feel like Don Quixote looking for the Holy Grail. It is becoming tragic. Why do I persist? I am going to be an old man with no one to care for me. But there is a big part of me that still believes the right one *is* out there. You have to help me. Either that or I'm cursed.

G: (I wonder to myself: Am I to be Sancho Panza? Does he want me to help him maintain the illusion? What if I challenge the reality of his quest?)

Matthew's scenario presents a vivid illustration of how the addictive act serves to ward off both neurotic and psychotic levels of anxiety. On the one hand, these addictive acts (spending hours on internet dating services, perfecting his bio, choosing different photos, having them airbrushed so he looks perfect) are an attempt to avoid the anxieties of the phallic-oedipal phase. On the other hand, they are a desperate attempt to master anxieties encountered at a much earlier phase, when separation from the mother arouses the terror of bodily disintegration, annihilation, and a sense of inner death.

Matthew is a 41-year-old, successful doctor, arrested in his capacity to love. He can only aspire to adult, intimate relationships. Three years ago we began analysis, one year after he terminated a five-year psychotherapy. He told me his previous analyst had labeled him a hopeless narcissist, incapable of getting beyond himself, shaming him continually for his inadequacy.

One thing he was really good at, he told me, was dating. He had perfected it. He was lucky enough to have many opportunities to meet women, but no relationship lasted. He would be enchanted, then abruptly disinterested. The "disqualifying process" would begin suddenly. He paused for a moment, and seemed embarrassed to continue. I waited, gently nodding my head. "I don't want you to think I'm superficial," he continued. "But it always seems to be for physical reasons, like her breasts are too small, or her hips are too big, or I don't like the curve of her jaw." What really had him worried was that this disqualifying process was beginning earlier and earlier. He felt he was the quintessential, swinging bachelor, with an empty life. He had lost hope. The consequential emptiness caused him tremendous anxiety which he often self medicated with drugs and alcohol.

As he told me the details of his story and the narrative deepened, he became less communicative. Silences overtook him. He seemed caught in a trance, a deadened state. I felt myself becoming anxious and perplexed. My silences deepened the spell he was in. When I called attention to these gaps or "holes in connection," as we came to understand them, he would become alert and enlivened again. Psychoanalysis, with Matthew on the couch and me out of sight, seemed to precipitate a deadened self-state. It reminded me of how he abruptly lost interest in the many women with whom he had attempted relationships. The lively self that entered therapy disappeared, revealing a transference depression which indicated to me the repetition of an infantile depression taking place *in the presence* of the mother/analyst. How quickly this deadened mother transference was born of my silences.

To all outward appearances, Matthew was living a peaceful, successful life. He lived alone with his dog, Lefty, and had done so for twelve years. He had a successful medical practice and dated frequently. He had many male friends (all of whom were now married with children) with whom he spent less time than before. Being with his friends made him feel like he had never grown up. His friends and family often included him in their get-togethers and Matthew always brought Lefty. "Matt and Lefty, that's how we're known – like a couple," he said.

Matthew was the youngest child of three, with two older sisters. Mother had come from a middle-class, educated family and father from a working-class family. Mother's hopes were pinned on Matthew. He was to be the man her husband could never be. Father constantly disappointed mother. He worked hard but "never amounted to anything," according to mother. He was never around, and of little importance in the family, except as an object of derision. Father faced bankruptcy while Matthew was growing up and Matthew remembers this as humiliating for his father. When home, father was shadowy, worked with his hands a lot, and hardly ever spoke. "It was like he was never there, except as an irritant. You know, he wouldn't remember her birthday or anniversary. I got to the point where I would send flowers to Mom and sign his name to make up for him."

Matthew was dominated by his sisters. He spoke of the eldest, Margaret, as being quite cruel to him while Mandy played more of a good mother role. He remembers being "picked on" all the time in school. Rhymes were made using his last name that mortified him. He was told he was oversensitive. He remembers no one attending his birthday party. Waiting by the door, he eventually learned his mother had forgotten to send the invitations. He remembers Dad pinning up his report card for everyone to see how average he was. And all the hurt and humiliation. Mostly he remembers the emotional climate of home . . . the raging spells or emotional deadness of mother, absences of father and the fighting when he was home. Mother's rage evoked both fear and aggression in relation to women. Matthew felt his emotional and sentimental life was greatly unfulfilled, leading to ongoing depressive affects. He wondered if he hadn't always lived with low-grade dysthymia.

Matthew's maternal grandfather had died the year Matthew was born. His mother was hospitalized briefly for a serious depression toward the end of his first year and remained alternatively morose and explosive. His mother suffered greatly from this loss. By age 5, Matthew remembers vividly his mother's suffering and making a deal with himself that he would strive to make her happy in a way that Dad could not. He always felt responsible for her.

Our work revealed several different mother imagos that often danced across his mind: inconsolable mother, screaming mother, dead quiet mother, angry raging mother, comforting mother. We moved through panic and longing, followed by deadness. He recalled mother's bouts of depression: dark, brooding, vegetative states in which she enveloped him. "Nobody was ever good enough for her. Everyone disappointed her. We could never get it right. She judges everyone."

The bitter gulf between his parents became Matthew's problem. He was convinced he could right this wrong, that he could give her the gift of himself, although he often spoke of the cold comfort he received as he lay next to her and she slept, unmoved by his presence.

André Green (1986) wrote of the mother whose "heart is not in it" (p. 151). Rather, her "sorrow and lessening of interest in her infant are in the foreground" (p. 149). He charted the cascading consequences of a child attempting to bring back to life a depressed, bereft, or absent mother. This resuscitation becomes the mission of the subject's life. And so Matthew struck a brutal bargain, unconsciously, it appeared. He would remain mother's boy, and have no other woman before her.

> A recent example illustrates this arrangement nicely. He mentioned that when he leaves mother's house after Friday night dinner, he always tells her he is going home, even if he has made other plans. He wants her to know that he leaves her for no one else.
>
> Remaining "mom's boy" was repeatedly reflected in the transference. In the beginning, he titrated our meetings, so as not to really commit, but not to leave me either. When he lay on the couch, he always used a pillow to cover his genitals. He felt and acted as a boy. Always a boy. "I still tie my shoes like a 5 year old with two loops first, then tied together."

A series of mechanisms has allowed him to stay true to his unconscious bargain (identification with the object, compulsive mentation, compulsive sexual behavior and autoerotic retreat in hopelessness). These mechanisms allow him to maintain the chain link between himself and his deadened, internal mother. With Matthew, I feel all he has is *what he is missing*. Green (1986) calls this state the "negative sublime" (p. 147). The absent other becomes the graveyard of the subject.

I knew I had to find a way to be vitally present with Matthew to help release him from the grip of the dead mother. My task was to seduce him into living in the present.

In the initial phase of analysis, problems of narcissism took center stage. Matthew felt shallow and impotent. When Matthew does achieve in any small measure at work or socially, he is profoundly dissatisfied with the results. His sense of impotence was expressed cognitively in his belief that he had severe memory loss, less than average intellectual ability, and maybe a learning disability? A neurologist and an Alzheimer specialist found his functioning normal. He was so convinced that his intelligence was impotent that I sent him for testing. His IQ was in the ninety-third percentile. Matthew was also impotent to love.

In the next stage of analysis, infantile depression mirrored the sudden loss of mother's life forces. A child can interpret loss of maternal vitality as the consequence of his drives toward her. For Matthew, having an inaccessible father left him with no place to take refuge.

Further analysis focused on classical oedipal conflicts and pregenital fixations. Avoidance of the oedipal was manifest in the following: Matthew knew he must remain mom's boy and show no signs of sexuality. He recalled never having posters of pinup girls in his room like his friends did.

He avoided all mention of the sexual world in his mother's presence. He was embarrassed whenever a romantic scene was portrayed on television if mom was present. He is careful to leave sexuality out of our relationship. I am the mother, he the boy. Any sexuality between us is experienced by him as incestuous. In this way, he retains his mother in an earlier form. If mourning for that mother does not take place, his development will remain arrested.

Matthew approached analysis in a task-oriented way. He was very attached to it and spent much time engaging in intellectual gymnastics. It was very difficult for him to immerse himself in his feelings. He preferred to arrive with objectives to achieve and enjoyed the intellectual sorting out of things. His intellectual narcissism was reassured by the search for meaning that we did together. This is what engaged him. I told him gently that I felt he was more attracted to the analysis we did together than to the relationship we were building. I held fast to what I saw as my task that was to seduce him out of the cold comfort of ideas into the vitality of relating.

> G: You know, I often feel like we are analyzing someone else together in detachment, that you and I are observers of a third person.
>
> M: (Laughing) Thanks for indulging me. I indulge you too, you know. It really makes me feel like we are creating something together. I don't get this feeling stuff, this relationship with you stuff. But I trust you. I don't trust your science. So, I go along. (The session was drawing to a close.) So, what can I take home with me today? Can you give me a recipe, some homework to do?
>
> G: (All of these efforts I understood as protective devices against rising emotions.) I've got it. Your homework can be, "How long can you hold onto in your mind what happened here today in our connection?"

I learned that it was important for me to resist silences and bring a vital, engaged self to Matthew. Winnicott's transitional space was relevant for me, a place where we could creatively and emotionally engage and evolve, an open space in which to play, and play with ideas rather than be dominated by them.

Being with Matthew is pleasant. I look forward to our sessions. One cannot help but love him. He is charming, considerate and grateful. Time goes quickly. He is open to self-examination. Initially he called me his "safety net." From the beginning, he has been open to talking of his feelings about me. Those feelings mostly concern my wellbeing. I suspect this is his fear of losing his safety net.

Matthew is vigilant. He announces the end of our time before I can, reminiscent of how he must leave women before they leave him. I work hard to keep him alive in his feelings as he remains in the intellectual realm much of the time. I often feel I am gathering him emotionally into life while a strong force pulls in the opposite direction. We have constructed a lively dyad, but one that can change at any point. My silences are deadening to him. His intellectual rumination is deadening to me. Mostly I am stuck in my role of the yearning one and he in his role as the lost one, resigned to his fate. One is lively; one is near dead.

> The sense that Matthew was more attached to the analytic process than to me was pleasantly punctuated by a brief communication one day. He spoke of arriving early to my office (the first session of my day, always). I was five minutes late. "I felt a twinge of panic thinking you might not show up. It meant nothing. It's hardly worth mentioning," he said. That same week, however, he cut back sessions to twice weekly from three times.

> M: The therapy is too expensive for me right now. It's costing too much.
> G: Too much emotionally to risk my bailing on you?

The day he cut back the sessions, he brought me a gift of a stylized mirror, suggesting a narcissistic retreat and what might be construed as a form of linking object (Volkan, 1981). He may have been telling me what he needed, that is, to know who he is, something that has never been reflected back to him. Recognition as a separate, unique being through what is reflected in mother's eyes, would be destined to give him not only his mirror image, but also what he represents for his mother. In Matthew's case, his mother's attention and intensity of feeling were diverted from him toward painful situations that excluded him. Her gaze likely reflected nothing, like unmirrored glass. Or, she may have sought in Matthew her own reflection, a confirmation of her own identity, as typically seen with children of narcissistic mothers.

Volkan (1981) tells us that a linking object is used in pathological mourning to keep away the pain of mourning. I believe Matthew realized my importance to him in those few minutes I was late but could not let it be so. I believe the mirror was an externalized, concrete attempt to deal with his ambivalence, to both retain me (with gift giving) and destroy my impact (through decreasing our sessions). Mirroring was important for Matthew because that is precisely what was lacking in his growing up.

The path to mourning his dead (year two)

> One year ago, Matthew's dog Lefty developed terminal cancer. He had made reference only briefly to his dog in the therapy, but when his condition was known, Matthew told me it was important to him that I meet Lefty and he would like to bring him to our next session. Lefty's cancer rendered him

unable to climb the stairs to my office, so Matthew carried this very large dog up the steep staircase. He laid him on the floor. I petted him and gave him biscuits as Matthew began to tell me the story of how Lefty had come into his life. Matthew's roommate had found him at the Humane Society twelve years ago. Shortly thereafter, he moved out, leaving Matthew with the dog. Matthew tried to give him away while on a Humane Society walk to raise funds for abandoned dogs. A fellow walker shamed him into keeping Lefty, telling him that he could not just give him away as he had adopted him and had a responsibility. Matthew provided good custodial care even though he did not want him. Lefty appeared to have insinuated himself slowly into Matthew's heart. "He is the reason I go home at night." In anticipation of his loss, he said, "I can't bear to look around the house. I see signs of him everywhere.

Finally sorrow found vent in tears. Matthew wept openly for the first time as he itemized signs of Lefty that would live on: claw marks on the wainscotting, smudges on the window, a corner of his couch eaten. Tears welled in my eyes, as I shared in his sadness. Unbeknownst to himself, he had become attached to this dog. "Signs of him everywhere to keep him in your heart," I said.

The following session he said in desperation:

I know I have said to you that I just don't know what an emotion really is. But last session, I recognized one. You know how I would do anything to avoid that, but afterwards I felt more real somehow. You know, I look at my father and I am not able to feel for him. [His father's health is failing]. I hate that. I feel fake with my false empathy but last session, here, I really felt!

I remarked that his sadness was a valuable experience. To my delight at the next session, Matthew held fast to this new vitality.

When I left here last time, I cried in my car on the way back to my office. I appreciated your kindness so much. You were really feeling for me. I felt: Wow, my analyst cares about me!

Lefty died last June. Matthew began a mourning process. When he told me the news, we both cried as he recounted each and every detail of Lefty's dying day. He worried if he had done enough, whether his hand was on Lefty at the precise moment of his death as he drove him to the vet and whether he had administered enough morphine to keep him comfortable. He told me how he clipped some of his fur so he would always have part of him. Every detail was hypercathected, and highly important. He told me that Lefty had left an indelible mark: "Losing Lefty woke me up after twelve years." He began to go through the stages of mourning, beginning by sharing his loss with me. He was finally able to symbolize and process affects related to loss, including aggression as well as grief.

M: Just as you said, it will come over me in waves. I'm OK for a while, then it washes over me. There is a good feeling to it too. I'm feeling.
G: The pain is bittersweet?

When Matthew is able to experience his emotions, we are both able to feel alive, rather than one of us being deadened in the presence of the other. Matthew would talk to me of how Lefty was becoming a distant memory, then his memory would come flooding back.

The house is so empty. For a single guy it is very sad. I am at a pivotal point in my life. Comfort was my house, my profession, my car and my dog. Someone pulled their finger out of the dike and my emotions are flooding me. I'm forty-one and mourning the loss of a dog!

This period was characterized by dreams about mouths hemorrhaging, wounds opening and unstoppable floods. Although he was in a lot of pain, I was encouraged that Lefty had facilitated a bridge to mourning and that Matthew could share his grief with me. "He meant the world to you," I said.

Matthew loved his dog unconditionally. The reciprocity of love (and control over his love object) made Matthew feel safe for the first time with an animate object. In contrast, Matthew felt great ambivalence toward his mother, the primary object in his life. Sporadically, he has been dealing with this ambivalence and, in particular, his hostility. At times, I feel mother is almost gone, then she resurfaces and claims him with a vengeance. The feeling I have most difficulty with is the pull toward mutual resignation. It can be seductive. I find myself giving up hope sometimes and accepting the fates. Then I try to nudge him out of his despondency. His passivity at times threatens to deaden me and run us both off the rails. I make an effort to enliven him. My activity and interest in him wakes him up to the relationship. Over the past few years, I chart progress by the evolving feeling states within myself. When we began treatment, I felt deadened much of the time. Now, I feel a deep and moving empathy most of the time. A while ago Matthew said:

M: I don't feel connected with anyone.
G: Sure you do. You are connected to me. I can feel it.
M: You can? (he said with delight).
G: Yes, I can.

For the past year, we have been in the throes of mourning. Sometimes it is foreground. Other times, his compulsive seeking holds sway and we have empty sessions. I believe we are working on what Green (1986, p. 164) called "constituting absence" where there was once nothingness. Matthew is finally linking feeling and thoughts so that the thought has a felt sense. To feel the thought, refers not only to linking emotion and cognition but also to embodying a lived object relationship that links self and other, affect and object, past and present. Those "felt thoughts" are incubated within our relationship in the texture of the encounter between us.

For example, when I reminded him last summer that I was going abroad, he panicked briefly. "What if I meltdown, what should I do?" I gave him the name of my colleague, reassured him I would be back and said goodbye. He has built a bridge to me and is now able to miss me. He told me he wanted to increase the sessions when I return. He appears to be re-engaged (in my leaving?), less fearful and more ready to go forward. "I thought of having someone in my life. I'm trying not to focus on negative things and superficial things," he said.

As his therapist, I believe I have become a bridge to future relationships. I am a new, trustworthy object. We are building a space that allows for internal restructuring. He has to be seduced into "this world," out of the tomb, just as we do with failure to thrive infants who seem to have little interest in the vitality of life. I have found it crucial to be aware of the oscillations between the vitality that is possible and necessary and the dead spaces that are ubiquitous in him. I am fully aware of Matthew's ambivalence to his unmourned object (mother), the hostility that alternates with undifferentiated love that is so often replayed in our relationship. He pushes me away in many preemptive strikes. Then, as he moves closer to me, he struggles with fears of falling into needing me. He oscillates between separation anxiety and intrusion anxiety that signal the weakness of boundaries between ego and object. We are mostly feeling and thinking together through painful states, whereas in the past they were largely actualized.

Two months ago Matthew began the session by telling me he has been waking up every morning to a jazz station on the radio that Mary, a woman he had been dating every once in a while, had tuned to.

M: Maybe I kept it there because it reminds me of her. Maybe, I hold onto her that way.

G: Yes, like the signs of Lefty in your house that remind you that he is in your heart.

M: That's it. I find myself once in a while . . . I'll be driving and remember Lefty sitting in the back seat where he always sat looking out the window. I'll look over and try to imagine him there. Or, I'll be at home and have a flash of where he sat and I will say out loud, "Lefty, I miss you." I'll catch myself a few times yelling out his name. I don't expect a response. It feels contrived. I had a dream that woke me up. I was feeling such pain crying out for him. It was heart wrenching, audible sobs that awakened me from my sleep. To wake up and see that he wasn't there where he always was beside me on the bed . . . I am melancholic. He was one of the few constant things in my life. Where is this wailing coming from?

G: You can't believe it is you?

M: I can't believe it. You know it's not enough to carry the memory inside. I want a response, a light to flicker, something to move. It's too empty to accept that one is gone forever. I try to apply it to myself. Over the last week, I try to remind myself how mortal I am. I'll read a period piece and think about the famous personalities or the slaves in Egypt who built pyramids. Each body, each personality, each represented a life with hopes and dreams, hopes and dreams that we build on the ashes of previous generations. At 1000 AD they were thinking the same things as me. In 1000 years my bones will be lost forever as well. What is really important is to have a relationship, to have children. To enjoy life while it is here. You know I can picture myself screaming out Lefty's name four or five times. I know it is not only about Lefty but it's about reaching out for a loved one. Sometimes I scream his name at the top of my lungs, clenching my fist like in Munch's painting, *The Scream*. It's not just Lefty! It's: Help somebody! Somebody who loves me. Help me. Where are you?

G: That's the question that reverberates.

M: The last few days I have been frantically seeking again. I was OK the whole day after our session. But I want someone to love. I was on line day and night. I had six dates on the weekend. Try fitting that in. I'm battling against time. You and I have a pact. I will find a woman by my forty-second birthday. I fantasize the speech at my wedding that tells everyone how I love this person . . . without my looking at one of the bridesmaids out of the corner of my eye.

G: (I bring him back to the emotion from which he runs into frantic, seeking mode, looking for the narcotic. I am reminded of the day I was late and he was waiting in his car in the usual place. He always parks in the same spot until I arrive, and get settled. Then he comes up. I reflect on the twinge of panic that he felt when I did not show up at the usual time, after which he cut back the sessions. Very gently, I guide him back to those unbearable feelings.) Matthew . . . will you come back to: "Help me. Where are you?"

M: You hit the nail on the head today. It's the one thing today that made my gut turn over. You know, I never thought about *The Scream* and *who* he is screaming at. Is it the Universe? Is it an injustice? Pain? Maybe psychological pain . . . Did you ever see the Glade commercial, the guy with the tie with a picture of *The Scream* on it and cigar smoke all around him. Once the face on the tie got wind of the smoke, it screamed harder. So now I can think of air freshener when I see *The Scream*.

G: Perhaps there is something noxious in the other that the screamer is running from. Calling out to the other and screaming at the other at the same time.

M: Yes, the screamer is looking for peace of mind. And not to be force-fed it. (He is silent for a long time.) I remember my mother made chocolate cake. We were having it for dessert. It was my favourite. I tasted a little piece before dinner. She was so angry. So angry that she made me sit down and eat the whole cake. I was gagging and crying. She wouldn't let me stop. It was so awful. She wanted to teach me a lesson. I guess she really did do that. Be careful of too much of a good thing. You will choke on it.

G: Oh, my goodness. How terrible. Looking for something delicious and comforting and being sickened by the very thing you loved.

M: Yes. I just want peace of mind. (He is crying softly now.) Like the Screamer.

G: From whom? From what?

M: From something greater, from someone greater.

G: Anyone who will respond and comfort?

M: Yes, A greater being than his poor helpless self. Someone with the *answer*. A woman. Could be you.

G: Do the words of the answer matter when you are so distraught or might it be the music beneath the words? (Matthew is visibly shaken by this. Without his words, he is left with his feelings.)

M: The Screamer has been screaming into a vacuum. That's the problem. There is no one there. But you are here. I really feel you are here. It is such a new feeling for me. I just thought of the oddest project, to superimpose my face on the screamer . . . OK, now I'm finished. Time's up. (As usual Matthew has been vigilant. He must announce the end before I do.)

Facing fears

Following is a fragment from a session two months ago. Matthew's avoidance of his psychic pain has waned considerably. He is feeling more entitled to a woman and family of his own. He arrives breathless.

M: I don't know where to start. As I was driving here I was thinking how fears control people. I saw a guy walking with a kid. It was great. His life is going the way it should. I realize that irrational fears have kept me out of my own life, frozen with my mother. I started to think of fears as ghosts and that I have to have the courage to face them.

G: Yes. A wise analyst (Loewald, 1960) once said that we need to turn our ghosts into ancestors.

M: Yes and leave them in the graveyard. I like that. (He reflects silently.) You know, I was thinking of the last survivor of Vimy Ridge who just died this week. He was 103 years old. You know, my Dad was in the Second World War. He spent it in trenches living on a mud island in the Bering Strait. What about your father? Was he in the war?

G: Yes, he was in the airforce.

M: What was he like?

G: (It seemed important to him to know more. I wonder if he is drawing on the courage of men who went before him, who had enemies to fight, to help him fight his fears.) My father lived life to its fullest. He flew Spitfires and lost many of his buddies in daily runs. It was very hard for him. He used to read Omar Khayyam and Rudyard Kipling to inspire himself. He learned to live for the moment, I think, and that stayed with him his whole life. (Matthew wanted to know if he was happy, what it was like for me to have this father. I brought it back to him.) Did your Dad tell you war stories?

M: He put himself in danger in his search for land mines. Pretty scary work. He showed me pictures of himself in uniform. He looked very manly. I was surprised. And in the face of death, he looked full of life too. (He is silent for a while.) Thanks Gail, it means so much to me that you shared something personal with me. You must miss him. (He turned over and put his face in the pillow and cried.) You know, I never saw that father in the pictures, the manly man. I only saw him as a disappointment, the way my mother did. Weak somehow.

The analytical work now called him to assume the position of an adult man, and a paternal function. This brought on another period of anxiety: his unconscious knowledge reminded him that this meant submitting to the same fate as his father, namely to be castrated and destroyed by the powerfully destructive, phallic mother. He had no doubt as to the final outcome of the primal scene: mother destroys father.

Filling the emptiness (presently)

Matthew has begun to acknowledge and tolerate the emptiness he always avoided. His compulsive behavior has all but disappeared. We continue to gain further insight into his fear of "nothingness." Following is a fragment of a session where he recognized himself for what he felt to be the first time.

M: I feel so good I have maintained what happened here between us for four days. (This following a session where there was a significant connection between us.) It was a catharsis last session, some emotional piece went into place. I will recline today. I'm in a dark place. Last night I saw the film, *About a Boy*, with Hugh Grant. I'm going to watch it again tonight. There's a line in there where this girl, Rachel, says to him: "First you bored me. I thought you were blank. Then you interested me. But now I see you really are blank." (The character Hugh Grant played posed as a single father so he could meet more women at a single parent group where he would be seen as sensitive and interesting.) When he heard that comment, he stood up and walked ramrod straight out of the restaurant. He was filled with shame. There was nothing to say. You see, he was seen in his emptiness. Then, and only then could he be real. I recognized myself! That's what I am afraid of seeing . . . that I am like vapour, not a substantial self. I can take any shape to please others. But, I decided, no more. I am going to be honest with myself and just speak honestly to others. This is how I will substantiate myself.

G: You seem very shaken, but relieved, too. You have been terrified by what you see is your non-existence. But you feel reflected back through this character. That's a beginning. (The fragility of Matthew's childhood sense of self is evident in his terror of looking into the voids and realizing that he does not know who he is or, worse, if he exists at all.)

M: Yes. There is something about accepting your blankness finally. Then maybe you can start filling it up. Maybe. Like the character. That

12-year-old boy who kept visiting him just kept hanging around him and needing him. He didn't realize how he was being a father figure to his own inner child through that boy. Once you let one person into your heart, the doors open, I guess. This guy let the boy in.

G: Like you let Lefty into your heart unbeknownst to you. He insinuated himself into your heart.

M: (Matthew is very emotional, holding his head, rocking as he does when he is very sad. After mastering his emotion, he continues.) And then, I guess I let you in. But, I pay for you. Although I can't help thinking that you like me too. That you see something real in me. Just like the girl saw the Hugh Grant character. He was empty, missing something vital. He lived in images like me, giving them what he thought they wanted.

G: Like with your mother, you had to be who she needed.

M: Yes, so I didn't know who I was. You told me many times that I was an island unto myself. It's just the way this guy was. He thought of himself as an island, too, but he said islands can be part of island chains connected under the ocean. So I'll aim for that. I may be an island for a while, then I will make links. You know, this boy who insinuated himself into Hugh Grant's life was twelve years old. Lefty was with me twelve years.

Matthew continued to wrestle with the problem of psychic survival and the need to reassure himself of his subjectivity. He thought of those "holes in connection" now as empty spaces where the other was absent, so he did not exist. These sessions were characterized by his inability to stay on the couch for several weeks. He seemed to need to feel his existence confirmed in my eyes.

Conclusion

Patients who have lost a parent by death in early childhood may hold onto an unconscious fantasy that the dead parent remains alive. A similar process occurs in the case of the child who psychically loses a parent. There is a massive loss that is often incomprehensible to the young child, particularly because there has been no actual loss. The unconscious bargain is an attempt by the child to hold this contradiction at bay, to deny and preempt the loss. Such a bargain encapsulates the child in early dynamics that allow no room for future, palpable relationships with others. It is as if the patient has decided to remain with the dead. I believe this is what Matthew and I struggle with day by day, that is to say, the pull of the identification with the deadened mother who keeps him entombed.

In Sophocles' play, Antigone says, "I owe a longer allegiance to the dead than to the living: in that world I shall abide forever." Her remark underscores the Herculean task of bringing patients like Matthew from the seductive land of dead objects. Death and life forces are in constant tension. These forces are a clinically felt phenomenon for all of us. When the death forces hold sway, we are stuck in the tomb of the past. In such states, no thought is possible, only circular rumination, precluding the process by which loss may be thought through emotionally to become memory. Memory means distance from the experience. Distance means we are no longer in the grip of the lost object, and can go on living.

Note

1 In *Civilization and its Discontents* Freud (1930, p. 117) wrote: "The poets and philosophers before me discovered the unconscious; what I discovered was the scientific method by which the unconscious can be studied."

References

Freud, S. (1930) *Civilization and its Discontents. Standard Edition*, 21: 57–145. London: Hogarth Press, 1961.

Green, A. (1986) The dead mother. In A Green, *On Private Madness*, pp. 142–173. London: Hogarth and Institute of Psycho-Analysis.

Loewald, H. (1960) On the therapeutic action of psychoanalysis. *International Journal of Psychoanalysis*, 41: 16–33.

Volkan, V.D. (1981) *Linking Objects and Linking Phenomena*. New York: International Universities Press.

Chapter 6

Beyond the consulting room

Ritual, mourning and memory

Joyce Slochower

Psychoanalysts write a great deal more about the acute experience of loss and the mourning process than about its lifetime sequalae. Death is dramatic; our response intense. Yet long after the immediacy of death and associated pain have eased, we continue to remember and sometimes to mourn those we've lost, even when our experience of loss was not exceptionally traumatic. For many, this process involves finding a way to mark and honor the memory of a loved one, of memorialization.

Memorialization, a crucial aspect of human experience, allows us to re-find and reinforce memory, countering our (perhaps equally strong) need to forget, to sidestep loss and the pain, fear, guilt, or rage that death evokes. While psychoanalysis provides a setting in which loss can be mourned and worked through, it does not easily support the process of memorialization, of ritual observance over time. Indeed, psychoanalysts have paid scant attention to the dynamics embedded in memorial rituals, probably because we tend to locate therapeutic action within the treatment structure, and to view what happens "outside" as less profound, less deeply integrated.

To memorialize, we must leave the consulting room. The very personal act of memorialization is best expressed in rituals, secular and religious, that involve symbolic or literal acts which allow the mourner to contact, revisit, and re-create memory.

Acts of memorialization often occur at sites of physical memorial (e.g., cemeteries). Bassin (1998) has suggested that these "dead" physical memorials may, over time, displace our need to mourn onto an external object, depriving us of necessary mourning work. If we are to create a time and space within which loss and remembrance can be both activated and contained, we must find a way to imbue the concrete with symbolic meaning.

Memorialization functions in this way by helping the mourner remember, linking past to present. This is especially central to the experience of traumatic loss. In *The Mourning After* Bassin (2004) described a yearly ritual performed by a group of Vietnam War veterans known as Rolling Thunder. The name of their organization (Rolling Thunder, Inc.) refers to the thunderous bombing campaign against North Vietnam in which many of them participated. Once yearly, these veterans ride en masse on their motorcycles to the Vietnam Veterans Memorial in Washington DC, enacting the coming home parade that the veterans never had. Bassin suggests that this parade embodies the trauma to which they were exposed; the roaring motorcycle engines mimic the sound of the planes and the bombs they dropped. In this ride, the veterans revisit *and* re-experience the past in the company of those who shared the trauma, honoring the memory of their dead while reliving the experience of traumatic assault and loss. The ride is also a political act, an attempt to draw attention to the plight of those missing in action or prisoners of war, a protest against marginalization (Bassin, personal communication).

The site of the Vietnam Veterans Memorial, a wall filled with names of the dead, is a symbolic burying place. Flowers and other mementos are left at the site as if it were a cemetery. The reflective quality of the stone allows the visitor to see the names of those who died while also seeing their own image in the stone (Bassin, 2004).

The members of Rolling Thunder have a special need to mourn; their lives were traumatically altered by war experiences. Those trauma are reflected in symptoms of post-traumatic stress disorder and a variety of other physical and psychological disabilities.

All traumatic losses (the death of a child, the sudden death of a loved one, death caused by natural disaster, war or terrorism) are assimilated and mourned, if at all, with great difficulty and often result in arrested or pathological mourning processes (Kavaler-Adler, 2003). Acts of memorialization serve a crucial therapeutic function in the face of these trauma.

In contrast, non-pathological, "ordinary" mourning is traditionally viewed as a time limited process that comes to a natural end. Psychoanalysts have tended to address the acute experience and working through of loss rather than the long term, normal sequelae of the mourning process (Klein, 1940; Bibring, 1953; Jacobson, 1957; Bowlby, 1960, 1980; Winnicott, 1964).

Freud (1917) conceived of mourning as a form of psychic separation from the lost object. He believed that this "normal" variant of depression would be resolved as the libido slowly and painfully is detached from the loved individual, leaving the mourner free to cathect a new love object, to recover from mourning and move on with life.

In some respects, Freud captured the phenomenology of grief. The raw shock, grief and loss that follow death subside with time. Longing for the deceased gradually diminishes as the ordinariness of life takes over and the mourner returns to the everyday and attaches to new love objects. But this recovery does not necessarily imply a lost connection with the deceased. Rather than decathecting the love object, the mourner may identify with and introject that object, thereby symbolically sustaining an otherwise lost relationship (Abraham, 1924).

The shape of the inner tie with the lost object reflects the nature of our relationship with the deceased. While relatively unconflicted object ties tend to be connected to more positively colored affective states, most of our intimate relationships are not entirely unconflicted. Volkan (1981) emphasized the problematic effect of feelings of aggression in mourning. Gaines (1997) suggested that many other kinds of emotional states interfere with maintaining the continuity of our connections. Whatever its affective coloration, the process of internalization helps the mourner relinquish the real relationship by solidifying the inner object tie (Loewald, 1962). From this perspective, the mourner's continued attachment to the deceased is not a pathological phenomenon, but an integrative one (e.g. Rubin, 1985; Klass, 1988; Silverman et al., 1992).

Loss and the evocation of memory

However much the pain of death fades and becomes integrated, we do not altogether "get over" the loss of loved ones. The immutable presence of loss in our lives is reflected in the ease with which memory is evoked. Those memories may be associated with a wide range of affect states. The quality of the relationship being mourned (e.g., the relative weight of nostalgia, remorse, loss, etc.) and the context in which the loss occurs, color both affect and memory. Feelings about the deceased emerge in response to a myriad of stimuli – major life cycle events (weddings, funerals), the anniversary of the death, a return to the family home – momentarily flooding us with grief, guilt, pleasure, anger, feelings associated with the lost connection.

It is not surprising that tears are shed at funerals, both for the one whose life is being remembered and also for other losses. Even the mundane – a powerful film, a familiar place, smell, object – pulls us back in time and affective state to memories of lost loved ones. Cleaning out my country house, I came upon a gardening book that had been my mother's. Seeing her familiar handwriting evoked a pleasurable nostalgia and sadness as I envisioned her in her housedress, hair tied back in a scarf, tending vegetables in the now overgrown garden. I never tasted the vegetables she grew, yet the gardening book brings up a wealth of body memories associated with the housedress she wore while holding me. Those memories are connected to the experience of normal, rather than traumatic mourning, yet they triggered affect long after the period of acute mourning had passed.

The role of ritual in mourning "ordinary" loss

From a traditional psychoanalytic perspective, it is not altogether clear that memorialization is necessarily a part of "ordinary" mourning. Although on one level, every loss is a trauma, on another, expectable losses are less shocking, unexpected or horrifying than simply sad. These "normal" losses confront us all and permit some anticipatory mourning to occur, perhaps diminishing the need for acts of memorial over time. However, in contrast to the more traditional assumption that normal mourning is a circumscribed process, it is my belief that even expectable (relatively non-traumatic) losses require moments of mourning and memorialization across the lifespan (Gaines, 1997). The function of these acts of memorial is similar to that characteristic of traumatic loss.

Acts of memorial take us outside of the treatment setting, for the psychoanalytic process is not framed in a way that supports this kind of ritual. For some, this is a profoundly private experience. At times of strain or sadness, my patient Jane periodically visits the grave of her beloved cat that died many years ago. There, she is enveloped by feelings of warmth. She experiences the physical presence of her cat's soft body on hers as an emotional tranquilizer that relieves her sadness. The death of her gentle, caring grandmother many years earlier (symbolically represented by her cat) was similarly internalized. Jane thinks of her grandmother and shifts into a comforting affective state associated with soothing images of soft laps and warm cookies, images that counter the depressive affect with which she struggles.

Jane has creatively constructed a personal act of memorialization that she uses both to access memory and to comfort herself. Like the mourner who makes solitary visits to the grave of the deceased, leaving behind flowers, letters, and poems, and like those who quietly cherish keepsakes that embody the memory of the lost loved one, Jane mourns alone. She is a private person who abhors group ritual and is unusually able to access and work with inner states. Her experience illustrates how the individual can create a memorial ritual and engage that ritual over time to good therapeutic effect.

Many of us, however, cannot mourn alone so easily. We need structure, affective triggers, formal ways of marking our losses and having those losses witnessed. We need to remember in a space wherein we feel recognized and where our experience of loss is linked with that of others. Those who witness our losses provide an intersubjective context within which we are recognized, validated and supported (Bassin, 1998; Grand, 2000).

When the sense of loss is shared by many (for example, those who lost loved ones in the September 11 terrorist attacks), we more easily find a community of mourners to both witness our loss and mourn with us. However, predictable (i.e., relatively non-traumatic) losses that occur in a (post)modern world characterized by dispersed extended families and diluted social structures are less easily mourned within the community context.

My patient Michael had an ambivalent relationship to his father, who died shortly after Michael began his analysis. At the time of that (partially expected) death, Michael mourned deeply, working over a range of feelings (grief, rage, guilt, longing) over months. Michael emerged from this prolonged period of mourning feeling older, sadder, and mostly at peace with the loss. Our analytic work moved on; the death of his father no longer dominated Michael's experience.

Nearly a decade later, Michael married and started a family. For the first time in some years, memories and painful affects associated with his father's death re-emerged. As Michael watches and plays with his children, he is acutely conscious of his father's voice, a voice that is, at different moments, admiring, supportive and critical. Michael's experience of himself as a more demonstrative and loving parent than his father is associated with feelings of regret ("If only I could have reached out to *him*"), longing ("How I wish he were here to see my kids") and a quiet sadness ("I never got what I needed from him"). These thoughts re-evoke and cement Michael's memory of his father and shift aspects of his self-experience. Michael thinks of his father when he cuddles his toddlers, supporting a new vision of himself ("I am a better parent") and soothing himself by connecting to the experience of self as child ("I am soothing my child as I wish I had been soothed"). Michael is beginning to find a way of identifying with his father's shyness, a shyness that felt like rejection to Michael, but more likely reflected his father's own fear of rebuff ("He wanted to give me more, he really did love me, but was afraid to show it").

Michael's ongoing work on his relationship to his father does not, I believe, reflect an incomplete mourning process, but rather the progressive integration of a complex, internalized object relationship. The re-emergence of affects and conflicts related to his father's death supports Michael's development, deepening his self-experience in the context of that rich inner tie.

Although our psychoanalytic work has gone very well, Michael feels the need to address his loss outside the dyadic analytic context. An only child who lives far from extended family and outside a cohesive community, Michael longs for a way to mark his loss and share it with others. He has none. He does not belong to any community or religious group and feels ethnically dis-identified. Michael expresses envy toward friends who are involved in community or extended family life, but has not found a point of entrée into those worlds for himself. He finds comfort in bringing memories of his father to me, but longs to memorialize his father's passing through some ritual act.

Cultural and religious rituals represent an antidote to the experience of absence by creating a formal structure that facilitates mourning. Such structures serve multiple purposes. They help the mourner cope with death and provide an organized context that helps the mourner's community provide needed comfort. Such rituals also introduce death into the community of non-mourners. Memorial rituals may thus help the community anticipate and imagine loss, providing an antidote to the denial of death (Becker, 1973) that is ubiquitous in so much contemporary culture.

Many cultures and most religious traditions have ceremonies with which to mark death and anniversaries of these losses. Some of these are secular: Mexicans observe the Day of the Dead; Israelis observe Holocaust Remembrance Day[1]. Other ceremonies occur within a religious frame: Roman Catholics have a memorial mass; Muslims read a portion of the Koran; Jews sit *shiva*, say *kaddish* and *yizkor*.

Psychoanalysts do not often explore the dynamic function of these kinds of rituals because of the heavy ideology with which they are laden. Most mourning ritual carries specific beliefs about the meaning of death, the relationship to the dead, and the location of the dead vis-à-vis the living (see Ashenburg, 2002 for a discussion of mourning ritual across history and culture).

On one level, psychoanalysis has replaced religious beliefs with a combination of the rational and the illusory (Slochower, 2006). We embrace a depth of conviction about the curative power of psychoanalysis that sometimes borders on the illusory, but we shy away from religion, belief in god, and the "magical" belief system with which religious and some cultural practices are imbued. In shunning those rituals that we do not practice, we lose an opportunity to explore the interface of culture and psychology, to deepen our understanding of the dynamic function of experiences that occur beyond the consulting room.

I would like to further explore the dynamic function of community acts of memorialization in instances of ordinary mourning, using my own experience with Jewish mourning (*shiva*) ritual to illustrate this process. This chapter builds on a previous essay (Slochower, 1993, 1996) about the therapeutic function of *shiva* that I wrote following the death of my father.

Traditional Jewish custom calls for a seven-day period (*shiva* means seven) during which the mourner "sits," that is, formally mourns the loss of a close relative (parent, sibling, spouse or child) by remaining at the home of the lost relation or at one's own home, refraining from all social and work-related activities while receiving "callers" who come for the express purpose of comforting the mourner.

Shiva ritual alters virtually every aspect of standard social behavior. The mourner is symbolically separated from the community (Kraemer, 2000) in a variety of ways. For example, the mourner wears a ripped garment, sits on a low seat, does not wash, wear shoes, or work. The mourner is not expected to rise to greet or otherwise entertain the caller. The caller, in turn, waits for the mourner to initiate conversation, allowing the mourner to use the *shiva* space in the way that best meets personal needs. The mourner does not offer or serve food to visitors, but is, instead, fed by others[2].

Although the religious meaning behind many of these rituals primarily concerns beliefs about the dead, sin and the afterlife (Kraemer, 2000), *shiva* customs can have an extraordinarily therapeutic effect that facilitates mourning. These customs establish barriers against superficial social interchange and prescribe behaviors that symbolically express the subjective state of grief. For example, the mourner tears a garment either upon hearing of the death or at the funeral and wears that garment throughout *shiva*; bathing is avoided (unless the mourner finds this excessively difficult); the mourner sits on a low seat which symbolizes a lowered emotional state; the mourner is fed by others (like a sick or vulnerable person) and is forbidden to serve her[3] guests.

Shiva tradition creates an emotionally protective setting that is reminiscent of the therapeutic holding environment (Winnicott, 1964). The community of callers supports that holding experience by being reliably present, non-impinging, yet responsive. Like the parent whose protective presence permits a sense of "going on being," the *shiva* caller acts as a witness for the mourner but does not intrude on the mourner's experience with her own agenda, allowing the mourner to be the single subject in the mourning context. Within the *shiva* space, the mourner is free to experience and express a wide range of affective states without attending to the reactions or needs of the caller, for the mourner is not expected to be able to shift out of her own frame, to engage in mutuality (Winnicott, 1971; Benjamin, 1995).

In this acute phase of mourning, the mourner is often psychically alone in a state of grief, connected primarily to the deceased, perhaps linked in pain with others who share the loss, but more tenuously connected to others whose lives have not been disrupted. The structure created during *shiva* allows us to be alone in the presence of the (m)other (Winnicott, 1958) – for the subjectivity of the visitor is subordinate to that of the mourner. Like other therapeutic experiences, *shiva* ritual permits the mourner to use people within that community without regard for their needs (i.e., ruthlessly).

Despite the heavy emphasis on the mourner's need within the *shiva* context, Jewish tradition introduces the needs of the community into the mourning space in small ways. There is an intrinsic tension between the mourner's need to mark her loss and the community's need to get on with life and to celebrate it. Aspects of that tension are embodied in the structure and calendar of *shiva*. At those times when community ritual collides with the mourner's need to mourn, *shiva* is interrupted or cancelled in deference to religious laws concerning the observance of these holidays.[4] Here, the community need to celebrate overrides the mourner's need to mourn.

The caller (who is not expected to stay long) does not say goodbye, but often ends the visit with a traditional phrase ("May you be comforted among the mourners of Zion and Jerusalem"). This phrase reminds the mourner of the wider communal context, both historical and contemporary, within which her personal loss occurs. She does not mourn alone, but is not expected to acknowledge this reality.

Other traditional farewell statements (e.g. "May we next meet at a celebration [*simcha*]") also locate the mourner's very private experience of loss within a broader social frame that creates a symbolic link to the life from which the mourner has temporarily withdrawn. It is as if the caller holds and articulates the idea of life and continuity, connecting the mourner's solitary pain to that of others and also to life outside the mourning space. The mourner, however, is not required to explicitly acknowledge these linkages.

Shiva lasts a week. At its conclusion, the mourner is expected to return to work and, to some extent, to life. A week, of course, is an insufficient period in which to mourn, and Jewish law and custom dictate aspects of the mourner's behavior for the first thirty days following a death (*shloshim*) or, in the instance of a parent's death, for the full year thereafter.[5] In recognition of the mourner's continued state of grief, activities associated with pleasure are traditionally avoided during this period. Many males refrain from shaving for the first thirty days following a death. Males and females may refrain from wearing new clothes, attending parties, musical events, or other large-scale celebrations. (Exceptions are made for mourners celebrating a child's bar or bat mitzvah or wedding. Here, the need of the community to mark the joyous event, without diminishing it, overrides the parent's need to observe a state of mourning.)

Many mourners attend daily services for thirty days (or a year following a parent's death). The mourner (in traditional communities, only males; in non-orthodox and many modern orthodox communities, women as well) continues to say *kaddish* (prayer for the dead) for this period. This memorial prayer can be recited only in the presence of others (in orthodox synagogues, by a minimum of ten men; in conservative and reform synagogues, by ten people of either gender). This ritual, traditionally observed several times during the service, is marked by a sudden quality of silence in the congregation, as those in mourning recite the prayer aloud and are joined by non-mourners who "answer" by reading selected lines of the prayer, supporting a momentary holding experience within the communal context. In some congregations, only mourners stand during *kaddish*, symbolically "announcing" to the community that they are in mourning; in other communities, all members stand with the mourner, underscoring a sense of communal solidarity.

For those mourners who say *kaddish* daily for either *shloshim* or for the year, the synagogue group (usually including many others saying *kaddish*) tends to become a cohesive community that holds each mourner during this longer mourning period. This custom quite literally pulls the mourner back to the community context, linking her both to others who are mourning and to the community as a whole.

Mourning ritual across the lifespan

The end of *shloshim* (or a year following a parent's death) marks the conclusion of formal acts of mourning. While the mourner is expected gradually to return to "ordinary" life, Jewish tradition includes acts of ritual memorialization across the lifespan. A variety of rituals are performed on the yearly anniversary of a death (*yarhzeit*). At services on the preceding *shabbat*, a memorial prayer (*El Moleh*) for the deceased is often recited. Most light a special candle that burns for twenty-five hours beginning on the eve of the person's death. Some fast, study, or give charity to mark this anniversary. It is also customary to sponsor *kiddush* (a celebratory meal following services) and when possible, to lead services. Many name a baby after a deceased relative, thereby linking the dead to the living (in Sephardic communities, children are named after living relatives as well; this is considered to be a way of honoring them).

On each *yarzeit*, the mourner recites *kaddish* in synagogue. This act has particular power when members know one another and can identify the person for whom *kaddish* is being said. In some synagogues, the names of those observing *yarzheit* are publicly announced and a memorial prayer is read aloud.

On four other yearly occasions, a brief memorial service entitled *yizkor* is integrated in ritual holiday observance. *Yizkor* (literally meaning "he will remember," but more colloquially meaning remembering or remembrance) is recited on *Yom Kippur* (Day of Atonement) and on the last day of the three other major Jewish festivals (*Sukkot*, *Passover*, and *Shavuot*). It is not uncommon for Jews who have some connection to ritual, but who rarely attend synagogue, to make a point of participating in at least one of these *yizkor* services.

The particulars of the memorial service vary among congregations both within and outside the United States. In the United States (especially in non-orthodox settings), the *yizkor* service is frequently introduced with a psalm and sometimes with a short talk that sets the tone for the service. Separate prayers for lost loved ones (mother, father, and other relatives) are read silently; the mourner inserts the name of each lost relative into a prayer. Many congregations in the United States follow these individual prayers with a communal memorial prayer, either recited by the community or by the individual leading the service. In some, but not all communities, *kaddish* is then said communally. Finally, it is common (but not universal) to conclude the *yizkor* service by either reading or singing Psalm 129 (The Lord is my shepherd . . .).

Part of the *yizkor* prayer includes a promise to "perform acts of charity and goodness" in the name of the deceased. That pledge honors the dead and, perhaps, represents a concrete attempt at expiation on the part of the mourner, a giving back to the lost object who is no longer there to receive love or remorse in symbolic form.

Memorialization: creating meaning from ritual

Ritual observance, like other acts of memorial, requires affective context that *creates* meaning out of ritual. When the *yizkor* prayers include introductory or concluding psalms, remarks or a communal *kaddish*, access to feelings of loss is facilitated. I once attended a bar mitzvah held at a hotel, where people from many different Jewish communities came together to celebrate. The rabbi, noting that many of those assembled did not know one another personally, rather extraordinarily asked all those who were saying *kaddish* that day in honor of a relative's *yarzheit* to briefly speak about the person whose loss they were remembering. Half a dozen people did so. The experience of listening to strangers flesh out the face and quality of their relationship to the lost loved one created a sense of community, breaking down the experience of isolation, replacing it with a sense of recognition (Benjamin, 1995). This rabbi creatively constructed an act of memorialization, transforming what could have been a pro-forma ritual into one imbued with affect and memory.[6]

The recitation of *yizkor* can be a powerful act of memorialization even for those who are not otherwise observant. Shortly after we began working together, my very secular patient Amy mentioned that she would be attending synagogue to mark the fifteenth anniversary of her mother's death. Amy, who lives the life of an urban academic, is a somewhat offbeat, vital person with considerable emotional depth and a capacity for joy and sadness. Although Amy grew up in a mostly non-observant family, she was exposed to Jewish ritual in her grandparents' home and she sat *shiva* for her mother with other relatives. Amy had a deeply emotional response to that ritual, although she felt no desire to become more involved in religious practice.

In the years since her mother's death, Amy experienced and worked over that loss, addressing feelings of ambivalence, guilt and conflict. Now, many years later, I see no evidence that she suffers from unresolved or pathological mourning. Amy is engaged in life and not in death. While she struggles with anxiety and has difficulty in some of her relationships, she is not burdened by depressive affect or longing for what "was". Yet Amy is drawn to ritual observances that commemorate her mother's passing, regularly attending synagogue on the anniversary of her mother's death. On those occasions, she lights a memorial candle in her home and recites *kaddish* in synagogue. There is a special pain associated with this anniversary; in our sessions Amy briefly returns to the subject of her loss. The act of honoring her mother's memory, concretized in the solitary acts of lighting a memorial candle and reciting *kaddish* for her, serves a multitude of purposes. Amy enacts, simultaneously, her love for her mother and the sense of loss at her absence. She makes symbolic reparation by attending synagogue and at the same time honors her mother's memory.

Amy's somewhat urgent need to be at services for *yizkor* stands in contrast to her lack of interest in religious observance at other times. What pulls Amy to synagogue on these occasions? She tells me that she finds comfort in the act of remembering, in marking her mother's passing. When she recites the memorial prayer, Amy briefly and intensely re-experiences the vitality of their connection. Sometimes she experiences the *yizkor* service as intensely sad and is flooded by guilts, painful memories of how she failed her mother. At other times, she re-finds pleasure in that connection, evoking memories of happy occasions and loving contact between them. Following each *yizkor*, Amy's grief quickly dissipates. The memorial process does not catapult Amy into a state of depressive longing. Instead, *yizkor* stimulates memory, creating a link to her mother that she finds simultaneously painful and comforting.

My understanding of the power of these acts of memorialization was deepened when I lost my own mother two years ago. I, too, found myself in synagogue, now saying *yizkor* for both parents. This very brief act of memorial had a power that took me by surprise. Before, I had mourned one parent but knew I had another. Now I was an orphan, alone with my losses and pains, flooded by memories that no one shared with me. I thought of my mother's last, painful days, her lonely, perhaps avoidable death, my love for her. This loss was fresh, and these thoughts and feelings were expectable. As I moved from reciting the *yizkor* prayer for my mother to one for my father, I found myself thinking of him (now gone over a decade), with fresh intensity and sadness about how much of my children's lives he had missed. That association took me, in turn, to memories of my maternal grandmother, whose loss was even more remote. *Yizkor* took me back to thoughts of her in the kitchen, baking, as I played with her precious china bowls at her feet. Suddenly I was back in Brooklyn, in an apartment I knew only as a young child, now vividly remembered for the first time in years.

The memorial service not only allowed me to mourn a recent loss, but also evoked feeling and memory related to losses that were otherwise relatively remote. This is the function of memorialization – to evoke memory and affect – and, in a contained context, to both stimulate and support affective experience that has been diluted by time.

When ritual fails

Both *shiva* and post *shiva* ritual are highly formalized. Although the structure they create has enormous therapeutic potential, that same structure may inhibit, rather than facilitate mourning, just as physical memorials may inhibit, rather than support, the grieving process (Bassin, 2004). There is, for example, no place within the *shiva* tradition wherein to formally mourn a loss other than that of parent, sibling, spouse or child, yet other losses may call for such ritual. While Jewish tradition calls for a year of mourning only in the instance of a parent's death, other losses (e.g., of child) can be profoundly traumatic, and insufficiently memorialized in thirty days. When *shiva* observance is interrupted or cancelled because a holiday intervenes, the mourner's need to mourn is displaced by the community's need to celebrate, and *shiva* fails the mourner. In large, anonymous synagogues the power of community tends to be diluted and *yizkor* observance can feel pro-forma. In very traditional communities, women may be unable to comfortably say *kaddish*, left without access to this potentially comforting ritual.

At other times, ritual fails because the observing community is unaware of its meaning or unable to support it. Following my father's death, I went to a local synagogue. The service was very sparsely attended. I was the only woman there. Although *kaddish* was recited several times, the men seemed not to hear my *kaddish*, which I recited alone, without hearing the group respond. Not surprisingly, I left feeling more pained than soothed.

Mourning and mutual recognition

Psychoanalytic work tends to move from the experience of object relating toward object usage or collaboration (Winnicott, 1971; Slochower, 1996), that is, toward increasing recognition of the Other (Benjamin, 1995). The work of mourning seems to follow a similar trajectory. In the intense period of grief immediately following death, the mourner needs a space that is largely protected, in which there is little room for intersubjectivity. Rituals associated with the shock of death, burial and *shiva* place heavy emphasis on individual needs in the absence of a demand for interconnectedness or mutual recognition. While even during *shiva*, a few ritual elements pull the mourner toward an awareness of the Other, it is in the months and years following death that ritual observance reflects the mourner's increasing ability to move out of that interior space and to take in the experience of the Other. *Yizkor* ritual folds the process of the personal into a broader community context, allowing us to mourn together, thereby supporting both our separateness and connectedness.

Where *shiva* creates a solitary therapeutic holding space, the *yizkor* service, more remote from the acute experience of loss, occurs in a wider space that provides room for both inner experience and emotional linkage with others. *Yizkor* creates a double experience of utter solitude and intense connection, and at each *yizkor*, I find myself both connected to personal memories and pains, yet acutely aware that those around me are grieving too. As I recited prayers for my parents, just behind me stood a friend whose husband had died when her children were still toddlers. Across from me stood a middle-aged woman who had lost both husband and son, a friend who mourned her unborn children, a woman who lost her brother far too young, another who mourned the recent and tragic death of both child and husband. No one moved to comfort others during the brief service. Tears were shed privately, for our losses were our own, and comparisons and gestures of comfort were profoundly out of place. My losses were, and were not, unique; I did not mourn alone.

In my community, the *yizkor* service concludes with the singing of a psalm. Communal singing is a powerful vehicle through which affect and memory can be contacted and expressed, and the haunting melody both triggers and assuages grief while creating a context that contains it. Singing together establishes a holding space (Solomon, 1995) for the group. In his discussions of music and creative process in Greek culture, Orfanos (1997, 1999) has described the power of music in creating a potential space and facilitating collective mourning. In line with his description, I felt intensely *with* myself, connected to my losses, yet held by the intense, soothing affect embodied in the swell of voices around me.[7]

Where acute confrontation with death leaves us in a state of intense distress, unable to respond to the Other as a separate subject, mourning across the lifespan may best occur in the context of community where individual pain and loss are recognized and shared. There is comfort in the awareness that the pain of our own loss is both separate from, yet connected to, that of others. In the very long aftermath of the void created by death, the commonality of loss is sustaining and nurturing.

The *yizkor* ritual takes place in transitional space (Winnicott, 1951), creating room for both connection and separateness, for merger and isolation. We do not challenge the experience of linkage *or* of isolation, just as we do not challenge the "reality" of our loved one's simultaneous absence and presence (Bassin, 2003). By invoking the memory of our dead, we paradoxically experience *and* deny the pain of loss. Rather than choosing between renunciation and denial, we simultaneously confront our losses and affirm their internal aliveness (Bassin, 1998).

Yizkor represents one example of many types of cultural and religious acts of memorialization that occur in a communal context. These rituals may serve a crucial function in allowing the individual to integrate the experience of aloneness and loss within an intersubjective context that reaffirms life in the face of facing loss.

Ritual and existential meaning

Yizkor is a ritual created for the mourner. It addresses the particulars of our losses and gives us an opportunity to remember and mark them. It is not surprising that so many non-mourners flee the synagogue space during *yizkor*. To remain there forces a confrontation with vulnerability and the danger of loss. Yet even for those who leave, the very existence of rituals like *shiva* and *yizkor* introduces a peripheral recognition of the existential realities of living and dying. The non-mourner leaves the room, knowing that one day she too will be there saying *yizkor* for a lost loved one.

In recognizing and memorializing death, we confront our (non-pathological) concerns about the meaning of life, and perhaps of death as well. We may begin to assimilate the reality of our vulnerability and that of others. We have an opportunity to momentarily mourn other losses, of persons, opportunities, time.

The mourning process is never fully resolved but, instead, is lifelong. We need opportunities to remember, relive and even to grieve again for those we've lost and for those we will lose. That need may be best met by periodic rituals, whether personal, cultural or religious, which take place within a group context. Such rituals not only help mark our losses, but also support the gradual integration of death into life, allowing us to anticipate other deaths (even our own). Acts of memorialization are an abiding, immutable human need that can enrich psychoanalytic experience and our understanding of the dynamics of loss.

Acknowledgements

I thank Lew Aron, Donna Bassin, Andy Druck, Beverly Druck, Sue Grand, Joseph Kaplan, David Kraemer, Sharon Penkower and Ann Wimpheimer for their very helpful comments on an earlier draft of this chapter, Eugene Tereshchenko for his stellar editorial help and Minyan M'at for providing a context in which memory is honored.

Notes

1 In Israel, on Holocaust Remembrance Day (*Yom haShoah*), Israelis, both secular and religious, observe a minute of silence to commemorate the death of those lost in the Holocaust. A siren sounds everywhere in the country; people stop and stand still and silent wherever they are; in cars, offices, shops. In this brief, powerful moment, loss is memorialized in the context of a community, indeed, a country, of mourners. Then, the siren stops and life goes on.

2 See Lamm (1988) for an excellent discussion of all aspects of Jewish mourning and references to relevant Jewish texts. More recently, Lamm (2004) has detailed many of the "do's" and "don'ts" of *shiva* calls, focusing on the mourner's need to mourn.

3 Throughout this chapter, I use the female pronoun to refer equally to people of both genders.

4 The precise timing of the death in relation to major holidays determines whether *shiva* is observed in a truncated fashion, or not at all.

5 Parallels to many of these *shiva* and post-*shiva* rituals may be found in the customs of Italian Catholics from small towns in Southern Italy (and even today in small towns in Sardinia) where, for example, the mourner remained at home and received visitors for about seven days following a burial, refraining from celebratory activities for the next thirty days, and dressing in black for one year (Maria Luisa Tricoli, personal communication).

6 I wish to acknowledge Rabbi Saul Berman who so creatively responds to human need.

7 In many orthodox synagogues, the *yizkor* service is limited to the recitation of the memorial prayer. The absence of rituals that pull the community together (for example, communal singing or communal *kaddish*) may dissipate the emotional

power of *yizkor*. The function of this ritual as an act of memorialization is profoundly enhanced by its communal dimension, and can be bleached of meaning in its absence.

References

Abraham, K. (1924) A short study of the development of the libido, viewed in the light of mental disorder. In *Selected Papers of Karl Abraham M.D.*, pp. 418–501. New York: Basic Books, 1968.

Ashenburg, K. (2002) *The Mourner's Dance*. New York: North Point Press.

Bassin, D. (1998) In memoriam: "memorialization" and the working through of mourning. Paper presented at the Doris Bernstein Memorial Lecture, Institute for Psychoanalytic Training and Research, and the American Psychoanalytic Association Meeting, New York.

—— (2003) A not-so-temporary occupation inside Ground Zero. In J. Greenberg (ed.) *9/11: Trauma at Home*, pp. 195–203. Lincoln, NE: University of Nebraska Press.

—— (2004) *The Mourning After* (unpublished film synopsis).

Becker, E. (1973) *The Denial of Death*. New York: Free Press.

Benjamin, J. (1995) *Like Subjects, Love Objects*. New Haven, CT: Yale University Press.

Bibring, E. (1953) The mechanism of depression. In P. Greenacre (ed.) *Affective Disorders*, pp. 14–48. New York: International Universities Press.

Bowlby, J. (1960) Grief and mourning in infancy and early childhood. *The Psychoanalytic Study of the Child*, 15: 9–52. New York: International Universities Press.

—— (1980) *Loss: Sadness and Depression*. New York: Basic Books.

Freud, S. (1917) Mourning and melancholia. *Standard Edition*, 14: 237–258. London: Hogarth Press, 1957.

Gaines, R. (1997) Detachment and continuity. *Contemporary Psychoanalysis*, 33: 549–570.

Grand, S. (2000) *The Reproduction of Evil*. Hillsdale, NJ: Analytic Press.

Jacobson, E. (1957) Denial and repression. *Journal of the American Psychoanalytic Association*, 5: 61–92.

Kavaler-Adler, S. (2003) *Mourning, Spirituality and Psychic Change: A New Object Relations View of Psychoanalysis*. Hove, UK: Brunner-Routledge.

Klass, D. (1988) *Parental Grief: Solace & Resolution*. New York: Springer.

Klein, M. (1940) Mourning and its relation to manic-depressive states. *International Journal of Psychoanalysis*, 21: 125–153.

Kraemer, D. (2000) *The Meanings of Death in Rabbinic Judaism*. London: Routledge.

Lamm, M. (1988) *The Jewish Way in Death and Mourning*. New York: Jonathan David.

—— (2004) *Consolation*. Philadelphia, PA: Jewish Publication Society.

Loewald, H. (1962) Internalization, separation, mourning and the superego. *Psychoanalytic Quarterly*, 31: 483–504.

Orfanos, S.D. (1997) Mikis Theodorakis: music, culture, and the creative process. *Journal of Modern Hellenism*, 14: 17–37.

—— (1999) The creative boldness of Mikis Theodorakis. *Journal of Modern Hellenism*, 16: 27–39.

Rubin, S. (1985) The resolution of bereavement: a clinical focus on the relationship to the deceased. *Psychotherapy: Theory, Research, Training and Practice*, 22(2): 231–235.

Silverman, P.R., Nickman, S. and Worden, J.W. (1992) Detachment revisited: the child's reconstruction of a dead parent. *American Journal of Orthopsychiatry*, 62(4): 494–503.

Slochower, J. (1993) Mourning and the holding function of shiva. *Contemporary Psychoanalysis*, 29: 352–367.

—— (1996) The holding function in mourning. In J. Slochower, *Holding and Psychoanalysis: A Relational Perspective*, pp. 125–138. Hillsdale, NJ: Analytic Press.

—— (2006) *Psychoanalytic Collisions*. Hillsdale, NJ: Analytic Press.

Solomon, M. (1995) *Mozart*. New York: HarperCollins.

Volkan, V.D. (1981) *Linking Objects and Linking Phenomena*. New York: International Universities Press.

Winnicott, D.W. (1951) Transitional objects and transitional phenomenon. In D.W. Winnicott, *Through Pediatrics to Psychoanalysis*, pp. 229–242. New York: Basic Books, 1958.

—— (1958) The capacity to be alone. In D.W. Winnicott, *The Maturational Processes and the Facilitating Environment*, pp. 29–36. New York: International Universities Press, 1965.

—— (1964) The importance of the setting in meeting regression in psycho-analysis. In D.W. Winnicott, *Psychoanalytic Explorations*, pp. 96–102. Cambridge, MA: Harvard University Press, 1989.

—— (1971) *Playing and Reality*. London: Tavistock.

Part III

Childhood and adolescence

Chapter 7

On losses that are not easily mourned

Michael O'Loughlin

At the beginning of his book *On Private Madness*, André Green (1986) ruminates on why he writes. Apart from the obvious reasons that he gleaned from his own analysis, Green states that fundamentally he has no choice: his writing is driven by his own sublimated urges. In my case, the answer is much less clear. While those who know me intimately will affirm that I use intellectual pursuits, especially reading, in a sublimating manner, my relationship with writing is much more tortured. It seems that I write to seek answers, but the act of writing is so fraught with resistance that it would appear that I have a strong aversion to whatever truths I might find. Ironically, I find my work as analyst and professor performative and vivifying. It is only in the totally solitary act of writing, in which my mirror image gazes back at me from the screen of my computer, that I face an inner emptiness that paralyzes me.

I am the sad clown. Those who encounter me in performative mode are moved to new emotional places and I experience a lightness of being in the interpersonal milieu that I have evoked. Yet, left to face myself, everything seems flat. This summer, for example, I taught a weeklong institute for teachers and psychologists on the emotional lives of children. As a capstone project on the final day, one group of students set up a playroom and all thirty-three of us played with children's toys for an hour. I felt transcendent. Then I came home to write . . . this promised chapter about depression . . . or rather to ruminate about depression and flee back into reading others' writings because the prospect of placing my own words on paper became too anxiety provoking.

I am drawn to psychoanalytic writers who have the capacity to locate themselves explicitly in their work. It is somehow comforting to know that what Green termed "private madness" – the mirror image of my inner psychosis – is not mine alone. Perhaps all clowns are sad, and perhaps it is a clown's capacity to elicit an uncanny connection in audience members to their inner psychosis that is the true source of the clown's pathos. Green (1986) notes that Harold Searles was pre-eminent among analysts in his capacity to "break the law of silence" (p. 15) and bring to life the dialogical relationship between his private madness and his capacity to work with patients. Paradoxically, while Searles was astute at using his own "private madness" as a therapeutic foil for his patients, he was also acutely aware of how easily the therapeutic encounter – much like the writing encounter for Green – could provide a sublimating escape from the analyst's own psychosis rather than an opportunity for new analytic inquiry: "I surmise that not a few work-addicted analysts tend, as I do, to unconsciously defend themselves against an undeniably sustained experiencing of their own individual life by keeping themselves immersed in the collective lives of their patients" (Searles, 1979, p. 159).

Perhaps, then, the opportunity to confront my own emptiness is a gift. I imagine myself as the clown meditating in his dressing room prior to a show. It is by reaching inward that I find ways of connecting to what, following Green (1999), I will refer to as the "objectalizing/disobjectalizing functions" that keep me connected, yet leave me alone among people. I have no way of knowing precisely what inaugural loss or deprivation might serve as the source of this emptiness but, just as my patients do, I can imaginatively reconstruct links between known experiences and potential early correlates of those experiences that, at a minimum, provide me with an imaginary narrative of my life that "explains" my sense of loss and names the unnamable, free-floating worry I experience when I leave myself free enough of intellectual pursuits to allow it to surface.

All writing is autobiographical. I am no longer willing to hide in my writing because that makes me feel like an impostor. When I stare at my reflection, I recognize that I am compelled to come clean. Perhaps I am finally beginning to experience what my analytic training taught me at an implicit level: becoming an analyst is really about being able to construct a narrative of one's journey into analysis. What set out to be a chapter on depression, an intellectual discourse on loss of vitality and feelings of emptiness, ends up, inevitably, as a tale of the intrapsychic encounter between self and other in the consulting room. More fundamentally, it is a tale of my reluctant journey as an analyst to confront the deeper, darker layers of my own psychic formation, driven by my recognition that analytic insight and self-understanding are deeply intertwined.

Circa 1952: on absence in presence – an abject hospital tale

When I was an infant, I suffered from severe projectile vomiting for a period of two or more years. I spent most of that time in the local county hospital. There were occasional interludes when I was allowed home. I had two siblings, one and two years older, respectively. My dad worked all day, and my whole family was perched precariously on the precipice of poverty. The little time that I spent at home, my mother tells me, was frenetic. When

I vomited at home there were no spare linens, and my mother did not have running water, let alone a washer or dryer. Thus, my illness caused serious domestic upheaval as well as lots of worry. It was far from the idyllic holding relationship Winnicott (1964, 1968) might have hoped for.

Meanwhile, at the hospital, my mom and dad were advised to visit me as infrequently as possible, as their presence invariably upset me and times when they could actually hold me were strictly limited. My mom tells me that when she visited, she would peer longingly at me through the window. The hospital was so anxiety provoking for me that, to this day, I experience anxiety when I hear or see an ambulance. As a child, I would stand paralyzed and "go white as a sheet" whenever an ambulance passed. This experience resulted in arrested development; I reached all of my early developmental milestones about two years behind schedule. My life was saved when my dad, ignoring the doctor's advice to order a coffin for me, transferred me to the only other hospital in town where, in due course, I responded to treatment. The taxi driver who picked me up for my final trip home at age 2 was convinced that I was a newborn.

Today, my son and daughter are both emergency medical technicians, and both are embarking on careers in medical fields. Meanwhile, hanging in my office is a photograph given to me in 1987 by one of my students, a gifted amateur photographer. The picture is a headshot of a chalk statuette of an elegantly coiffed, 1940s style woman staring wistfully at the world through the grimy window of an antiques shop. At the time, I did not make much of it, but today I stand in awe of my student's uncanny sensibilities. Why did he shoot this particular image? Why, of the thousands of images in his portfolio, did he choose this one as his parting gift to me? I perform my emotions expressively in my teaching and in this course on human development, I had focused particularly on loss, death and dying. I suspect that in so doing I worked through some of my own experiences of loss and thereby unconsciously allowed him a window into the absence within.

My childhood illness was not easily forgotten. I lived on a restricted diet until I was 14. Reminiscent of the invalid boy, Colin, in Frances Hodgson Burnett's *The Secret Garden*, (1909) I was labeled *delicate* throughout my childhood. I lived much of my childhood vicariously, envying the heartiness of Dickon in *The Secret Garden*, but identifying much more with the suffering children that peopled Dickens' novels. I bled for characters such as Smike, David Copperfield and Bob Cratchit's invalid son, Tiny Tim. Although my early losses were intellectualized and sublimated to some extent, I never had the opportunity to name and symbolize them fully. They were part of my make-up in some nameless sort of way.

Poltergeists are invisible. Yet they have a way of making their presence felt. So, too, with my inner losses. They are my perpetual companions, a spectral and silent presence in my subjective experience of self. That is the part of me that gives off an aura of sadness and causes me to feel dislocated and not belonging in the presence of others. It is often quiescent. Yet, like the poltergeist that is disturbed by new inhabitants occupying its ghostly mansion, excessive gaiety, loss, or loneliness, evoke intimations of unease and loss in my consciousness, insofar as experiences as unanchored and nameless as these can be said to be conscious at all.

March 1985: the leave-taking

When my father entered his final illness in the winter of 1985, I was still a graduate student in New York. I abandoned school for six weeks to return to Ireland to be at his bedside. He had a terribly painful illness, yet the leave-taking, though lonely, was tranquil. Buttressed by his enviable religious faith in a better after-life and by the comforting presence of his family at his hospital bedside, my dad left this physical world. After the funeral, an inordinate crowd of mourners came back to our house to eat, drink, and remember my dad. The revelry and absence of any *naming of loss* became unbearable for me. I fled to my childhood bedroom to escape or perhaps indulge the *unspeakableness of my loss.*

Circa 1987: on absence *in* loss – another leave-taking

Those among us who are exiles or emigrants know the dislocations that come with crossing borders and developing hybrid identities. I found an anchor to help me sustain myself through this struggle in a fellow traveler named Patrick. He was a year or two older than me and a veteran border crosser. Patrick died of leukemia when he was 37. His doctor and a small group of us stood at his deathbed and granted his last wish that we share parting sips from a six-pack of Budweiser as he put the best face he could on what neither he nor any of us could name – his imminent death. Fifteen years later, I was finally able to visit Patrick's wife at their home without being suffused by depression and a desire to flee. During those years, I have never had the courage to listen to the audiotape of my remarks at the memorial service. The speech, as best I recall it, was a manic effort to protect all of us from annihilating grief by recreating the antic dynamic between Patrick and myself. Why do I now have the urge to listen to it?

June 22, 2002: extract from a dream

Dreams, of course, are the true poltergeists of the unconscious. Although I have revisited my family many times since I emigrated from Ireland, the trip I had planned for summer 2002 had some special significance as it was the occasion for a rare family reunion. Capitalizing on my return after an absence of five years, my sisters organized a surprise birthday party for my mom. My mom was 76 years old that summer, and this was the first time in her life that there had been a surprise party in her honor. I anticipated that my three sisters and I would attend, as well as grandchildren and relatives. My brother, who resided elsewhere in Europe, was noncommittal. The latest word I had was that he was too busy either to attend this event or to fly over to meet me during my visit. My brother had always resented the unearned privilege that accompanied my *delicate* status. The night before I departed I had a dream that included the following:

> We are attending a lavishly catered event. I greet my brother-in-law, Jackie – who, in real life is older – and I note that he looks much younger and happier than I. The table is all set and ready for dining and the moment comes for all of us to sit down. In my usual hesitant way I hold back a little to see where others choose to sit before taking my own seat. However, when I go to sit, all of the seats around the banquet table are occupied and there is no room for my brother and me. Everybody is eating and drinking with gusto. Nobody seems to notice that we are left out. I am holding a bowl of hearty chicken soup which, despite this being a catered affair, I know is made by my mother. Having no table on which to rest it, I balance it on my knee and try to break up one of the chunks of chicken. The chunk flies through the air and lands on my pants. In trying to catch it, I dribble the soup all over my clothes. I flee the room in confusion and change my clothes. My brother continues to eat his soup, and the others do not notice.

The actual party went according to plan, of course, and I derived some secret pleasure from my own sociability on that occasion. Nevertheless, my dream is a reminder that I have periodically approached an abyss of primitive dread, a sense of non-belonging. Similarly, in the days following the World Trade Center collapse, I experienced a form of abject depression that I can only assume accurately mirrors my earliest experience. As Kristeva (1982) notes, failing to find anything outside with which to identify – and unwilling or unable to convert my melancholy into rage that I might expel onto Arabs, Afghanis, or any demonized Other – I turned inward and encountered the loss at the center of my being.

Inaugural loss and its consequences

My interest is in free-floating forms of primitive dread and emptiness, their origins, and their manifestations in psychic experience. Inaugural losses occur during the presymbolic period and continue to live within us as unsymbolized experience. While I have had little difficulty in recognizing split-off experiences in my patients, it took me a long time to recognize that the nameless, free floating feelings of worry and dread that I experienced were actually markers for unsymbolized, inaccessible aspects of my own experience.

Psychoanalysis, Freud's pessimism notwithstanding, tends toward the optimistic and is often unreceptive to notions such as *inaugural loss* (Kristeva, 1982), *negativity* (Green, 1999), and the kinds of destructive impulses that Klein (1975) described as underlying the paranoid schizoid position. As Joan Riviere noted, "The concept of a destructive force within every individual, leading toward the annihilation of life, is naturally one which arouses extreme emotional resistance" (quoted in Rose, 1993, p. 134). Lacan's writings (e.g., 1968, 1977) leave us in no doubt, however, that the entry of humans into the symbolic realm, most particularly through language, is a painful process. Rose (1993, p. 131) reminds us that, for Lacan, psychic negativity is simply "the price that all human subjects pay for the cruel passage of the psyche into words."

The writings of Tustin and others at the Tavistock Clinic on the effects of autism (e.g., Alvarez, 1992; Tustin, 1992; Alvarez and Reid, 1999) and the work of others such as Bick (1968; see also Briggs, 2002) and Bion (1989, 1993) reveal the cataclysmic psychic consequences of an incapacity to enter the world of the other through symbols. Overwhelming dread appears to be at the core of the everyday presymbolic psychic experience of autistic people. They appear to lack the capacity to gain even the temporary reprieve from terror that nonautistic infants accomplish through projection that can, as Bion (1993) notes, ultimately lead to the reintrojection of metabolized, hence less terrifying emotions.

Many analysts do not routinely work with significantly autistic or psychotic patients. Our population typically includes patients who have entered the world of the symbolic. Nevertheless, all analysts still have the opportunity to work with the unsymbolized parts of patients' psychic experiences. Our capacity to work with these unsymbolized parts is what distinguishes psychoanalysis from other treatment modalities. More precisely, it is the capacity of the analyst to get in touch with unsymbolized or psychotic aspects of his or her own psyche and to use those therapeutically in the service of the patient that makes psychoanalysis distinctive. The repeated opportunity analysts have for working through their losses is surely at the root of the comforting adage that even if we do not improve our patients, we are no doubt helping to cure ourselves.

Depression without an apparent object

In her book, *Negativity in the Work of Melanie Klein*, Jacqueline Rose (1993) describes Klein as the "high priestess of negativity" because of her willingness to postulate a destructive or death instinct at the origins of psychic life. Contrary to "the idyll of early fusion with the mother" advocated, for example, by Winnicott, Rose tells us that "Klein offers proximity as something which devours" (Rose, 1993, p. 140). It is difficult to read Klein without experiencing a visceral response to the rage and destructiveness inherent in her vision of psychic development. Klein argues that it is *withholding* rather than symbiosis that is the catalyst for the delineation of subjectivity. Merger with an object produces tremendous narcissistic gratification. When this gratification is withheld, as it must inevitably be, the infant experiences a fundamental sense of loss. "For," Rose (1993, p. 151) notes, "the loss of the object forces a breach in the primitive narcissism of the subject, a breach which, in a twist, produces the object as its effect." The earliest object relations, therefore are negative, arising from an infant's need to find an object to contain its projections. Experiencing a surge of negative emotion, and lacking the capacity to process these feelings, the infant seizes upon an object, not for comfort, but to expel negative feelings. Rose summarizes Klein's inscription of subjectivity in the negative as follows:

> In these earlier papers it is stated over and over that the subject first comes to experience itself negatively. Self-alienation gives the colour of the subject's coming-to-be: "nothing good within *lasts* . . . the first conscious idea of 'me' is largely coloured by painful associations".
>
> (Rose, 1993, p. 152, quoting from Riviere)

Rose (1993) points out that "For Klein the mother rapidly comes to be experienced as bad" (p. 153). In the ordinary course of things, Rose suggests, object relations "are 'improvements' on and 'protections against' primordial narcissistic anxiety; distrust of the object is better than despair" (p. 152). This is a dark view of the psychic life of the infant, a view that suggests suffering is inevitable. Object relations from a Kleinian perspective are not idealized. While Klein does discuss reparative functions, her work does not allow us to imagine a relational world without suffering, disappointment, and inevitable loneliness. In the best of relational worlds, with an available good-enough-mother, the infant projects psychotic anxieties. These anxieties are returned with reasonable reliability in metabolized form by an attuned caregiver. In situations where "maternal reverie" fails and the infant is, instead, exposed to "a willfully misunderstanding object" (Bion, 1993) or, as happened with my mom, an absent object, the consequences, while not as calamitous as an autistic psychosis, are significant.

> Normal development follows if the relationship between infant and breast permits the infant to project a feeling, say, that it is dying, into the mother and reintroject it after its sojourn in the breast has made it tolerable to the psyche. If the projection is not accepted by the mother

the infant feels that its feeling that it's dying is stripped of such meaning as it has. It therefore reintrojects, not a fear of dying made tolerable, but a nameless dread.

(Bion, 1993, p. 116)

In her work, *Melanie Klein*, Kristeva (2001) notes Klein's point that even in the depressive position complete integration of the ego is never possible, and therefore loneliness and feelings of separation from the maternal object are inevitable. She cites Bion's fantasy of having a twin as a fantasy of integration of the ego that eliminates these splits. However, as Kristeva notes, when integration fails we are liable to experience a sense of non-belonging, a feeling with which I am all too familiar. Alternately, Kristeva (2001) notes, "One can defend oneself against too great a dependence on the external object by thrusting oneself upon the internal object," and this results in solitude being transformed into "an omnipresent feeling of forlornness" (p. 112).

Using a phenomenological approach, Kristeva has attempted to elucidate the psychic consequences of these kinds of losses. In a variety of writings, Kristeva (1982, 1989, 1991) focuses variously on manifestations of loss as expressed in symptoms of uncanny strangeness, abjection, and melancholia. In *Powers of Horror*, for example, Kristeva describes how formless feelings of loss lead to an experience of abjection:

There looms, within abjection, one of those violent, dark revolts of being, directed against a threat that seems to emanate from an exorbit-ant outside or inside, ejected beyond the scope of the possible, the tolerable, the thinkable. It lies there quite close but it cannot be assimilated . . . When I am beset by abjection, the twisted braids of affects and thoughts I call by such a name does not have, properly speaking, a definable *object*.

(Kristeva, 1982, p. 1)

Kristeva conceptualizes this type of abject loss as arising from the inability to identify with an object in the world. This leads to a turn inward, a turn toward the emptiness that arises from an inaugural loss of significant proportions:

If it be true that the abject simultaneously beseeches and pulverizes the subject, one can understand that it is experienced at the peak of its strength when that subject, weary of fruitless attempts to identify with something on the outside, finds the impossible within; when it finds that the impossible constitutes its very *being*, then it is none other than abject. The abjection of self would be the culminating form of that experience of the subject to which it is revealed that all its objects are based merely on the inaugural *loss* that laid the foundations of its own being.

(Kristeva, 1982, p. 5)

In *Black Sun*, an examination of melancholia, Kristeva distinguishes two forms of depression. According to classical psychoanalytic theory, she notes, "Depression, like mourning, conceals an aggressiveness toward the lost object" (1989, p. 11). An act such as suicide, therefore, is not only an act of aggression against the self, but also a reflection of hatred for the introjected object. Of more relevance, here, is the second form of melancholia posited by Kristeva. She suggests that often in narcissistic individuals, "Sadness would point to a primitive self – wounded, incomplete, empty" (Kristeva, 1989, p. 12). This sadness is the "archaic expression of an unsymbolizable, unnameable, narcissistic wound" (p. 13). For such persons, sadness itself becomes the object, and suicide merely a merger with sadness (p. 12). The center of mourning for a depressed narcissist is not an object, but rather an archaic attachment to an unsymbolizable object, which she refers to simply as the "Thing." The "Thing" is "an insistence without desire" (p. 13) that leaves the depressed person with a profound sense of having lost something supremely good, but having no name for that lost object. Such a person, steeped in melancholia, is left without memory, without words, without desire, and could easily seek relief through suicide: "The Thing is inscribed within us without memory, the buried accomplice of our unspeakable anguish. One can imagine the delights of reunion that a regressive daydream promises itself through the nuptials of suicide" (p. 14).

Kristeva's ideas are consistent with the Kleinian perspective articulated above. Her broad-brush approach offers a useful window into the phenomenology of formless loss. It should be noted, however, that except in her more recent work on Klein (Kristeva, 2001), Kristeva argues that the inaccessibility of unsymbolized experience is due to repression. I believe, following Klein, that splitting is a more likely explanation because of the inaccessibility, and non-neurotic characteristics of this nameless anguish. Green (1986) clarifies the distinction this way: "The return of the repressed gives rise to signal anxiety. The return of the split-off elements is accompanied by feelings of severe threat, of 'helplessness' (Freud's *Hilfosigkeit*), 'annihilation' (Klein, 1946), 'nameless dread' (Bion, 1970), 'disintegration' or 'agonies' (Winnicott, 1958, 1964, 1968)" (Green, 1986, pp. 77–78).

Green (e.g. 1986, 1999; see also Kohon, 1999) has devoted a considerable amount of his writing to exploring this phenomenon. He speaks of blank psychosis as a radical solution to catastrophic object loss. Such a loss, rather than leading to repression results, instead, in a massive decathexis of emotion and a blank state of mind. Green's (1986) discussion of introjected maternal depression, the dead mother syndrome, is illustrative. By dead mother, Green is not referring to literal death, but rather to the effects on an infant of an emotionally dead mother. A catastrophic event such as the death of a child or a miscarriage is liable to throw the mother into a deep depression. The effect on the infant is "a brutal change in the maternal imago" (Green, 1986, p. 149) in which the vitality of the mother disappears. The blankness comes from the loss of meaning that occurs, in particular if the infant has nowhere else to turn to seek a metabolic outlet for his or her emotions. The crisis deepens when the infant, having exhausted available psychic defenses, such as "agitation, insomnia, and nocturnal terrors" (p. 150), turns instead to "decathexis of the maternal object and the unconscious identification with the dead mother" (p. 150). Green (1986) characterized this not as a psychotic break, but as a breakdown only in a very specific area of emotional functioning, "a hole in the texture of object-relations with the mother" (p. 151).

Modell (1999) offers another example. He describes a mother who, by virtue of her own psychic difficulties was unable to allow her child a mind of his own. The merger between the mother's mind and her son's mind caused the child to fail to identify his own psychic uniqueness and to feel psychically alive. As Green notes (1986, p. 152), the child may simply feel "forbidden for him to be."

The ego's attempts at repair involve the construction of what Green (1986) calls a "patched breast," a splitting off of the emptiness – the hole in the ego – and an attempt to replace it with sublimatory activities such as intellectual achievement, and an attempt to seek pleasure through auto-erotic excitation which allows for the sensation of pleasure without engagement with an other. In the area of intimate relations, predictably, the person remains vulnerable.

> In this area, a wound will awaken a psychical pain and one will witness the resurrection of the dead mother, who, for the entire critical period that she remains in the foreground, dissolves all of the subject's sublimatory acquisitions, which are not lost, but which remain momentarily blocked.
>
> (Green, 1986, p. 153)

The patient, upon meeting a new love object may feel ready to love, believing that the dead mother trauma is excised, but the patient will fail, Green (1986) tells us, "because his love is still mortgaged to the dead mother" (p. 156). In a worst-case scenario, the emptiness the patient feels becomes the only alive part of the self – the absence becomes the presence, the dead becomes the living.

Arrested in their capacity to love, subjects who are under the empire of the dead mother can only aspire to autonomy, Green wrote. Sharing remains forbidden to them. Thus solitude, which was a situation creating anxiety and to be avoided, changes sign. From negative it becomes positive. Having previously been shunned, it is now sought after. The subject nestles into it. He becomes his own mother, but remains prisoner to her economy of survival. He thinks he has got rid of his dead mother. In fact she only leaves him in peace in the measure that she herself is left in peace. As long as there is no candidate to the succession, she can well let her child survive, certain to be the only one to possess that inaccessible love.

Shades of Norman Bates and his darling mother in Hitchcock's *Psycho* (1960)! Indeed, as was the case with Bates' enactment, Green (1986) tells us that behind the blank mourning there is a "mad passion" of which the dead mother remains the object. The eternal fantasy of such patients is "to nourish the dead mother, to maintain her perpetually embalmed" (p. 162).

In more recent work, Green (1999, 2002) has attempted to situate his thinking about blank mourning within a larger structural theory of the work of the negative in psychic formation. Citing clinical instances such as the ones discussed, and the increasing prevalence of threats of mass destruction in the world, Green argues for the need to rearticulate the death drive as the motor of self-destruction. Green conceptualizes a life drive and a death drive. He argues that the purpose of the life drive is to ensure an "objectalising function" (1999, p. 85), by which he means the capacity to create and invest in meaningful object relations. In terms of the death drive, he cites clinical instances of the type discussed earlier, including "catastrophic or unthinkable anxieties, fears of annihilation or breakdown, feelings of futility, of devitalisation or of psychic death, sensations of a gap, of a bottomless hole, of an abyss" (p. 84). The purpose of the death drive is decathexis, a process Green labels "deobjectalisation." Contrary to the kind of mourning that sometimes accompanies loss, Green argues that this decathexis is characterized by an inhibition of the mourning function. This process, which involves what Bion would call attacks on linking, is at the heart of what Green (1999, 2002) terms negative narcissism – negative, because of the presence of significant self-abasement, and what Green calls "an aspiration to nothingness" (2002, p. 6).

Clinical implications

Decathexis, splitting, and attacks on linking – symptoms of the kind of blank or formless depression under discussion here – make analysis challenging. In addition, the analytic relationship requires the co-construction of a new relational experience, and this requires the suffering person to turn away from solitude toward acknowledging an other. Since wordless, formless anguish is presymbolic, the task of the analyst, as Kristeva (2001) notes, drawing on Segal and Bion, is for the analyst to use symbolism to enable the patient to transform unformulated *beta* elements into thinkable, *alpha* elements, to experience mourning for an unnamable, unrepresentable archaic object. From the perspective of countertransference, this requires the analyst to stay with the patient's unsymbolized experience long enough to work with it symbolically. This, of course, makes demands on the analyst's archaic objects and the analyst's capacity to live with his or her archaic experiences, yet not be bound by them in the same, unsymbolized manner as the patient.

Nancy

When Nancy presented for treatment, she was in her thirties. Early on, she brought in a picture of herself, at about age 3, gazing adoringly at her father, who was working under the hood of the family car. She produced no picture of her mother. The definitive crisis in Nancy's life came when, in her early teens, her parents, long in a conflicted marriage, divorced. Nancy's father left during a bitter dispute. Nancy was forced to live with her mother. She could not handle the abandonment by her father. She went through periods of blank despair: a flight into drugs for a year; hospitalization for a psychotic break; and the development of severe, schizoaffective symptoms, accompanied by bouts of self-abasement, severe paranoid ideation, ideas of reference, and occasional delusions. Nancy abandoned her therapist of thirteen years without accepting a single session to explore termination issues. Sitting in my office three times weekly, she almost never made eye contact. She usually stared fixedly at the floor and said she really had nothing to say. She appeared to experience the most profound anger, but it always came out verbally as the mildest of recriminations, most often directed towards her mother or herself, but never at her idealized father.

By the time she began treatment with me, Nancy had resumed an exquisitely delicate relationship with her father, some fifteen years after the catastrophic break. As we began to flesh out her family history, she was explicit that we could talk about and change anything as long as it did not affect her relationship with either parent. These parameters, designed to protect her attachment to the emptiness that replaced the object, were to eventually prove fatal to the therapy. The predominant mode in our sessions was silence, punctuated by bouts of self-abasement, and anxiety lest I attack her. I found the silences extremely hard to bear. I began to doubt my competence and constantly feared she would abandon therapy. It took a considerable amount of work in supervision for me to recognize that her extreme isolation was evoking my own inner losses. I often experienced relief when she canceled a session. She showed little desire to speak of the external world, and seemed terrified of her internal world. My supervisor's exhortations to me to join in her paranoid state rather than interpret from outside were initially puzzling and frightening to me. I often found myself perceiving her as waif-like and marginal. For a long time I walked on eggshells in her presence. She was constantly fearful that I would take over her mind. I was fearful she would flee. Then I began to wonder if I was feeling her paranoia and I wondered if it was really me who wanted to flee the paranoid isolation we created. As I became more comfortable living in the deathly shadow of her paranoid structures, some life entered the room. I caught a furtive smile from time to time, flirted a little, and pursued her when she canceled sessions. We even shared an occasional joke. I began to see a determined, interesting, and competent woman hiding behind the fragile shell she showed the world. Eventually I began to wonder if the fragility was an artful construction.

My suspicions about her fragility as an artifice were reinforced when Mother induced her to move back home under her care. The dynamic of their relationship was such that whenever Nancy exhibited signs of illness, Mother became solicitous and adopted a good mother role. However, whenever Nancy exhibited signs of thinking her own thoughts, Mother became extremely fragmented, enraged, and controlling. At such times, Mother would goad her until Nancy began to scream. After the fight, Nancy would eventually experience remorse and resolve to be a more caring, dutiful daughter. During their worst fights Nancy, lacking any self-soothing capabilities, would flee to the bathroom, screaming and retreating into paranoid isolation. Mother would eventually remind her that she, Nancy, was sick and Mother was only doing things for Nancy's "own good."

Mother suffered from severe anxiety and depression and had tremendous difficulties with boundaries. I referred Nancy to a new psychiatrist for medication management and Mother accompanied her to make sure, in Nancy's words, that she "got her story straight." I began to work with Nancy to help her distinguish her own thoughts from the overflow of psychotic anxieties she received daily from Mother. Gradually, Nancy began to set her own boundaries and began to use me as a resource to figure out where to draw the lines and to understand which psychosis belonged to her, and which belonged to Mother.

Nancy's professional life stabilized. She began dating casually, joined a sports league, and started interacting socially with long forgotten friends. She negotiated typically complex social situations such as family weddings and parties with greater ease. The more Nancy improved, the more Mother appeared to descend into rage-filled tirades, accusing Nancy of being ungrateful for all that Mother did for her. Did she not know how much Mother sacrificed on her behalf? Mother urged Nancy to resign her professional position and stay home all day. Torn by guilt and pressed by Mother, Nancy agreed to accompany her on a vacation to a foreign country. During the vacation, Mother was extremely fragmented, and complained continuously. Nancy struggled valiantly to maintain boundaries but finally reached breaking point. She called me from a foreign city. I reminded her of how to hold on to herself in the presence of Mother. She did, but was wracked with guilt at thinking her own thoughts and not absorbing Mother's stuff. She was a bad girl, a failed daughter. The only way to make things up to Mother would be to become more dutiful and obedient. The therapy was making her life harder, highlighting the splits she experienced between self and Mother.

Nancy terminated therapy at that point, after eighteen months of treatment. She did agree to a few sessions for termination. Feeling that I had conceded defeat to Mother, I was rather depressed. I later learned that Nancy had moved out from home shortly thereafter, and was again living independently.

Not knowing Nancy's early history, it is impossible to delineate a possible relationship between early losses and later trauma. However, even from the brief description offered here, it is evident that Nancy suffered serious ego disintegration as a result of a traumatic abandonment. Her situation was compounded by the absence of a metabolizing figure. Instead, her mother compounded the problem, further negating Nancy's existence by using her as a container for her own psychosis. Nancy's identification with her father may have precipitated her mother's persistent attacks on her. The end result was that Nancy suffered attacks on her capacity to make meaning, entered deep melancholia, and for many years lived in unspeakable anguish, having the kind of nameless loss at the center of her psyche that Green (1986) discusses as characteristic of negative narcissism.

Nancy lacked a capacity for mourning, due to her inability to symbolize her experience. In many respects, she was "forbidden to be." Her lengthy treatment, of which her work with me was only a small part, consisted of: (1) encouraging Nancy's capacity to symbolize her experience; (2) engaging her in the kinds of dialogue that restored her capacity to think for herself and to restore absent links; and (3) fostering her desire and capacity for autonomous living. An ultimate goal, toward which small steps were taken, was to assist Nancy with engaging the possibility of moving from her terrified, distrustful object-relational state to a new form of objectalization in which mutual relations might become possible.

Nicole

Nicole entered once weekly therapy in her late twenties. She has no recollection of her mother as other than depressed. Disappointed in love both from her own mother and from the man she had hoped to marry, Nicole's mother chose a partner based on practical considerations. Nicole reports that her mother has lived her whole life in suppressed anger, bitter toward men, burdened by her two daughters, soothed only by alcohol. At age 20, Nicole entered a relationship with an obsessive, alcoholic man that endured for a number of years. Nicole soothed herself through eating and heavy marijuana smoking. Her relationship ended under rather traumatic circumstances. Nicole returned home very depressed and sought therapy. Her relationship with her mother immediately reverted to its old pattern. Her mother, as always, was hypercritical and resentful of her presence in the home. She also resented the unspoken bond between Nicole and her father. Nicole had a deep longing for sexual and emotional intimacy, but was terrified of entering a new relationship.

For three years, our sessions had a numbing sameness. Nicole loved to come to sessions, and found in them a source of relief. She poured out the events of her week reportorial style and I felt induced to sleep. Sometimes her thoughts came out in a jumble, as if she were thought disordered. I noticed there was a correlation between Nicole's mental state and her mother's. When her mother had a bad week, Nicole was depressed and fragmented. When mother was occasionally solicitous, Nicole was elated, but this rapidly turned to depression, as she knew that this was temporary, serving only as a reminder of longing and loss. While she was cowed by her mother at home – and not helped by a docile and largely emotionally absent father – at work Nicole was very aggressive, suggesting that beneath the depression and fragmentation there was anger and life.

Many sessions had a manic quality. It was as if Nicole was desperately trying to connect, but even more desperately trying to keep me at bay. I had difficulty helping her symbolize her experience. My "dead mother" interpretations were of little help. "I know, that's why I hate my mother" was her typical response. By absorbing her experience without retaliation, I managed to keep her engaged in therapy, though I felt little accomplishment in this.

In the past two years, significant change has occurred in Nicole's life. She has earned a credential for a new profession, spent a year living on her own, took a new position, and moved into a new apartment with her partner with whom she has shared a relationship for more than a year. This is not to suggest that all of her issues have been resolved. Her relationship with her mother may have improved on the surface largely because they now see each other infrequently. She continues to experience considerable levels of self-abasement and melancholy and is still fearful of touching that loss at the center of her being, even though she is well aware that metabolizing it is necessary to mitigate pain. In addition, despite her bad, first partner experience, she appears to have chosen a new one who needs considerable caretaking. Nicole has some identification with her passive father, a man who has devoted his life to caring for her disconsolate mother.

Nicole's life has many elements that are suggestive of a dead mother introject. She has considerable difficulties with intimate relations, and rather than a securely introjected object, her thought confusions and bouts of melancholia and self-abasement suggest an internalized emptiness of the kind discussed earlier as negative narcissism. Nicole has been deeply wounded, but has lacked a capacity to symbolize that injury. She devotes considerable effort to defending her mother. Nicole still has to struggle with intrusions from a decathected object. Despite these difficulties, Nicole has struggled to create a new "third" in her relation with me. This co-construction has been hindered by her need to keep me at a distance. Yet, given the space to use the relationship on her own terms, Nicole has shown a capacity to develop and maintain a mutual relationship and is continuing in therapy.

Bringing analysis to life

Green (1986) suggests that the analyst should strive to create a revivifying experience for the patient with unmourned losses. He cautions against silence on the analyst's part, as this is likely to cause the patient to retreat into solitude. Staying with such patients, however, is not easy. People who have negative narcissistic qualities and experience blank mourning come to sessions filled with self-abasement and unspeakable sadness. They work to create a relationship in therapy that allows the confirmation and reproduction of those feelings despite a conscious desire to be healed. The likelihood is that the analyst who interprets from outside the patient's experience will contribute to the alienation of the patient and the objectification of their anguish. As the autobiographical introduction to this chapter suggests, it is my belief that the analyst needs to journey into his or her own losses in order to have the fortitude and sensitivity to engage the patient on a similar journey. What is needed is not didactic talk from an intrepid explorer who has already plumbed the depths and extracted nuggets of wisdom about inaugural loss. Instead, the humility of understanding the anguish of our own losses will allow us to tune our analytic ears to a register that allows us to absorb the patient's unconscious losses without the urge to either flee from or fix the patient.

References

Alvarez, A. (1992) *Live Company: Psychoanalytic Psychotherapy with Autistic, Borderline, Deprived, and Abused Children.* London: Routledge.

Alvarez, A. and Reid, S. (eds) (1999) *Autism and Personality: Findings from the Tavistock Workshop*. London: Routledge.

Bick, E. (1968) The experience of the skin in early object relations. *International Journal of Psychoanalysis*, 49: 484–486.

Bion, W. (1970) *Attention and Interpretation*. London: Tavistock.

—— (1989) *Learning from Experience*. London: Karnac.

—— (1993) *Second Thoughts: Selected Papers on Psychoanalysis*. Northvale, NJ: Aronson.

Briggs, A. (ed.) (2002) *Surviving Space: Papers on Infant Observation*. London: Karnac.

Green, A. (1986) *On Private Madness*. New York: International Universities Press.

—— (1999) *The Work of the Negative*. London: Free Association Books.

—— (2002) A dual conception of narcissism: positive and negative organizations. Presented at *Journal of the American Psychoanalytic Association* Conference, "Narcissism Revisited: Clinical and Conceptual Challenges," Mount Sinai Hospital, New York City, February 23–25.

Klein, M. (1946) Notes on some schizoid mechanisms. In M. Klein, (ed.) *Envy and Gratitude and Other Works, 1946–63: The Writings of Melanie Klein*, pp. 1–24. London: Hogarth Press, 1975.

—— (1975) *Envy and Gratitude and Other Works 1946–1963*. New York: The Free Press.

Kohon, G. (ed.) (1999) *The Dead Mother: The Work of André Green*. New York: Routledge.

Kristeva, J. (1982) *Powers of Horror: Essays on Abjection*. New York: Columbia University Press.

—— (1989) *Black Sun: Depression and Melancholia*. New York: Columbia University Press.

—— (1991) *Strangers to Ourselves*. New York: Columbia University Press.

—— (2001) *Melanie Klein*. New York: Columbia University Press.

Lacan, J. (1968) *The Language of the Self: The Function of Language in Psychoanalysis*. Baltimore, MD: Johns Hopkins University Press.

—— (1977) *Ecrits: A Selection*. New York: Norton.

Modell, A. (1999) The dead mother syndrome and the reconstruction of trauma. In G. Kohon (ed.) *The Dead Mother: The Work of André Green*, pp. 76–86. New York: Routledge.

Rose, J. (1993) *Negativity in the Work of Melanie Klein*. Cambridge, MA: Blackwell.

Searles, H. (1979) *Selected Papers on Countertransference*. Madison, CT: International Universities Press.

Tustin, F. (1992) *Autistic States in children*. London: Routledge.

Winnicott, D.W. (1958) The capacity to be alone. *International Journal of Psychoanalysis*, 39: 416–420.

—— (1964) The newborn and his mother. Lecture presented in Rome, April 1964. Originally published under the title "The neonate and his mother". *Acta Pediatrica Latina*, 17, 1964. Reprinted in D.W. Winnicott, *Winnicott on the Child*. New York: Perseus, 2002.

—— (1968) Communication between infant and mother, and mother and infant, compared and contrasted. Lecture in a public series about psychoanalysis known as the Winter Lectures, Marylebone, London, January 1968. Originally published in British Psychoanalytical Society, *What is Psychoanalysis?* London: Baillière, Tindall & Cassell, 1968. Reprinted in D.W. Winnicott, *Winnicott on the Child.* New York: Perseus, 2002.

Chapter 8

Looking at the film *American Beauty* through a psychoanalytic lens

Parents revisit adolescence

Anita Weinreb Katz

In this study of Sam Mendes's Oscar-winning film *American Beauty* (1999), I will follow the theme of the developmental journey: the ongoing effort to lay claim to one's life. This laying claim to a life of one's own is one of the primary tasks of adolescence, but not only of adolescence. Separation and adulthood are not achieved in one fell swoop. The search for an authentic, satisfying life of one's own can be a lengthy, if not lifelong, endeavor (Levinson, 1978; Anthony, 1993).

To do the work of adolescence, a child must create within him- or herself psychic space for both childhood and adulthood, for experimenting with new identities, new beginnings, and new endings (Blos, 1985). The child's parents must do the same, since each new beginning for the child is potentially an end for the parents, and each new ending potentially a beginning. Between the issues left over from the incomplete work of the parents' own youth, and the adjustments demanded by the awkward, repeated efforts of their child to separate, the parents of adolescent children are under a lot of stress with regard to their own identities (sexual and otherwise) and with beginnings and endings in their own lives (Benedek, 1970).

I believe strongly that parents do not just react when a child's adolescence engulfs a family. They *do* react, of course, but they *act*, too – that is, they also re-engage their own adolescent passions and conflicts. The turmoil of having an adolescent, therefore, is heightened for the parents by individual regressions of their own. Regressions of this kind are responsible in no small part, I think, for what has come to be known as the "mid-life crisis." They may result in uncharacteristic behavior in both parents, which in turn disturbs to a greater or lesser degree their relationship with each other, and with their children. I want to show how this phenomenon is illustrated and elaborated in *American Beauty*.

I first focus on the embattled Burnhams: Lester, Carolyn, and their teenage daughter, Jane. Once upon a time, we are led to believe, the Burnhams got along better than they do at present. "We used to be happy," Lester says. But something has surely gone wrong, because they are not happy now. Jane is separating from her parents by the usual adolescent means of criticism and withdrawal. In the past, her openness to them had filled some of their pressing emotional needs. Her growing separation, as well as her physical maturation, has shifted both intrapsychic and inter-personal balances in the two parents, and something has broken down (Loewald, 1980). *American Beauty* is the story of this breakdown and what comes of it. I will use this story to illustrate my hypothesis about adolescent re-engagements and the work of separation and growth that is always waiting for us, if we can open ourselves to it (Katz, 2002).

Let me try to show you what I am talking about by delving beneath the manifest content of this film. I think you will see why I believe that Lester and Carolyn were indeed revisiting their own adolescent issues, not just reacting to their daughter's. Lester laments the fact that Jane no longer talks to him. They used to be pals. He wonders, "What happened to us?" My answer to his question is that his daughter's adolescence stirred up in her parents a parallel revisitation of their own adolescent passions, conflicts, and separations. The father's unresolved adolescent issues are reawakened now in the context of his daughter and his wife. Carolyn is also revisiting intense adolescent longings and losses, and feels rejected by the unchar-acteristic withdrawal of her husband and child. The parents' separate pre-occupations with their unfulfilled needs, and the intensity of their wishes to fulfill them, have left Lester and Carolyn withdrawn into private worlds, intolerant of the incursions of others, and unwilling to relinquish their fantasies long enough to be emotionally available to, and supportive of each other as real, demanding persons (Benedek, 1970).

Jane is a "typical" 16 year old. It appears that her parents' desires for love and recognition are directed toward her. Although she once was happy to fulfill them, now she can barely tolerate either her mother or her father. She has distanced herself from them, and is confused by feelings that cover the gamut from murderous rage to fear, desire, and love.

In true adolescent style, although she pushes both parents away, she still needs and wants them. Neither parent can deal with her rejection and still be sensitively available to her; nor can either support the other to that end. On the contrary, they are disappointed in and defensively detached from each other, while they compete for Jane's now scarce love and support (Colarusso, 1990).

Jane has a best friend, Angela. To cover up her fear that she is "ordinary," Angela talks big about using sex to get what she wants. Jane's father, Lester, is obviously enchanted with her. Angela loves and encourages this enchant-ment. She flaunts it aggressively with Jane, who finds it disgusting, but is also jealous. Jane herself bonds with Ricky, the odd, intense, 18-year-old boy next door. Angela calls him a freak, but Jane knows her own mind. She and Ricky make an attachment that facilitates their work of separation. While Jane's adolescent struggle is interesting, I want to focus on what it evokes in her parents, and on the difficult, parallel journeys it catalyzes in them.

In the beginning of the film, Carolyn is very tightly laced and lonely. Her passions in this now bitter, arid marriage are displaced onto raising perfect American Beauty roses and acquiring power as a realtor. Lester supported her real-estate work, and still submits to her obsessional need to create a "romantic" atmosphere in the house, even though he finds this "romance" sterile and loveless. He feels shut out and unappreciated. Rejected sexually and emotionally by his wife, and deprived of the old pleasures of physical closeness with his newly taboo daughter, he feels dead. He comments bitterly that the high point of his day is masturbating in the shower.

The alienated Lester encounters Ricky at a stuffy party where Ricky is working as a waiter. They bond around their mutual defiance of authority, smoking marijuana and laughing. When Carolyn fetches him to go home, Lester says, "Okay, Mom."

His adolescent recapitulation hits full stride when he quits the job he hates (engineering a good monetary deal for himself by threatening to expose the fraudulent hypocrisy of his employer/father). He begins to feel powerful and happy. He is galvanized by his crush on seductive Angela. He gets a job as a hash-slinger at a fast food place, drives around singing with joy and aggression, "American woman, stay away from me! American woman, let me be!" and buys a red Firebird, all of which evoke for him the 1970s, when the teenage Lester still felt the world was open to him. It is hard not to believe that he has regressed to his own adolescent issues, and is reworking his sense of self and identity (Loewald, 1979).

Lester wants to feel loved and recognized. He comes alive in his fantasies of a perfect woman. Significantly, he always imagines Angela embedded in crimson rose petals, suggestive of the American Beauty roses to which Carolyn is so passionately attached. Despite the overtly arid and angry relationship with his wife, Lester seems still to desire her.

Thus we see Lester reopening his developmental growth, endeavoring to become a strong, independent man (Anthony, 1970). When his wife catches him masturbating in bed, for instance, and attempts to humiliate him, instead of cowering as he used to, he expresses his rage at her refusal to have sex when he then suggests it. He decides to get in shape, lifting weights and jogging.

Carolyn also is revisiting her adolescent issues. As her own sexual and aggressive tensions intensify, she at first reinforces her obsessive-compulsive defenses – creating the "house beautiful" and growing perfect roses. She despises weakness and failure, in herself as much as in others. When she cries out of sadness or disappointment, she cruelly slaps her own face to shut herself up, and tries to program herself to be upbeat. She relies upon superficial "show" to defend against the "messiness" of her strong feelings. She is the more fragile of the two parents. In the beginning, at least, she lacks compassion for either herself or her husband. So controlling and judgmental is she that at first the viewer, too, is hard put to feel for her. On repeated viewings of this film, we understand more of the pain covered up by her brittle, rigid exterior.

Still, she is not easy to live with. She cannot relinquish control sufficiently to listen to others. Lester, frustrated and infuriated by this, finally gets her attention by throwing a plate of food against the wall of their exquisite dining room. Carolyn knocks on Jane's door looking for comfort, but Jane rejects this bid for alliance and dismisses both of her parents as freaks, which leaves Carolyn feeling alone and furious. Although Jane's developing autonomy is experienced by her parents as abandonment, it also highlights the incompleteness of their own adolescent quests for autonomy and fulfillment (Benedek, 1970). Carolyn is not yet able to recognize that her own need to separate is as important as Jane's, so Jane's response – "I'm not in the mood for a Kodak moment" – enrages Carolyn. She slaps her daughter's face, as she had earlier slapped her own.

Despite herself and despite her fears, Carolyn's sap is also rising. She begins an affair with an arch-rival in the real estate business, whose apparent power she covets. His name is Buddy Kane, but he calls himself "the King." She rebels against Lester and her daughter, and returns to her own adolescent journey, submitting to a powerful father figure whose strength she hopes to borrow. Her relationship with Buddy reconnects her with both her feminine and masculine strivings. She surrenders to them and to an authentic desire for sexual pleasure and independence. Buddy offers to teach her the secrets of his success. He also initiates her into the thrill of pistol practice, and she gets high on the phallic power that this affords. Like her husband, she too begins to drive around singing defiantly. Her theme song is, "Nobody had better rain on my parade" (Katz, 2002). Carolyn is now able to find joy in passions she was afraid of before. Her juices, like Lester's, are starting to flow again. She, too, is finding her own inner strength.

Amidst all of this wild activity, Lester and Carolyn are growing – fighting with each other openly now, but approaching each other, too. When she discovers Lester's new car, Carolyn confronts him angrily about not having consulted with her. He stands his ground, compliments her on her new haircut (acquired for Buddy's benefit), approaches her on the couch, and begins to kiss her. Intrigued by his new assertiveness and by his loving gaze, she opens up and enjoys his love and attention. Defensively, she pulls away from him when she notices a beer in his hand, taken over by fear that it might spill on her $4000 couch. In upbraiding him, the moment is destroyed. Carolyn still confuses surrender with enforced submission (Ghent, 1990; Katz, 1990), and so fears her desires for love and sex with Lester. She returns once again to her obsessional defenses, and he gets angry at her for caring more about the couch than about him. They still do not feel safe with each other (they are too afraid of being taken over) but they are taking more risks.

When Lester discovers Buddy and Carolyn kissing, Buddy, fearful of reprisals, splits the scene forever. Lester tells his wife that he won't be passive and submit to her any more, essentially relinquishing his old sado-masochistic posture (Katz, 1990). The double blow leaves Carolyn feeling weak, helpless, and frightened. Gun practice gives her a quick high, but she still feels small and tries to shore herself up, saying to herself over and over, "I will not be a victim," and entertaining murderous fantasies against Lester. Her new capacities for power and passion fuel her own developmental journey.

While all this is going on, Jane's bond with Ricky next door is deepening. At first she was scared and annoyed by his surreptitious videotaping of her, but after the blow-up with her mother, she poses for him in her window, experimentally baring her breasts. She becomes intrigued with him, reciprocating his voyeurism with assertive, exciting exhibitionism. They surrender to each other and fall in love.

Ricky himself comes from a family that is even more troubled than Jane's. Whereas Jane's family is struggling with the normal stresses that adolescence creates, Ricky's has reacted to his adolescent journey by breaking down altogether. We see his mother as a shadowy figure, depressed, and nearly catatonic. His father is a brittle, homophobic, retired marine colonel, a caricature of machismo. He is abusive, violent, abandoning, and invasive, infantilizing his son in a desperate attempt to turn back the clock to the greater comfort he experienced with Ricky as a young child. Neither of Ricky's parents is capable of revisiting adolescence with its demands that they surrender (at least temporarily) to the fantasies within them. Their rigidity and fragility leave them helpless in the face of their son's adolescence which they experience as unrelievedly traumatic (Katz, 2002).

Ricky himself, however, has a distance on his situation that Jane does not yet have on hers. Ricky and his father once shared a special bond, but this was disrupted when Colonel Frank Fitz caught his son, in the first flush of adolescent rebellion, smoking marijuana at 15. He cast him out of the house and sent him to military school. Ricky, not a compliant adolescent, got himself expelled from that school. His father beat him, leaving the enraged Ricky to struggle with his own violent impulses. After the beating, Ricky tells Jane, a kid in school picked on him for his haircut, and Ricky snapped. He wanted to kill the kid, and would have, he believes, if they hadn't pulled him off. That's when his dad put him in the mental hospital where they drugged him and kept him for two years. When Jane says, "You must hate him," Ricky, sensing his father's inability to love him in any way other than this perverse, sadomasochistic one, defends him, saying with compassion, "He's not a bad man."

Now out of the hospital, Ricky's obsessional videotaping of the world of objects and people helps him preserve his perspective, and his sanity. He also protects his budding autonomy by living a double life, keeping his controlling, intrusive father in the dark about the things that matter to him. For a while he still appears to be daddy's adored, adoring little boy, but he has continued to smoke marijuana secretly, has developed a very successful business selling it, and has been foiling his father's periodic requests for "wiss" samples by substituting drug-free urine acquired from a client.

Ricky begins to come out in the open when he admits to his father that he has a girlfriend. This dismays Colonel Fitz, who deeply needs his son's love and cannot bear his son's separating from him. His own repressed desires distort his understanding of Ricky, and lead him to dangerous misinterpretations. He catches a glimpse of a transaction between Ricky and Lester; in fact it's a marijuana deal, but Colonel Fitz concludes they have a sexual connection. He projects his own repudiated fantasies onto Lester and Ricky. When Ricky comes home, he beats him brutally, saying, "I'd rather you were dead than be a faggot." Ricky's work of separation, however eccentric, is well under way, and he maintains his sense of himself even under this attack. He refuses to hit his father back even when his father, seeking any kind of reconnection with his son, begs him to. He refuses to submit to his father's view of life and is able to realize, not without compassion, what "a sad little man" the Colonel is.

After the fight, Ricky asks Jane to leave home with him. She agrees, and tells Angela about her intention. Angela once again attacks Jane and Ricky as freaks, but Ricky defends Jane and challenges Angela's pretensions, exposing the fears and jealousies that she tries so hard to conceal.

We see a poignant scene between Lester and the now bereft Angela, in which Lester declares his yearning for her. "You're the most beautiful thing I've ever seen," he says, and begins to undress her. She encourages him in an attempt to reassure herself of her own desirability, but he comes to his adult senses when he realizes that she is a frightened girl underneath her sexual bravado. In a beautiful, transforming moment, he refuses to let Angela submit to him. He covers her with a blanket, reassures her that she is beautiful, that everything is okay, and that any man would consider himself very, very lucky to be with her. He then takes her into the kitchen and feeds her, a metaphor for his new and comfortable capacity to be a confident and authentic adult, with the psychological space and perspective to help the next generation through their own adolescent turmoils – an attitude that Erikson (1950) has called *generativity*. Thus Lester helps Angela return to her own precociously rejected adolescence, at peace with herself, and no longer hiding behind her pretensions (Anthony, 1970).

Lester has returned to the parental stance, having, I believe, gone through a tremendous adolescent regression and reworking. Angela also has visibly returned to a less defended, more authentic self. Lester asks her about his own daughter, admitting how hard it is for them to talk to each other these days. Angela tells him that Jane is in love. He says with appreciative pleasure, "Good for her" (Erikson, 1950). His recent re-engagement with his own issues of love, power, and autonomy has made it possible for him to empathize in a new way with his daughter. Wistfully he recalls how happy he was with his wife when Jane was younger. He looks at a photo of Carolyn, Jane, and himself, and smiling says, "I feel great!" (Colarusso, 1990).

When we see Lester begin his journey as the father of Jane's adolescence, his control over his sexual and aggressive impulses is shaky, I presume because his defenses have become destabilized in the face of his own reawakened adolescent passions (Loewald, 1979). In connecting with his fantasies of power and sex, of overthrowing and outsmarting the authorities, and in breaking out of the bondage he experienced at work and in his marriage, I believe he became able to negotiate his own conflicted desires in a healthier manner. He could then give up fantasies of perfect, idealized self and other, feel good about himself, however flawed, and be genuinely happy when his daughter finds love with the boy next door. His new compassion and strength also allow a renewed appreciation and love for his wife.

Meanwhile, Lester's new vitality has attracted not only Angela, but also Ricky's father, whose brittle homophobic controls have collapsed during the adolescent revisitation brought on by his own child's physical and psychological maturation. Reawakened passions can have a dark side and, in *American Beauty*, that side is played out in Colonel Fitz. This harsh, repressed man, whose mantra is "structure and discipline," uses rigid controls to defend against unmetabolized homosexual yearnings. He is in turmoil over his son's adolescence, and the passions and conflicts it has revived within him. Ricky was once a small child whom he could control and love without danger. His love for the now sexually mature Ricky terrifies him, and his rigid defenses against it have become destabilized (Benedek, 1970). He alternates between treating Ricky as the child he no longer is, and occasional violent beatings. These last-ditch defenses break down. Colonel Fitz hates what he cannot bear to acknowledge in himself. Stirred by Ricky's physical maturation and his own adolescent urges rising up (Katz, 2002), he displaces the homosexual desire that overtakes him onto Ricky's supposed partner, Lester, who then becomes the object of his desire.

Right before Lester's encounter with Angela, Colonel Fitz approaches Lester in the garage where he is working out. Colonel Fitz can barely talk. He is shaking, soaking wet from a drenching downpour like the torrent of feelings that is inundating him. Misinterpreting Lester's concern for him, he kisses Lester in a sudden breakdown of his fragmenting defenses. Lester gently tells him that he has the wrong idea. His new security and psychic strength as a person and as a man are marked by the calm, gentle way he responds to this frantic advance. But Lester's compassion and lack of anger cannot spare the vulnerable Colonel Fitz a humiliation so deep that he eventually must silence the witness to it. In an attempt to reinstate his manhood, he stalks Lester – who himself is in a contented reverie of newfound peace – shoots him, and kills him.

This somber denouement makes clear that there are no more guarantees in a second adolescence than in a first one; parental revisitations of early struggles with desire and separation do not necessarily eventuate in growth; severe repression is potentially far more dangerous than a rich fantasy life, however wild and chaotic it may occasionally be. In this movie, it is not the people with the rageful and sexual fantasies, but only the person *without* inner truth – the person who cannot bear to know what's inside of him – who solves his problems by killing the object of his desire.

For Carolyn and Lester, revisitation of their adolescent journeys brings not only pain and disappointment, but also joy. For the Fitz parents, there is only pain and decompensation.

I keep wondering why the director foretells Lester's death as the film opens; death is present from the very beginning. Although we see lives being transformed throughout, we know that one life will be over by the time the movie ends. Why does Lester have to die just after struggling so to achieve a new inner and outer balance, and having achieved a new, vital sense of self and other? Why is this flowering so tragically and violently cut off just as it is beginning to be enjoyed? It seems so senseless. Perhaps this is the director's point: we all die. How we come to death is beyond our control. Development is risky. All we can do is make the journey in the most meaningful way we can. This journey may be a search for inner truth, but to find truth doesn't guarantee life, only the capacity to live fully and authentically. There are no guarantees how others will receive what we give or do not give. Perhaps this says something powerful and humbling to us as analysts as well.

In one passionate scene of their bonding, Ricky shows Jane a video in which a discarded bag (a piece of trash) dances in a buffeting wind. This is a dance of life to Ricky, breathtakingly beautiful and moving. Something ugly is lovingly accepted, and in the acceptance is transformed. The bag, too, displays the beauty of acceptance in its surrender to the wind. This movie is about surrendering to the wind, a metaphor for the life force and the life course.

Laying claim to a life of one's own in the ongoing journey of life involves surrender (not enforced or unthinking submission) but willing surrender to knowledge – knowledge of the fantasies, feelings and conflicts within the self, and knowledge of what is out there. Rilke (1986) poetically captures this concept: "He who pours himself out like a stream is acknowledged at last by Knowledge: and she leads him enchanted through the harmonious country that finishes often with starting, and with ending begins."

So the forces of growth and the forces of death interact in *American Beauty* in complex ways, as they do in life, and perhaps particularly in adolescence. While Lester is enduring the final, decisive confrontations of his own life, Carolyn is becoming a woman who can enjoy her own phallic power and aggression, test out in fantasy its violent potential, and still rediscover her love for the husband at whom she feels such rage. Tragically, her achievement comes too late for a happy ending with Lester, now dead at the hands of a man who could neither entertain nor contain his own fantasies.

The difference between fantasy and action is poignantly portrayed at the end of this movie. Carolyn comes home with the fantasy of killing her husband, repeating with rage, "I will not be a victim." Then she throws her gun in the hamper, hugs his clothes hanging in the closet, and crumples to the floor weeping – very different from her crying before – allowing herself to mourn the idea of his death, as previously she could not. It is not clear whether she has already seen that he is dead. Her fantasy of gaining power by killing him has been shaken. She has become sufficiently strong in herself to face the reality of what she would lose if he were actually to die. She recognizes that the person she wanted dead was also the person she loved. This integration of the loved and hated husband, the result of her struggles, marks a transformation in her that will endure, in spite of the tragic reality of Lester's death (cf. Klein, 1975).

Conclusion

Parenthood affords adults many opportunities to regress to, and potentially rework, past and present intrapsychic issues in parallel with their children. So does analysis, as patients regress and re-experience buried feelings and stir them up in their analysts, as well. What's so hard, as well as rewarding about what we do is that these feelings, and the longings and conflicts that go with them, provide opportunities to revisit our own deeper issues, and thereby become more open to our patients, more able to hear and interpret so that both they and we grow in the process. If we cannot tolerate our own revisitings, we may fail our patients by foreclosing, or acting out, their deepest desires and fears.

References

Anthony, E.J. (1970) The reactions of parents to adolescents and to their behavior. In E.J. Anthony and T. Benedek (eds) *Parenthood: Its Psychology and Psychopathology*, pp. 309–324. Boston, MA: Little, Brown.

—— (1993) Psychoanalysis and environment. In G.H. Pollock and S.I. Greenspan (eds) *The Course of Life*, Volume 6: *Late Adulthood*, pp. 261–310. Madison, CT: International Universities Press.

Benedek, T. (1970) Parenthood during the life cycle. In E.J. Anthony and T. Benedek (eds) *Parenthood: Its Psychology and Psychopathology*, pp. 185–206. Boston, MA: Little, Brown.

Blos, P. (1985) Toward an altered view of the male Oedipus Complex: the role of adolescence. In P. Blos, *Son and Father: Before and Beyond the Oedipus Complex*, pp. 135–173. New York: The Free Press.

Colarusso, C. (1990) The effect of biological parenthood on separation-individuation processes in adulthood. *Psychoanalytic Study of the Child*, 45: 179–194.

Erikson, E.H. (1950) *Childhood and Society*. New York: W.W. Norton.

Ghent, E. (1990) Masochism, submission and surrender: masochism as a perversion of surrender. *Contemporary Psychoanalysis*, 26: 108–136.

Katz, A. (1990) Paradoxes of masochism. *Psychoanalytic Psychology*, 7: 225–242.

—— (2002) Fathers facing their daughters' emerging sexuality: the return of the Oedipal. *Psychoanalytic Study of the Child*, 57: 270–293.

Klein, M. (1975) *Love, Guilt and Reparation & Other Works, 1921–1945*. London: Hogarth Press.

Levinson, D.J. (1978) *The Seasons of a Man's Life*, pp. 221–256. New York: Ballantine.

Loewald, H.W. (1979) The waning of the Oedipus Complex. *Journal of the American Psychoanalytic Association*, 27: 751–776.

—— (1980) Comments on some instinctual manifestations of superego formation. *Papers on Psychoanalysis*, pp. 326–341. New Haven, CT: Yale University Press.

Rilke, R.M. (1986) The Sonnets to Orpheus. New York: Touchstone. Quoted in Zornberg, A.G. (1995) *Genesis: The Beginning of Desire*. Philadelphia, PA: Jewish Publication Society.

Chapter 9

Reclaiming the relationship with the lost parent following parental death during adolescence

Glenys Lobban

Since 1987 I have worked with a large number of adults who lost a parent when they were children or adolescents, but suspended the mourning process. This was resumed only after they had entered treatment as adults. The suspension often occurred because the surviving parent could not facilitate or tolerate the child's experience of grief, and no alternate route to mourning, such as therapy, was available. These patients typically entered treatment because their careers and love relationships were stalled and unsatisfying, and they were not consciously aware of any unresolved issues related to the parent's death.

In the course of my work with these patients I was privileged to share in their mourning process and see it unfold, which taught me a great deal about the nature of mourning. My work with these patients raised many questions for me regarding analytic assumptions about the mourning process and the definition of successful mourning and I will address these in my chapter.

My approach to understanding mourning is to define the loss as a loss of a relationship. The relationship with the lost person is a rich, multifaceted, "relational matrix" that spans Mitchell's three dimensions of self, object and the intersubjective, all "subtly interwoven" (Mitchell, 1988, p. 33). My patients' relationships with their parents encompassed their perceptions of the parent and their attachment; the way the parent viewed them and how this influenced how they saw and valued themselves; and a rich tapestry of co-constructed, intersubjective experiences that signified the unique way of being, feeling and connecting particular to them and their parent. Bromberg (2001) would define this as the "self state" connected to the parent. I believe that each mourner needs to create her own version of what was most salient to her in her own particular, multifaceted relationship and that this is part of the work of mourning.

Most of the psychoanalytic literature on mourning has focused solely on the impact of loss of the object (see Frankiel, 1994) and not on all the dimensions of the relational matrix. Very few authors have discussed the ways in which the death of a loved one can impact on the self. Some exceptions are Jacobson (1965), Joffe and Sandler (1965), Tyson (1983), and Lerner (1990). The reverberations that a death can induce in the intersubjective experience, co-constructed by the person and her loved one, have been largely ignored. An exception is Mitchell's (1999) description of an adult woman whose mother was killed in a car accident when she was 5 years old. Mitchell explored the impact of maternal loss on all facets of his patient's relational world.

In my view, "successful mourning" involves a creative process where the mourner fashions her own image of her relationship with the lost person that she can carry with her into her future. The attachment to the lost loved one continues after the person dies. We survive loss by extracting and holding onto the features of our relationship that are essential to us. Paradoxically, when the mourner holds on to an aspect of the relationship in this way, it also enables her to move on with her life. She is able to move forward because she has transported some aspect of the relationship and connection with the lost beloved into her present and future. She is able to accept the finality of the beloved's death because she has found a way to transcend that finality.

In the traditional psychoanalytic literature on mourning, the assumptions regarding what constitutes "normal" or "successful" mourning are very different from those which informed my work. In this literature, the "normal" outcome of mourning is defined as "detachment of all feelings and attachments from the lost object" (Baker, 2001, p. 56). Any other resolution is defined as pathological (Baker, 2001). Freud was the first theorist to espouse this detachment position on the mourning process. Baker reviewed the psychoanalytic literature on mourning and found that the views of most analysts in the western hemisphere were still "consistent with Freud's original theorizing" (Baker, 2001, p. 56). The detachment construct contradicted the belief held by many of the world's cultures that death recreates, but does not sever, important bonds which "remain inextricably part of the self" (Shapiro, 1996, p. 550). Ironically, Freud's personal accounts of his own experiences with mourning indicated that he had difficulty achieving detachment (Silverman and Klass, 1996).

In "Mourning and Melancholia," Freud (1917) developed his position. He stated that mourning was not "normal" unless the internal tie to the beloved was excised and totally converted into an ego identification. He stated that mourning was normal only when the mourner is able to totally "sever the attachment to the nonexistent object" (p. 255). For many years, Freud's assumption that successful mourning required total detachment from the beloved, and renunciation of the tie to this person was accepted as fact by the majority of psychologists who dealt with mourning. It was believed that a person would not be able to develop a new attachment unless the old bond was severed (Silverman and Klass, 1996). Analysts accepted Freud's goal as truth and were unaware that this shaped how they listened and intervened when their patients grappled with loss and mourning. If an analyst views her task as that of exorcising her patient's connection to the real lost parent, she will focus on different issues from an analyst who sees her task as that of helping the patient to tolerate the poignancy of longing for and missing the lost parent. The assumptions that an analyst makes about what constitutes "normal" or "successful" mourning will influence the type of resolution chosen by the analyst's patient.

New approaches to the definition of the goals of mourning have recently been suggested by Silverman and Klass (1996), Gaines (1997), Ogden (2000a, 2000b) and Baker (2001). These authors point out that the connection to the lost person continues. They question the value of the detachment position. Baker (2001) suggests that we broaden our definition of successful mourning to include more than just identification with the lost person. He views mourning as a transformative process which is "normal" or "successful" (p. 56) when it includes the "creation of an internal relationship that allows the bereaved to maintain some tie with the inner representation of the love object but that also leaves room for investment in new relationships and new activities" (Baker, 2001, p. 68).

Ogden (2000a, 2000b, 2001) has discussed the creative act contained in mourning. He suggests that a central aspect of the mourning process is the creation of something "adequate to the experience of loss" (2000a, p. 66). This creation, which can take any form, represents "the individual's effort to meet, to be equal to, to do justice to, the fullness and complexity of his or her relationship to what has been lost and to the experience of loss itself" (p. 66). Ogden (2001) suggests that the analyst's task is to describe the uniqueness of the particular patient's "experience of grieving" and not to prescribe an outcome (p. 294). Bernstein (2000) also sees mourning as a creative act, one where the past and the present can coexist in a new form. She argues that Shimon Attie's photographic series entitled "The Writing on the Wall" constructs a "memorial space . . . a world in which the past filters through the present, casting its own shadows upon a world that never existed in this way before" (Bernstein, 2000, p. 355).

Silverman and Klass (1996) suggest a new way to define the purpose of the bereavement process based on the assumption that resolution of grief involves a "continuing bond that the survivor maintains with the deceased" (p. 3). They argue that grieving culminates in a Piagetian style accommodation where "people seek to gain not only an understanding of the meaning of death, but a sense of the meaning of this now dead or absent person in their present lives" (p. 19). Evidence of these continuing bonds has been shown in many situations where adults suffer loss including spousal loss (Conant, 1996; Moss and Moss, 1996) and loss of a child (Klass, 1996).

The process of mourning in children and adolescents has been widely researched (see Frankiel, 1994; Sussillo, 2005). The Massachusetts General Hospital and Harvard Medical School Child Bereavement Study is a longitudinal prospective study of how parental death impacts on children aged 6 to 17. Silverman and Nickman (1996) have analyzed data gathered during this study to try to understand the process of mourning in children and adolescents. They found evidence of a continuing bond to the lost parent that was similar to that found in the adult studies already cited. They argue that the child's relationship with the deceased changes over time. The child accepts the finality of the parent's death but continues to maintain "an active, two way relationship with his or her dead parent" where "the dead and the living are able to communicate and pursue their relationship" (Normand *et al.*, 1996, p. 109).

I will describe my clinical work with two patients whom I will call Ruth and Michael. They each experienced the sudden, unexpected death of their father during adolescence. Both fathers died as the result of a heart attack when they were less than 50 years old. My patients felt that their mothers would be unable to tolerate their terror, grief and anger about the father's death. The mother was their only remaining source of emotional support. They had to preserve the relationship with her at all costs, so they dissociated these feelings and the whole self state associated with them. During treatment, the mourning process, which been frozen, held in suspended animation since adolescence, was reactivated or reanimated. The work of Bromberg (1993, 1994, 2001) on dissociation helped me to understand why my patients had originally suspended their mourning process and why it had been reactivated in their adult treatment.

My patients brought their pain into treatment, along with a conviction that I would be like the mother, and would not register their pain or be able to endure it. This pain was dissociated. They were not conscious of it and could not frame it in language. As treatment progressed, I began to experience the particular pain that each of these adults had tried to render invisible. Once I became aware of what I was feeling, I tried to experience their pain and put my experience of it into words. This enabled my patients to register and experience their grief. Eventually they were able to describe it in words. Once they had experienced the pain, anger and terror induced by the father's death, they were able to recapture many memories about their relationship with him. They distilled some essential features of their relationship with their father and these invigorated and vitalized them. They were each able to experience the self state connected to the dead father and render it cognitively. It could then coexist with other self states. They were able to accept the finality of the father's death because they found a way to transcend that finality. Both found a way to construct a version of their relationship with the father that they could carry with them for the rest of their lives. They each made a work of art that signified what they had created. Ruth painted a portrait of her father to bring to her wedding. Michael created a volume of poems about connection between fathers and sons.

Ruth

Ruth was a 28-year-old painter who entered twice-weekly therapy because she felt unable to move forward in her career and had never had a serious relationship with a man. She was the middle child in a family from the American Midwest. When she was 14, her father, an academic, died suddenly of a heart attack at home in the middle of the night. Ruth experienced her mother as unavailable after her father died. She had to get a job to support herself and her children and was constantly tense and busy. Ruth felt her mother did not want herself or the children to be sad and that it was Ruth's job to "just be cheerful."

In therapy Ruth was taut and affectively muted. The sessions felt very bleak and flat. I frequently had a headache when they ended. I think my bleakness and headaches were my first taste of Ruth's pain. Initially Ruth did not discuss her father's death. Instead, Ruth's relationship with her mother was the major focus of the transference. Prior to her father's death, Ruth had not felt in tune with her mother, who was warm and maternal, but practical and prosaic, unable to understand Ruth's sensitivity or her deep connection to fantasy. She hoped her mother would change after her father died and would be able to hear and tolerate her pain. Instead her mother coped with her own grief by becoming businesslike and obsessive, so she was even less emotionally available.

When she entered treatment, Ruth hoped to be understood, but expected that I would also not be able to tolerate her pain. Initially she treated therapy like school, seeking assignments and goals, filling the sessions up with minutiae. She was very surprised every time I pointed out her need to keep things task oriented, as she assumed each time that she was responding to my need for order. After about a year and many tests, Ruth seemed to finally decide that she could ask me to tolerate pain. She described what she termed sudden "weird" moments which occurred when she was walking alone at night. Suddenly she would have to stop walking because a great big hole or chasm would open up in front of her in the sidewalk. These experiences had begun the year after her father died. She had never told anybody about these holes. She hastily assured me that she knew they weren't really there. She would wait till she calmed down and the hole closed, then continue walking. When I asked her what she felt when the chasm opened, Ruth said she felt terror and pain and wanted to run "so bad" but couldn't because then the "hole might spread." When she revealed the existence of the holes I felt extremely frightened. I did not connect my feelings to anything in her history or my own history. I was afraid her anxiety would destabilize her and doubted my ability to help her cope with it. I felt surprised, caught off guard, as I had not anticipated that her flat, muted exterior concealed such intense pain and terror. I did not share my reaction with Ruth at that time because it was too intense for me to process sufficiently. Instead, I stayed closer to Ruth's conscious experience and talked with her about the holes. She was enormously relieved that I could talk with her about them and this enabled both of us gradually to go deeper within the experience of the holes and to face the fear they engendered.

I began to understand that the terror and pain of the chasms must be linked to Ruth's feelings about her father's death and suggested this to her. For a long time she did not believe that I really wanted to know about her reactions to her father's death and she could not access them. Finally she was able to talk about some of her feelings. She had felt constant guilt since her father's death. She blamed herself for his death. She had not done her evening chores the night he died. He got angry with her, then did the chores himself. She felt the argument had been the last straw for his heart. Eventually Ruth was able to stop blaming herself for her father's death. She realized she got a sense of control from blaming herself, and that this, while painful, was preferable to feeling fate was so arbitrary. She recalled more of the circumstances of the night her father died. He was rushed to the hospital. Her mother went with him, leaving the children alone for hours, waiting by the phone for news. Eventually her mother called and told her he had died. Ruth felt totally alone and bereft.

As Ruth talked about her father's death, I continued to feel intense fear. I kept recalling the image of her at 14, alone by the phone after she heard that her father had died. I began to comprehend that the fear I felt was a fear of death, of mortality. I did not share my fear with Ruth, but I shared my hypothesis about the origin of my fear. I suggested that as she sat there alone, she must have registered for the first time that death can hit at any moment and she must have felt great pain and terror, similar to the feeling engendered by the holes that appeared in the road. Ruth was gradually able to access her terror. She suggested that her fear of a chasm opening up in the road and engulfing her was her fear of "death just grabbing me or someone I love with no warning." We speculated that Ruth must have felt that terror and horror on the night her father died. She felt she could not voice this terrifying insight to her mother. She also could not hold on to her connection to her father without voicing her pain at his death and her terror about mortality, so she had dissociated a whole self state connected to her father.

Ruth was gradually able to admit to her anger at her father for dying and leaving them and she was able to verbalize her longing for him, but she still did not have a rich, vital fund of memories about the bond between her father and herself. After three years in treatment, Ruth met a man who was capable of a mutual, loving connection. They lived together for a year and finally got engaged. Her fiancé was anxious to set a wedding date and meet her mother and siblings, so they took their first trip to her hometown in the Midwest. Ruth told me in the last session before the trip that she and her fiancé planned to visit her father's grave, her first visit in about ten years. On her return, Ruth called me in a panic and requested an emergency appointment. She was usually calm and contained, but arrived completely hysterical. I felt as if someone else inhabited her skin. Even the tone and timbre of her voice had altered. She had decided she couldn't set a wedding date and should call off the wedding. She burst into tears and said,

> I can't plan for the future, settle down, look ahead, because I don't know when Dad will come back or what he will want to do then and I have to be ready for whatever it is. I feel so disloyal about Alan (her fiancé) filling my father's place. I'm supposed to keep that place warm for him. If I don't keep it open he won't be able to come back. It's a betrayal if I let someone else into that space. I have to stay by the grave waiting. I have to stay just the way I was at 14. The problem is I lose my Dad if I take this relationship with Alan, though I think my Dad would really like Alan and wanted a relationship like this for me.

In this session, Ruth's dissociated self state (Bromberg, 2001) that related to her loss of her father, was present and palpable to us. It became possible to seek "linkage" of "multiple realities being held by different self states" (Bromberg, 1994, p. 544). As Ruth described her beliefs about her father's return, there was a dialogue of different perspectives.

> I know it sounds so weird to say I believe he's coming back. I think I felt how could he be dead, it happened too quickly and the hand I felt in the coffin wasn't him, it was cold and hard. The adult me is more skeptical about his return but I'm afraid the other me, the little girl waiting for her Dad, will break through.

She elaborated on this idea of the little Ruth as our work progressed, accessing many memories of herself in relation to her father. The little girl who was evoked in her father's presence was daring, creative and spontaneous. Her father loved her artwork. It was he who identified her talent, found a teacher in a distant city and drove her a hundred miles to art class every Saturday. She loved those drives and their separate Saturday world.

They would go to a museum or movie and talk about all kinds of things including her art. He was warm and relaxed. She had great fun and felt they shared a special connection. She felt he knew the artistic, creative facet of her self and that her mother, a more prosaic soul, could never tune into that part of her. "I cannot access the real creative painter within me as my father was the only one who enabled me to show that piece of me."

Once Ruth had recognized the existence of the little Ruth waiting for her Dad, something shifted within her. She went through a period of profound sadness as she accepted that he would never actually return. She began to experiment with the idea that she might be able to access the creative facet of herself even though her father was not there to evoke it. She tried talking about her art to me and to her fiancé. Eventually Ruth and her fiancé set a wedding date. The week before the wedding, she told me she planned to bring her father to the wedding. "I've stopped waiting for him. Instead I've pulled him into the present. I've painted his portrait and it's coming to the wedding." Since this time, Ruth has produced an impressive body of work dedicated to her father. She is also the mother of two children. The portrait she painted of her father hangs in her living room.

Michael

Michael began treatment at the age of 35 because he was feeling depressed following the death of his maternal aunt. Initially he came twice a week. After two years, he began analysis four times a week and this continued for about five years. Michael was the youngest of three boys. He grew up in a pro-fessional family in an affluent Californian suburb. He was a talented, enthusi-astic child who pursued many creative interests, but felt that neither of his parents could empathize with his creativity. He felt unwanted, an afterthought, an outsider in his family, and longed to feel part of a united family. Michael's mother became a librarian although she had hoped to be a dancer. She was a frenetic, vivacious woman who needed Michael as her audience and took credit for his creativity. His father, an accountant, disliked his job and was frequently irritable and unavailable to Michael. The father felt he had failed because he had not gone to medical school. He often withdrew to his study to work or paint dark, depressing landscapes. When we began our work, Michael described himself as a poet and jazz musician. In order to support himself, he did temporary office work. Following graduation from college, Michael did a graduate degree abroad in creative writing. His poetry achieved significant recognition for a year or two, but by the time he began treatment he was writing only sporadically and did not know how to reactivate his creativity.

When Michael was 12 years old, his father had a sudden heart attack as the family sat watching TV. He died a few hours later. Michael's mother became clinically depressed. She told Michael that she also wanted to be dead. She lay on her bed, inert and unable to talk. She was remote and inaccessible for about six months. Michael's maternal aunt hired a full-time housekeeper to care for Michael and his older brother, a senior in high school. Michael's mother was totally unable to help Michael with his feelings of loss. He felt she needed him to act happy. He tried to throw himself into activities but he felt continually frustrated and unsuccessful.

Michael had experienced many losses by the time he began treatment. When he detailed these to me, he described them in a dry, bitter, highly intellectual way. He was not aware of any pain or sadness related to his father's death. He could not really remember his father as a real person and couldn't feel anything about him. He thought that something had happened the night his father died that had changed him, but he could not remember what had occurred. As he described his life, he calmly said things like,

> Life has two levels. There is apparent normality, but that's just covering up a nightmare. I lost my family at 12 (when his father died) and then I lost it again totally at 14 (when his mother remarried). Our family wasn't so great before. It was kind of a dilapidated house, but it totally crumbled to pieces when I was 14.

I would reverberate to the sense of devastation that these comments conveyed, but he was detached from their bleakness and pain.

Michael described a dream very early in treatment. In the dream, he was in my office with me. A third person, a man, was present in the room. Halfway through the session the man interjected a comment and Michael turned to me, awaiting my reaction. He was surprised when I let the man remain and did not object to his presence. He said the man reminded him of the father of one of his friends. Later we decided that the dream was about Michael bringing his father, and the self state connected to his father, to therapy.

In the first years of treatment, Michael dealt with his anger at his father and mother for not being empathic to him, and his guilt about his father's death and his mother's depression. Michael was extremely angry with his father for neglecting and disparaging him. When his father died, Michael blamed himself. Michael felt his rage and competitiveness had killed his father. He shared his fear of the power of his anger with me, but was convinced that the anger would terrify and horrify me. As the treatment progressed, I experienced different aspects of Michael's dissociated anger and used these experiences to help verbalize his anger to him.

As Michael shared his memories of his relationship with his father with me and began to experience his pain and anger, he also recalled times they had spent together that were positive. He said:

> I had a sense of buoyant exhilaration and empowerment and that was abruptly pulled out from under me, like a rug, with my father dying. I had the power to move my mother before my father died and to move my father. When my father died and my mother was unavailable, I couldn't move either parent. It was devastating and it undermined all of my self-confidence. I lost the happy, sparkling part of myself that got others to sparkle back.

Later Michael understood that the "sparkling" part was connected to the assertive, autonomous facet of himself that he had dissociated along with his anger. He had finally let himself know and symbolize his experience of that part of him. Once he felt that the "sparkling" part of him could exist in the present, Michael's excitement about his work mushroomed. He began to take his poetry more seriously, wrote prolifically and published a book of poetry about his relationship to his father. When treatment ended, Michael had achieved considerable creative success as a poet, was editing a poetry publication, and mentoring younger artists. He felt he had recaptured the autonomous, sparkling part of himself and that he was able to evoke a sparkling response from others.

Michael had a recurrent fantasy after his father's death that caused him to feel fear and terror. In the fantasy, Michael saw himself as a spaceman attached by a cord to a spaceship. Suddenly the cord broke, and he went spiraling off into the depths of space. He knew that he could never return and would be alone forever. Whenever he talked about this fantasy, I felt deep, bleak sadness. Near the end of the treatment, Michael was able to grapple with the bleak, sad feelings associated with his fantasy and its connection to the night his father died. He recalled that he was sent to the end of the driveway to wait for the ambulance, then he spent that night and the next day at a neighbor's house, totally isolated from his family. Michael realized he was the spaceman disappearing into space.

Towards the end of his treatment, Michael said:

> I'm not the same. I've woken up and been reborn. A defrosting is occurring. I'm letting my feelings in and out. I'm not holding myself so stiff and rigid. I'm letting myself feel things. I'm not so self-protective. I've stepped off the spaceship and I'm flying through space under my own steam and it is scary.

He had a series of dreams about himself and his father that indicated he had learned how to "stand in the spaces between realities" (Bromberg, 1993, p. 166) and integrate his different self states and ways of seeing himself and his father. The dreams began with a father of 44 (the age at which his father died) and a 12-year-old Michael, and culminated with his father as an older man interacting with the current day Michael in a variety of situations where they were "talking man to man." Michael felt so happy in the dream that he started to cry. When the sequence ended, Michael said:

> My father is buried now, but for years I carried him inside me, a large homunculus. Now I can finally put a cover on his grave. I can bury my Dad and survive alone. I feel like superman and I feel really sad.

Discussion

How can we understand what happened in these two treatments? I am going to try to answer that question by offering an extended metaphor. Ruth and Michael each arrived at my office with a suitcase that was invisible to them. These suitcases contained memories about them in relation to their fathers and rich tapestries of intersubjective connections they had each woven with their fathers. These invisible, self state suitcases were bound tightly shut by ropes of pain and anger that they also could not register. The suitcases stood in the corner of my office until I registered the searing pain and noticed them. I pointed out first the ropes, then their suitcases. The suitcase was not something either of them could deal with alone. It took each a long time to believe I would risk touching the pain and rage, and try to untie the ropes and discover the contents of their relationships with their fathers. Finally, we broached the pain and anger together, and then Ruth and Michael were each able to show me the contents (their connection with their father). They verbalized and symbolized their feelings about their fathers. They sorted through the contents and decide what they wanted to leave behind and what they wanted take with them into their adult life. They tried things on to see if any of them were suitable to incorporate into current relationships. Each created an image of their relationship with their father that they could carry with them into their adult life. Ruth made a painting that captured that image. Michael created a volume of poems about fathers and sons. By the end of treatment, they were able to give away the suitcases as they no longer needed them. The remaining, salvaged contents could intermingle freely with the other facets of the self.

There are some issues of general importance that are illuminated by these cases. The first is related to the crucial role of the surviving parent in enabling the child to experience grief (see Silverman and Nickman, 1996).

If the surviving parent is not available to witness the adolescent's grief, then it will be extremely difficult for the child to face it alone, and she may dissociate it. The problem is that the surviving parent has her own unbearable burden: to experience and manage her own grief; cope with all the practical necessities related to the death of the spouse; and facilitate her children's mourning. The surviving parent may succumb under the burden of her own grief, as Michael's mother did, or she may be like Ruth's mother and have difficulty acknowledging her child's pain. It is often difficult for the surviving parent to mourn as this requires that she can retain hope and believe that the family will ultimately survive the traumatic loss. It is important that a clinician working with any member of a family that has suffered parental loss appreciate that the burden of loss rests on the surviving parent, and that this is indeed enormous. Some clinicians have tried to find ways to help the family cope with their pain, such as parent–child bereavement groups where therapists work with parent and child to help them experience their grief, and to enable the parent to tolerate the child's pain (Schoeman and Kreitzman, 1997). When the adolescent or child agrees to enter individual therapy, the therapist can help her experience and bear her pain. Therapy will be successful only if the surviving parent can allow the adolescent to develop such an intimate relationship with an adult other than the parent.

Another general issue is the adolescent or child's ability to tolerate mourning. Even in cases where the surviving parent can tolerate her child's grief, this does not guarantee that the child can face her pain. Not all children or teenagers who have recently suffered a catastrophic loss are willing to engage in therapy. They frequently fear their feelings and resist exploring them. They are afraid their feelings will be overwhelming to them and to their peers.

> I saw a 15-year-old girl in consultation shortly after the sudden death of her father. She was very angry at fate and could not access any sadness, though she had been very attached to her father. She said:
>
>> I can't feel this now. I have to be normal and be with my friends and go to school and play on my field hockey team and hang out. If I feel sad about my Dad, I won't be able to function and be a regular kid.
>
> Another adolescent lost her mother at the age of 13 but did not tell anyone at her new high school. She told me that the fact that she had no mother made her feel "weird," different from all the other kids. She did not want to think about her mother's death or feel any of her feelings connected to it. These adolescents tried to avoid grief and were therefore not available for therapy. I hope that they, like Ruth and Michael, were able to mourn later on in their lives.

Conclusion

In conclusion, let us consider the impact of the analyst's assumptions about what constitutes "normal" or "successful" mourning. Ruth and Michael created a new, continuing relationship with the lost parent during our work together. This resolution occurred because I made certain assumptions about what constituted "successful" mourning. Freud's "detachment" (Baker, 2001, p. 56) position on mourning felt counter-intuitive to me. It did not describe my personal resolutions when I have suffered significant losses. I was raised in Africa where ancestors were always accorded space in the current life of the self and the tribe. I assumed that the final outcome of the mourning process would be the creation of something related to the complex interrelation with the parent that the person could call her own and carry with her into life.

Ruth and Michael created a new internal relationship with the lost parent that they could retain while continuing to form new attachments. The therapeutic outcome would presumably have been different if they had worked with an analyst who had a different set of assumptions about what constituted successful mourning and espoused the goal of detachment. Of course, I assume that the assumptions that I made about "successful" mourning are more correct than those of the detachment variety, but this too is only an assumption. I believe that it was easier for my patients to experience the painful feelings associated with their loss when they believed that they would be able to carry some aspects of their connection with the dead parent with them into their present and future. It is possible that these assumptions would not help all patients to experience their grief. Even the requirement that grief be experienced and processed rests on its own set of assumptions. It important that analysts who work with mourning and grief acknowledge that we are all operating with assumptions about what constitutes "normal" mourning and that these are assumptions, not truths (see Goldner, 1994).

My work with Ruth and Michael demonstrated that it is deeply traumatic for a child or an adolescent to lose a parent. The adolescent experiences the horror of loss. In addition, she discovers that the arbitrary hand of fate can strike anyone at any moment, and discovers the reality of her parents' and her own mortality. Dylan Thomas protested the fact of mortality when he exhorted his dying father, "Do not go gentle into that good night. Rage, rage against the dying of the light" (Thomas, 1951, p. 926).

In order to be helpful to an individual who lost a parent as a child or adolescent, the analyst needs to be open to experiencing the full magnitude of the child or adolescent's loss, and the pain and rage it provoked. An adolescent can survive and transcend such a loss better if the adults in the environment do not flinch from acknowledging its horror. When we acknowledge this, we can help the bereaved person process their feelings, and achieve a resolution where the connection with the lost parent can remain a live and vital force in the person's present and future.

References

Baker, J.E. (2001) Mourning and the transformation of object relationships: evidence for the persistence of internal attachments. *Psychoanalytic Psychology*, 18(1): 55–73.

Bernstein, J.W. (2000) Making a memorial place: the photography of Shimon Attie. *Psychoanalytic Dialogues*, 10: 347–370.

Bromberg, P.M. (1993) Shadow and substance: a relational perspective on clinical process. In P.M. Bromberg, *Standing in the Spaces: Essays on Clinical Process, Trauma and Dissociation*, pp. 165–187. Hillsdale, NJ: Analytic Press, 1998.

—— (1994), "Speak! That I may see you": some reflections on dissociation, reality and psychoanalytic listening. *Psychoanalytic Dialogues*, 4: 517–547.

—— (2001) The gorilla did it: some thoughts on dissociation, the real and the really real. *Psychoanalytic Dialogues*, 11: 385–404.

Conant, R.D. (1996) Memories of the death and life of a spouse: the role of images and sense of presence in grief. In D. Klass, P.R. Silverman and S.L. Nickman (eds) *Continuing Bonds*, pp. 179–196. Washington, DC: Taylor and Francis, 1996.

Frankiel, R.V. (1994) *Essential Papers on Object Loss*. New York: New York University Press.

Freud, S. (1917) Mourning and melancholia. *Standard Edition*, 14: 237–258. London: Hogarth Press, 1957.

Gaines, R. (1997) Detachment and continuity: the two tasks of mourning. *Contemporary Psychoanalysis*, 33: 549–571.

Goldner, V. (1994) Theoretical metaphors in psychoanalysis. *Psychoanalytic Dialogues*, 4: 583–594.

Jacobson, E. (1965) The return of the lost parent. In R.V. Frankiel, *Essential Papers on Object Loss*, pp. 233–250. New York: New York University Press, 1994.

Joffe, W. and Sandler, J. (1965) Notes on pain, depression and individuation. *Psychoanalytic Study of the Child*, 20: 394–424.

Klass, D. (1996) The deceased child in the psychic and social worlds of bereaved parents during the resolution of grief. In D. Klass, P.R. Silverman and S.L. Nickman (eds) *Continuing Bonds*, pp. 199–215. Washington, DC: Taylor and Francis, 1996.

Lerner, P.M. (1990) The treatment of early object loss: the need to search. In R.V. Frankiel, *Essential Papers on Object Loss*, pp. 469–481. New York: New York University Press, 1994.

Mitchell, S. (1988) *Relational Concepts in Psychoanalysis*. Cambridge, MA: Harvard University Press.

—— (1999) Attachment theory and the psychoanalytic tradition: Reflections on human relationality. *Psychoanalytic Dialogues*, 9: 85–107.

Moss, M.S. and Moss, S.Z. (1996) Remarriage of widowed persons: a triadic relationship. In D. Klass, P.R. Silverman and S.L. Nickman (eds) *Continuing Bonds*, pp. 163–178. Washington, DC: Taylor and Francis, 1996.

Normand, C.L., Silverman, P.R. and Nickman, S.L. (1996) Bereaved children's changing relationships with the deceased. In D. Klass, P.R. Silverman and S.L. Nickman (eds) *Continuing Bonds*, pp. 87–111. Washington, DC: Taylor and Francis, 1996.

Ogden, T. (2000a) Borges and the art of mourning. *Psychoanalytic Dialogues*, 10: 65–88.

—— (2000b) A picture of mourning: commentary on paper by Jeanne Wolff Bernstein. *Psychoanalytic Dialogues*, 10: 371–375.

—— (2001) An elegy, a love song and a lullaby. *Psychoanalytic Dialogues*, 11: 292–311.

Schoeman, L.H. and Kreitzman, R. (1997) Death of a parent: group intervention with bereaved children and their caregivers. *Psychoanalysis and Psychotherapy*, 14: 221.

Shapiro, E.R. (1996) Grief in Freud's life: reconceptualizing bereavement in psychoanalytic theory. *Psychoanalytic Psychology*, 13: 547–566.

Silverman, P.R. and Klass, D. (1996) Introduction: what's the problem? In D. Klass, P.R. Silverman and S.L. Nickman (eds) *Continuing Bonds*, pp. 3–27. Washington, DC: Taylor and Francis, 1996.

Silverman, P.R. and Nickman, S.L. (1996) Children's construction of their dead parents. In D. Klass, P.R. Silverman and S.L. Nickman (eds) *Continuing Bonds*, pp. 73–86. Washington, DC: Taylor and Francis, 1996.

Sussillo, M. (2005) Beyond the grave – adolescent parental loss: "Letting go" and "Holding on." *Psychoanalytic Dialogues*, 15(4): 499–528.

Thomas, D. (1951) Do not go gentle into that good night. In R. Ellmann and R. O'Clair (eds) *The Norton Anthology of Modern Poetry*, 2nd. edn, pp. 926–927. New York: W.W. Norton, 1988.

Tyson, R.L. (1983) Some narcissistic consequences of object loss: a developmental view. In R.V. Frankiel, *Essential Papers on Object Loss*, pp. 252–267. New York: New York University Press, 1994.

Chapter 10

Darth Mader

The dark mother

Sara Weber

Several years ago I received my first in a series of child psychotherapy cases referred by Family Court. These cases keep me up at night. The children cannot rest securely in the face of their parents' distortions and hatred. They are often forced to take sides in battles far beyond their emotional maturity and capacity to manage. The case I discuss here will explore the vicissitudes of one child's attempt to find her own mind in a toxic environment.

Have you ever seen the "reality" TV show *The Chamber*? (One can only hope it is off the air before you read this chapter.) In it, the skimpily clad contestant is strapped spread-eagle onto a chair that looks like something out of a Frankenstein movie. The chair glides the contestant backward into a "torture" chamber. Electrodes strapped to certain muscles induce involuntary contractions. Sometimes the chair rotates over billowing flames as if roasting the contestant on a spit. Alternately, the temperature in the chamber falls below zero, the contestant is splashed with icy water and gale force winds might blow. All the while, the contestant is trying to answer trivia questions for cash. Terror and normal reactivity must be dissociated (held at bay) to win. If you lose, you are weak, bad, and "a loser." If you lose, you feel as though you have lost your mind. An argument can be made that if you win, you have lost your mind, too. A complete taking in of the experience and its meaning would be deeply disturbing, but you would, at least, perceive the reality of the situation.

Perhaps this game assumes a certain belief that the TV producers will not let you get hurt. You rely on them not to really hurt you. After all, it is all just a trick. But what if it isn't? What if you choose to be a contestant thinking it will be fun, good for your acting career, or on a dare? Hoping in short to show the world what a cool person you are, confirming that you have enough inner strength in a dangerous world. What if, instead, you find yourself anxious, having nightmares, unsure of yourself and everyone else? Your having consciously chosen, even if naively, to be subjected to this treatment makes you feel worse. Perhaps what you have agreed to was deeply masochistic. Why did you do this? Perhaps you are actually trying to master or understand some early, partially, or never apprehended childhood abuse.

Emmanuel Ghent (1990), in his article entitled "Masochism, submission, surrender: masochism as a perversion of surrender," discusses the profound motivating force in all of us for an experience of faith he calls "surrender." What he means by surrender is the sense that one is living in a way that feels authentic, spontaneous and vital. Forces of growth feel unimpeded. Surrender is not to another person, though it evolves in the environmental atmosphere created by mother and child. It is much like Winnicott's (1954) true self. One has a sense of personal integrity and feels at home in relation to others. Submission and masochism are perversions of efforts to find a true self, caused by defenses and compromises aimed at warding off dread. Submission is to a person, idea, impulse or fear. It is a "clinging to" that resists the forces of change, learning, thinking for oneself and growth. Conversely, the true self allows a blossoming of life in what feels like a balance of effort and ease.

From what substrate does a true or false self arise? Ghent says, "There is, however deeply buried or frozen, a longing for something in the environment to make possible surrender" (1990, p. 109). Eigen (1981) reminds us that we need to have an area of faith from which this true self can arise. It is an outgrowth of the clear realization of self-and-other differences from which, in turn, thinking and being evolve. For human beings this area of faith is rooted in the parent, usually the mother, and child relationship. Ghent says, "Faith, surrender, the beginnings of creativity and symbol formation all intersect in the world of transitional experiencing" (p. 109) when the baby lives in a faith born of the bond with the mother. That faith is prior to a clear realization of the differences between self and other. Growth requires successive rounds of disorganization of previous cognitive and emotional perceptions of one's reality followed by a reorganization that includes new ideas and experiences. Object relations based on merger and projection give way to a vital sense of differentiated self and other via a process of digestion of the other that involves a thorough emotional penetration of them.

How do we find this differentiated true self if those people who make up the most essential parts of our environment are constantly impinging on us? When they are profoundly perverted and demand that we support their perversions or lose their love? When they require us to submit to them for their mental stability? How does one come to discover oneself when one's parents see not their child but a bundle of projections? The intrusiveness of these projections interferes with "coming into being." How do we discover our true self, one that can think and differentiate from our parents, when we have no faith in them, or when our need for faith in them costs us the truth?

Growing up with even one parent who is intensely paranoid, enraged, and vengeful, is the psychic equivalent of a real torture chamber engendering submission and masochism. Severely challenged is your fundamental belief that your parents are really doing things in your interests, yet you hold onto the illusion of their goodness because you need an "area of faith" from which to develop. In doing so, you twist yourself into all sorts of false positions.

In such families, prior to clear differentiation of self and other, the child lives with danger and toxic emotions. The child may be subjected to torrents of venom from one parent regarding the other. The child may become the object of the venom when perceived as "taking the side" of the other parent or in any way frustrating the one parent. Fits of irrational rage abound. Every hurt the child experiences is used as an opportunity to malign the other parent, no matter whose fault. Normal nicks of parental differences become festering infections that threaten to require amputation of the other parent. Object loss is a constant threat.

Abusiveness and neglect are denied, irrelevant. Everything is blown out of proportion. Outright lies abound. Worse still, subtle, insidious half-truths and lies couched in longed-for love cause deep confusion and leave residues of irresolvable trauma. How do these children find their true selves in this frightful storm? Rarely are they helped to process reality in keeping with *their* interests. Rarely is a decision made because it is best for the child, rather than in relation to its effect on "the case." Rarely does a disturbed parent admit fault.

Through all this, both parents expect the child to carry on without any trouble at school, and to be well behaved with them. The child is never supposed to behave as the parents themselves do. Remarkably, some of them, like the one I will shortly discuss, behave incredibly well, building up a repertoire of alternative self-states held at dissociated distance with frightful, enormous effort. A child shows a certain set of beliefs with one parent, and an opposing set of beliefs with the other. They feel false, unintegrated and ashamed. They dread what may come. Collisions of these states cause traumatic effect and affect. The collisions may lead to a devastating sense of being "bad" or "evil," but they can be important moments for enduring truth and mental health. The psychic cost of these dissociations and collisions is enormous.

In order for a family to need an appointed Family Court judge to tell them to put their child in treatment, at least one parent must be severely disturbed, usually in a way that otherwise allows them to continue to function in the world. The other parent, if not equally ill, may be masochistic or schizoid. The child may seek refuge in the saner parent, or join the psychotic one's reality to turn against truth. More usually the child tries to have it all, desperately trying to find a way to avoid schism between the parents and within him or herself. How impossible to salvage all the pieces! The parents cannot allow it. One's own need to be grounded in reality or in a stable relationship forces a position. The dilemma is a terrible choice. Choose to share a parent's psychotic, skewed, hateful reality, or be without a parent, both internally and in the world. How do you find the space for the forces of growth to evolve?

This chapter describes one child's heroic efforts to resolve these issues, and to grow up with integrity despite a mother so psychologically ill that the court denied her custody.

The mother had lost custody of her then 4-year-old daughter because she was drawing her daughter into her paranoid worldview, which included accusations that the father had sexually abused the daughter. Apparently the child had learned a "story" about what her father had done to her, much as one learns a nursery rhyme. Too young to understand the consequences of the story, she naively recited it to whomever her mother told her to tell (but only when her mother was in the room). Armed with considerable evidence that I did not know for many months into the treatment, the court's forensic psychologist felt that the mother's capacity for destroying this child's mind was too toxic to be allowed to continue. The father was convinced to sue for custody. This mother, coping psychotically with her own early abuse, sincerely believed that she was protecting her child. Within this context, the mother–child relationship was warm, loving and playful. The daughter, drinking in her mother's love, was drinking in the poison of her mother's psychotic thinking. Worse, she had innocently become an agent of her mother's psychosis. Her "area of faith" was rotten. The warping effects of this were wearing down her capacity to think. Nonetheless, the bond between them was powerful. Both the daughter and mother were shocked, unprepared for the sudden separation, and the sudden attack on the integrity of their love for each other.

I shall call this child Lucy, the feminine equivalent of Luke. Lucy, you shall see, grafted the *Star Wars* story of Luke Skywalker and his father, Darth Vader, onto her own very similar creation. When I first met her, Lucy was in a pact with the devil. She had sacrificed herself so as not to lose her mother. She had begun to realize that the stories she told were lies that implicated her father and anyone who threatened her mother, and she was not happy about it, but she was more profoundly in agony over the loss of her mother.

Each stage of development requires renegotiation, renewed trauma, loss and mourning. This is the story of Lucy's successful negotiation of this dilemma through her latency years, and her re-entry into horror at the beginning of her preteen years.

As part of a custody battle, the court had ordered a forensic evaluation. After hours with mother, father, daughter and all possible pairings of the three, the forensic psychologist concluded that the mother was quite paranoid and unable to make reasonably empathic judgments regarding her daughter. The father seemed quite appropriate with, and supportive to the child, and was himself psychologically stable. The mother had accused the father of physically attacking her and sexually abusing the child. The mother had apparently coached her daughter on what to say to people about what her father had done to her, using an odd sort of childlike language. She taught her to describe a game called "ding-dong" which involved the little girl playing with her father's penis. A therapist friend of the mother heard the child's story and reported it to the Bureau of Child Welfare. Investigation proved negative. The mother wrote many clearly psychotic letters to the forensic psychologist stipulating how the father should conduct himself while with the 4-year-old daughter. For example, the mother required the father never to be within 1700 feet of the child. The Law Guardian and the forensic psychologist convinced the father to seek custody, not just visitation. Notably, the psychologist found this child unusually unable to verbalize facts about her life. She could not even name her preschool teacher. Thinking had been compromised by her attachment to her mother's skewed thinking.

Uninformed of the findings of the forensic psychologist, I met each parent before meeting Lucy. Each seemed interested in proving the other a monster. Both were very interested in the child. The mother accused the father of sexually abusing the then 5-year-old daughter. Her evidence was hard to follow and rather bizarre. Her apparent desperate desire to protect her daughter from harm could not keep the facts from getting hopelessly mixed up. The father's countercharge was that the mother was paranoid. Hurt and defensive (he still expected to be accused of molesting the child), he fell back onto a European aristocratic arrogance. Nonetheless, his deep compassion for his daughter was apparent in the way he described his daughter's agony when the judge, making a radical decision, removed the child from the mother's custody, forcibly and traumatically, in the courtroom. He was genuinely sensitive about her feelings of being parted from her mother.

New to the divorce court system, I was skeptical. (I am still deeply skeptical.) I did not know the judge, or the forensic psychologist who had evaluated the parents. I did not know whom to trust, if anyone. Unbeknownst to me, I was perfectly in line with Lucy's state of mind. She had many pieces of "data" that did not add up. Although she seemed unperturbed by the impossible coexistence of various facts, her intensity made it clear that she was deeply agitated.

Lucy eagerly entered my office on her own, accompanied to her first session by her mother, who had visitation that day. A competent, vivacious 5-year-old, she required minimal introductions. Heading straight for the dollhouse, she immediately began a story that she was to work over weekly for four years, until it lost its power. In this story, a very frightening-looking, scantily dressed, female, GI Joe figure, with red hair, scary eyes and battle attire, was immediately named the "Evil Lady." The other figure in the play, simply known as "the girl," was innocent looking, pig-tailed, with bobby socks, all in pink. Before she spoke, while she examined the toy figures, her body was alert to the sounds of her mother leaving my waiting room to get a cup of coffee. The moment the outer door closed, she whispered that the Evil Lady was trying to control the girl's mind. The Evil Lady got the girl to do evil, and tell lies. Though the girl figure tried to get away from the Evil Lady, she was often overpowered by her mind controlling spells and magical, witch-like powers. Before the play could come to its own conclusion, ever vigilant, she heard her mother enter my waiting room. The play stopped in its tracks. After some anxious clean up, she ran out to her mother and hugged her with what appeared to be great hunger.

As the weeks went by, we lived simultaneously in two worlds, seemingly unaware that one depiction of reality had anything to do with the other. The mother of the transitional play space was evil; the mother of the interpersonal world was wonderful and painfully missed. Consciously and profoundly, this child was haunted by the trauma of having lost her mother. She told me about the horrible experience of going to the courthouse, assuming she would be going home with her mother. While there, someone took this unsuspecting child into another room. Then the judge told her she could not go home with her mother; indeed, she could not see her mother for a week, and then only every other weekend. Moreover (I do not know if she understood) her father now had custody of her. She fell apart, torn from her mother.

For a year or two she told me this story, emphasizing how angry she was with the judge. This is one of the few "facts" of her life she talked about. (Perhaps this is the only "fact" that both her parents and she agreed upon, thus it had consensual validation.) Sometimes she talked about it at the same moment that she played out a scene in which the "Evil Lady" kidnapped, plotted against, or wiped out the mind of the girl. She was genuinely heart-broken about the loss.

Most of the time I was sure the Evil Lady was her mother, but sometimes it seemed like it was the lady judge who took her from her mother. Always there was for me a bewildering split between the relationship of the characters in her play and the overt relationship with her mother. On the days her mother picked her up, she ran out, jumped into her arms and smothered her with loving affection. The mother reported no acts of resistance, only that the child constantly expressed a desire to live with her. Clearly, I needed to tread with care so as not to impeach the desperately needed, real mother.

On the surface, no one would ever know how troubled this child was. There were no complaints about her behavior at school or home. She was cooperative and competent, rarely got upset, made friends easily. Her teachers found her to be well adjusted. She did what she was told without argument, and well. Her adjustment in the world was remarkable. She behaved as though no one knew about her predicament. She had different personas and thoughts for each situation, including therapy.

Her capacity for dissociation allowed her to describe in the transitional space of therapy how evil her mother was, while in the sphere of actual relationship to her mother she held onto a "good mother." A ritual in therapy helped create the transitional space. Each week, without fail, she would run into my office and "hide" in the same place. I would have to say how much I missed her, wonder where she was, then "find" her. Once "found," she could play out her concerns about her mother's evil attempts to control her mind until, without reminder, she would know time was almost up. Then, she would sit in my chair and have me spin her a number of times in each direction, seemingly uncasting the spell we had woven over our time and space. We had carved out a special place where she could explore her feelings about her mother without impingement. I made sure never to get ahead of her with "reality" words. I had great fun playing out the Evil Lady's dastardly deeds. She made sure that no one else could know what we were doing. Many things even we could not speak of fully.

Every week, for two years, we played some variation on the theme of the Evil Lady. Early on, she would punctuate her play with real wetting accidents during the sessions (I found out later that they had been happening at home as well), until we discovered, in the play, that the Evil Lady had checked the "girl's" vagina for signs that she had been molested. Once again, though never spoken of directly, through the transitional play, the wetting was cured. Some weeks, the Evil Lady was more effective at overpowering the girl than others. She developed the means to fight off the mind-controlling efforts of the Evil Lady.

As various court reviews of the custody decision came up, the mother's, and thus the Evil Lady's efforts became more extreme. Each time, the real-life mother had Lucy tell their therapist friend the story of her father molesting her at age 4. This friend repeatedly called Child Welfare. Upon each investigation, Lucy had to undergo physical examination, even though the report was about something that had happened when she was 4 years old. Nothing was ever found and Lucy, when not in the room with her mother, denied anything ever happened. Still, it was very clear I should never say anything about these examinations, who the Evil Lady was, what roles she and her mother played in reporting this old charge over and over again or what our play had to do with her real life. Her relationship to her real mother, her need for her, was too strong to explore the shame of what was really happening. Further, it seemed very important that I not influence her and become the Evil Lady myself. Any action on my part would destroy our transitional space that was so crucial to the possibility of her becoming real.

When Lucy was 8 years old, things broke down. A court decision was coming up. Mother told me she had proof that the father was a pedophile, but it was in a foreign language. She had lost the translation and did not know where the person who had sent her the "proof" lived. The "proof" she reported to me was vague innuendo. In addition, Mother told me that Lucy had told her about doing all the housework at her father's house, including the bathroom, dishes, garbage and cooking. Mother believed (incorrectly) that Lucy was her father's housekeeping slave. She was puzzled, however, by a different lie she had uncovered. Her daughter had told her that she was in a concert at school, but that Dad would not let mother come. Angry that she was not notified, she inquired of Lucy's teacher. There was no concert. For the first time the mother accepted the fact that Lucy was saying things that were not true. While she was unable to generalize from this example, she was truly puzzled and interested in why. This opened a door for Lucy to begin to think about the lies and to question her own behavior.

Soon thereafter, I had my only emergency school contact in this case. For the first time, Lucy was breaking down in school, crying all the time, unable to work or play. Immediately following the teacher's report, Lucy came into my office and had a huge tantrum, finally to reveal with words what she had been showing me in the play. She had been lying to give her mother what she wanted to hear. Lying about the sexual molestation, about the concert, about the housework, all of it. She felt deeply ashamed of herself for having done so. Soon she began to tell me that her mother was crazy. She described her strange religious beliefs, and very peculiar friends. She began to express dread at having to visit her mother, and at her mother's pressuring her to hate her father.

The play went on, but picked up a new twist. Having seen the movie *Star Wars*, she pulled out my space Legos and created a whole new scene. The evil figure was now called Darth Mader, the dark mother. Darth Mader had a base and space ships and was constantly trying to take control of the base and space ships of the "good" figure. Much time was spent building good controls and warning systems for the "good" side. Her use of the Star Wars myth added a hope that someday, as Luke did for his father Darth Vader, she could help bring her mother back from the "dark side" and reconcile.

Now we could talk about her mother and specific crazy things mother did to scare Lucy. Around this time I saw her mother walking around an abandoned part of lower Manhattan. I wondered if she might be prostituting herself, or was she simply walking around "crazy"? Her mother also began to show up over one hour late to pick Lucy up from her sessions. Lucy was my last session on Friday evenings. I felt that I could not leave her alone to worry about her mother, so we puttered in my office, doing art projects and homework. Lucy told me about her mother's strange rituals and superstitions. The first time mother was so late to pick her up, I asked what had happened and suggested she call if she were delayed. I was then subjected to an angry rant. Somehow it was my entire fault. Lucy continued to greet her mother with a big hug, but it seemed more and more staged to keep her mother from flipping out.

Nonetheless, there were times when she was truly in the grip of the "Evil" side of her mother and believed her mother's paranoid version of reality. Once when her father was waiting for her at the end of her session, she ran to slam the door shut on him and stay in the safety of my office. She looked genuinely frightened and told me that she was afraid of him. Within a few seconds, this look disappeared and she walked out the door. I was very concerned. Like Lucy, I had never completely dropped the possibility that her father *was* doing something to her. When I tried to discuss this in the next session, she could not really connect to what she had been feeling in the previous session. Aware that she lived in irreconcilable states of reality she said, "Sometimes I need my Dad to drag me across the gulf because I can't swim."

Around this time, her father became seriously involved with a woman who took in Lucy wholeheartedly. With a new safety net, Lucy became empowered to "know" who her mother was and to reject more and more parts of her. I came upon Lucy and her soon-to-be-stepmother in a bakery. Lucy looked like a different child. She was relaxed, looking younger, softer, less on guard than I had ever seen. They left holding hands. Lucy was briefly a normal 9 year old.

Soon her mother found out about this woman and poured on jealous rage. Mom tried yet again to fight for custody, called in the molestation charge (which was finally dismissed without a physical examination, thanks to the power of computer records) and redoubled her efforts to turn Lucy against her father and his girlfriend. This time it did not work. The experience of being in a family, including the stepmother-to-be's large extended family, gave Lucy a grounding she had never had. Lucy was more able to describe the peculiarities of her mother and to express wishes that she see her less and less. After several months, we terminated therapy, although we all assumed she would need to return.

I was hoping to tell a triumphant story, but things have taken a bad turn. Several things tested the unequivocally positive relationship with father and girlfriend. First, her father and girlfriend went on a vacation without Lucy. Lucy told her father that she wanted to stay with her new extended family and not even tell her mother that they were away. Lucy felt abandoned and left out. Months later, the father and girlfriend married. Within a few months, they were expecting a new baby and moved into a new apartment. All of this made Lucy very happy, but when they rearranged the apartment for the baby to come, she felt pushed away from the warm center of the family. Her mother proffered psychological poison that Lucy would alternately taste to assuage her hurt, then avoid because of its toxicity. Toward the end of the pregnancy, the mother and stepmother got into a physical fight. The mother ended up with scratches on her face. All this really threw Lucy profoundly. Soon after the baby was born, Lucy felt displaced in her father's and step-mother's hearts. Intrapsychically, she retreated to her mother's side, where she was sure of being the most important one. Although now she could verbalize how crazy her mother was and voice her confusion, she became more controlled by the dark side.

Lucy would tell her mom how much she hated the baby, while she portrayed a different Lucy to her father and step-mom. They told me how loving she was to the baby. More disturbing, however, was that for the first time Lucy, now in middle school, began to have serious social problems. She began to see some girls as "enemies," and tell stories to others, including her father, about them. Her father arranged for her to travel by subway to school with some other girls. The mother felt, probably rightly, that the father should take Lucy to school. She made sure that Lucy knew how she felt. Caught between the two parents, Lucy tried to cover for her father and began making up more and more far-fetched stories to her mother. Trying to be the perfect child for her father, and unclear if the need she had to have her father take her to school was part of her mother's craziness, she told him different far-fetched stories. Confused, Lucy arrived later and later so that she could no longer travel with the other girls, telling her father that they pushed her down the subway stairs. The father, in a sleepless haze after the arrival of the new baby, did not pick up on her dilemma and take her to school. I imagined that she would arrive at this new middle school after a panicky, lonely trip, and begin to try to deal with the intense social complications of the preteen years by making up more stories. Soon she lost even those friends who had initially been on her side as they learned about the lies. I learned all this from her father when he called to tell me that Lucy needed to come back to therapy.

Lucy continues to lead several lives, but the pressure of identity formation and teenage self-consciousness is making dissociation difficult to maintain. She is trying to be each parent's perfect child, unable clearly to recognize her own needs since she is so befuddled by her mother's use of them, and freshly afraid to separate from her mother as she enters puberty. She is now deeply confused and submerged in the "dark side."

Will she be willing to return to therapy? I have two concerns. The first is that just before we ended therapy, I became the mother's enemy as well. In addition to our battle over picking up her daughter on time, the mother had become aware that I had sent a letter to the Law Guardian diplomatically recommending that the custody arrangement not be reopened. (I had been reluctant to do so in order to protect my neutrality and Lucy's transitional space, but there was an imminent danger of the entire case going back to court.) Mother staged a confrontation with me in front of her daughter, telling me that she would pray for me because I "lacked a mother's heart." She punctuated her prayer by leaving, in my waiting room, the most deadly fart I have ever smelled. Lucy gracefully got her mother out of my office. Clearly able to deal with her mother in a differentiated way, Lucy was able to laugh in the next session as Darth Mader threw stink bombs. At first the fact that I was the mother's enemy was not a problem. Later, as her newly constituted family began to be less of a solution for Lucy, that position took on a different light. I fear that Lucy is now afraid to come back to therapy because it would betray her deeply needed mother. More profoundly, I think Lucy fears a return to therapy, dreading the emotional trauma of the collision between realities she knows is coming. Will she let me "drag her across the gulf"?

The ebb and flow of Lucy's need for her mother and her mother's mental illness have had a strong influence on her capacity to verbalize and mediate social reality. For this child, using language to express truth can be done only when she is sufficiently held by her father's benign world, or when her mother can be enough in touch with reality to see her daughter as a separate human being. Lucy is unable to risk the aggression inherent in disagreeing with her mother's version of reality. Wanting to be a "good girl," she has submitted to becoming the false caretaker self with the mother, and as "good" as she can be with the father and stepmother. She fears that each time she passes from the "evil" side to the truth, the experience will be catastrophic humiliation and loss. No doubt, as she gets older, she will become increasingly conflicted about what she is doing, ever more aware that what she has constructed to try to hold her world together holds too many contradictions and will not work. For now, Darth Mader is still controlling her mind. Lucy has submitted to the dark side of her mother. Truth and growth of a true self are held hostage by the need for a mother. It is not yet safe to apprehend completely who her mother is and what effect she has had on her. Each fresh opportunity for clarity is instead subverted by dread. It is unthinkable to acknowledge her mother's destructiveness and the shame of her own corrupted behavior while she is negotiating the shoals of puberty. For now, we hold onto the faith that there is a "centrality, despite its buried secrecy, of a longing for the birth, or perhaps the rebirth, of true self" (Ghent, 1990, p. 110).

References

Eigen, M. (1981) The area of faith in Winnicott, Lacan and Bion. *International Journal of Psychoanalysis*, 62: 413–433.

Ghent, E. (1990) Masochism, submission, surrender: masochism as a perversion of surrender. *Contemporary Psychoanalysis*, 26: 108–136.

Winnicott, D.W. (1954) Metapsychological and clinical aspects of regression with the psycho-analytical set-up. In D.W. Winnicott, *Through Paediatrics to Psycho-Analysis*, pp. 278–294. New York: Basic Books, 1975.

Part IV

Violence and terror

Chapter 11

Sometimes a fatal quest

Losses in adoption

David Kirschner

The *quintessential adoptee*, to quote an adoptee friend of mine, author/
psychologist Betty Jean Lifton (1988), was Oedipus. Had Freud been an
adoptee, he would have known that the pivotal issues in Oedipus' complex
were abandonment and loss, a need to reconnect with genetic roots and
buried, dissociated adoptee rage. Oedipus' search for his past evolved into a
fatal quest, in large part, because he was not told the facts of his birth –
that Laius, not Polybus, was his biologic father and Jocasta his birth
mother. He had voyaged to Delphi to seek the truth from the Oracle, but
was rewarded only with a cryptic message, that if he returned to his own
land he would kill his father and marry his mother. The fact that he had
been adopted by Polybus after being abandoned by Laius was kept from
him, as the truth of their birth is often kept from most adoptees. The
consequence was parricide and incest. We are left to consider the possibility
that on a deeply unconscious level, Oedipus knew exactly what he was
doing when he killed his father and took his mother to the marital bed: he
was both taking revenge for having been abandoned as an infant and
reconnecting with his genetic past.

Abandonment and loss are core issues in adoption. Loss of the birth
mother is a *primal wound*, says adoptive mother/author Nancy Verrier
(1993), likely no less profound than loss of significant relationships through
death, separation or divorce. In adoption, however, there is also a *loss* of
origins, *loss* of identity and *loss* of a completed sense of self. All members of
the adoption triad experience profound loss. Birth parents lose their
children, adoptive parents lose their dream of a child they wanted to
conceive, and adoptees lose their birth families. Unlike other situations of
traumatic loss, the adoptee's need to grieve is too often *not validated* by
society, or understood by the adoptive family.

Speaking of adoption loss, Jean Paton, the grandmother of adoption
reform (Paton, 1968) wrote me, when she was age 82:

> I believe that there are two traumas in the average adoption life history.
> One relates to the rejections one has received in the search. The other

seems to come from nowhere else except the separation trauma, from the birthmother. It lies so deep that one is lucky if it comes to life and can be unearthed.

If loss is not recognized, how can grieving and healing take place? It is only when the losses of adoption are addressed, that the gains of adoption can be more fully realized. Kubler-Ross (1997) has identified five stages that are worked-through in *normal* grief and mourning. Recognizing these stages of grief can reassure adoption triad members that they are experiencing appropriate feelings, even though grieving in adoption is different in some distinct ways from mourning a death. With death, there is at least a concrete ending that initiates the rituals of grieving. In adoption, there is no death, and no clear ending, but rather a kind of limbo, which has been described as similar to mourning a loved one who is missing in action.

In a landmark double murder case in 1986, I testified for the defense that 14-year-old Patrick DeGelleke had killed his adoptive parents (by setting their bed afire) as he felt that only by their dying could he be freed to search for and find his birth mother. When I suggested to Patrick that his birth mother, Barbara, might *not* be alive, his response was "but if I found out for sure that she was dead, at least then I could see her grave." Young Patrick, incidentally, was obsessed with fire, and with the story of the Phoenix, the mythical bird that is consumed by fire, but is reborn and rises in beauty from its own ashes. Patrick acted-out his festering adoption issues, but many adopted children internalize their pain and curiosity, rather than hurting the adoptive parents' feelings, or risking another feared rejection. Consequently, it is not uncommon for adoptees to remain stuck at the first stage of grieving, *denial*, or the second stage, *anger*, or the fourth stage, *depression*.

Adoption loss has been described as the only trauma in the world where the victims are expected by the whole of society to be grateful. Psychologist/ author Betty Jean Lifton, a mother figure of adoption reform, has called the secrecy based adoption system, *"the game of as if."* She wrote:

> Everyone pretends *as if* the adoptee belongs to the family raising him or her . . . The adopted parents embrace the child *as if* it were their own blood and ask the child to live *as if* this were true . . . Inherent in this process is the expectation that the child regard the birth parents *as if* dead, if not literally, then certainly symbolically.
>
> (Lifton, 1988, p. 14)

Many adoptees, in fact, have even been told the lie that their birth mother *was* dead. One notorious/high-profile example of this kind of lie was David Berkowitz, the so-called "Son of Sam" serial killer, who terrorized New York City in the 1970s by shooting and killing young women in parked cars. Berkowitz, always told the lie that his biologic mother had died giving birth to him, nonetheless searched for and found her alive. She did not measure up to his idealized fantasy image. When he met her, she introduced him to a half-sister he never knew existed, whom she had kept, while giving him up for adoption. Shortly after this ill-fated reunion, the killing spree began, in the same section of New York City, the borough of Queens, where he had met his birth mother and sister. I speculated then (1975) that he was repetitively killing young women in mating situations to prevent other unwanted little David Berkowitzes from being conceived in parked cars and later abandoned, as he fantasized that he had been.

There is little doubt that adoption at its roots was meant to exist on a base of death and rebirth, writes adoption-activist Shea Grimm (2002). The adoptee was, and is, meant to be *reborn* (into the adoptive family) as if they are dead to their birth family, and the biologic family is dead to them. This concept is echoed in state adoption laws and court rulings, perpetuating the deep-seated notion that death and rebirth is intrinsic to adoption, and so a system of sealed records, falsified birth certificates, secrets and lies evolved to facilitate this process. Consequently in adoption, there is too often *no* acknowledged grief, *no* meaningful mourning, and *no* closure. Just a festering wound that cries out to be healed, so that the adoptee can truly bond, give and receive love, have a solid sense of self and identity, and not get stuck in pathological grief and unrealistic fantasies (of birth parents) that may last a lifetime.

There should/can be a rebirth/transformative experience in adoptees, but this is possible only in a climate of openness, honesty and validation that allows for grieving first. Where there is a failure to mourn, there will be a failure to bond.

Recent trends toward more honesty and openness in adoption, and increasing acceptance of the need of some adoptees to search (for their birth parents), has resulted in new beginnings and transformative experiences, in many adoptive families. Yet original birth records remain sealed in all but five of the fifty US states. Most adoptees continue to be frustrated and blocked in their search for information, closure and/or hope for a reunion with birth parents.

Since the early 1960s, I have seen hundreds of adoptees, adoptive parents, and birth mothers in psychoanalytic therapy. Since 1986 I have testified as a forensic psychologist in more than twenty cases of adoptees who have killed (usually parricides, but also serial killers and killers of strangers) around the United States. I have repeatedly emphasized (Kirschner, 1980, 1988, 1990, 2006) that the vast majority of adopted children grow up to be psychologically healthy, productive, law-abiding citizens. I have also said (Kirschner, 1992, 1993, 1995, 2006) that there is a *spectrum* of adoption-related issues/problems ranging from the essentially "normal" ones that *most* adoptees present and resolve to ego "splitting" or dissociative disorders (Kirschner and Nagel, 1996) for which only a small subgroup of adoptees at the extreme end of the spectrum are at risk. While it is just a small percent who are prone to commit violent crimes, we should pay attention to this group for, as criminologists Jack Levin and James Alan Fox (1985), Ken Magid (1988), and Joel Norris (1989) point out, adoptees are over-represented in the criminal justice system and adopted serial killers have become household names.

Despite a wealth of clinical data and many replicated studies, with consensual validation among most mental health professionals in the adoption field indicating that adoptees are at greater psychological risk (Steed, 1989), there is still controversy about whether or not children of adoption are more vulnerable/at risk for emotional problems. Authors such as adoptive parent Elizabeth Bartholet (1993), adoptive father/sociologist William Feigelman (1986), adoptive mother Florence Klagsbrun (1986), and adoption agency lobbyist William Pierce (1990) all argue/maintain that adoptees are *not* any more prone to suffer from emotional/psychiatric problems than non-adopted individuals.

Adoption per se does *not* necessarily give rise to psychopathology. It must, however, be considered a risk factor, perhaps a precipitating one, in some families that are dysfunctional in terms of core adoption issues and parent–child interactions. Fortunately, not one of the hundreds of adoptees treated in my practice has ever killed anyone (thank G-d), though they all presented issues of loss, identity, anger/rage, etc., similar in kind, if not degree, to the twenty forensic cases who did act out in homicidal violence. What differentiates the few who kill from the vast majority of adoptees who work-through their issues of loss, abandonment, and identity and go on to lead productive lives? Why in these extreme cases is there pathological mourning, and an ultimately Fatal Quest instead of the healing, transformation, and new beginning that is often seen so dramatically, especially in the psychoanalytic treatment of adoptees? What can be learned from these cases at the extreme end of a spectrum?

For one thing, almost all of the twenty adopted killers whom I have seen *had* been in therapy (in childhood and adolescence), often with a number of different therapists, but the adoption issues were left virtually untouched in their treatment, and their therapists were *not* psychoanalytically oriented. Many therapists tend to minimize adoption as an issue in child and adolescent treatment. They often unwittingly enter into a folie à trois with the parents and adoption agency in which the adoptive family is viewed as being no different from birth families. Sociologist and adoptive father David Kirk (1964) believes this "denial of difference" as opposed to a realistic "acknowledgment of difference" is key to parenting emotionally healthy, adopted children. Therapists should also be aware that the transference of adopted children is quite special, and arises from the distorted parental images of many adoptees. The therapist may come to represent the birth parents and the patient may be intensely ambivalent, feeling both a strong need for attachment and a powerful fear of rejection. He or she will invariably attempt to sabotage the treatment. Adoption-sensitive, analytically trained therapists are best equipped to deal with this resistance.

My review of extensive treatment notes and reports on the twenty adoptees who killed suggests that their treatment was *not* adoption-sensitive, and did *not* focus on these issues. Almost all of them, as teenagers or young adults, had attempted to search for their birth mothers, but were blocked (by a closed adoption system) in this quest. Ironically many did have reunions *in prison*, as defense attorneys or investigators *were* able to find information on birth families in almost every case. In my opinion, had they been raised with openness and honesty; had their treatment been with therapists who were sensitive to adoption issues; and if they had been able to find their birth mothers *prior* to the events (the Son of Sam case notwithstanding), the killings would never have occurred.

This is not to say that reunions are always wonderful. Usually they do not result in long-term, close relationships. Reunion with the birth mother does, however, bring the adoptee back to the primal trauma. Revisiting this trauma, filling in the gaps and testing reality, no matter how unpleasant or painful, is often a major step in the healing process. In every case of the adoptees who killed, split fantasies of *all-good or all-bad* parent figures, dissociated adoptee rage, and the acting-out of an unconscious *compulsion to repeat*, was at the heart of the deed.

In *Beyond the Pleasure Principle*, Freud (1920) describes cases where patients display an unconscious need to recreate and repeat the primal traumas of their childhood, in successive relationships. He states, "There really does exist in the mind a compulsion to repeat which overrides the pleasure principle . . . and this compulsion to repeat is part of the death instinct" (p. 24). Nowhere, in my opinion, is the connection between traumatic loss, pathologic grieving, the death instinct and repetition compulsion more dramatic than in cases of adoptees who kill.

For example, in 1989 I examined then 45-year-old Steve Catlin, accused of killing his fourth and fifth wives, as well as his adoptive mother, with paraquat poison. Steve's third wife, Edith Ballew, raised suspicion about the deaths. The bodies were exhumed, traces of poison were found. I was called in to see if adoption issues could explain Steve's motivation and mitigate against the death penalty. When I evaluated him in prison in Bakersfield, California, I asked how he felt about being adopted. Steve, a macho kind of guy, started crying and said, "I can't believe you're asking me that. No one ever asked me how I felt about adoption before." When questioned what he had been told about his birth parents, Steve said that his biologic father was a Royal Air Force pilot during World War II who met his mother while training in the United States. He fell in love with her, went back to war, and was killed in the Battle of Britain. His birth mother, so he was told, upon learning of her lover's death, committed suicide by *poisoning* herself. I asked Steve whether he believed this story. He answered, looking me straight in the eye, "Ma Catlin would never tell a lie." But Steve poisoned Ma Catlin, his adoptive mother. Subsequent investigation revealed that the entire story was a fabrication. His birth mother had not poisoned herself. She was, in fact, still alive. Three other women *were* dead however, poisoned by Steve who, I'm convinced, was in the throes of a fatal quest, a need to revisit his primal trauma, repetitively killing symbolic mother figures, poisoning them as, he believed, his birth mother killed herself when she abandoned him as an infant.

Joel Rifkin, the most prolific serial killer in New York State history (Pulitzer and Swirsky, 1994; Kirschner, 2006), was also on a fatal quest, a pathological search for his birth mother, when he killed seventeen young women in the New York City/Long Island area from 1989 to 1993. Adopted as a newborn, Joel played out his role of the "good adoptee" at home where adoption was a taboo subject, virtually never discussed, in a family atmosphere of almost total denial. "We never talked about adoption in our family, not even close to really talking about it," Joel said. He spontaneously used the term *dissociation* to describe his adoptive mother Jeanne's tenacious denial of the importance of his adoption. Even the psychotherapists who treated him in childhood and adolescence (for "dyslexia," would you believe?) sided with this resistance, avoiding discussing adoption. Joel always fantasized about his birth mother and was convinced she was a prostitute (though she wasn't).

My first meeting with Joel was shortly after his arrest in 1993. Over the next twenty months, we met for more than 110 hours in the Nassau County and Suffolk County, Long Island prisons. Though he thought of searching for his birth mother when away at college, he never did anything about it because, as he told me, "I didn't want to hurt my parents' feelings." Instead, he carried out this quest pathologically, in the throes of a (bizarre) repetition compulsion. Explaining that he always felt lonely, terribly lonely prior to each killing, and he would then troll for prostitutes, whom he felt a strong bond with, to counter his painful loneliness. Symbolically, even consciously, he identified the women he killed with fantasy images of his birth mother. He had no *conscious* anger toward them and described only a bond of affection with prostitutes from whom he sought the nurturing love he felt had been denied him. It was in their world that he sensed he belonged, feeling strangely at home. It was for these women, he insisted, that he felt nothing but affection. Though amnesic for the killings (which he called the "events") and what triggered them, Joel had total recall for the "disposals" of his victims, and his bizarre need to first return with the dead bodies intact to their source (where he searched for and found them) before dismembering them. If he did not return with the dead women to the source (scene of his symbolic reunion), he said, their life energy would not stay with him, to nurture him and counter his loneliness. In a tone as rational as a biology professor describing the body's need for nourishment, Rifkin explained that he needed the life-energy of these women – each his symbolic mother – to survive emotionally, to fill the void and counter the pain that was always inside him. For this energy to nurture him, the women had to be dead first. If they remained alive, he reasoned, the energy would stay with them. In death, their life-energy would be released and absorbed into the body of their killer.

Parke Dietz, the prosecution psychiatrist in Rifkin's only trial, testified that Joel's motive, pure and simple, was "sexual sadism." I submit however, that even if there were elements of sexual sadism in Joel's acts, this did not fully explain his complex motivation. In *Civilization and its Discontents*, Freud (1930) could well have been analyzing Joel Rifkin in writing about the death instinct as follows:

> It is in sadism, where the death instinct twists the erotic aim in its own sense and yet at the same time fully satisfies the erotic urge, that we succeed in obtaining the clearest insight into its nature and its relation to Eros. . . . In this way [by destructive behavior] the instinct itself could be pressed into the service of Eros, in that the organism was destroying some other thing, whether animate or inanimate, instead of destroying its own self.
>
> (Freud, 1930, p. 78)

A great value in studying extreme cases, such as these adoptees who kill, is that they can demonstrate in pristine form, issues that may affect other adoptees, on a spectrum ranging from normal/minor to severe/extreme. "The importance to society of future research on this problem (adoptees who kill) is that only by acknowledging that it exists can we obtain the data and understanding to treat, and we may hope, to prevent further tragedies" (National Association of Homes for Children, 1986, p. 6).

References

Bartholet, E. (1993) *Family Bonds: Adoption and the Politics of Parenting*. Boston, MA: Houghton Mifflin.

Feigelman, W. (1986) Don't stigmatize the adopted (letter to the editor). *The New York Times*, March.

Freud, S. (1920) *Beyond the Pleasure Principle. Standard Edition*, 18: 3–64. London: Hogarth Press, 1955.

—— (1930) *Civilization and its Discontents. Standard Edition*, 21: 57–145. London: Hogarth Press, 1961.

Grimm, S. (2002) Sealed records and adoption reform: an historical perspective. www.bastards.org/activism/reform.htm, March 31.

Kirk, D. (1964) *Shared Fate*. New York: Free Press.

Kirschner, D. (1975) Son of Sam and the search for identity. *Adelphi Society for Psychoanalysis and Psychotherapy Newsletter*, June: 7–9.

—— (1980) The Adopted Child Syndrome: a study of some characteristics of disturbed adopted children. *Report of the South Shore Institute for Advanced Studies*. Merrick, NY: South Shore Institute for Advanced Studies.

—— (1988) Is there a pathological adoption syndrome? Paper presented at the American Adoption Congress National Conference, Boston, MA, May.

—— (1990) The Adopted Child Syndrome: considerations for psychotherapy. *Psychotherapy in Private Practice*, 8: 93–100.

—— (1992) Understanding adoptees who kill: dissociation, patricide, and the psychodynamics of adoption. *International Journal of Offender Therapy and Comparative Criminology*, 36: 323–333.

—— (1993) Understanding Adoptees Who Kill. Paper presented at the national convention of the Council for Equal Rights in Adoption, New York City.

—— (1995) Adoption psychopathology and the adopted child syndrome. *Directions in Child & Adolescent Therapy*, 2: 3–13.

—— (2006) *Adoption: Unchartered Waters*. New York: Juneau Press.

Kirschner, D. and Nagel, L.S. (1996) Catathymic violence, dissociation, and adoption pathology: implications for the mental status defense. *International Journal of Offender Therapy and Comparative Criminology*, 40: 204–211.

Klagsbrun, F. (1986) Debunking the Adopted Child Syndrome. *Ms Magazine*, October.

Kubler-Ross, E. (1997) *On Death and Dying*. New York: Scribner.

Levin, J. and Fox, J.A. (1985) *Mass Murder, America's Growing Menace*. New York: Plenum.

Lifton, B.J. (1986) How the adoption system ignites a fire. *The New York Times*, March 1.

—— (1988) *Lost and Found: The Adoption Experience*. New York: Harper & Row.

Magid, K. (1988) *High Risk: Children without a Conscience*. New York: Bantam.

National Association of Homes for Children (1986) *Caring*, 11: 4–7, Millbrook, NY: National Association of Homes for Children.

Norris, J. (1989) *Serial Killers*. New York: Anchor.

Paton, J.M. (1968) *Orphan Voyage*. New York: Vantage.

Pierce, W. (1990) "Family secret," *CBS News: 48 Hours*. Cable News Network. November 28, transcript 132.

Pulitzer, L.B. and Swirsky, J. (1994) *Crossing the Line: The True Story of Long Island Serial Killer Joel Rifkin*. New York: Berkley.

Steed, C.A. (1989) Children of adoption: are they at greater psychological risk? A critical review of the literature. Paper, University of Minnesota Counseling and Student Personnel Program.

Verrier, N.N. (1993) *The Primal Wound: Understanding the Adopted Child*. Baltimore, MD: Gateway Press.

Chapter 12

What is paranoia in a paranoid world?

Transference and countertransference in the wake of the World Trade Center attack

Veronica Fiske

In the aftermath of the World Trade Center attack, both therapists and patients in New York City have suffered from the loss of perceived safety in the world as well as in the therapeutic setting. We have all been bombarded with images of the dead and sensory experiences of smelling the smoke and tasting the dust that remind us of the burned bodies of those who died. Living in this atmosphere of the crematorium, therapists and patients struggle to find some kind of relief or equilibrium. When listening to repeated accounts of terror by those patients who were at or near to "Ground Zero," therapists may experience vicarious traumatization. When successive clients described flashbacks to their escapes, I, too, began to have intrusive visual images of terrified crowds, imagined hearing the clattering of feet desperately running down endless flights of stairs, and felt the choking panic engendered by being enveloped in blinding dust clouds. While safety is particularly disrupted for trauma survivors, therapists may also be subject to feelings of vulnerability both from vicarious trauma and, in this present situation, from the actuality of living in a threatened environment. Furthermore, this climate of fear did not descend on a vacuum; both patients and therapists have their own histories of previous experience of trauma and ways of coping. Finding clarity about how to conceptualize the way clients respond to this extraordinary situation becomes difficult. What is paranoia when there is a real threat?

On the morning of September 11, I walked out of my private office in downtown Manhattan and joined the crowd of stunned pedestrians standing in the middle of Sixth Avenue. We silently gazed at the clearly visible tail end of a plane sticking out of the World Trade Center surrounded by an aureole of flames. This surreal moment floats in my mind as the beginning of the end of normality for New York, my work, my patients, and myself, for some time to come. By the next day, my office was behind the first set of barricades limiting access of all cars and non-residents. Walls became covered with the poignant flyers of photos of the so-called "missing" from the Word Trade Center. The pictures were mostly family photos showing smiling men and women at family gatherings, on holiday and in the office. We all knew the "missing" were really dead. Everyday, going to my private practice, I had run the gauntlet of hundreds of faces of the dead, symbols of grief and denial of unimaginable tragedy. Each flyer represented a family that had gone down in flames along with the buildings. They always made me cry a little. At the same time, I was guiltily aware that I experienced a certain excitement at being close to the war zone and longed to work more directly with victims for reasons that included wanting to be helpful but also wanting to regain a sense of control in a somewhat voyeuristic way.

Initially I had facilitated a critical incident debriefing with the emergency medical technicians (EMT) who had been sent to the site. They had lost many co-workers. One of them had been buried for seven hours. As a group, they traditionally espoused values of being tough and unaffected by trauma. "Oh we've seen it all before," one young man explained. When I said I thought that was not quite true, he agreed, but said his only problem were a number of somatic complaints. Eventually stories of the experience began to unfold, coupled with fears they might appear weak. A young woman asked, "Is it OK to cry all the time?"

Two work partners described getting separated at the site. They commented on how strange it was, not being able to see the terrain and being approached by the wounded and frightened victims for medical assistance. Despite this, they were calm and not afraid as long as they were together. However, their cell phone wasn't working and the female partner felt impelled to go and telephone her family to tell them not to worry. When she emerged from the building, the dust cloud was worse. She could not find her partner. She began to panic and fear she might be lost forever, peering through the gloom, unable to get her bearings. Her male counterpart grew afraid and uncertain when she did not return and began desperately shouting her name. They felt it was a miracle when they finally found each other. "Your partner is everything," the woman said. They also told me that the ones who suffered the worst, the ones who had pulled their friends' bodies out of the rubble, did not want to talk about it at all.

I could easily relate to these workers' reliance on their toughness. They had selected a job that is extremely intense even in less drastic times. I, too, felt drawn to intense experience. I had often chosen adventures in my life and even as a clinician had appreciated working with more disturbed and traumatized clients. I imagine that these choices may reflect both some reaction formation and also a way to avoid the deadening of dissociation by transforming it into excitement. I was uncomfortably aware that I was quite disappointed that the more traumatized workers did not want to talk to me. The violence of the attack, and perhaps the symbolic castration of the towers, held an almost erotic fascination for me; I wanted to hear horror stories.

Thus I was excited when I was referred a 35-year-old, divorced, Guyanese woman named Mia as part of an assistance program to help victims of the World Trade Center attack. She had worked a temporary job on the twenty-fifth floor of Tower 1. She described how she was so terrified when the plane hit, she felt paralyzed. Some colleagues were saying they should stay put. Her co-worker, Trudy, insisted they immediately go down the stairs. She vividly described how she kept stopping, but Trudy kept dragging her on. She saw people going up the stairs or who had stopped, and later realized they probably had not made it. It was hard to see. Smoke was everywhere. She kept asking to stop but Trudy forced her to keep running down. She lost her shoes in the process but Trudy did not let her go until they were outside. "Trudy saved me," she said.

> There were clouds of dust and it was hard to know where we were. We asked some people where to go. Trudy went off to try and get the Staten Island ferry and I went to go uptown. My feet were bleeding on the stones. At one point I remember kicking a foot in the rubble and I didn't know if it was alive or dead or whether it was attached to a body.

I asked her what she most wanted to forget. It was when she turned and saw one of the people who jumped off the higher floors land right behind her. She kept seeing him. A young man in a gray suit and black shoes. She kept seeing his shoes. She also kept smelling the smoke everywhere, even when others could not. In my clinic office, where I could smell nothing, she kept saying "Don't you smell it? I'm choking."

Prior to the attack, Mia had exemplified the idea of an immigrant success story. Her father had died when she was young, resulting in considerable financial hardship. When she came to the United States at age 19, she was determined to establish herself. She learned some secretarial and book-keeping skills and worked two and three jobs until, at the age of 32, she succeeded in buying her own house in Rockaway, near Kennedy Airport. After the attack, she became a different person. She was unable to take public transport and was often unable to leave the house. She had difficulty making her therapy appointments at the right time. Her need to talk about her trauma was coupled with feelings that no one could understand who had not had the same experience. I tried to express confidence we could work through this together, but I began to feel uncertain whether being a witness to her experience was going to be enough to help her. "I keep thinking a plane may crash into my house," she said. Probably due to my own anxiety vicariously re-experiencing her horror story at every session, I foolishly tried to reassure her that was unlikely. Her vivid flashbacks to falling rubble and falling bodies were too intense to be mollified.

On November 12, the impossible happened. An American jet crashed into Rockaway, about two miles from where she lived. When I heard about it, I thought of her immediately and called. "You see," she said sadly, "Everyone told me it couldn't happen – but it did." She missed her next few sessions and told me in telephone conversations she had moved her bed and all possessions into her basement and was barricaded in, unable to go upstairs, let alone outside. Her family was bringing her food. Her cousin stayed with her when she could. On top of this, she was in a financial crisis, unable to work or to pay her mortgage and her bills. When I finally did see her, she told me she had gone to apply for financial assistance at a Red Cross center, but they were all evacuated because there had been a bomb scare. Furthermore, she had discovered that her rescuer, Trudy, had not made it to Staten Island. Despite having escaped Tower 1, she had apparently been buried when the second tower collapsed. This final horrible irony made me feel as if we were both buried under the weight of too many traumas. "Is this too much for you?" she asked, perceptively. I became aware that although listening to her story held a grim fascination for me, I was feeling increasingly incompetent to assist her therapeutically. I commented that while her experiences were certainly too much, I was willing to hear them. I also admitted being troubled that I was not sure how to be helpful. She brightened up at this and said she did not want to talk about the horror any more. Her goal was to regain her life and focus on the future, not the traumas. We began discussing concrete ways to achieve this, including selling her house (to avoid living by the airport), going back to school, or moving to Florida with family members. Although I might not have had her traumatic experience, joining together in feelings of helplessness paradoxically allowed her to regain her previous motivation to succeed.

As it happened, the best remedy for Mia was something I had never even considered. At the next session, she came with a beautiful little dog tucked into her coat. The dog gazed at her adoringly and licked her face. She now had to leave her house several times a day to walk the dog. "I love him so much," she said, looking happy for the first time since I had met her. Not long after, she moved away to Florida.

Later, I discovered that dogs were used very effectively with withdrawn children at the Pier 94 Family Assistance Program services for victims of 9/ 11 (Coates et al., 2003). Once the children were able to make contact with the dogs, they became more responsive to staff.

Melanie Klein (1946) characterized the paranoid-schizoid position as the developmental phase when good objects are introjected and bad objects disowned and projected. If the persecutory fears inherent in this stage are too strong, then the necessary integrations of love and hate, hope and despair, rupture and reparation are impeded, compromising the working through of the depressive position. This failure may then lead to regressive reinforcement of persecutory fears as fixation points for later severe psychopathology. If previously traumatized patients already tend to resort to the defenses of splitting and projective identification, it is hardly surprising that these tendencies have recently increased. For therapists, already subject to their own fears, these responses may prove difficult to tolerate and metabolize. Furthermore, the paranoid-schizoid position tends to be temporarily re-evoked in all of us when external threats predominate.

The week following September 11, I was scheduled to move jobs in the city hospital where I work. My new assignment was working an outpatient clinic, taking over the practice of a colleague, Dr. S., who specialized in the treatment of Dissociative Identity Disorder. Taking on someone else's patients is always a difficult situation for both patients and clinician. As the replacement for a much loved therapist, the new clinician inevitably evokes feelings of anger and resentment for being a poor substitute and, on some level, is seen as having caused the loss. Added to this was the new trauma of September 11. It was not surprising that several of these patients had resorted to an increased use of the rageful aspects of their personalities.

The first patient I saw on my new job was Michelle, a slender, 50-year-old African American woman with a history of severe, early-childhood, sexual and physical abuse. She came to our first meeting wearing a skin-tight jeans and denim jacket ensemble, complete with a large American flag transposed onto the jacket, which was decorated with red, white and blue sequins. She also wore a red, white and blue sequined cap. "I am only wearing red, white and blue from now on," she said, glaring at my green dress. "You're not American, are you?" I admitted that was so and asked to whom I was speaking. She scornfully said she was Sandi, her angry persona. "Dr. S. could always tell." She went on to express fury that American Muslims had objected to racial profiling. "We blacks have always had to deal with this. And we are American. We have fought for America, to keep it Independent." As she continued to pour racial and national scorn on Muslims, I felt increasingly that it was also I that was being attacked. I asked her if it was hard for her to have a new therapist who was white and not American. She gave me a withering look. "I don't even know you. Why should I care about you? And Dr. S. was white. But she was good!" She scowled at me. She did not comment on my nationality. She then continued her diatribe by laughing at recent cases of Muslims being physically assaulted and even killed following September 11. "If they don't like it they should go back to where they came from." She was the first of several patients to express these sentiments. I felt nauseated and assaulted at the end of this session.

In their attempts to regroup fragile egos, and to regain a sense of control, some previously traumatized patients resorted to racist diatribes and to railing against all foreigners. As a foreigner, I felt I was being attacked as the potential assassin, or the "other," during these outbursts. What part of this was a projection of their paranoia of being persecuted and what part was my paranoia about being different in an increasingly xenophobic world was hard to determine. At times, some patients seemed like terrorists to me in the implacability of their hatred of others. At times, I believe I was viewed as an alien invader. Attempts to discuss possible transference issues were scornfully shot down. In fact, being white and European, I was probably not always their idea of the alien. It may have been my paranoia in my identification with the other that made me feel personally attacked. Under threat, we all reverted to a Kleinian, paranoid-schizoid position.

My ambivalence about how to respond to the crisis was out of sync with my surroundings. The United States as a whole seemed determined to maintain a dichotomy between "us" and "them" in order to pursue war. In the name of safety and patriotism, civil liberties were disrupted. President Bush declaimed, "You're either with us or you are with the terrorists" prior to bombing Afghanistan. My own history as a cultural outsider with anti-war and anti-establishment sentiments suddenly seemed frighteningly unacceptable in this simplistic New World. I was unable to endorse the mainstream patriotic ideal, not because I did not care about the victims, but because I also identified with the other potential Afghani victims. As my co-workers, friends and patients became more and more identified with being American, with concomitant hatred of the terrorist, I became increasingly identified with the other. As their enthusiasm for bombing Afghanistan increased, I kept seeing children in Afghan villages getting shot.

My own paranoia began to increase in direct proportion to the number of American flags on display. I no longer saw them as symbols of solidarity and support, but as exclusionary, dangerous symbols of war. I feared for the future because of what the United States might do. I felt responsible for my adopted country, but powerless and voiceless to affect it. I feared that America's aggression and desire for revenge would further incite terrorists. I feared my nonconformist beliefs would make me a target. I was afraid to speak, thinking I would be attacked. In New York, questions about the advisability or morality of ongoing bombing did not seem to be acceptable ideas to express, even within the analytic community.

I had been working with a number of paranoid patients prior to September 11.

One of the most challenging was Ursula, a 70-year-old, married woman I had been seeing privately, once a week, for about two years. A colleague who was treating her son and hoped to rescue him from her clutches had referred her to me. This son had been hospitalized for such severe anorexia that he had to be placed on a respirator to survive. The anorexia had been largely the result of chronic addiction to Valium. He had rarely left the house in the preceding twenty years. Ursula had provided the Valium after doctors refused to continue to prescribe it. "What could I do?" she said. "He got so upset without it."

Ursula is an obese woman who looks younger than her stated age. She usually dresses casually in cheap stretch pants with long T-shirts decorated with applique designs. Her heavy make-up is always flawless and her bleached-blond hair elaborately coifed. It is still possible to see she must have been very pretty when young. Her reason for seeking treatment was that she felt stressed both by her son's illness and by her mother's recent death.

She is the middle child of a second-generation, Catholic, Irish-American family. She had an older and a younger brother. Her father was alcoholic. Becoming increasingly dysfunctional during her childhood, he was eventually unable to work. She described her mother as a good, hard-working woman who had had to both raise the family and clean offices to support them, so had little time for her. Ursula was her father's favorite and described herself as a beauty but her mother appears to have preferred her brothers. She described several traumatic events when she was young. Her father would take the kids far from home, leave them outside some bar, and forget about them. They would then have to find their own way home. On one occasion when she was about 5, she was left on the subway, resulting in a lifelong fear of public transportation. Despite this, she never blamed her father, but felt he could not help himself. As a late teenager, when her father already had cirrhosis of the liver, she used to sneak him alcohol. When I asked why, she said she felt "sorry for him." At 19, she married a quiet, dull man largely because of her need for stability and her fear she might not be able to retain her virginity for long. They had three children (a son, then two daughters).

Initially, she was hesitant to tell me many things and refused to let me write notes. Her presentation was confusing and vague. Her speech was tangential. She frequently misused words, rarely finished sentences, would never say what period of her life she was talking about, and refused to name people she was talking about. Instead, she would whisper in a conspiratorial way, "You know – that guy!" It turned out there were many different "that guys!" Early on in her marriage, she had regularly gone dancing and drinking with a girlfriend on Saturday nights and had a number of different lovers. One of these men prostituted her to his friends, about which she had confused feelings. She enjoyed the attention and liked feeling she was helpful to her lover, but had a vague idea that this was not quite right. She was a lot guiltier about a Jewish lover about whom she cared deeply. She even contemplated leaving her husband for him, but was afraid of losing her family. Eventually they broke up and she never again had an affair.

Following the end of this relationship, she had what she described as a "nervous breakdown" and went to a psychiatrist. This visit had been traumatic for her and she always refused further psychiatric care. For some weeks, she was unwilling to say what it was that the psychiatrist had done. Eventually she admitted that the terrible wrong he had committed was to ask, "Do you think people use you?" Despite having no prior connection with this psychiatrist, nor having told him her history of sexual infidelities, she believed he somehow knew all about her. Furthermore, she saw hidden meanings in his statement. "You know what he meant?" she asked. "He meant, 'Do you think people Jews you?'" She was surprised I did not immediately understand this obvious connection. This combination of paranoid fears that others knew about her past coupled with delusions about secret messages in words, images, or music proved to be a pattern. She felt others were communicating with her when she had any associations to her youthful indiscretions, even though they had occurred some forty years earlier. Thus she became anxious when she saw a laundry van with the logo, "Aphrodite," because she had once attended a club of that name and assumed the van driver knew about it. She saw a newspaper picture of a female police officer that looked like her, and assumed it was a message that she might be exposed. She heard a 1950s pop song that had been her favorite playing in a store and thought the storeowners must know something. Eventually we developed a language to talk about these concerns when I commented that she "read too much into things." She began to question her delusions.

Lacan (1966) characterizes psychosis and paranoia as being defined by the foreclosure of the Name-of-the-Father (the paternal function). The Name-of-the-Father sets in place the symbolic order, allowing for the acquisition of language, with its underlying structure, and confers identity on the subject (positions him in the symbolic order). In psychosis, there is a hole in the symbolic order, resulting in disturbance of both language and identity. For Lacan (1966), a diagnosis of psychosis cannot be made without a disturbance in language.

Ursula, who had no access to a reliable paternal figure, exemplifies such a deficit in the symbolic order. Her language is vague and idiosyncratic, with frequent neologisms. She constantly questions who she is, and cannot differentiate between her mental associations and external reality. In Lacanian terms, without the symbolic Other, she is faced with the imaginary other who negates and kills her. In paranoia, the phenomenon of persecution is part of the category of imaginary relations.

It was difficult to deal with her vicious tirades about people she deemed as "others." Struggling with issues of identity, she often expressed puzzlement as to what group others thought she belonged to. "I know I'm Irish but maybe they see me as Italian or Jewish." These categories made up her set of "us" versus "them." For everyone else, Ursula was remarkably indiscriminate in her racial and group abuse. She railed against African Americans, Mexicans, Guyanese, Chinese, etc. She reserved particular scorn for anyone who did not speak English. She was outraged hearing foreign languages, in part because she felt excluded. "This is America," she would say. "They should speak English or go back to where they came from." She expressed hatred against Democrats and homosexuals. All these groups were ugly, disgusting, and dirty. With the least provocation, she verbally attacked any group member with whom she came in contact. Whenever she perceived a slight or a threat, she went for the jugular. When her son was hospitalized, she was outraged that the hospital staff cast aspersions on her competency as a mother and implied that she was somewhat to blame for her son's illness. She triumphantly told me about calling a black nurse a junkie with AIDS because she looked at her "funny," and telling the psychiatrist his mother must have been garbage to have made her son a faggot. Each session represented a challenge for me, as she spewed her vitriolic rage against others. I felt silenced by fear of my unexpressed dislike of her at these times. When I became exhausted from her hatred, I found myself goaded into challenging her beliefs and behavior. This was always entirely unsatisfactory.

After September 11, both her paranoia and her rage against the "other" increased. She was furious the attack had not been prevented and blamed liberals for allowing immigrants into the country. She not only thoroughly endorsed the bombing in Afghanistan but also thought many other countries should be bombed as well. When I asked what countries she had in mind, she said, "All them Pakistinians, Muslims, Guyanis, Hindus." When I attempted to clarify that Pakistanis and Palestinians were not the same nationality and that Hindus were not a nationality but a religious group, she was scornful. "They're all the same. If they're not with America, we should bomb them." She became increasingly suspicious that most of her immigrant neighbors might be terrorists, largely because they used cell phones. She hurled abuse at a woman who bumped into her on a crowded street because she was wearing a headscarf. In October, she told me she had a terrible scare. She had gone to buy a loaf of Wonderbread and had become frightened because the cashier was wearing some headdress and she concluded he was "one of them Pakistinians." Three days later, she developed a tiny blister on her finger and concluded that there must have been Anthrax in the bread. Only going to the doctor and getting tested slightly alleviated her terror. Aware of my own paranoia at this time, I empathized with her fears of malevolent others and commented on how difficult it was to be in a world that felt so unsafe. At last I could better tolerate and metabolize her fury.

Shortly thereafter, I began to respond differently to both her paranoid ideas and racial attacks. I found myself affectionately laughing at her. Initially a little surprised, she quickly joined me and laughed as well. "I know," she would say. "You think I'm reading too much into it" or, "You think I'm too hateful." We would laugh together, despite seeing things differently. No longer feeling I was silently colluding with her paranoia and racism freed me to work more effectively.

Writing about September 11, Susan Coates (2003) noted:

> Trauma and human relatedness can be seen as inversely related terms. The greater the strength of human bonds that connect an individual to others, and the more those bonds are accessible in times of danger, the less likely it is that an individual will be severely traumatized and the more likely it is that he or she may recover afterwards.
>
> (Coates, 2003, pp. 3–4)

While the immediacy and severity of the danger experienced obviously impacts the extent of traumatic responses, resilience in the face of trauma is mediated both by the security of early attachment in childhood and by the availability of present social support. Many authors have written about the importance of human connection as a protection against traumatic response and a lack of connection as exacerbating it. Thus, in a study of London children during the German Blitz, Anna Freud and Dorothy Burlingham (1943) noted that children were less upset by the bombing than by evacuation to the country as protection from it. Bretherton (1995) described how hospitalized children may be more traumatized by separation from parents than by surgery itself. Similarly, Fairbairn (1943) reported that soldiers were prone to breakdown when disconnected from their commanding officers.

When examining both my own and my patient's responses to the trauma of September 11, it was this need for human bonds to reduce paranoia that was most striking. Being a foreigner without family in the United States undoubtedly exacerbated my paranoia. Conversely, discussing my feelings with friends relieved it. The EMT workers I met clearly stated that connection with their partner was of primary importance in coping with trauma. Mia, who suffered multiple traumas and had lost her father at an early age, was initially less resilient. It was her connection with her dog, and perhaps my improved ability to resonate with her helplessness, that allowed her to begin to recover. Ursula, although less directly impacted by the actual events, was more vulnerable to any perceived threat, because of deficits in her early attachments. It was only when I could engage with her that we could escape our previous hostile enactment. She was also therapeutic for me. Seeing my fears in her delusions allowed me to play again. In a dangerous world, where splitting and projection became the defense of choice, feeling more connected helped diminish paranoia.

References

Bretherton, I. (1995) The origins of attachment theory: John Bowlby and Mary Ainsworth. In S. Goldberg, R. Muir and J. Kerr (eds) *Attachment Theory*, pp. 50–84, Hillside, NJ: Analytic Press.

Coates, S.W. (2003) Introduction: trauma and human bonds. In S.W. Coates, J.L. Rosenthal and D.S. Schechter (eds) *September 11: Trauma and Human Bonds*, pp. 1–14. Hillside, NJ: Analytic Press.

Coates, S.W., Schechter, D.S. and First, E. (2003) Brief interventions with traumatized children and families after September 11. In S.W. Coates, J.L. Rosenthal and D.S. Schechter (eds) *September 11: Trauma and Human Bonds*, pp. 23–49. Hillside, NJ: Analytic Press.

Fairbairn, W.R.D. (1943) The war neurosis: their nature and significance. In W.R.D. Fairbairn, *Psychoanalytic Studies of the Personality*, pp. 256–288. New York: Routledge, 1994.

Freud, A. and Burlingham, D. (1943) *Children in War*. New York: Medical War Books.

Klein, M. (1946) Notes on some schizoid mechanisms. In M. Klein (ed.) *Envy and Gratitude and Other Works 1946–1963*, pp. 1–24, New York: Delacourt Press/ Seymour Lawrence, 1975.

Lacan, J. (1966) *Ecrits: A Selection*. Trans. A. Sheridan. New York: Norton, 1977.

Chapter 13

Just some everyday examples of psychic serial killing

Psychoanalysis, necessary ruthlessness, and disenfranchisement

Mark B. Borg

> Efficiency and progress is ours once more.
> (Jello Biafra, 1980)

When I was a candidate in psychoanalytic training, one of my supervisors made a passing comment that has remained with me as a faint, yet reverberating echo. She said of the patient we were discussing: "She lacks an absolutely necessary ruthlessness." This necessary ruthlessness, as I understood my supervisor then and am using the term now, is the ability to inattend and dissociate extremely anxiety-provoking stimuli – stimuli that, when integrated into one's ongoing sense of self, are detrimental to one's psychological functioning. These are the stimuli which, unblocked by "necessary" dissociative defenses, cause us to experience a chaotic overflowing of unsymbolized affect – what Sullivan (1953) called "uncanny emotions." I hypothesize, therefore, that ruthlessness is necessary in the maintenance of one's ongoing, continuous experience of oneself in the world. In this chapter, I delineate some of the essential ingredients of a culture of ruthlessness and go on to explore the maintenance of necessary ruthlessness in three analytic patients. I approach the issue with the assumption that the ability to maintain necessary ruthlessness exists along a continuum from total ruthlessness (i.e., complete indifference to the plight of others) to the total breakdown, over time, of the ability to maintain this necessary defensive barrier. My three cases explore different points on this continuum. One will also be used to examine the possibility that we can, if we explore our own ruthlessness, find a constructive balance point.

A culture of "necessary ruthlessness"

Western societies in general seem to be breeding pools for the development and proliferation of remedies – social, personal, and cultural – for just about anything that might cause discomfort. This includes not only pain and anxiety, but also their derivatives: irritation, frustration, sadness, anger, and so on. These remedies might serve as *palliatives* that reduce our pain and suffering at the cost of losing any and all hope of recovering from whatever causes underlie the symptoms that are being alleviated (Borg, 2004a). These remedies help individuals to dissociate awareness of the suffering around us. They shore up our capacity for necessary ruthlessness. On this note, I wrote:

> Human – that is, emotional – responses to everyday stimuli are increasingly pathologized, and we are increasingly promised the obliteration of all personal suffering. Yet at the core of all these *human responses* to suffering that need remedy is a deep sense of empathy with the struggles of existing at this time in this society, in a state of perpetual dread over the immense social problems that infect those around us, and that seem (and often are) insurmountable.
>
> (Borg, 2004a, p. 215)

It seems in our society it is the experience of empathy that is most feared, most defended against, and most abstained from – as if compassion is the ultimate contagion that, if experienced in full force, would lead to break down.

Some of the essential characteristics of a culture that unconsciously implements *necessary ruthlessness* are consistent with the sociological analyses of Bellah *et al.* (1985) who described a general American movement toward *liberal individualism*. They asserted that the definitive aim of life in such a society is to promote fulfillment (in the form of increased satisfaction and decreased discomfort or pain) for individuals instead of groups or communities. By individualizing fulfillment, people in such a culture are set up to, and supported in the practice of ignoring (dissociating) the suffering of others, enacting ruthlessness as a status quo approach to living, making it seem (and often actually be) *necessary*. The underside of the argument presented by Bellah *et al.* – and others, such as Amitai Etzioni (1991) – is a kind of "new communitarianism" that defines *community* as prior to individual rights and calls for a return to traditional social institutions such as religion and the family (Bell, 1992; Samuels, 2001). The new communitarians largely uphold the liberal Western tradition, criticizing deviations or threats to this tradition (Ellin, 1999). In this process, they wind up repeating the elitist underpinning of the very system they criticize, becoming the watchdogs of their own version of the "good life."

Other authors have analyzed the pervasiveness of this liberal individualism perspective in many social and cultural institutions (including psychotherapy and the social sciences) in capitalist societies, particularly the United States (Taylor, 1992; Richardson *et al.*, 1999). However, there is a sense that some of the ways that the major critiques of liberal individualism themselves have been framed supports a kind of "America as Empire" philosophy (Clarke and Hoggett, 2004; Garrison, 2004; Johnson, 2004) that overlooks crucial issues related to race, class and gender bias (Giroux, 2003; Clarke, 2004; Schultheis, 2004). As a character defense on a societal level, the necessary ruthlessness underlying liberal individualism allows us to avoid acknowledging the social consequences of a sanctioned perspective that supports fulfillment for some and suffering for others. As this perspective becomes rigidified, it functions as an ideology. By ideology, I mean, "those values and assumptions about the world which have implications for the control and allocation of limited resources" (Knox, 1995, p. 3). Consistent with such a notion of ideology, control and allocation processes are dissociated; problems and fulfillments become increasingly individualized, separated from their social and cultural influences and etiologies (Said, 1993; Zizek, 2004). The inability to empathize with both self and other diminishes the potential for subversive or revolutionary processes to exert any impact on societal transformations or daily functions. The phenomenon is clearly expressed in the final volume of the *Dune* saga, when Frank Herbert (1985) states that "Rules are often an excuse to ignore compassion" (p. 78). Nowadays there are many examples of compassion being pushed aside in favor of rules and regulations that diminish our awareness of our collective fragility.

When awareness of pain and suffering – whether on the level of individuals, communities, or groups – is reduced through the use of necessary ruthlessness, what remains is a form of chronic crisis that is so muffled that even those who suffer from it don't know how to respond. This process not only supports a "victim-blaming ideology" (Ryan, 1971), but also establishes a framework for defining social problems in terms of social conditions (e.g., poverty, racism, poor healthcare) and the groups that allegedly engender them (Seidman and Rappaport, 1986; Warren, 2001). The conditions inherent in the dynamics of necessary ruthlessness concretize the split between the subjectified self and the objectified (or "inanimate") other (Fanon, 1968; Freire, 1970; Blackwell, 2003).

I hope to show in the following case examples how certain aspects of these cultural dynamics may become internalized and enacted in our relationships with those around us (including analysts and patients) and contribute, as well, to our own sense of self.

Malfunctioning ruthlessness

Over the course of a three-year analysis, Deborah, a middle-class African American woman in her late twenties, became increasingly unable to pass a suffering stranger on the street (in New York City) without experiencing acute anxiety. (Deborah is the woman that my supervisor was addressing when she mentioned the lack of "necessary ruthlessness.") She ruminated incessantly about a vast and undifferentiated category of people who were homeless and mentally ill. Her experience of "those who suffer" had collapsed into a monolithic symbol that served to limit her needs, indict her frivolous desires, and expose her wishes as the petty complaints of a "spoiled child." Deborah "recognized" the absurdity of her own wishes and desires in the glaring contrast that confronted her gaze each time she left her apartment. She asked herself, "How can I live with the injustice of how much I have versus how much others need?"

Deborah's father died when she was 4 years old. Her family had attempted to save her from the loss by denying the impact of his death, and she had feelings of betrayal about this. Apparently her father had engaged in a similar denial right up until the moment of his death, when he called her from the hospital to say goodbye. "What," she wondered, "did my father do to suppress, for me, his unbearable emotions?" Her sense was that he had expended his very last breaths in his attempt to save her from his (or perhaps her) suffering. Was her father in extremis while she, a child, ruthlessly went on wanting and needing? Deborah lived from then on in a perpetual attempt to answer the unanswerable question: Whose needs should have been met – her father's, the man who was dying, or his 4-year-old daughter's? She recognized what she imagined to have been his unbearable emotions in the eyes of the homeless and mentally ill. It was not until well into her analysis that she began to recognize this process whereby she had forfeited her capacity for ruthlessness and to assess the damage to her professional and personal life that was the result. As it turned out, this was not a forfeiture she was willing to reverse. Upon termination, Deborah moved to Arizona where she imagined that she would be less exposed to the suffering of others, and so not have to lose her "compassion."

"But that would be illegal"

Another patient, Jeff, began his session in a clearly exasperated state, revealing that he had been accosted in the street by "one of those crazy homeless people." This statement was ironic, considering that this 32-year-old, Caucasian man was the director of an agency that worked to house such (mentally ill/homeless) people in the Bronx. "What happened?" I asked. Jeff said that as he approached my office, an apparently homeless man had asked, "Do you have a quarter?" In an act that my patient recognized as being somewhat "strategic" (his euphemism for aggressive), he did not answer. The man then shouted, "Don't you speak English?" Jeff turned to him and, "uncharacteristically, but calmly" said, "Fuck you." The homeless man, now a few paces away, dropped his bag and began to approach Jeff. Jeff, dropping his briefcase, also began to move toward what he was imaging would be physical contact (another euphemism – a fight). "What entitles you to my money?" he hissed. "At least I asked," said the man, "I could have just killed you." Infuriated and terrified, Jeff said, "Come on then." At that point, the homeless man stopped, looked into Jeff's eyes and said, "You mean you want to fight?" My patient also stopped and was silent. The man went back to his bag and picked it up. "But that would be illegal," he said, and began to move on, leaving Jeff stupefied and trembling.

What had happened? Jeff and I explored this interaction which we came to refer to as a "border crossing." Although humiliated by his increased awareness of his own capacity for ruthlessness, Jeff also began to experience a sense of paradox: in order to be able to be compassionate in his day-to-day work, he had to be able to dissociate his ongoing experience of the very pain that those with whom he worked lived with constantly. Jeff was willing to explore what this interaction said about him and his relationship to his work, as well as about our interaction (Why did he feel so ashamed? Why did he experience my questions about the interaction as being so judgmental? etc.).

This interaction was a crossing wherein, from Jeff's point of view, a generally unseen *Other* (who had been, in an instant, summed up as homeless and, perhaps, mentally ill) became a real obstacle to the well-honed image that he used to navigate his way through his life. The man had somehow invaded the boundaries of Jeff's generally integrated, continuous, well-defended sense of self. After all, Jeff had been in analysis for three years and had attained some sense of what existed beyond those (conscious) boundaries, and even of how he himself had been historically forbidden to see, let alone exhibit, those contents. Did the homeless man suddenly manifest what lay beyond those seemingly impenetrable socially constructed walls? Had an aspect of himself that Jeff thought had been securely put to rest (i.e., killed) suddenly been resurrected?

Or inversely, Jeff wondered, had he somehow inadvertently stumbled into the position of denying existence to the homeless man? Was he one of those who deprive and withhold? One of those who withhold, most essentially, the acknowledgment of existence? In an act of defiance and protest, that man had pushed his subjectivity across a threshold of regulated spatial and emotional distance to evoke a near-violent moment of co-participation that refused suppression. Perhaps this was a (or another) last-ditch effort for this man to, if not reclaim his humanity, at least turn the tables on an archaic, generally condoned, enacted murder.

In the borderlands

Jeff and I began exploring this "experience in the borderlands." He had been forcibly yanked out of his position of necessary ruthlessness. He had a sense that the area that he inhabited without it existed at the boundary of his own defensive system, and that the emotions that ignited within him in his engagement with the homeless man were not actually alien to his experience. It was as if the interaction suddenly outlined the perimeter (perhaps uncomfortably close) of his own sense of marginality; as if it brought him too close to some implicit and standardized measuring stick against which he could never measure up.

Fuery and Mansfield (2000), considering the violence inherent in identity formation and maintenance, suggest that "the identifying group consolidates its sense of collective selfhood by nominating and defining what is other to it. The identity thus created inscribes two kinds of possible selfhood, therefore: the identifying self, and the counter-identified other" (p. 145). This process is the reduction of the other to the same (or self). The other loses his/her/its independence, and becomes merely an inferior (or otherwise outwardly projected) version of the dominant self. And, of course, a version of self that, in comparison, offsets one's own feeling of lack. The other, therefore, is represented as a sort of blind spot in the standard economy of representation – a blind spot sustained by necessary ruthlessness.

The function of identity is to stabilize our experiences in the world, to make ourselves something that will not only be secure, but also be continually validated by the world around us. The something that we appear to be must be something that has meaning to (is valid to) others, and to the massive, impenetrable social forces that others represent. We do not so much express our inner natures in our identities as we perform identities in order to give the impression that we have a recognizable, orthodox, acceptable, inner nature (Butler, 1993, 2003). In this performance, guilt, over-identification, and a usually warded-off aggression offset the standard collusion that generally plays out along the surface where multifaceted, internally sustained, identity conflicts become an environmentally (externally) focused category.

An exclusive focus on category provides distance from both the subjective individuality of the *Other* and the more general culture in which he or she lives. This focus wards off anxiety-provoking experiences of *Self* and *Other* that may give rise to impenetrable self-protective biases. Yet what sort of interactions do such defenses perpetrate across the *Self/Other* border? Historically, murder. The *Selves* who colonize "new" territories have historically licensed genocidal treatment of *Others* (e.g., indigenous ethnic groups) based upon whether or not they measure up to the standards of a self-defined "human enough-ness."

Perhaps in the borderlands these things of memory, things unconsciously silenced, things that were thought to have been transcended, appear in our vision, pulling us back into our breakable bodies. After all, the threat of death is constantly, if implicitly, evoked in our perpetual struggle for presence.

Hegeman (1995) has said about the process of enculturation and the anxiety that it can evoke that

> security operations arising from interaction in the interpersonal field can bring about a fear of "otherness": a stranger who does not know or follow the cultural conventions we are familiar with can behave unexpectedly and induce a great deal of anxiety.
>
> (Hegeman, 1995, p. 831)

This being the case, what would it mean to have empathy for such a person? To relinquish the ruthlessness? Would empathy and compassion require that Jeff relinquish the well-established "self-system," that is, self-experience in the context of anxiety-reducing security operations (Sullivan, 1953) that allowed him to do his job, not to mention his other routinized daily activities such as leaving his apartment, entering the subway, and so on? Would he lose the ruthlessness that allowed him not to see? And if he *were* to see, would he then see how close he himself was to not measuring up to what he believed were the requirements of his own cherished image of a functioning, successful individual in this society? Perhaps, then, the silent presence of the suffering *Other(s)* would explode into the absent space that inhabits Jeff's gaze when he looks through men such as the one he had just encountered, a man who refused to be left for dead by the silence of the unseeing.

Jeff's necessary ruthlessness collapsed in his interaction with the man who asked him for money, and Deborah lost it over time as she walked the New York City streets. These examples suggest there is a message revealed in the ruthlessness. It was spoken to the cold, unconsciously calculating machinations of a ruthless, narcissistic cynicism, a cynicism adopted by those of us inner-city dwellers who believe that we live within the margins, a cynicism that perhaps has as its motto: you do not exist if you are inconvenient.

The killer in the cross-hairs

One of my patients, Joyce, *is* mentally ill and homeless. She told me that this allowed her to experience (chronically) the "killer" in others. She felt "murdered," she said, by every act of cold, cruel indifference that was perpetrated upon her when she met the hopefully averted eyes of others as they passed her on the street. She described feeling a kind of death each and every time this happened to her – and it happened often. But what is it like for the killer who finds himself in the cross-hairs of the one who was supposed to have been killed? Jeff knew. I found out too, as I dodged a half-full cup of coffee that flew toward my head as Joyce terminated her two-year, three times per week psychoanalytic treatment with me. In that moment, and in the transference, I was the incarnation of every cold-blooded or apathetic killing that Joyce had suffered in her years of homelessness.

Joyce began treatment at age 39, after a year in a New York City homeless shelter between repeated psychiatric hospitalizations. Throughout our work, as I shifted in the transference from typical (not-to-be-too-enticed-by) object to needed (and fairly exciting) subject, Joyce's experience of being humiliated, chronically objectified, and ignored became increasingly clear to her and to me. It also became clear, after about a year of treatment, that every practitioner she had dealt with (and, with her history, there were literally hundreds) had ultimately disappointed her. When that happened, her pattern was to stage rather severe attacks in her attempts to destroy the disappointer. She enacted destruction through litigation, reports to licensing boards, claims of fraud, and so on, made against those, such as myself, who represented the apathy of the system toward her conditions.

Interestingly, both of her parents had been physicians, and had expected her to be one as well. They both died unexpectedly within a month of each other when she was 17. As she puts it, she was "orphaned." Soon after that, she was placed against her will in her first psychiatric hospital. She was released after about a year, deemed incompetent to handle her own affairs (including her inheritance), and given the status of "mentally disabled" (complete with Medicaid and Medicare benefits). So prepared, she began a lifelong pattern of chronic hospitalization and homelessness.

In the period I am reporting, we had been discussing some alternatives to Joyce's pattern of attacking the very practitioners to whom she turned for help. A month or so earlier, she had begun to write "hate" letters to the White House, complaining about her poor treatment by her numerous practitioners. This was immediately after 9/11. (Joyce's treatment is covered more thoroughly, specifically her reaction to 9/11, in Borg, 2003.) The letters were perceived by the White House staff as being quite threatening and Joyce was hospitalized for three weeks. She brought with her to the session I am describing a large shopping bag full of a new onslaught of threatening letters. Instead of sending them, she planned to give them to me for "safe-keeping." It was in the act of handing me the bag of attack letters that Joyce suddenly shifted her sights to me, and began blasting away. Could it be that in that act, the bag became the symbol of *her* necessary ruthlessness? In the moment of relinquishing it, did she become impossibly vulnerable, too overwhelmed by her experience of what it would be like to exist without it?

With her coffee-cup missile, Joyce took back her own ruthlessness and her capacity to categorize me as "practitioner," objectifying me and leaving me with a powerful, ongoing countertransference dread of an (actual) counterattack (that is, that she would report me to state boards, etc.). Oddly enough, aside from the termination of her treatment, no counter-attack ever came. In fact, the endless calls that I, as her analyst, had received from her caseworkers, her doctors, and the staff at local psychiatric hospitals throughout her treatment ceased completely after that. In the moment when she threw the coffee, I learned what it's like to be absolutely *taken out* − I no longer existed in her world.

Homeless and mentally ill

Deborah and Jeff seemed, at times, to be able to make use of the silent, death-like surface of the homeless/mentally ill category as a highly functional (albeit defensive) blank screen. This surface served as a "convenient" repository for submerged needs, desires, and generally dissociated self-states. Joyce, on the other hand, lived to ensure that the necessary ruthlessness of others would be anything but convenient − although she certainly had repositories of ruthlessness of her own. The fact of categorized difference is probably as powerful a trigger (and container) for the projection of unacceptable impulses, with resulting prejudices toward the object of the projection as we have in our culture (Holmes, 1992). Consistent with this statement, Fuery and Mansfield (2000) comment that:

> Each identity requires an inferior other that can be measured against it. The other is not something outside and alien. It is a necessary part of the identity that thinks it is using the other as something to define itself against. The outside is truly inside. The difference is truly part of the same.
>
> (Fuery and Mansfield, 2000, p. 62)

To assure my three patients' own continuous, fluid sense of existence (and to ward off the anxiety of non-existence), it appeared the individual subjectivities of numerous others had to be compressed into the static presentation of a stereotyped *Other*. In exploring such processes, Sullivan (1964) states that "anxiety and its complex derivatives prevent the progressive discrimination of significant differences between given persons and inadequate . . . stereotyped personifications" (p. 311). In one broad stroke of necessary ruthlessness, these two specific (anxiety-provoking) conditions (homelessness and mental illness) become crystallized and solidified into one vast category, a semiotic warehouse for all those who exist in society-sanctioned silence in the borderland world of the disenfranchised: "homelessmentallyill."

In this objectification, the homelessmentallyill category embraces those perceived as a threat to those inside the margins, those who fall outside our implicit bioeconomic pact to behave, to conform, to produce, to consume, to buy, to sell. Inhabitants of this category are disqualified as citizens, and emerge as a symbol of the wild fragment of nature that must be systematically disavowed. This is not a new kind of thinking. In 1764, Le Tronse, who was a judge at the presidial court of Orleans, published a treatise on vagabondage. In his evaluation, vagabonds are those who "live in the midst of society without being members of it, who wage war on all citizens, and who are in the midst of us in that state that one supposes existed before the establishment of a civil society" (quoted in Foucault, 1977, p. 88). Le Tronse went on to suggest that such people should be hunted down and killed "like wolves," as they are far more threatening. The idea of the homelessmentallyill as a crude reminder of our own primitive potentialities, and the threat that this poses to "civil society," has a long history.

As an example of such objectifying practices, psychiatric epidemiological studies since the 1960s have shown that the prevalence of psychiatric disorders is extremely high among American homeless people, with a broad consensus emerging that of the homeless people residing in shelters, about one-third have significant mental illnesses (Breakey and Thompson, 1995). Yet there is some discrepancy of opinion as to whether these illnesses are a cause or a result of homelessness (Cohen, 1993). Experience and research findings suggest that homeless people are a heterogeneous lot. Although a steely, impervious homogeneity is attributed to homelessness, and it serves as a trigger for the stimulus–response nature of the transferential reactions explored within this chapter, homeless people do not constitute a distinct class of individuals (Smith *et al.*, 1993). In fact, the National Institute of Mental Health has identified eight major subgroups among the homeless: (1) street people; (2) chronic alcoholics; (3) situationally homeless; (4) chronically mentally ill; (5) dually diagnosed (substance abuse and psychiatric disorder); (6) homeless families; (7) homeless children and adolescents; and (8) HIV infection (Breakey and Thompson, 1997). But how much heuristic penetration can we expect from an epidemiological study? Does not that research methodology in and of itself provide a repetition of the very circumstance that I am discussing in that it must compress the vast diversity and the many unique subjectivities and individualities of actual people into objectifiable categories and almost equally anonymous subcategories?

In one such study of the "epidemic" of homeless mentally ill persons, the authors state that the "outrage" of the American public has little to do with concern for the people in this condition and more to do with "visible signs of failures of our social and health care policies" (Breakey and Thompson, 1997, p. ix). This system breakdown, evidently, is the cause of a massive form of collective defense, characterized by a generally hopeless attitude about the epidemic proportions of homelessness in the United States. Society-level security operations are created against the anxiety that were we (that is, I) to fall into this status, I, like those who are there now, would be stuck there.

To think about the workings of such a societal system conjures up the notion of Erich Fromm's (1941) "social character." Invoking this specter, and Fromm's explicit forebodings regarding it, Hegeman (1995) suggests that within such a character formation, "successful adjustment to society could produce psychopathology" (p. 830). In this society, some (the homelessmentallyill) suffer from an inability to adapt while others (my three patients, myself, etc.) suffer from the compromises they have made in order to adapt (Fromm, 1955). Directed specifically against homelessness and mental illness, perhaps as a screen for the displacement of other concerns about system-wide failures, this adaptation allows us to maintain a blind spot around the notion that were we to fall (into that death-like silence) there would be nothing to catch us.

The surface and its meaning(s)

In the clinical cases mentioned above, the surface of "homelessmentallyill" became a reflector of transference and countertransference reactions: that is, my patients' reactions to the homelessmentallyill, and my dread of being targeted by Joyce's rage the way so many other practitioners had been. The surface became that which my patients used to organize (project) warded-off emotions, feelings of inferiority, and self-states that could extort silence in the context of murderous threats to well-established, long-held images that my patients (and their analyst) used to navigate their way through the outer world.

In many conquered civilizations throughout history, the language, rituals and cultural styles of the conquered were forbidden, subsumed under, incorporated (via bastardization) into the spoken and written word of the conqueror (Sardar, 1997). Any so-called minority group is defined as such not through some kind of numerical weighting, but rather through the possession or dispossession of a voice (hooks, 1994). Once access to the system of languages/discourse is denied, then subjectivity is lost and people become like objects (Kristeva, 1982).

From the psychoanalytic perspective, the question becomes: what lies beneath the surface – the surface of writing, speaking, and even of existence itself? Generally speaking, what we usually come up with is meaning. This being so, the search for meaning reflects a cult of authority that encodes social interaction into the lexicon of meanings surrounding the experience of agency and authenticity. Whose existence is authentic? Whose way of being manifests agency? Official, or dominant, culture attempts to impose unitary models of interactive legitimacy on an otherwise dynamic social field, educating us in "correct" models of being. Meaning from this perspective becomes a sort of tyranny; it imposes a widespread social system that both narrows and distorts the possibilities of human existence.

Jeff's interaction with the homeless man became increasingly complex as we found different ways to re-engage with it. Perhaps more understanding of the need for ruthlessness and the use we make of it would allow us to handle it better than exhortations against it; perhaps we could make better choices about how we see, hear, and think about, as well as what we want to do with, the crisis of serious social problems that confront us (e.g., homelessness, mental illness). In counterpoint to Sullivan's (1954) clinical approach of "participant-observation," we generally manifest non-participant/non-observation with such problems. Whether consciously or not, we do experience and respond (even if through inaction) to such chronic crises, or at least to the voices of those who whisper (or scream) at the peripheries of our existence.

Efficiency and progress

In 1980, responding to the terrifying possibility of a weapon of mass destruction that would kill humans while leaving the fruits of their labor intact (buildings, property, etc.), Jello Biafra of the punk band the Dead Kennedys offered his version of Swift's satirical "modest proposal." In the song "Kill the Poor," he states sarcastically:

> Efficiency and progress is ours once more
> Now that we have the Neutron bomb
> It's nice and quick and clean and gets things done
> Away with excess enemy, with no less value to property
> [makes] No sense in war but perfect sense at home.

This song captures the sentiment of this chapter. I read it less as a nihilistic "proposal" about what (in actuality) should or could be done (to the poor, the homeless, the mentally ill), but as what, at the psychic level, is done each and every day – and perhaps with necessity.

"Speak! That I may see you," suggests Bromberg (1994, p. 517). The image of the *Other*, however, remains unseen (and, hence, unheard) as disturbing images (and muffled voices), such as the whole vast category of homelessmentallyill, and thereby becomes dissociated from meaning. After all, how can I see you, feel you, hear you, touch you when, to maintain the integrity of my own sense of self, I must dissociate your existence with a precise and "necessary" ruthlessness?

In opposition to the idea of a complete, whole subject (person), both Freud (1930) and Sullivan (1953, 1964), long before the current multiplicity of self theories, postulated that the subject was infinitely fragmented, split, and often at odds with him- or herself and the social environment. This fragmentation is, of course, endlessly anxiety-provoking. Therefore, the stimuli (people) that remind us of it must, if at all possible, be neutralized, if not obliterated completely – killed repeatedly as they arise, serially, as if each potentially disturbing image must be shot down before it enters our awareness in a kind of unconscious skeet-shoot.

It is my impression that we have in our culture a significant investment in maintaining categories of *Otherness* that reinforce our collective tendency to use them as focal points for the projections and dissociated self-states that we find most unacceptable. Freud (1917) referred to a similar process as "the narcissism of minor differences." The narcissism of minor differences formula goes something like this: although two groups may seem alike, they have minor differences; rituals are developed to maintain these minor differences and keep a psychological barrier between the opposing groups that absorbs the flow of aggression and, at least in times of peace, keeps the groups from killing each other (Volkan, 1988).

Our opportunity to work on problems such as homelessness and mental illness is limited by our institutionalization of these categories. This limitation is upheld by our limited professional appearance in the outside world, in community contexts, where such a vantage point might be challenged and opened up to new possibilities (Borg *et al.*, 2001; Borg, 2004b). Winnicott (1958) spoke of the developmental process as one wherein "ruthlessness gives way to ruth, unconcern to concern" (pp. 23–24). Although he was referring to early problems between parents and children, he was also speaking about the facilitating environment and its role in development and personhood, much as I have been discussing at a broader societal level.

We cannot simply impose "ruth" on our patients or on our world. Moments of true ruth often come as a shock, even a severe blow, to the defensive system – or perhaps as a result of such a shock. All three cases presented here reveal this shock that comes when indifference gives way to compassion, when (necessary) defenses break down and reveal the (suffering) other as subject, when the other becomes the serially killed self resurrected.

Of my three patients, only Jeff was willing to explore both the need for ruthlessness and the potential to survive unprepared moments of compassion. In the slow expansion of Deborah's ruth, she lost her capacity to defend against the suffering of others to such a degree that she had to regress to an "ideal" world where suffering no longer existed. As we saw in the case of Joyce, the unprepared, shocking compassion one might feel toward others has the capacity to induce panic, when the necessary categorization of *Other* breaks down and leaves one vulnerable to one's own fragile state.

This shift from ruthlessness to ruth, from indifference to compassion was, in each case, painful; it did not come without a price. Living in a city like New York, where the suffering of others is rampant and efforts to intervene in it feel daunting, if not futile, ruthlessness may be a necessary defense if one is to survive. Awareness of the pain of another's condition is what this shift is all about. We cannot naively assume that this will be possible at all times. We have all, most likely, had to make adaptations that allow us to exist and function (maintaining "efficiency and progress") in "civil society." In many ways, our necessary ruthlessness brands us as, in cyberpunk author Neal Stephenson's (1995) terminology, "veterans of that elongated state of low-intensity warfare known as society" (p. 286). How can we close the gap between necessary ruthlessness and the generally dissociated, empathic connections that, perhaps at times necessarily, remain unlinked between those inside and those outside of the borderlands? If we do not address this gap, then perhaps we might assume that the reason why we never used the neutron bomb was because we did not need to.

References

Bell, D. (1992) The cultural wars: American intellectual life. *Wilson Quarterly*, 16: 74–107.

Bellah, R., Madsen, R., Sullivan, W., Swindler, A. and Tipton, S. (1985) *Habits of the Heart: Individualism and Commitment in America*. Berkeley, CA: University of California Press.

Biafra, J. (1980) Kill the poor. *Dead Kennedys: Fresh Fruit from Rotting Vegetables*. San Francisco, CA: Alternative Tentacles.

Blackwell, D. (2003) Colonialism and globalization: a group-analytic perspective. *Group Analysis*, 36: 445–454.

Borg, Jr., M.B. (2003) Psychoanalytic pre war: interactions with the post-apocalyptic unconscious. *Journal for the Psychoanalysis of Culture and Society*, 8: 57–67.

—— (2004a) A zombie storms the meathouse: approximating living and undergoing psychoanalysis in a palliative care culture. *Psychoanalysis, Culture and Society*, 9: 212–233.

—— (2004b) Venturing beyond the consulting room: psychoanalysis in community crisis intervention. *Contemporary Psychoanalysis*, 40: 147–174.

Borg, Jr., M.B., Garrod, E. and Dalla, M.R. (2001) Intersecting "real worlds": community psychology and psychoanalysis. *The Community Psychologist*, 34(3): 16–19.

Breakey, W.R. and Thompson, J.W. (1995) Mental illness and the continuum of residential stability. *Social Psychiatry and Psychiatric Epidemiology*, 30: 147–151.

Breakey, W.R. and Thompson, J.W. (1997) Psychiatric services for mentally ill homeless people. In W.R. Breakey and J.W. Thompson (eds) *Mentally Ill and Homeless*. Amsterdam: Harwood Academic.

Bromberg, P.M. (1994) "Speak! That I may see you": some reflections on dissociation, reality, and psychoanalytic knowledge. *Psychoanalytic Dialogues*, 4: 517–547.

Butler, J. (1993) *Bodies that Matter*. New York: Routledge.

—— (2003) Violence, mourning, politics. *Studies in Gender and Sexuality*, 4: 9–37.

Clarke, S. (2004) *Social Theory, Psychoanalysis and Racism*. New York: Palgrave Macmillan.

Clarke, S. and Hoggett, P. (2004) The Empire of fear: American political psyche and the culture of paranoia. *Psychodynamic Practice*, 10: 89–106.

Cohen, C.I. (1993) Poverty and the course of schizophrenia: implications for research and policy. *Hospital and Community Psychiatry*, 44: 951–958.

Ellin, N. (1999) *Postmodern Urbanism*. New York: Princeton Architectural Press.

Etzioni, A. (1991) *A Responsive Society*. San Francisco, CA: Jossey-Bass.

Fanon, F. (1968) *The Wretched of the Earth*. New York: Grove.

Foucault, M. (1977) *Discipline and Punish*. New York: Vintage.

Freire, P. (1970) *Pedagogy of the Oppressed*. New York: Continuum.

Freud, S. (1917) Taboo of virginity. *Standard Edition*, 11: 191–208. London: Hogarth Press, 1957.

—— (1930) *Civilization and its Discontents*. *Standard Edition*, 21: 57–145. London: Hogarth Press, 1957.

Fromm, E. (1941) *Escape from Freedom*. New York: Rinehart.

—— (1955) *The Sane Society*. New York: Rinehart.

Fuery, P. and Mansfield, N. (2000) *Cultural Studies and Critical Theory*. Melbourne, Vic.: Oxford University Press.

Garrison, J. (2004) *America as Empire: Global Leader or Rogue Power?* San Francisco, CA: Berrett-Koehler.

Giroux, H.A. (2003) *The Abandoned Generation: Democracy beyond the Culture of Fear*. New York: Palgrave Macmillan.

Hegeman, E. (1995) Cross-cultural issues in interpersonal psychoanalysis. In M. Lionells, J. Fiscalini, C.H. Mann and D.B. Stern (eds) *Handbook of Interpersonal Psychoanalysis*, pp. 823–846. Hillsdale, NJ: Analytic Press.

Herbert, F. (1985) *Chapterhouse: Dune*. New York: Ace Books.

Holmes, D. E. (1992) Race and transference in psychoanalysis and psychotherapy. *International Journal of Psychoanalysis*, 73: 1–15.

hooks, b. (1994) *Outlaw Culture: Resisting Representations*. New York: Routledge.

Johnson, C. (2004) *The Sorrows of Empire: Militarism, Secrecy, and the End of the Republic*. New York: Metropolitan Books.

Knox, G.W. (1995) *An Introduction to Gangs*. Bristol, IN: Wyndham Hall Press.

Kristeva, J. (1982) *Powers of Horror*. New York: Columbia University Press.

Richardson, F., Fowers, B. and Guignon, C. (1999) *Re-envisioning Psychology: Moral Dimensions of Theory and Practice*. San Francisco, CA: Jossey-Bass.

Ryan, W. (1971) *Blaming the Victim*. New York: Random House.

Said, E.W. (1993) *Culture and Imperialism*. New York: Alfred A. Knopf.

Samuels, A. (2001) *Politics on the Couch: Citizenship and the Internal Life*. New York: Karnac.

Sardar, Z. (1997) *Postmodernism and the Other*. London: Pluto.

Schultheis, A. (2004) *Regenerative Fictions: Postcolonialism, Psychoanalysis and the Nation as Family*. New York: Palgrave Macmillan.

Seidman, E. and Rappaport, J. (1986) *Redefining Social Problems*. New York: Plenum.

Smith, E.M., North, C.S. and Spitznagel, E.L. (1993) Alcohol, drugs and psychiatric comorbidity among homeless women. *Journal of Clinical Psychiatry*, 54: 82–87.

Stephenson, N. (1995) *The Diamond Age*. New York: Bantam.

Sullivan, H.S. (1953) *The Interpersonal Theory of Psychiatry*. New York: Norton.

—— (1954) *The Psychiatric Interview*. New York: Norton.

—— (1964) *The Fusion of Psychiatry and Social Science*. New York: Norton.

Taylor, C. (1992) *The Ethics of Authenticity*. Cambridge, MA: Harvard University Press.

Volkan, V. (1988) *The Need to Have Enemies and Allies*. Northvale, NJ: Jason Aronson.

Warren, M.R. (2001) *Dry Bones Rattling: Community Building to Revitalize American Democracy*. Princeton, NJ: Princeton University Press.

Winnicott, D.W. (1958) The sense of guilt. In D.W. Winnicott, *The Maturational Process and the Facilitating Environment*, pp. 15–28. Madison, CT: International Universities Press.

Zizek, S. (2004) *Organs without Bodies*. New York: Routledge.

Part V

Death instinct?

Chapter 14

Notes on negativity

Karen Lombardi

As a graduate student in New York City in the 1970s, I was trained within an ego psychological model. I rebelled against most of this training, based on a drive theory epistemology that seemed to blame us for our thoughts, desires, even our creativity, which were seen as ways of escaping our forbidden desires and the murderous forms these were thought to take. Kill your father to marry your mother; kill your mother to marry your father. The best you could hope for was Freudian sublimation (or endless Lacanian metonymic elision, though Lacan was not part of my training).

During those graduate school days, while plowing through the meta-psychology of the ego and its impossible applications to clinical life, I came upon René Spitz's (1957) lovely, slim monograph, *No and Yes*. His volume was devoted to an exploration of the early development of the ego through language, which Spitz characterized in terms of the baby's first utterances of no and of yes. Although I translated this into my own terms (there is my negativity again), there was something compelling in the idea that early language allowed us a window through which to view the baby's sub-jectivity, constituting itself through the no as well as the yes. This idea has stayed with me throughout my own musings on theory over the years, and especially in my clinical work.

Negativity and the death instinct

In psychoanalysis, refusal, negation, denial, and disavowal are all aspects of the clinical concept of negativity, which is seen to have its roots in the death instinct. In Freud's (1920) theory, the death instinct is a metapsychological concept based on the law of entropy of the physical universe which he translated as the primary impulse of living organisms to seek death. Although the concept of the death instinct has been rejected or ignored by many schools of contemporary theory, it does find modern expression in the concept of negativity as elaborated most notably by Klein, Lacan, Kristeva, Matte Blanco, and André Green.

In accepting Freud's death instinct, Klein goes further than Freud by developing it into a primary psychic experience, placing the fear of death (and the fear of one's own destructive potential) at the root of persecutory anxiety. It is the fear of death, not the fear of castration or the fear of separation, which is, for Klein, at the root of all anxiety. For Freud, death was an instinct in an abstract and species-specific sense, not in an individual and experiential sense. He argued that one cannot fear what one cannot conceive, and that it is psychologically impossible to form a positive idea of anything so negative as being nothing. Contrary to Freud, Klein argued that if we cannot form an idea of being dead, we can certainly form an idea of, and fear, the experience of dying (see, e.g., Money-Kyrle, 1955).

To underscore the differences between the Freudian and Kleinian concepts, Freud posits an organismic impulse to seek death (the law of entropy), while Klein posits a primary psychic impulse to fear and avoid death. We might call the Freudian concept a positive death instinct (as in attraction), and Klein's a negative death instinct (as in the anxiety of avoidance or denial).

How is negation tied to the death instinct? In perhaps his most object relational paper, "Negation" (1925), Freud states: "Affirmation – as a substitute for uniting – belongs to Eros; negation – the successor to expulsion – belongs to the instinct of destruction." He went on to say that "The performance of judgment is not made possible until the creation of the symbol of negation has endowed thinking with a first measure of freedom from the consequences of repression" (Freud, 1925, p. 239).

Negation destroys the unity of the subject at the same time that it introduces the symbol, which allows for separation and for thinking. Klein develops this notion through the concept of the paranoid-schizoid position, which presents the split subject as a condition of human living. Affects, experienced from the earliest phases of life, which break down into experiential qualities of good and bad, love and hate, creation and destruction, constitute primary divisions in the subject. Negativity, in its projective and expulsive aspects, is what constitutes the self, by separating me from not-me experiences, at the same time that it threatens to destroy the object. In order to maintain ties to objects, the subject must further split itself in two, with the need to preserve the other further threatening the self. Negativity, then, is intimately involved with the constitution and destruction of the links between subject and object.

Negativity and symbolization: clinical examples

In the clinical literature, Klein and Winnicott present cases wherein negativity figures in a central way. Klein's early (1930) paper on symbol formation presents Dick, a 4-year-old boy with simultaneous failures in language and object relations. Though Klein categorizes Dick's difficulties in terms of schizophrenia, we might recognize, through her description, autistic features: severely delayed language development, echolalia, considerable insensitivity to his own pain, physical awkwardness, lack of coordination, indifference to human contact, lack of anxiety, inability to take the other's perspective, lack of symbolic play, and so on. Klein alludes to the deficits in his relationships that help explain the state of Dick's existence:

> Possibly his development was affected by the fact that, though he had every care, no real love was lavished on him, his mother's attitude to him being from the very beginning overanxious. As, moreover, neither his father nor his nurse showed him much affection, Dick grew up in an environment rather poor in love.
>
> (Klein, 1930, p. 233)

Klein understands Dick's incapacities in terms of premature, exaggerated identification with an attacked object, leaving him with an unbearable sense of his own sadism. In other words, Dick was seen as identified with an anxious mother whose love and vitality were dead, leaving him feeling like a robber or killer of the missing vitality and love. In speaking of the mother's relationship to Dick, Klein recognizes an important, positive strain in his personality – negativity. "Dick's mother could at times clearly sense in the boy a strong negative attitude which expressed itself in the fact that he often did the very *opposite* of what was expected of him" (Klien, 1930, pp. 221–222). In this negativity Klein recognizes Dick's will, and his nascent capacity to separate himself from the deadness of his mother while at the same time living in terror of his own sadism and destructiveness.

Winnicott (1971) introduces his concept of negativity through the discussion of a schizoid patient whose sense of loss was elevated to the real. Separated from her parents during the war and evacuated to safety,

> she completely forgot her childhood and her parents, but all the time she steadily maintained the right not to call those who were caring for her "uncle" and "auntie," which was the usual technique. She managed *never to call them anything* the whole of those years, and this was the negative of remembering her mother and father . . . From this my patient reached the position, which again comes into the transference, that the only real thing is the gap; that is to say, the death or the absence or the amnesia.
>
> (Winnicott, 1971, p. 22)

In communicating to Winnicott that only loss was real to her, she said, comparing him to her former analyst, "You may do me more good, but I like him better. This will be true when I have completely forgotten him. The negative of him is more real than the positive of you" (p. 23).

For Klein, and Winnicott after her, negativity is an essential quality of psychic functioning that allows for symbolization to occur. However, negativity as void, as non-vitality or death, as a gap, is negativity in its more pathological aspects, and may leave the individual in a state of psychic foreclosure. Green (1986) extends negativity as a void or absence by relating it to his concept of the dead mother introject. While normal aspects of the negative are constitutive and creative, pathological aspects of the negative result in the fading of the symbol and place the mind under the threat of being destroyed. Green suggests that the symbol's fading may be related to unbearable separation, which is usually described in terms of aggression. I would add that lack, non-presence, and the terror of a terri-fying presence may also occupy the space of unbearable separation. Such a non-presence is not a loss that can be mourned, but an emptiness, a void, a blankness. In too-long absences (and in the presence of deadly objects), non-existence takes possession of the mind, and the symbol fades. It is the void that then becomes real.

The use of an object allows us to recreate what we have destroyed and to create new and non-existent objects. When we haven't that capacity, what Green (1999) calls the disobjectualizing function (a concept tied to the death instinct) strips objects of specific individuality or personal meaning, so that they become fetishistic dead objects. "The so-called death instinct becomes an inclination to self-disappearance. It is linked less with aggression than with nothingness" (p. 220).

The positive and negative of negativity

Negativity is the necessity of subjectivity, a lifeline, a foreclosure, a void, and a death. How can it be all these things? How can it be itself and its opposite? In Freud's theory, life instincts stand counterposed to death instincts; the law of entropy is always at work. Because it divides (I am not you – I eject you – I reject you), negativity is seen as an expression of the death instinct. Because it divides, negativity is also seen as essential to the exercise of judgment, thinking, and the constitution of the ego itself. No must stand in relation to yes; yes must stand in relation to no. I am you must stand in relation to I am not-you; you are me must stand in relation to you are not-me.

In the development of the symbol and theory of the split subject, Klein expands Freud's view. Tying negation to processes of introjection and projection, particular attributes will be introjected when experienced as good, and projected or made alien to the self when experienced as bad. The original lack of differentiation between what is subjective and what is objective – what is inside ourselves and what exists out there in the world –

is taken up by Klein when she speaks of object relations beginning at the breast. The first encounter with the other sets in motion these introjective and projective mechanisms, whereby we take in and expel psychic experiences in relation to the other, forming the basis for phantasy and subjective existence. Negation, which forms one half of continuous introjective-projective cycles, is seen as belonging to the "instinct" of destruction, while affirmation, which Freud calls the substitute for unity, belongs to Eros.

For Klein, negation is an embodied experience, framed in terms of the earliest experiences at the breast: "I should like to eat this; I should like to spit it out" (Freud, 1925, p. 237). For Klein, as well as for Freud, negativity is coexistent with the emergence of the ego. Particularly for Klein, however, negativity is born of passion. Klein assigned meaning and affect to the death instinct by transforming it from a metapsychological concept to a psychic reality. The destructiveness of hatred – I spit this out, this is bad, this is the not-I of me – standing in opposition to living identification – I take this in and embrace it as part of me – is the stuff of unconscious phantasy. This phantasy life, this psychic reality, comes to be formed not on the basis of "knowledge," in the conscious, cognitive sense, but on the basis of affects. Kleinians speak of affects, particularly anxiety, as being experienced by the infant in simile; for example, to feel like death. Negativity – the destructive force of the personality – is what constitutes the self as it threatens the object. One exists in the not, in the no, as well as in the I of the beholder, for to feel the existence of the self is to be simultaneously continuous and discontinuous with the object.

Living in two places at once: yes and no

Matte Blanco (1975, 1988) affords us a window into the simultaneity of knowing and not knowing, of thinking and being simultaneously in different and contradictory registers. The simultaneous existence in the yes and the no is captured in his fundamental antinomy. Negation, which consists in the slicing of reality, exists in relation to affirmation or unity. Affirmation or union is not privileged over negation, as one cannot exist without the other. Using mathematical set theory, Matte Blanco describes the forms of logic most commonly used in conscious processes as asymmetrical, and the forms of logic that most commonly correspond to unconscious processes as symmetrical. Asymmetrical modes of experience, governed by difference, exist simultaneously with symmetrical modes of experience, governed by similarity or the obliteration of difference. Symmetry is always wrapped in asymmetry. That is, modes of thinking and relating that slice reality into categories and relations governed by differentiation exist simultaneously with modes of thinking and relating based on radical equivalence, where one thing tends mysteriously to become every other thing.

The human dilemma, as well as the human project, is to live simultaneously in opposing and mutually informing states, one based on unity or the impossibility of differentiation, the other based on the language of distinction, hierarchy, and difference. The fundamental antinomy is the contradiction to pure reason that results from our basic, irresolvable coexistence in these antithetical logical states. In terms of human relatedness, the continuity of subject and object, to the point where difference is not discernible, coexists with the fundamental alienation of subject and object, each then simultaneously constituting and destroying the other. Extending Klein's notion of the split subject, this antinomy operates internally within the subject, not only between the I and the you, but between the I and the me.

Living predominantly in the negative presents an irresolvable contradiction. The ability to distinguish, in an asymmetrical mode, allows for separate subjective existence at the same time that it destroys the unity with the other. This very ability to refuse, to separate, to disidentify, which is necessary for subjectivity to come into existence, is tied to the very destructiveness of the personality. Normal aspects of the negative are able to preserve a semblance of positivity at the same time that unity is destroyed. Pathological aspects of the negative tend in the direction of obliteration, where the very attempt to constitute the self through refusal leads to a refusal of an intimate and personal creative life. In Kleinian terms, when sadism is too strong and negativity holds sway, symptoms of a paranoid-schizoid nature result. In Green/Winnicottian terms, when absence predominates and pathological negativity holds sway, symptoms of a schizoid or negative narcissistic nature result. In Lacanian/Kristevan terms, when the negativity of lack holds sway, symptoms of an obsessional or perverse nature result.

How can we live in two places at once? Klein, Kristeva, and Matte Blanco each speak of bivalence, although in different ways. For Kristeva (1979), negativity is a bivalent process, consisting of knowledge of x and disavowal or repudiation of x. She offers Freud's (1938) classic example of the boy who notes his mother's lack of a penis but nevertheless continues to think she has one. For Kleinians, bivalence may be thought of as the simultaneity and interpenetrability of the paranoid-schizoid and depressive modes. The Kleinian version of Kristeva's example would be an attack upon the mother's possession of the desired/persecutory penis at the same time that there is recognition of the loving desire for the caring mother whom we have attacked. For Matte Blanco, bivalence is a theoretical position only, marked by either-or relations in the asymmetric mode. What Kristeva calls bivalent, Matte Blanco calls bi-logic, the simultaneous existence of asymmetrical and symmetrical logics. The asymmetrical would differentiate the boy and his penis from the mother and her vagina (her not-penis), while the symmetrical would join the boy and the mother in an omni(im)potent phallic metaphor.

Summary

The intimate, oscillating, co-constructing, simultaneous relationships between negativity and affirmation can fuel wondrous developmental projects pertaining to separation, autonomy, symbolization, creativity, intersubjectivity, intimacy, and other important matters. This positive potency is one edge of the sword, the other being the negative domain of psychopathology, annihilation, destructiveness, and other dark variables. Further investigation of the links between these realms may add substantially to our understanding of both some of the most positive and some of the most negative aspects of life.

References

Freud, S. (1920) *Beyond the Pleasure Principle. Standard Edition*, 18: 3–64. London: Hogarth Press, 1974.
—— (1925) Negation. *Standard Edition*, 19: 235–239. London: Hogarth Press, 1961.
—— (1938) *An Outline of Psycho-Analysis. Standard Edition*, 23: 144–194. London: Hogarth Press, 1964.
Green, A. (1986) The dead mother. In A. Green, *On Private Madness*, pp. 142–173. New York: International Universities Press.
—— (1999) The intuition of the negative in *Playing and Reality*. In G. Kohon (ed). *The Dead Mother: The Work of André Green*, pp. 205–221. London: Brunner-Routledge.
Klein, M. (1930) The importance of symbol formation in the development of the ego. In M. Klein, *Love, Guilt and Reparation*, pp. 219–233. London: Hogarth Press, 1975.
Kristeva, J. (1979) The true-real. In T. Moi (ed.) *The Kristeva Reader*, pp. 214–237. New York: Columbia University Press, 1986.
Lacan, J. (1977) *Ecrits*. London: Tavistock/Routledge.
Matte Blanco, I. (1975) *The Unconscious as Infinite Sets*. London: Duckworth.
—— (1988) *Thinking, Feeling and Being*. London: Routledge.
Money-Kyrle, R.E. (1955) An inconclusive contribution to the theory of the death instinct. In M. Klein, P. Heimann and R.E. Money-Kyrle (eds) *New Directions in Psychoanalysis*, pp. 499–509. London: Maresfield Library, 1977.
Spitz, R. (1957) *No and Yes: On the Genesis of Human Communication*. New York: International Universities Press.
Winnicott, D.W. (1971) *Playing and Reality*. London: Tavistock.

Matte Blanco, the death drive and timelessness

Ross M. Skelton

In the Preface to *The Unconscious as Infinite Sets*, Matte Blanco (1975) tells his readership that the book is a starting point for new developments:

> The first refers to the question of God. If the findings of Freud on this subject are reformulated in terms of the approach presented here, then the immanent notions about God, interpreted as "bi-logical" experiences, lead to interesting perspectives. The second (development) concerns the so-called Death instinct which, if viewed again as a bilogical conception, instead of as an instinct, seems to provide fresh insights into the nature of life.
>
> (Matte Blanco, 1975, p. xix)

Rodney Bomford (1990) has taken up the question of God in his article, "The attributes of God and the characteristics of the unconscious." I propose to take up Matte Blanco's interpretation of the death drive that seems to provide fresh insights into the nature of life.

Freud and the death drive

The death drive hypothesis put forward by Freud contains two main strands: the repetition of old experiences and the resistance to change which he thought lay at the basis of human experience.

The compulsion to repeat and timelessness

Freud's idea of repetition compulsion was to find its final formulation in the "Death" drive. One of the chief actions of the death drive is to repeat past experiential structures that manipulate the subject like a puppet. Someone in the grip of repetition is in the grip of an alien will and, through analysis, may come to know the extent of this alienation. Already in the "Papers on technique" of 1914, Freud mentioned the compulsion to repeat. In "The Uncanny" (1919a), he referred to the fact that a person can feel compelled to repeat earlier scenes in his or her life which were certainly not pleasant. He was already considering human motivations that were "beyond" the pleasure principle before he entitled his next paper *Beyond the Pleasure Principle* (1920). Whereas in "The Uncanny" he considers repetition as a psychological phenomenon, in the later paper he wants to make it an "instinct" or drive. In what follows, we (like Matte Blanco) shall not be concerned with the question of whether or not it is a drive.

At the outset of *Beyond the Pleasure Principle*, Freud notes that people who have had accidents often repeat this same experience in their dreams, again and again without change. He remarks: "This astonishes people far too little" (1920, p. 13). He explains repetitions in terms of attempts at mastery of a difficult emotional experience. He cites the case of a little boy who is distressed by the absences of his mother. The boy conceives a game whereby he can make a cotton reel appear or disappear when *he* chooses. In this game, the cotton reel represents his mother. He can, thereby, practice "letting mother go." By enduring the absences of the cotton reel, he can achieve mastery of the separation experience. As Freud (1920) says: "At the outset he was in a passive situation – he was overpowered by the experience; but by repeating it, unpleasurable though it was, as a game, he took on an active part" (p. 16).

Although many people master experiences by repeating them, many others do not. They are therefore condemned to repeat painful experiences without achieving any mastery over them, or learning from the experience. To adapt one of Freud's own examples: a man who has been scorned in his family may have failed to master this painful experience through its being repeatedly experienced. If this man eventually goes into psychoanalysis, he may contrive to get himself scorned by the analyst. This will be part of the so-called "transference repetition." As Freud says:

> He is obliged to repeat the repressed material as a contemporary experience instead of, as the physician would prefer to see, remembering it as something belonging to the past. These reproductions, *which emerge with such unwished-for exactitude*, always have as their subject some portion of infantile sexual life.
>
> (Freud, 1920, p. 18, my italics)

What I think Freud is highlighting here is the fact that, say, a humiliation experienced thirty years ago acts just like a fresh experience when it is touched off today. To put it more dramatically, he is saying that the experience has become "timeless." Thus for Freud, timelessness and repetitions are linked. When an early experience is touched off, it is as if the intervening years had never happened.

In *Beyond the Pleasure Principle*, the following passage occurs: "As a result of certain psychoanalytic discoveries, we are today in the position to embark on a discussion of the Kantian theorem that time and space are necessary forms of thought" (Freud, 1920, p. 22). What Freud means here is not certain. He could be alluding to the fact that, according to Kant, we humans wear spatio-temporal "spectacles" and have knowledge of only what we perceive through these spectacles. Certainly for an unconscious repetition to be reclaimed from timelessness by psychoanalysis it will have to be analyzed *into* time. But how are we creatures of time to get into contact with timeless repetitions?

In the Introductory Remarks to the "Wolf Man," Freud (1918) says the physician "must behave as 'timelessly' as the unconscious itself . . . By submitting on a single occasion to the timelessness of the unconscious he will be brought nearer to vanquishing it in the end" (pp. 10–11). As we know, as soon as the Wolf Man felt relief from Freud's analyzing, he immediately gave up working in order to avoid any further changes. This brings an alternative view: there is resistance to the opening out of time-lessness into time in the form of a *stasis* or a reluctance to change on the part of the patient. Thus we can see changelessness and timelessness as to some extent the same thing. With this discussion, we seem to be entering a rather eerie, alien world of timelessness and changelessness. This impression is borne out by a remark of Freud's in "The Uncanny": "Whatever reminds us of this inner 'compulsion to repeat' is perceived as uncanny" (1919a, p. 238).

Resistance to change and masochism

To return to our earlier example of the patient who repeatedly contrives to feel himself scorned, we can further notice that it is clearly masochistic. A person who feels compelled to repeat actions painful to himself is sub-mitting (albeit unconsciously) to an alien tyrant. For this reason, Freud includes masochism as a vital ingredient of the death drive. He will now give masochism a more privileged place in his theory than ever before.

Throughout Freud's early career and up to his 1919b "A child is being beaten," masochism was derived from an original sadism. It was seen as aggression turned against the self. By the time Freud wrote *Beyond the Pleasure Principle*, he was beginning to think that perhaps masochism was not a derivative of sadism but that there might be an original or "primary" masochism. By the time he wrote his 1924 "The economic problem in masochism," primary masochism has become a working assumption. According to this new hypothesis, we are born with an internal drive to self-destruction. In order to survive its disintegrative effect, we project it outwards onto others. Freud says:

> The libido has the task of making the destroying instinct innocuous and it fulfils the task by diverting that instinct to a great extent outwards . . .

[helped by the musculature] . . . towards objects in the external world. The instinct is then called the destructive instinct, the instinct for mastery or the will to power.

(Freud, 1924, p. 163)

This then is Freud's later theory of human aggression. An original masochism or passivity is transformed by projection into aggression against others or mastery of our own painful experience. Masochism is a remainder of self-destructiveness that has not been projected outwards. This primacy of masochism illuminates the deep feelings of guilt suffered by those unfortunates who apparently wish to endure punishing experiences. The so-called "pale" criminals, whose primary compulsion is to repeat crimes, illustrate the desire to be caught and punished in order to assuage a guilt of which they are unconscious.

The reader may be wondering what the compulsion to repeat, or even primary masochism has to do with death in the so-called death drive. Freud theorizes that just as the compulsion to repeat seeks to install an earlier state of affairs as reality, so also the self-destructive tendency seeks to install a much earlier state of the person, namely when they were not yet alive, in a non-living state before conception. Psychotic patients seem much more at home in this dead world; their very future seems embedded in the past. In a broad general sense, for Freud, the primary impulse in human beings is to "seek" death whereas, we shall find, for Melanie Klein the impulse was to fear and avoid death.

Klein and the death drive

Klein, following Freud, emphasized that the internal destructive attack projected outside resulted in paranoia. This can be clarified by a political analogy. Imagine a country in a state of internal faction fights. In a situation fast approaching the complete breakdown of law and order, the government hits on the strategy of declaring war on a neighbouring country. This external threat has the effect of mobilizing all troublemakers into the army to defend the country. The countryside and towns return to a state of relative peace and harmony, with this difference: the whole country (though stable) is now in a state of paranoia at the threat of war. This in turn feeds aggression towards external citizens now called "the enemy." From this analogy, we can see how Klein believed that the death drive amounted to this: we are all (unconsciously) in anxious dread of internal annihilation.

Traditionally in psychoanalysis, the fear of death masks castration anxiety or even the fear of losing all capacity for pleasure. Now, with Klein, it can be seen as masking the terror of mental annihilation. This then, for her, is our existential root – the dread of annihilation.

Klein fastens on the primary masochism aspect of Freud's account of the death drive rather than on the repetition compulsion viewpoint. Almost alone among analysts, she championed the unpopular Freudian concept of an internal destructive function. This eventually enabled her to secure the notion of a primitive, early superego. For Klein, the initial fierce projection of self-destruction outwards is one of the first survival strategies of the early ego. These hostile projections become the early superego. This superego of the first months of life is considerably more frightening in its effects than the Freudian superego which is formed, we are told by Freud, in the ashes of the Oedipus complex between the ages of 3 and 5.

Finally, it should be said that Klein emphasizes destructiveness in human nature, based on her deep understanding of, and attraction to, Freud's death drive.

Matte Blanco and the death drive

Unlike Klein, Matte Blanco does not link aggression and the death drive. He goes to some pains to distance himself from her views. At times this distance is not as great as he might have wished, but it does remain true that his main perspective is Freudian.

He claims in his *The Unconscious as Infinite Sets* that the death drive is "an important intuition of Freud expressed in an imperfect way" (1975, p. 379). More explicitly, in his "The four antinomies of the death instinct," he wrote: "I believe that the concept of the Death Instinct was Freud's most significant attempt to study the relationship which exists between the structure of the logic of the unconscious and the structure of the material world" (1973, p. 450). This is an oblique reference to "bi-logic," the bivalent logic of the physical world, and the ambi-valent or even paradoxical logic of the psychic reality of the unconscious.

Matte Blanco thought that the death instinct represented a clinical discovery for Freud which, in the context of classical logic, can only be expressed as paradox, or in the form of antinomies. For example, in psychotic and near psychotic states, we find patients who say that they are both alive and dead. In fact, Freud (1938) says in his *Outline of Psycho-Analysis*:

> Urges with contrary aims exist side by side in the unconscious without any need arising for any adjustment between them. Either they have no influence whatever on each other, or, if they have, no decision is reached, but a compromise comes about which is nonsensical since it embraces mutually incompatible details. With this is connected the fact that *contraries are not kept apart but treated as though they were identical*.
>
> (Freud, 1938, p. 169, my italics)

This is the reason why Matte Blanco (1973) chooses to explicate the death instinct through four antinomies or paradoxes. He argues that it is only in this way that our spatio-temporal perspective can apprehend a completely non spatio-temporal psychical reality of which the death drive allows us a glimpse – the timeless repetitions of childhood.

But what exactly is this timelessness? We recall that Freud said repetitions "emerge with such unwished-for exactitude." It is as if some pattern that is now occurring is experienced as happening for the very first time. From this perspective, the unconscious is fixed in an eternal present. In the idealist philosophies of Hegel and Bradley, time is unreal: only "now" is real. In Eastern philosophy, we meet the same notion. This idea of timelessness is central to the Zen experience. The achievement of *satori* or enlightenment is shown in the subject by an experience of the Absolute Present. As Suzuki (1972) wrote: "to hear the cry of the crow even before it was uttered" and to see our own "original face" before we were born. This is the root source of our reality via an original, Absolute Present. According to Zen, ever since Ignorance asserted itself, we take great pleasure in dividing reality into pieces. We divide time into years, months, and into what Heidegger was later to call "clock-time."

This timeless, indivisible mode of being, so favored by Matte Blanco can, according to him (and to Zen) only be approached by way of paradox or antinomy. In the One, opposites coincide; Life and Death are identical, yet from the spatio-temporal point of view they are polar opposites. Another example: from Freud's Darwinist perspective, life tends to preserve itself, but from the point of view of the death drive, life tends to destroy itself.

Matte Blanco (1975) makes a special note that Freud described the death drive as a tendency to return to a previous state. Freud (1920) says: "We shall be compelled to say that the aim of all life is death and, looking backwards that inanimate things existed before living ones" (p. 5). This encourages Matte Blanco (1975) to extend Freud's famous analogy: for just as the salmon returns to the river from the sea in order to spawn, so the human being longs to return to the indivisible, symmetrical mode of being which can only be perceived by us in contradictions. He writes: "There must almost inevitably be a confusion between this mode and death, which we are used to identifying with lack of movement" (Matte Blanco, 1988, p. 218). In other words, death evokes for us a stillness – the absolute stillness of the indivisible mode. The "drive to death" is really the pull into absolute symmetry – the stillness of pure Being.

Matte Blanco's notion is caught exactly by the pre-Socratic philosopher Parmenides (quoted in Barnes, 1987):

> Only one story, one road, now
> is left: that it is. And on this there are signs
> in plenty that, being, it is ungenerated and indestructible,

whole, of one kind and unwavering, and complete.
Nor was it, nor will it be, since now it is, all together,
one, continuous . . .
Hence it is all continuous; for what is approaches what is.
And unmoving in the limits of great change it is beginningless
and ceaseless, since generation and destruction
have wandered far away, and true trust has thrust them off.
The same and remaining in the same state, it lies by itself,
and thus remains fixed there. For powerful necessity
holds it enchained in a limit which hems it around,
because it is right that what is should be not incomplete.
For it is not lacking – if it were it would lack everything.

(Barnes, 1987, p. 134)

It is interesting that the last line contains the "all or nothing" thinking of the unconscious. Even more significant for Matte Blanco is Parmenides' exclusion of destruction or aggression from this realm.

Discussion

As already mentioned, Freud believed that in some sense we all strive for death whereas Klein saw us as living in the shadow of a death by internal annihilation. Matte Blanco seems to follow the Freudian alternative and shuns the Kleinian one. However Grotstein, in his 1996 review of Matte Blanco's (1988) second book, *Thinking, Feeling and Being*, has this to say: "Symmetry ultimately constitutes a powerful implosive force that putatively pulls the subject backwards and inward to primary identification, which is the indivisible state" (Grotstein, 1996, p. 1055). Whereas Matte Blanco seemed to be retreating from the Kleinian idea of annihilation, Grotstein reminds us that a person can become lost in the implosive force of the symmetrical, indivisible mode of being. Let us look further than annihilation and death-like states and examine the broader question of human aggression.

According to Matte Blanco (1988), aggressive phantasies are situated where symmetry meets asymmetry, where the indivisible mode is translated into heterogenous experiences. He notes that aggression can be experienced as infinite. It can also be experienced as distant and unreal. An apparently mild dream of a cat can be experienced as a tiger. As he explains, aggression may be felt to be nuclear from one point of view, but from another point of view experienced as an infinity contained within finite limits. Clinical experience confirms both these views. Aggression does tend to be felt as very intense and it tends to irradiate widely. In other words, the unconscious "similarizes" in aggression over ever larger classes at a deeper and deeper level of the unconscious. Interestingly, he notes that "nuclear" aggression may, from the symmetrical position, be perceived as unreal and unworthy of consideration.

One reason for aggressive phantasies and anxiety could be the dread of being overcome by the indivisible mode of psychical reality in the guise of what Grotstein (1996) called "primary identification." We sense the infinite mode with a mixture of fascination and fear. The anxieties that its proximity evokes can lead to very aggressive emotion that also engenders a feeling of catastrophic fusion. Matte Blanco (1988) seems to be suggesting that aggression guards the boundaries of symmetrical Being. It protects us from fusing with the "indivisible One." By this account, the psychotic is the moth that flew too close to the flame (of Truth), a view endorsed by Bion, Laing and many others.

On the one hand, Matte Blanco (1988) recognizes high levels of aggression when he says: "It seems possible that aggression may tend towards an infinite degree of intensity at deep levels and yet be perfectly in keeping with peaceful normality" (p. 170). On the other hand, he says: "As we proceed to still lower levels, the notion of aggression begins to lose its meaning. Indeed at the level of spacelessness-timelessness (absence of asymmetrical relations), aggression and conflict are both alien and inconceivable; so, also, is thinking" (p. 170). Matte Blanco is making the claim that aggression is not a part of our essential "human" nature for, at the level of the indivisible One, aggression is unreal.

It is interesting to notice that between his 1973 paper on the death instinct and the 1988 book *Thinking, Feeling and Being*, there is an evolution in Matte Blanco's thought. He makes a point of separating himself from the Kleinian position in making it quite clear that aggressiveness and the death instinct should not be considered to be the same thing. As we have seen, he does more than this. He makes the dramatic point that the so-called "drive to death" is not for a mere mortal death, but a desire for the absolute stillness of the indivisible mode – a longing for that state when all stirrings are still.

Matte Blanco argues that Klein's idea of the death drive projected outwards at the beginning of life could be reinterpreted as follows:

> The new-born baby finds himself disturbed in his "immobile peace" by the irruption, for the first time, of various sorts of very intense desires and impulses which are highly heterogeneous or asymmetrical, yet full of symmetry, as their intensity shows. He then tries to avoid conflict – creating asymmetry in order to remain at a deep level of symmetry in the womb. This results, so far as his development already allows him, in a confusion of self and external world and does not rid him of his intense feelings, for he is now in a symmetrical world.
>
> (Matte Blanco, 1988, p. 218)

This conception of human nature is markedly at odds with that of Klein for whom aggression was primary and is indicative of Matte Blanco's struggle with himself about human aggression. These two conflicting views of human nature come out very clearly in Rayner's (1995) *Unconscious Logic* (pp. 69–73) in a difference of opinion between the author and Elizabeth Spillius, a Kleinian. The difference amounts to this: for Klein there is aggression in the human being right down to the deepest levels, whereas for Matte Blanco, at the deepest levels, aggression (and change) is absent. In the words of Parmenides:

> Hence it is all continuous; for what is approaches what is.
> And unmoving in the limits of great change it is beginningless
> and ceaseless, since generation and destruction
> have wandered far away, and true trust has thrust them off.

References

Barnes, J. (1987) *Early Greek Philosophy*. London: Penguin Classics.

Bomford, R. (1990) The attributes of God and the characteristics of the unconscious. *International Review of Psychoanalysis*, 17: 485–492.

Freud, S. (1914) Papers on technique. *Standard Edition*, 12: 85–174. London: Hogarth Press, 1958.

—— (1918) *From the History of an Infantile Neurosis (the "Wolf-Man")*. *Standard Edition*, 17: 1–122. London: Hogarth Press, 1955.

—— (1919a) The Uncanny. *Standard Edition*, 17: 217–252. London: Hogarth Press, 1955.

—— (1919b) A child is being beaten. *Standard Edition*, 17: 175–204. London: Hogarth Press, 1955.

—— (1920) *Beyond the Pleasure Principle*. *Standard Edition*, 18: 3–64. London: Hogarth Press, 1955.

—— (1924) The economic problem of masochism. *Standard Edition*, 19: 157–172. London: Hogarth Press, 1961.

—— (1938) *An Outline of Psycho-Analysis*. *Standard Edition*, 23: 144–194. London: Hogarth Press, 1964.

Grotstein, J.S. (1996) Review of *Thinking, Feeling, and Being*: clinical reflections on the fundamental antinomy of human beings and world. *International Journal of Psychoanalysis*, 77: 1053–1058.

Matte Blanco, I. (1973) Le quattro antinomie dell'instincto di morte. *Enciclopedia*, 73, pp. 447–456. Rome: Enciclopedia Italiana.

—— (1975) *The Unconscious as Infinite Sets*. London: Duckworth.

—— (1988) *Thinking, Feeling and Being*. London: Routledge.

Rayner, E. (1995) *Unconscious Logic*. London: Routledge.

Suzuki, D.T. (1972) *Living by Zen*. London: Rider.

Part VI

Working with dying patients

Chapter 16

Lessons from hospice

When the body speaks

Sharron W. Kaplan

From 1980 to 1986, I worked full time with dying cancer patients and their families as the social worker on a home care hospice team. For years I knew this experience had affected me deeply. Later, as I began psychoanalytic work, I was vaguely aware my hospice experience was influencing my work as an analyst. Until the chance came to make a presentation at the conference on Deaths and Endings that evolved into this book, I never attempted to articulate any precise link between me as "hospice social worker" and me as "psychoanalyst."

Without any conscious intention, the emotional conditions of hospice drew me spontaneously into states of mind that I believe are insufficiently discussed in psychoanalytic writings. These states, which expand and heighten awareness of subtle sense perceptions, are well known in the realm of spirituality and are well articulated in the Buddhist tradition. In this chapter, I will first present my work with two patients who affected me powerfully, then I will discuss the power I find in subtle sense perceptions and memories.

In the interest of conveying both the sense impressions and the affective impact of my experience, I will use the format of free verse to present my clinical material. The ellipses in my writing (. . .) are inspired by the poet Alice Notley's (1996) *The Descent of Alette*. The intent is to "make the reader slow down and silently articulate – not slur over mentally – the phrases at the pace, and with the stresses, I intend . . . They may remind the reader that each phrase is a thing said by a voice" (p. v). I hope by slowing down, you will allow images to settle in. The longer the ellipse, the longer I hope you will allow your pause to be. Reading my clinical material out loud may facilitate this slowing down.

Clinical vignettes

Even as I rang the bell. . . . .of the modest garden apartment. . . . .I could hear. . . . .her screams. . . . . One of my first hospice visits. . . . .All I knew about Kitty. . . . .I had not met her yet. . . . .was. . . . . metastatic breast cancer. . . . .widespread bone metastases. . . . .Her husband explained. . . walking me through the living room. . . . .past the door to her bedroom. . . . . screams. . . . .steady. . . . . piercingly strong. . . . . . ."An ambulance is on its way. . . . .Her oncologist wants her in the hospital. . . . .probable spontaneous bone fractures". . . . .Screaming unabated . . . . . . I close my eyes. . . . . . .Surely she will not want. . . . .to talk with me. . . . .a stranger. . . . .a social worker. . . . . explore emotions of bone pain? . . . . .No way. . . . .I'll tell her. . . . .I'll return another day. . . . . . . Instead . . . . I cross the room. . . . toward her bedside. . . . .a memory arises . . . . .fifteen years ago. . . . .the second of my two children. . . . .born through natural childbirth . . . . .I kneel beside her. . . . .hear words come from my mouth. . . . ."I'm Sharron from the hospice team. . . . .you don't have to talk with me. . . . .you can send me away. . . . . but you might. . .want to listen to me. . . . .I may be able to teach you. . .something. . . . . that once helped me. . . . .when I was in great pain". . . . . What?. . . . . Was I saying?. . . . .Great pain? . . . . .I never said I had great pain. . . . .during those deliveries. . . . .all I was aware of. . . .was labor . . . . .I always said. . . . .Childbirth is well named. . . . . Labor. . . . . . .The breathing exercises I was taught. . . . .the hardest work I'd ever done. . . . .Aware of labor – Yes . . . . . Aware of great pain – No. . . . .Where were my words. . . coming from?. . . . . . . .Words kept coming. . . . .I was guiding her breathing. . . . . She was responding. . . . .I was remembering. . . . . breathing techniques. . . . .out of mind for fifteen years . . . . .breathing techniques to guide childbirth . . . . . . .And this?. . . . . Never thought to transfer. . .to other life events. . . . .How could I remember? . . . . . How could she be responding?. . . . . so easily. . . . . The pause between her screams . . . . .becoming longer. . . . . . . .Intensity . . . . .softening . . . . . . .pauses becoming . . . . . . periods of silence. . . . . . . screaming softer still. . . . . . .now only moaning . . . . .twenty minutes later. . . . . Kitty asleep. . . . . .I am shocked . . . . .What has happened?. . . . .She stays asleep. . . .until the ambulance arrives. . . . . .Later I learn . . . . . Yes . . . . .Kitty had multiple bone fractures. . . . .The breath work. . . . .eased bone pain. . . . .How could that be?

Now on a quest. . . . .for explanations. . . . . . .training next in. . . . . hypnosis. . . . .meditation. . . . . Buddhism . . . . .imagery. . . . .anything I can find. . . . . . . .Many patients follow. . . . .open as Kitty to anything. . . . .that might ease. . . . .their pain. . . . .their suffering. . . . .
Two years later. . . . .

In a hospital room. . . . .a handsome young man. . . . .lay sunken. . . . .in his pillow. . . . .blood gone from his gray pallored face. . . . .cheeks hollowed . . . . .On his right. . . . .in a chair. . .his mother sat . . . . . . shoulders slumped. . . . . . .There on his left. . . . .his father floated. . . . . . .disbelieving. . . . . .A nurse. . . . .bent over the young man's head. . . . .struggling with a suction tube. . . . . down his throat. . . . .gurgling sounds. . . . .nothing coming. . . . . "Don't fight me Johnny. . . . .just let it happen" . . . . .Eyes wide in terror. . . . .nothing. . . . .but more rasping and gurgling. . . . . "Sharron . . . . .Thank God. . . . .you are here. . . . .You can help him. . . . . Please". . . . . his mother. . . pleads to my eyes. . . . . Agony. . . . .Can I?. . . . .help?. . . . . him?. . . . .Now?. . . . . .Yes . . . .yes, I did before. . . . . .when we first met . . . .at his home. . . . teaching him hypnosis. . .self-hypnosis. . . . . engaged his imagination . . .his sense memories. . . . .before this cancer. . . . . . . .He relaxed into himself. . . . . .It was true. . . . he could release . . . .relax. . . . .play with his mind. . . . . . .even while the tumor. . .wrapped itself around his gut organs . . . . pain diminishing . . . . . .so he could. . . . .go out. . . . . .out till eleven . . . .with his pals. . . . .with his girl friend. . . . .a few times. . . . . Laughing. . . . . joking. . . . .sneaking a beer. . . . .or two. . . . .parents aghast . . . . .and joyous. . . . .

Months later. . . . .the call. . .to the emergency room. . . . .A nurse leaves his room. . . . . needle in hand . . . . ."Just gave him. . . .morphine. . . . . .his pain is. . . . .bad. . . . . . .It will take. . . . .at least twenty minutes to work". . . . . . . .He sees me. . . . .tries to smile . . . ."Hypnosis?". . . .he implores. . . . "Sure" . . . .my presence reminds him. . .of his skills. . . . . . . .He closes his eyes. . . . .I blabber on. . . .words . . .that have nothing to do. . .with the words. . .he speaks. . . . . . . .Yes. . . .one can speak . . . . .in a trance. . . . ."Sharron . . . . . Can you see me?". . . . ."What?". . . . . He repeats. . . . . "Can you see me?" . . ."Up here. . .on the ceiling. . . . .I can see you. . . . . I can see. . . . .that body . . . . . where the pain is . . . .It's great. . . .up here. . . . .I don't feel. . .that pain. . . . .down there. . . . .I want to stay here . . . . .for awhile. . . . . . Can you help me to?". . . . . "Sure". . . . . Now I am connected. . . . . "Let yourself be . . . comfortable. . . . . floating. . . . .up there. . . . . . .it doesn't matter. . .what I see. . .or don't see. . . . . . .so long as you know. . . . . how good it is. . . . .to simply feel that feeling . . . .of floating . . .up there . . . . .no need to return. . . . .until the pain has left. . . .that body". . . . . . What force . . . . .of nature. . . . .is engaged here?. . . . . . . Blew my mind. . . . .

Now. . . . .weeks later. . . . .in this hospital room. . . . . . .Here he is. . . . .He looks up. . . . .as his mother greets me. . . . .a flicker of warmth in his eyes. . . . . .I lean over. . . . .The nurse. . .still struggling with the suction tube. . . . .gives me space. . . . .I guide him. . . . .his labored breathing. . .too little to engage . . . . . .So

I call his attention. . .to the feel of the pillow. . . . . the mattress. . .supporting his body. . . . . . Nothing more important. . . .than the memory. . .of learning to trust. . . . .whatever comes. . .into awareness . . . . "There". . .sighs the nurse . . . ."I've got the phlegm out". . . . . .She stares at me. . . . "Who are you?. . . . How did you do that?". . .I reach into my pocket. . . . .to find . .my silver bullet. . . ready to call for Tonto. . . . .But. . . . . . . .I notice the air. . . . .Changed. . . . . .What is happening? . . .Pieces of paper on the floor. . . turn into dried leaves. . .blowing along the ground. . . .nurses scurry around . . .little animals. . . darting for cover. . .The air is charged. . . . .I realize we must leave. . .tugging at a nurse. . ."They need to be alone". . . .Three nurses and I leave. . .Minutes pass. . . . . .His father steps into the hall. . . . . "I think he is gone". . .tears flowing. . . . . .A doctor confirms. . . . . .His mother sobs.

Psychoanalysis and bodymind

Something powerful and something therapeutic occurred in my encounters with Kitty and Johnny. The process was repeated with dozens of other hospice patients. I do not presume that my interventions fall within the boundaries of what anyone calls "psychoanalysis." However, the power of the process that unfolded has illuminated and informed my psychoanalytic practice. My experience has made the integration of mind and body compelling and has provided a context within which I measure psychoanalytic theories.

Words came spontaneously, focusing attention to phenomena existing at a basic, non-verbal level of being. The possibilities for Kitty and Johnny to find release from pain and suffering emerged from this level. Words were related to preconscious and unconscious sensory awareness of these possibilities, not to conscious awareness. In this chapter, my argument is that if psychoanalysts developed more discriminating attention to subtle sense perceptions and subtle sense memory, listening more when the body speaks, we could expand and enhance the range of our effectiveness, and we might have greater understanding of where our therapeutic effectiveness already exists.

Psychoanalytic tradition recognizes and honors the realm of subtle sense perception and memory: free floating attention opens our perceptual field; Bion's (1961) "reverie" does the same; and dream work brings us into multiple levels of perception. Interest in subjectivity has led to concepts that help explain my experiences with Kitty and Johnny. However, I have found a fuller cognitive grasp of what happened through concepts from Buddhism. Buddhist psychology addresses levels of awareness not addressed in current psychoanalytic theory.

There are writers within psychoanalysis exploring the realm of subjectivity from perspectives that resonate with the ways in which Kitty,

Johnny, and I related. (Aron and Anderson, 1998; Rucker and Lombardi, 1998; Wolstein in Hirsch, 2000a; Newirth, 2003). Their work refines and extends Freud's (1923) "body ego" (p. 26). There is also a growing literature exploring the connections between psychoanalysis and Buddhism, a philosophical tradition which has never seen a split between mind and body (Ghent, 1990; Eigen, 1993; Molino, 1998; Epstein, 1999; Watson *et al.*, 1999; Safran, 2003). Before discussing that literature, I want to present relevant observations from the world of science.

Current discoveries question thinking that perpetuates splitting mind and body. Candace Pert, a biochemist who was Chief, Section on Brain Biochemistry, Clinical Neuroscience Branch, National Institute of Mental Health, with her colleagues at Johns Hopkins, isolated the first endorphins and other neuropeptides which, Pert (1997) proposed, are "molecules of emotion." I quote from the abstract to their 1985 breakthrough paper:

A major conceptual shift in neuroscience has been wrought by the realization that brain function is modulated by numerous chemicals in addition to classical neurotransmitters. Many of these informational substances are neuropeptides, originally studied in other contexts as hormones, "gut peptides," or growth factors . . . *Most, if not all, alter behavior and mood states* . . . Neuropeptides and their receptors thus join the brain, glands, and immune system in a network of communication between brain and body, probably representing the biochemical substrate of emotion.

(Pert *et al.*, 1985, p. 820, italics added)

The authors concluded, "The conceptual division between the sciences of immunology, endocrinology, and psychology/neuroscience is a historical artifact" (Pert *et al.*, 1985, p. 824). Pert (1986) recommended new vocabulary to reflect these discoveries: "The more we know about neuropeptides, the harder it is to think in the traditional terms of a mind and a body. It makes more and more sense to speak of a single integrated entity, a 'bodymind'" (p. 13). She went on to state in 1997: "The concept of a network, stressing the interconnectedness of all systems of the organism, has a variety of paradigm-breaking implications . . . Mind doesn't dominate body, it *becomes* body – body and mind are one" (Pert, 1997, p. 187). Doesn't this mean that if we wish to speak accurately about our emotional world, we need to adopt this new word, bodymind?

To support the breakdown of paradigms, Pert (1997) cited Eric Kandel's (1998) research that identified a psychosomatic network for memories extending between brain and body. The nerve ganglia are the conduits reaching in and near the spinal cord, into internal organs, and to the surface of our skin. Pert argued that we need new thinking consistent with the findings showing "emotions and bodily sensations are thus intricately intertwined, *in a bidirectional network in which each can alter the other*" (Pert, 1997, pp. 141–142, italics added).

Are we ready to breakdown paradigms that do not reflect the integration of "mind" and "body?" Are we ready to integrate thinking and interventions from different healing traditions? I believe Kitty, Johnny, and I were relating from a deep level of bodymind. If we acknowledge the findings that in the realm of emotion there is no mind–body split, it follows that our bodies are always speaking. Body speech, by necessity, will be through sense perceptions and sense memories, within ourselves and between each other. Recognition of bodymind calls for developing greater appreciation of the power of many levels of awareness.

Thinking within psychoanalysis is moving toward bodymind phenomena. Stolorow *et al.*, (2002) called attention to the effects of Cartesian thinking, arguing that "the isolated mind . . . is actually a myth of our culture" (p. 3). Aron and Anderson (1998) "called for renewed attention to the place of the body and somatic experience within a relational paradigm" (p. xxvii). Aron (1998), discussing "body ego," wished "to focus our attention on the place of the body in the mind's self-reflexive functioning, and the effects on the body when self-reflexive functioning is impaired" (p. 3). He reasoned, "The psychoanalytic situation entails two individuals jointly processing, experiencing, and reflecting on psychosomatic phenomena" (p. 3). He explored the idea, consistent with Pert's observations, of a skin ego based on the writings of Anzieu (1985) and Winnicott (1962) in which the skin is the differentiating membrane allowing us to identify boundaries as well as filter interactions.

Aron examined writings on breathing as a parallel model of ego (Eigen, 1993; Epstein, 1995). He credited Eigen (1993) for pointing out that psychoanalysts generally consider the hungers and frustrations of our appetites to be the central organizing feature of the body. We could turn to Eastern psychology and use the breath as an alternative model. Eigen suggested that

> partial identification with the breathing process provides the ego with a model of cohesion and interaction . . . Awareness of breathing points to the dual status of the self, the breathing self, as both subject and object and hence serves to enhance self-reflexive functioning.
>
> (Eigen, 1993, p. 23)

Is it not interesting that breath and breathing played such a pivotal role in my work with both Kitty and Johnny? Surely Eigen and Eastern psychology are emphasizing significant phenomena. Does not breath precede and supercede appetite throughout our lives? Was I helping Kitty to say within bodymind, "I still am because I am aware of my breathing?" With Johnny, I hope he had an easier death because we were saying, "You/ I will be no longer, because we are each aware that your breath is ebbing."

Engler (2003) reminds us that before postmodernism, Buddhism and yogic meditation traditions had evolved methods, including breath training, which enhance subjectivity by "deconstructing this construct of self, not so much to decide a theoretical or philosophical issue about 'reality' but to liberate oneself from what today we would call pathogenic beliefs or dysfunctional cognitions" (p. 88). Breath work may have liberated Kitty from an unspoken dysfunctional cognition that her death was imminent (she lived for six more months). When I stopped breath work by refocusing Johnny's attention to settling down into his mattress, he may have been freed from an unspoken, dysfunctional cognition that he could still fight for life.

In response to Aron and Anderson's (1998) call, Harris (1998) agreed that, "Psychoanalysis is a theory of body-mind integration, and relational theory must grapple with this project" (p. 39). She tied the importance of body-mind integration with the analytic tradition of interest in the analyst's subjectivity. This led her to propose "that the analytic instrument must have very deep and primitive processing abilities. Analysts must have access to and be comfortable with their subjective affect states and bodily reactivity if they are to experience and metabolize patients' communications" (Harris, 1998, p. 40). Harris challenged analysts to ground relational theory within our Freudian heritage "by rejecting a reified and simple biological base to psychic life and meaning. I am suggesting that we make a claim for a relational Freud" (p. 43).

Awareness

Benjamin Wolstein was a living example of "integration" of various modes of therapeutic being. As he said in an interview with Hirsch (2000a), "I've become a complex mixture of various things: a Western psychoanalytic mind, an Eastern Yogic body, and a Hasidic Jewish soul" (p. 193). While he made no direct references in that interview to the influence of his yoga practice on his thinking about the mutative dimensions of psychoanalysis, much of his language is congruent with Buddhism. In one of his summary observations he said, "The distinctive thing that makes a therapy psychoanalysis, I think, is this quest to enlarge the scope of awareness, so as to reintegrate unconscious, preconscious, conscious experience. It's an overall principle governing the exploration of direct experience" (p. 192).

My studies with Tibetan Buddhist teachers have given me the developmental theory that best explains what made my "direct experience" with Kitty and Johnny therapeutic and may provide specific links with some aspects of practice that make psychoanalysis mutative. In Tibetan psychology, as with Wolstein, enlarging the scope of awareness is at the heart of individual growth and practice for easing the suffering inherent in human existence. The respect Tibetans give to awareness is reflected by the many different words they have to describe various levels and dimensions of it. Our vocabulary (conscious, preconscious, and unconscious) is less precise and, consequently, our attentiveness less discriminating.

The Tibetan word for "mind" incorporates "mental energy" and the "awareness principle." Mind encompasses four levels of awareness, significantly expanding what we in Western cultures mean when we use the word "aware." The following is my summary of some key concepts in the teachings and writings of Tarab Tulku (1993,1999a):[1]

- Life begins at conception, as does awareness – at the pure energy level of awareness.
- In utero, a subtle body sense level of awareness develops to form our basic level of "mind."
- Capacities for energy and subtle body sense awareness remain with us throughout life, generally remaining unconscious, as we develop capacities for conscious awareness.
- The moment we engage our conceptual level of mind awareness, we disengage from our immediate sensory perceptions. That is, language takes us a step away from actual, live, direct experience.
- Movement of energy between all levels of awareness is inherent to human existence.
- Wellbeing evolves through free and expanding movement between all levels of awareness.
- All events leave energy imprints that affect that free movement of energy. These events begin in utero and continue throughout our lives.
- All levels of awareness contain the basic qualities of clarity, radiance, and reflection.

Surely we in Western cultures have made an error by ignoring fetal perceptions in our theories of human development. If we accept current research findings, then the Buddhist perspective is more attuned to reality than our thinking. We develop body perceptions from the moment of conception. A subtle body sense distinction between me and not-me starts before we are born. Acceptance of bodymind phenomena means a shift away from language as the primary tool of healing; it opens the field to exploring imagery as a more immediate representation of our actual, live, direct experience. This does not seem like such a radical shift for psychoanalysis given our foundation in working with dream imagery.

In relation to Kitty, I was responding on a level of awareness beyond the way we ordinarily use the term. Some people might say my work with Kitty and Johnny simply demonstrates how effective relaxation and hypnosis can be for symptom relief. While this may be true, I don't believe the efficacy of work with and in altered states is simple. To say my witnessing Kitty's pain simply brought previously dissociated memories into my consciousness may miss important subtleties of the process. Could one say Kitty's sensory experience radiated and resonated with my sensory memory of my experience during my two childbirths? There had to be some preconscious reflection within me to make the association and proceed spontaneously with a therapeutic response. I had no such direct personal experience to draw from with Johnny. However, from personal experience of being in deep trance states – one learns hypnosis by being in a trance state and I have used hypnosis effectively to control a heart arrhythmia induced by the stress of hospice work – I knew to be open to the unexpected.

Subtle sense perception and sensory memory

Kitty, Johnny, and I were relating through both subtle and non-subtle (called "rough level of mind" by Buddhists) sensory perceptions. We were relating subjectively at preconscious and unconscious energy levels of awareness. Some neo-Kleinian writers have emphasized the "subjective relational mode" of being. Rucker and Lombardi (1998), speaking from this perspective, present this mode as a complement to object relations. Their words seem congruent with fundamental teachings of Buddhism. They

> wish to move beyond the concept of the unconscious merely as that which is dynamically repressed or as that which holds dissociated contents, to a concept of the unconscious existing in dynamic relation to conscious processes, serving a linking or translating function between the internal and the external worlds, between self and other, in ways that are the source of intimacy, creativity, and discovery.
> (Rucker and Lombardi, 1998, p. 10)

Could it be that much of our creativity comes from subtle sense perceptions and memory stored in our preconscious and unconscious? Let's examine the breath. The body perception of sensory shifts arising from each breath is generally very subtle. These shifts have meaning generally out of conscious awareness. If I could do a study of analytic timing, I would hypothesize that the creative moment for many verbal interventions is signaled by a shift in patients' breath rhythm. The signals have considerable variety – from breath constriction signaling feeling threatened; or a deeper breath release that could indicate an integration of perceptions that the patient is about to articulate or needs midwifery assistance by the analyst to put into words; or very slow, quiet, abdominal breathing followed by words from deep in the belly, not the chest, representing deeply integrated, emotional truth.

I believe intuition is based in this area of subtle sense perception. Here is where trance states have great value, as shown in my work with Kitty and Johnny. Trance allows us to be more consciously aware of the specific, subtle perceptions that support our intuitive responses. I do not mean to suggest that this process is linear; it is multilayered.

Harris (1998) observed that while we may experience ourselves as a being in one body, "It is probably more accurate to see body ego as a set of layered ego states registering a number of spatiotemporal experiences of self, sometimes simultaneously, sometimes successively. Body and mind construct each other" (p. 49). In a similar vein, Aron (1998) stated, "The construction of a bodily self requires self-reflexivity, and self-reflexivity emerges through intersubjectivity" (p. 4). Is he not implying that to some degree we co-construct our bodyminds?

What would happen to our practice if we acknowledged that among the ubiquitous components of transference and countertransference are energy and subtle sense perceptions bridging body and mind to construct bodymind? Would the questions then become: To what degree and within what format do analyst and patient allow subtle sensory perceptions to become part of shared conscious awareness? Can we then ask with more open minds: How do we explore non-discursive experience? To what extent is that which has been called the ineffable rooted in experience grounded in bodymind? Can the ineffable be more known through greater bodymind sense awareness? Do we as psychoanalysts need to develop more fully our capacities to shift from language into the imagery level of relational experience?

Is there a connection between the analyst's openness to subtle sense perception, degree of presence, and interconnectedness on the level of subtle sense experience that will enhance the subjective relational mode? Is presence a key to working at the subjective relational level? For me, what is called presence rises out of being very connected to direct experience, moment to moment. It rises from trusting perceptions, spontaneity, and the unexpected. I open myself to awareness of subtle sensory relations by letting go of language to see where my non-verbal mind goes – going out of my mind, so to speak, as I did with Kitty and Johnny. As hospice social worker, I explored direct experience non-verbally. As psychoanalyst, subjective explorations become both non-verbal and verbal. Wolstein stated to Hirsch (2000a): "Real analysts use their real experience, their real feeling, their real thoughts, their real intuitions. And the more psychically real, I'm proposing, the more effective therapeutically" (p. 213).

Direct experience

While there could be evidence that Kitty, Johnny and I co-constructed our bodymind experiences, there is another dimension that may be separate from interdependency. Wilner (2000) described Wolstein as believing that "unconscious experience exists in the present tense. It leaps out from us in the here and now" (p. 269). Wilner (1999) summarized his own thinking about this dimension of awareness saying, "Another way of understanding unconscious experience, besides terming it 'unrelational,' may be to see it as not having a subject-object structure" (p. 269). He argued that such experience has no source or aim; no subject and no object. "It is emergent flow that may appear at any time, take any form, and disappear at any moment" (p. 269). The question becomes whether the analyst chooses to work openly with such spontaneous, unbidden experience which may disrupt detailed inquiry and the organization of clinical data.

When Wilner (1999, 2000) refers to the "unrelational," is he reflecting on the unconscious processing Pert (1997) refers to when she described bodymind as bidirectional within ourselves (p. 142)? From the Buddhist perspective, Engler (2003) described non-dual awareness as our natural mode of functioning. Buddhist "traditions therefore tend to nonlinear or 'discovery' models of practice: we're 'already enlightened' from this point of view. The task is to discover our natural state" (p. 67).

Although Kitty's physicians had not told her yet that she was terminal, I came to believe that she (like other hospice patients) knew she was dying through subconscious and unconscious direct experience of her internal condition – her natural state. Essentially, the inner, natural state of dying is unrelational, as is our breathing, and as is physical pain, although clearly my hospice experiences illustrate that these states can be significantly affected by relational phenomena.

By relating to Kitty through my direct experience of her breathing rhythms, I addressed more than her anxiety. Without conscious intent, we were giving each other many messages. She was crying out for help. My initial response was to leave, to feel overwhelmed and helpless, to do nothing for fear that any intrusion might do harm. Once my preconscious sensory memory woke me up, I called attention, non-verbally, to the immediate reality of her being alive. As long as she was breathing, she was alive. Moment by moment, we were sharing Eigen's "body aliveness." I was letting her know that while her husband sat feeling helpless in the kitchen, someone could respond to her with a Winnicottian hold. Through her breath quieting, she was telling me to continue, not to fear doing harm by being too active.

Rucker and Lombardi (1998) propose: "The unconscious is not simply a quality, or a structure equivalent to id, but a mode of being . . . [that] has the quality of being unconscious as a constitutive aspect of its nature" (p. 13). When Kitty's screams and Johnny's pleading eyes resonated within me, I spontaneously shifted internally into a mode of being that altered my consciousness. Working with altered states, practitioners slide into altered states along with their subject/patient, although there are differing degrees of internal engagement. Part of the process of altering consciousness is physical relaxation and release of critical judgment. Anxiety then diminishes. This process allowed me to respond creatively to Kitty and Johnny from my preconscious and unconscious experience. They, in turn, responded to me from their unconscious potentials.

Newirth (2003) developed what he calls a neo-Kleinian model of psychoanalysis focused on the "generative unconscious, integrating concepts derived from relational psychoanalysis, Klein, Winnicott, Bion, Matte Blanco, and Lacan" (p. xi). He outlined the meaning a subjective relational approach brings to day-to-day practice. Much of what he recommends is very compatible with the Buddhist perspective. He called attention to Freud's description of psychoanalysis as "wrestling with the demons of the unconscious" (Newirth, 2003, p. xiii). This imagery reflects an "active, two-person, *physical and kinesthetic experience* – one that captures the important moments of contact between patient and analyst as the psychoanalytic relationship evolves into an intense, personal reality" (p. xii, italics added).

Newirth focused on "five aspects of the analyst's participation that extend the usual two-person relational perspective" (p. xvii):

- Recognition of the dialectic between the analyst's volitional and unwitting participation in the transference–countertransference relationship.
- The analyst's capacity to regress to primitive states of mind.
- The analyst's ability to use reverie in the transformation of the patient's projected and acted-out, concrete, unconscious fantasies.
- Awareness of enactments and transitional experience that bring the lived unconscious fantasies into a symbolic realm.
- Appreciation of the analyst's subjectivity as an integral part of the development of the patient's subjectivity.

My work with Kitty and Johnny brought me into these dimensions of clinical practice. The spontaneous, naive nature of the dynamics between us validates, for me, Newirth's aspects of participation as rising from natural intrapersonal and interpersonal forces, even though we never shifted to words to gain a conscious level of insight. However, consistent with Tarab Tulku's structure of levels of awareness, I prefer to say that I accessed foundational levels of awareness in the realm of subtle sense perceptions. I prefer not to use the language of "regression to primitive states of mind." While I believe Newirth and I are talking about similar subjective states, the words "regression" and "primitive" have too many negative connotations suggesting immaturity to encompass the dynamic that occurred between Kitty, Johnny, and me.

Compassion

It seems to me that subject relations are linked to the mode of relating we call compassion. That realm is non-verbal, expressed through subtleties in tone, manner, air, level of focused attention, body language, and behaviors. It is a bodymind mode of relating. My responses to Kitty and Johnny were based in a visceral response that I believe has a universal human quality, something akin to people's wish to comfort a crying infant. Well into my six years in hospice, I became aware that while I had not sought the job, I was fortunate it had been offered to me. A moment of insight arose when I realized the work evoked and developed in me a tenderness and, I will not be shy here, a type of loving. This loving, for which I was grateful, is probably best called compassion. This is a bodymind phenomena.

Young-Eisendrath (2003), speaking from both a Buddhist and Jungian psychoanalytic perspective, looked at the association between compassion and transformation. She made an observation that describes my hospice work, and resonates with Wolstein and Wilner: "Compassion emerges spontaneously in unique and surprising ways" (p. 303). She believes there are aspects of cultivating compassion that psychoanalysts rarely fully describe: "The first is the patient's engagement in, and eventual awareness of, an unobjectionable idealizing transference" (p. 304). She views this as "the transference of the patient's own developmental potential for wisdom and compassion for self and other, as well as the patient's inherent capacity (however unconscious or nascent) to transcend suffering" (p. 305). This is a "containing-transcendent transference" (p. 308). A second aspect of psychoanalytic cultivation of compassion "is through the ongoing mutual inquiry into the patient's suffering" (p. 306).

It seems to me that Kitty, Johnny, and I were enacting, on a subtle sense level of awareness, both an idealizing transference and an ongoing, mutual, non-verbal inquiry into suffering. I provided a containing environment within which their inherent capacities to transcend their sufferings were released. As part of my containment of what they evoked in me through the radiance of their suffering, some preconscious form of inquiry at the subtle sense perception and sense memory level had to be going on. While we tend to think of "inquiry" as verbal, isn't it as much an attitude? On that level, inquiry can exist without words.

How often is the direct experience of the "way" we respond to our analytic patients more important than the content of "what" they and we say? How often does our self-reflection focus on the pacing, tone, and other qualities in the immediacy of the way we deliver communications to patients? Don't patients know the level of both body and psychic energy we put into the inquiry of suffering? Don't they sense the distinctions between when we speak from just our head, or from our head and gut, or from our head, gut, and heart? "Wolstein's Law" (Hirsch, 2000a) states:

> Every therapist is unique, every patient is unique, every dyad is unique.
> The wider the range of capacity that a therapist has, or, more exactly,
> capability, the greater the willingness to go into many different strange
> and secret places with patients.
>
> (Hirsch, 2000a, p. 188)

Acceptance of these strange, secret places makes it possible for a therapist
to work "in greater personal depth, beyond the borders of intimacy to the
threshold of love" (p. 188). I agree.

Hirsch (2000b) responded to Wolstein: "It may be, however, that an
imperative ingredient to helping patients reach their potentials is what has
been alluded to as analytic love" (p. 299). He clarified that he did not mean
psychoanalysis is a "love cure." I, also, don't mean to imply that the
compassion brought out in me by Kitty and Johnny led to a "love cure."
Hirsch picked up on "Wolstein's Law" about the uniqueness of each
psychoanalytic dyad with the qualification that

> none of these ways may be effective if patients do not feel profoundly
> known and cared for . . . It may not be possible for analysts to convey
> effectively what they see without a bond that can be loosely referred to
> as analytic love.
>
> (Hirsch, 2000b, pp. 299–300)

I would argue that this analytic bond, or love, has its roots in the realm of
subtle sense perceptions. That state, beyond the borders of intimacy, at the
threshold of love, exists in our bodymind, where Kitty, Johnny and I had
feeling for each other. Tarab Tulku (1999b) observed, "Love and compassion are basically the same, but love is more passive, just being there,
and compassion is active, wants to act. Desire and compassion both are
pushing to action" (p. 28).

In our final encounter, I see evidence that on all levels of awareness
Johnny knew his death was imminent. On my bodymind level of awareness,
I must have sensed his closed throat speaking to me of his panic. He drew
me to him, into a state of compassion, a force within me "pushing to
action." I was consciously focused only on helping him release the tension
that was impeding the nurse's attempts to prevent him from choking. When
I could not relate to his breath and shifted attention to the support of the
mattress, I believe I opened myself to preconscious perceptions that led to
my conscious awareness of the immediacy of his death through what
flickered like bizarre visual images, then flashed as insight. I felt electrical
charges in the room changing. How often are we aware of the electrical
currents in the room as patients present "charged" and "dead" commentary to us? Surely this is common experience. Is sensitive attention to
this "charge" related to that illusive quality known as the "timing that
comes with experience?"

Psychoanalysis and Buddhism

Along with others, I believe psychoanalysis and Buddhist practice have much in common, as well as significant differences (Ghent, 1990; Epstein, 1995; Molino, 1998; Watson *et al.*, 1999; Engler, 2003; Safran, 2003). Drawing from Buddhist philosophy, Engler (2003) presented four types of self-experience. All four are normal ways to experience self, although not all are equally common. Two types he sees as similar to Mitchell's (1993) two accounts of self in contemporary psychoanalytic thought: "self as multiple and discontinuous; and self as layered, singular, and continuous. The first type of self-experience is the focus of object relations theory; the second, the central concern of self psychology" (p. 54).

To these categories, Engler (2003) adds third and fourth types of self-experience and subjectivity. The third encompasses "moments in which there is full awareness without any reflexive consciousness of self" (pp. 58–59). These moments can, but need not be mystical. They happen when we are "just doing" a task, without anxiety or self-consciousness, or at times when we are absorbed in an activity. Athletes call this being in the "zone." It permeates experience across the arts, and is at the core of intimacy and love.

> It is surprising to realize how common such experiences are and how completely they permeate our life. And yet this mode of subjectivity has remained peripheral to psychoanalytic theorizing, just as we tend to downplay, dismiss, or ignore it in daily life.
>
> (Engler, 2003, p. 61)

Engler believes *non-dual* awareness characterizes this mode of subjectivity. It seems he is describing what happened to me. I was in a state where I was "unselfconscious but acutely aware, attuned to the realities of the moment" (p. 61). His description agrees with my experience that my internal tension and conflict either dissipated or was held in abeyance. I suspect the latter. Again, he described my experience when he said:

> The result is spontaneity in thought, will, and action. There are two aspects to this spontaneity. First, there is little or no sense that "I" am "doing" anything. Thoughts, feelings, actions occur, but they are not experienced as originating in or by "me." They simply occur as a response to the exigencies of the moment, fluidly, easily, spontaneously, unhampered by extraneous thought.
>
> (Engler, 2003, p. 61)

While we are all familiar with this "ordinary," unselfconscious subjectivity and non-dual awareness, the fourth self-state includes "non-ordinary" states that most Westerners, including most psychoanalytic commentators, consider beyond their areas of interest. These are the states of consciousness associated with meditation and spirituality. Engler (2003) points out that the Eastern "tradition identifies eight discrete levels of absorption, none of which have been recognized let alone incorporated into psychoanalytic thinking" (p. 63).

In a commentary on Engler (2003), Mitchell picked up on the third type of self-experience in which self-consciousness is suspended: "Engler is right to note the lack of attention paid to these states within psychoanalytic theory, with its reliance on structural concepts and its portrayal of the self as having properties like 'permanence' and 'constancy'" (Mitchell, 2003, p. 82). He pointed out that

> Sullivan, who regarded the self essentially as an anti-anxiety system, pointed toward, although he did not elaborate on, such experiences. In an evocative passage, Sullivan (1950) suggests that in a situation with no anxiety there would in fact be no self-system at all.
>
> (Mitchell, 2003, p. 83)

According to Mitchell (2003), Sullivan was criticized by theorists who believed in the importance of a unique, core self. He was accused of viewing people as purely conformist and adaptation oriented because he suggested that the function of the self is to steer clear of and handle anxiety. Mitchell noted:

> What these critics miss is that Sullivan was arguing, like Engler, that the self is a fundamentally narcissistic structure that disappears if there is no need for self-protection. That allows for something quite different to appear in experience. Unfortunately, Sullivan didn't elaborate on what such a no-self state would be like.
>
> (Mitchell, 2003, p. 83)

I wonder what contribution to this dialogue could be made by a "living master" of Buddhist philosophy and psychology such as Tarab Tulku. I suspect that Wolstein, Wilner, Mitchell, and Engler are circling around what Tarab Tulku articulates as various "energy" and "experiencing" levels of "mind-awareness principle." I am not sufficiently knowledgeable about Buddhist philosophy to observe anything beyond the wish to see more exchanges between masters from both traditions. When this occurs, the day-to-day practice of psychoanalysis will be enriched.

Surely I experienced Engler's third type of self-experience with Kitty and Johnny. My encounter with Kitty engaged my memory of trance states I went into (without knowing that was what was happening) during both my training for childbirth and the actual deliveries. I also went into low-level trances working with Johnny. I view these processes as part of the phenomena described by Ghent (1990) as "surrender." Like Wolstein, Ghent (personal communication) had strong ties to Eastern psychology and was a long-time practitioner of meditation.

Ghent (1990) noted a cultural factor: "In many people in our own culture the wish for surrender remains buried" (p. 114). Discussing the challenge surrender presents to psychoanalysts with a Western mindset, he said surrender encompasses more than a way of functioning. It is "characterized by a quality of need, mostly operating out of awareness, yet seemingly with a relentlessness that is not easy to account for in traditional psychoanalytic terms" (p. 113). It "might be thought of as reflective of some 'force' toward growth, for which, interestingly no satisfactory English word exists" (p. 110). Surrender engages the "letting go" that occurs in meditation, trance states, and the creative process.

Imagery

Some therapeutic models are more grounded in imagery than psychoanalysis, despite our roots in hypnosis and our ongoing foundation in dream analysis. Following the Buddhist position that language takes us away from the immediacy of sense experience, I would argue that it is imagery that represents bodymind and both subtle and "rough" sense perceptions and memory. To fully enter into subject relations, we must enter more fully into the realm of imagery and bodymind.

From Jungian analysis, Bosnak (2003) developed interventions to work with imagination and imagery to deepen our ability to work subjectively. Bromberg (2003) praised his work saying, "He has opened a clinical frontier . . . that can potentially lead us beyond the territory of dreams per se, into an enrichment of the total therapy environment" (p. 701). Bosnak (2003) reaches into affective states through imagery as well as dream work. He brings the patient into embodied images by addressing experience directly through descriptive language of sensory perceptions of whatever image arises. It is a more active mode of relating to patients than traditional psychoanalysis. Bosnak (2003) says, "A multiplicity of subjectivities is the norm, not the pathology . . . The main task of imaginal work is to let the variety of selves be aware of one another by networking them through the *craft of imagination*" (p. 688). He focuses on qualities embodied in images such as solidity, suppleness, and movement. These qualities represent affect. He initiates the embodied state through a safe point, such as entering a stone building to "harvest its solid strength" before entering white water, which is not a safe image. Sometimes he traces the energy of motion, such as fear of steepness. He repeatedly asks "What is it like to be in front of a wave? . . . What is it like inside the shaking?" (p. 692).

Bromberg's (2003) commentary on Bosnak highlights the value of this questioning. "What is it like?" helps the patient hold "two disjunctive self-states simultaneously" (Bromberg, 2003, p. 707). Bromberg emphasized his own belief in "'normal dissociation' – the natural hypnoid capacity of the mind that works in the service of creative adaptation" (p. 701). He wove together many concepts of current interest to psychoanalysts: "Magical field, dream space, embodied imagination, potential space, transitional space, the analytic third – each a slightly different version of our efforts to symbolize in language what we cannot not yet fully comprehend" (Bromberg, 2003, p. 699).

Imagery includes all five senses, not just the visual. With Kitty, I had the image of my own pain relief during childbirth. My words, guided by the rhythm of her breathing, one could associate to the rhythm of a lullaby and the movement of a rocking chair. I was essentially asking, "What is this like for her?" as I listened to the changes in her screams and watched her breathing change. I only continued because I could answer, "What I am doing seems to bring her comfort." Later I learned to ask all my patients, "Can you tell me what that was like for you?" after I offered a mind-body intervention, and they agreed to "give it a try." That question was woven into my work with Johnny after he accepted my offer to teach him "self-hypnosis" when I first met him. Isn't the question, "What is it like?" at the heart of empathy and compassion?

Conclusion

Are we ready to break down paradigms that do not reflect the integration of "mind" and "body"? Are we ready to integrate interventions from different healing traditions? Research in neuroscience requires the creation of paradigms even more expansive than those introduced by current psychoanalysts. Our ancestral roots in hypnosis warrant greater exploration. Hirsch (2000b) remembered that in supervision, "Wolstein would advocate yoga for us as a way to become more connected with our respective psychic centers" (p. 297). Engler (2003) addressed the contribution meditation and trance states could make to expanding our subjective awareness: "[Meditation] practice proceeds from the assumption that non-dual awareness is our natural mode of functioning. Practice simply calls attention to it, grounds us in it, and allows our natural functioning to function naturally" (p. 67). Recommending that patients meditate or develop other skills to expand awareness through altered states of consciousness could be a valuable adjunct to enhance the psychoanalytic process and deserves discussion.

If we have a "generative unconscious," as neo-Kleinians propose (Rucker and Lombardi, 1998; Newirth, 2003) and my experience with hospice patients seems to confirm, how do we address the subject? Newirth (2003) quotes Freud's (1905) warning, "No one who, like me, conjures up the most evil of those half-tamed demons that inhabit the human breast, and seeks to wrestle with them, can expect to come through the struggle unscathed" (p. xiii). I believe Kitty and Johnny showed me that there is a generative unconscious at the heart of which the angels of mercy reside in a wealth of subtle sense perceptions. Just as a commitment to engage in the struggle of psychoanalysis has its perils, deeply felt engagement (shall we call it love?), especially within the realm of subtle sense awareness, brings unsentimental blessings by the angels of the generative unconscious. Kitty and Johnny brought such blessings to me.

Note

1 Tarab Tulku is a high-level monk whom the Dalai Lama asked to preserve Tibetan philosophy and psychology. He has been Head, Tibetan Section, Royal Library of Denmark and Head, Tibetan Studies, Copenhagen University. Since 1994 he has developed and directed a school of psychotherapy with Lene Handberg, a Danish Jungian psychoanalyst. He is known in Europe, but not well known in the United States. In 1997, I was privileged to spend a week training with him and Dr. Handberg. Since writing this chapter, I sadly learned that Tarab Tulku recently died.

References

Anzieu, D. (1985) *The Skin Ego*. New Haven, CT: Yale University Press, 1989.

Aron, L. (1998) The clinical body and the reflexive mind. In L. Aron and F.S. Anderson (eds) *Relational Perspectives on the Body*, pp. 3–37. Hillsdale, NJ: Analytic Press.

Aron, L. and Anderson, F.S. (eds) (1998) *Relational Perspectives on the Body*. Hillsdale, NJ: Analytic Press.

Bion, W. (1961) A theory of thinking. *International Journal of Psychoanalysis*, 43: 306–310.

Bosnak, R. (2003) Embodied imagination. *Contemporary Psychoanalysis*, 39: 683–695.

Bromberg, P. (2003).On being one's dream. *Contemporary Psychoanalysis*, 39: 697–710.

Eigen, M. (1993) *The Electrified Tightrope*. Northvale, NJ: Aronson.

Engler, J. (2003) Being somebody and being nobody: a re-examination of the understanding of self in psychoanalysis and Buddhism. In J.D. Safran (ed.) *Psychoanalysis and Buddhism*, pp. 35–79. Boston, MA: Wisdom.

Epstein, M. (1995) *Thoughts without a Thinker*. New York: Basic Books.

—— (1999) *Going to Pieces without Falling Apart*. New York: Broadway Books.

Freud, S. (1905) On psychotherapy. *Standard Edition*, 7: 257–268. London: Hogarth Press, 1955.

—— (1923) The ego and the id. *Standard Edition*, 19: 3–68. London: Hogarth Press, 1961.

Ghent, E. (1990) Masochism, submission, surrender. *Contemporary Psychoanalysis*, 26: 108–136.

Harris, A. (1998) Psychic envelopes and sonorous baths: siting the body in relational theory and clinical practice. In L. Aron and F.S. Anderson (eds) *Relational Perspectives on the Body*, pp. 39–64. Hillsdale, NJ: Analytic Press.

Hirsch, I. (2000a) Interview with Benjamin Wolstein. *Contemporary Psychoanalysis*, 36: 187–232.

—— (2000b) Alone yet connected: response to the discussion. *Contemporary Psychoanalysis*, 36: 289–300.

Kandel, E.R. (1998) A new intellectual framework for psychiatry. *American Journal of Psychiatry*, 155(4): 457–469.

Mitchell, S. (1993) *Hope and Dread in Psychoanalysis*. New York: Basic Books.

—— (2003) Somebodies and nobodies. Commentary on chapter by Jack Engler. In J.D. Safran (ed.) *Psychoanalysis and Buddhism*, pp. 80–100. Boston, MA: Wisdom.

Molino, A. (ed.) (1998) *The Couch and the Tree*. New York: North Point Press.

Newirth, J. (2003) *Between Emotion and Cognition*. New York: Other Press.

Notley, A. (1996) *The Descent of Alette*. New York: Penguin.

Pert, C.B. (1986) Neuropeptides: the emotions and bodymind. *Advances*, 3: 12–18.

—— (1997) *Molecules of Emotion*. New York: Scribner.

Pert, C.B., Ruff, M.R., Weber, R.J. and Herkenham, M. (1985) Neuropeptides and their receptors: a psychosomatic network. *Journal of Immunology*, 135 supplement: 820s–826s.

Rucker, N. and Lombardi, K. (1998) *Subject Relations*. New York: Routledge.

Safran, J.D. (ed.) (2003) *Psychoanalysis and Buddhism*. Boston, MA: Wisdom.

Stolorow, R.D., Atwood, G.E. and Orange, D.M. (2002) *Worlds of Experience*. New York: Basic Books.

Sullivan, H. (1950) The illusion of personal individuality. In H. Sullivan, *The Fusion of Psychiatry and the Social Sciences*. New York: Norton, 1964.

Tarab Tulku (1993) *Tibetan Psychology and Psychotherapy*. Copenhagen: Tarab Institute.

—— (1999a) *Nearness to Oneself and Openness to the World*. Nijmegen, The Netherlands: Jewel Heart Transcript.

—— (1999b) Lucid dreaming: exerting the creativity of the unconscious. In G. Watson, S. Batchelor and G. Claxton (eds) *The Psychology of Awakening*, pp. 271–283. London: Rider.

Watson, G., Batchelor, S. and Claxton, G. (eds) (1999) *The Psychology of Awakening*. London: Rider.

Wilner, W. (1999) The un-consciousing of awareness in psychoanalytic therapy. *Contemporary Psychoanalysis*, 35: 617–626.

—— (2000) A legacy of self: the unique psychoanalytic perspective of Benjamin Wolstein. *Contemporary Psychoanalysis*, 36: 267–279.

Winnicott, D.W. (1962) Ego integration in child development. In D.W. Winnicott, *The Maturational Process and the Facilitating Environment*, pp. 56–63. New York: International Universities Press, 1965.

Young-Eisendrath, P. (2003) Transference and transformation in Buddhism and psychoanalysis. In J.D. Safran (ed.) *Psychoanalysis and Buddhism*, pp. 301–330. Boston, MA: Wisdom.

Chapter 17

A relational perspective on working with dying patients in a nursing home setting

Stephen W. Long

Psychoanalysis has a history of addressing matters related to death, including Freud's (1920) theorizing on the death instinct, and Melanie Klein's (1957) on the impact of this instinct on psychological development beginning in the earliest days of infancy. The death instinct has been looked at as an explanation for repetition, separation, experiences of psychological and physical disintegration, and aggression. However, other psychoanalytic authors (e.g., Winnicott, 1963; Bowlby, 1969; Mahler *et al.*, 1975; Stern, 1985; Blanck and Blanck, 1986; Beebe and Lachman, 1988) saw greater utility in focusing on the individual's experience of others early in development and the internalization of that experience as more crucial to explanations of psychological development than instinct. Many contemporary psychoanalytic authors and those whose thinking influenced these authors (e.g., Strachey, 1934; Jacobson, 1971; Stolorow and Lachmann, 1984–1985; Ferenczi, 1988; Mitchell, 1988; Ehrenberg, 1992; Bromberg, 1993; Hirsch, 1994; Aron, 1996; Slochower, 1996) have emphasized the impact of current relationships, particularly the one between analyst and patient, on the perpetuation or transformation of various aspects of the patient's psychological functioning.

This chapter addresses the importance of three psychoanalytic concepts, consistent with the contemporary relational focus in psychoanalysis – mirroring, the holding environment, and mutuality in the patient–analyst relationship – for working with terminally ill patients in a nursing home setting.

Mirroring

Psychoanalytic self psychology elaborated the concept of mirroring, the experience of having oneself accepted and confirmed by another (Kohut, 1971; Muslin, 1992). Mirroring is needed throughout life for the individual's optimal functioning (Mitchell and Black, 1995). In the analytic or therapeutic situation, the analyst engages in mirroring when the analyst's words and behavior reflect back to the patient what the patient thinks and feels in a way the patient perceives as accurate.

Mirroring Mrs. V

Mrs. V was 76 years old. She had a history that included a diagnosis of schizophrenia. Over the years, she received treatment with antipsychotic medications, largely on an outpatient basis. Though her behavior was retiring and somewhat withdrawn, her medical record showed no clear indications of her having had a debilitating psychotic episode in many years. She was admitted to the nursing home with left-side hemiparisis following a stroke that occurred a month after her husband of fifty years died. Her two adult children lived with their own families in distant states.

About a year after her admission, Mrs. V was diagnosed with pancreatic cancer. Shortly after that, she frequently reported not knowing where she was, though she was often reminded. When she left her room, she could not find her way back. She had mild to moderate memory impairment earlier, but after learning she was terminally ill, Mrs. V had marked difficulty remembering recent things. She also began stating, and presented as though she had profound difficulty hearing. The hearing aids that had previously been helpful were no longer of any use. She was very anxious and depressed.

I visited Mrs. V in her room, which is where she stayed nearly all the time, resisting staff efforts to encourage her to take part in available activities. She usually sat without even having the television on unless a staff member turned it on, suggesting that it would help her to have some stimulation.

Mrs. V explained she could not hear me when I spoke. However, she heard me say who I was after I said it quite loudly several times. She also heard me ask how she felt after I asked this loudly several times. Mrs. V said she felt very nervous and depressed. When I asked her questions, she typically said something like, "What? You know, I have trouble with my hearing. I don't hear very well. I know you're trying to say something to me but I just don't hear you." Not knowing exactly what to do, yet hoping to make some connection with her, when Mrs. V told me she was nervous and depressed I just restated what she had said of herself, "You're very nervous and depressed." Without hesitation, she responded, "That's right." She went on to say, "I don't know what's happening to me." I reflected back what I thought was the meaning of what she said, "What's happening to you is confusing." Mrs. V said, "Yes, and I can't remember things. I used to have a good memory. But now I can't remember from one minute to the next. I can't even carry on a conversation because I forget what is being talked about and I know I don't make any sense." Up to this point, my simply restating what Mrs. V said seemed to be followed by her saying more in a way that suggested she was hearing better. After what she said about her not being able to make sense in a conversation, thinking I would be allying myself with a more effective sense

of herself, I said, "Mrs. V, you were just talking with me and making sense."
Mrs. V looked blankly at me, then responded, "I know you're saying something. I just don't know what it is. I have a problem with my ears." Without
really speaking any louder, I returned to trying to mirror what Mrs. V was
expressing, "It's hard for you to hear me." Mrs. V then said, "That's right." I
continued by saying, "But it's pretty important to you that I hear you." "Well,
I get lonely. But I'm afraid to leave my room because when I do, I can't find
my way back again," she said. I responded, "It's good that I come to you. If
you had to leave where you are to find someone to be with you, you would
get confused and lost. That's pretty frightening." She continued, "I've been
very scared since my husband died."

In this excerpt from an early meeting with Mrs. V, anything I said that
was not a restatement, reflection, or mirroring of what she said or seemed
to feel, anything that was not validation or echoing (Feil, 1993; Bouklous,
1997) of her own subjective experience appeared to have a notably
disorganizing effect on her. Calling on her to consider thoughts or feelings
other than the ones she appeared to allow herself seemed to trigger an
increase in her experience of hearing impairment, confusion, and anxiety.
However, as I focused my participation with her on reflecting back to her
what she was saying, evidence of these symptoms declined.

Holding

Holding is an aspect of psychoanalytic treatment that is not directly aimed at
increasing the patient's awareness or understanding of the patient's psychological functioning (Slochower, 1996). It allows for elaboration of self-
experience. Holding may be seen as a metaphor for the analyst's attunement
or openness and responsiveness to the patient's emotional states. The therapeutic relationship can provide space, a holding environment (Winnicott,
1963), in which the patient's experience of self, others, and the broader
context in which they are embedded can be elaborated. In the relationship
with the analyst, there is room for the patient.

Traditionally in the psychoanalytic literature, holding has been addressed
as a metaphor for the mother–infant relationship (Winnicott, 1963). Here
the infant's dependency has been viewed as the paramount concern of
the mother while she offers sustenance, reassurance, and engagement.
Slochower (1996) points out that there is some overlap among this view of
holding, self psychology's concept of mirroring, and Mahler et al.'s (1975)
concept of refueling. All these concepts address the child's need for experiencing mother as present, unintrusive, yet responsive. The parent contains
the parent's affective processes, needs, agenda, providing space within

which the child can experience the child's self. This appears to facilitate the child's adaptive and changing experience of self, others, and the world.

Winnicott (1963), Kohut (1971), and Slochower (1996) have described therapeutic holding or similar processes as central to the treatment of patients having dependent, self-involved, ruthless, or hate-filled personality structures, and with patients whose characterological mistrust of others leaves them in a cycle of hope and despair. Slochower (1996) pointed out that holding may also be crucial for those with less fragile personalities, at times of overwhelming stress. Events like terminal illness, severely ill health, losses of mental and physical functions, of relationships, of possessions, and of social status can be such stressors. They can undermine or eliminate many of the things with which people define and give meaning to their lives, to their individual selves.

Holding Mr. D

Mr. D was an 84-year-old nursing home resident with terminal cancer. He had a daughter from whom he had been estranged for many years. Though still married, he had not seen his wife for more than twenty years. He made repeated trips toward the nursing home's front door, insisting that he could go home on his own, that he would be fine. This went on for a number of days. Each time, he was told about various aspects of the reality of his situation by a staff member. He was reminded, for example, that there was no one at home to help him with the things he needed. His response to these reminders was to quietly return to his room. Then two episodes occurred in which he screamed obscenities at the staff member who was trying to reorient him to the realities of his situation. In the third such episode, a psychological consultation was requested.

I arrived during the heat of the third episode. Mr. D was at the nurses' station shouting about being held prisoner against his will. Standing alongside him, I briefly listened, then said, "You're pretty ticked off."

"Damn right, I'm ticked off. These people won't let me go home," Mr. D responded.

"You want to go home and these people are getting in your way," I reflected back to him.

Mr. D continued, "That's right. They keep saying I need help. I don't need their damned help."

"You can take care of yourself," I mirrored back what he seemed to be saying.

Mr. D said, "I always have. I got work when I was 13 to help out at home. And I was never sick. If you were out sick, you didn't get paid back then." He was no longer yelling.

"It's important not to be sick," I said.

"Well, yes. You're not much use to anyone if you're sick," said Mr. D.

I responded by saying, "You need to be of use to people."

Since the door to the lounge was just a few feet away and we could be out of the hall traffic there, I asked Mr. D if we could go there and sit down to talk. He said that would be fine. As we walked, Mr. D asked who I was. I explained I was a psychologist.

"How do I get out of here and back home?" Mr. D asked as we sat down.

I said I was not sure what to tell him about that.

After a brief pause, Mr. D said, "Everyone in this place is dying. Last night my roommate died."

"That's pretty frightening," I said.

Mr. D continued, "I didn't really know him. He was in the room when I first came here. He didn't say anything though. He was too sick to talk. His family visited a lot. They were good people."

Mr. D went on speaking of the prison-like atmosphere he experienced in the nursing home, how useless he felt, how insignificant. He went on to talk of his early adulthood, of his work, and how most of his life he traveled around the country. Eventually, he spoke of his illness, his increasing fragility, and his approaching death.

Prior to our meeting, Mr. D had been relying a good deal on denial to deal with thoughts and feelings emerging due to his losses, declining health, and dying. He was unable to contain the anxiety, fear, and despair any other way but to deny his condition and take flight. Staff's directly confronting his denial by orienting him to the reality of his situation had not improved his psychological or behavioral functioning. In fact, it seemed to worsen how he felt and behaved. On the other hand, having his thoughts and feelings reflected back to him was followed by improvements in both his emotional state and behavior. As he was mirrored, he stopped shouting accusations about how staff members were jailers, and his attempts to abscond ended. Finally, Mr. D spoke of how difficult it was for him to become increasingly dependent and to know that he was near death. It seemed necessary for Mr. D to have the experience of what he thought and felt being accepted, made room for, held, or contained. Then he could tolerate more of his experience and admit it to consciousness, rather than try to escape it by taking flight or by battling with those he saw as not allowing him to escape.

Mutuality

Mutuality refers to reciprocation (Ferenczi, 1988). In therapeutic or analytic situations, it can be the interplay of the subjective experiences of analyst and patient (Aron, 1996). In relational psychoanalytic approaches, the patient's experience of the relationship with the analyst is the base upon which therapeutic gain is made. It is assumed that therapeutic experience of the relationship and, as it becomes tolerable for the patient, examination of the patient's experience of it, improves the patient's functioning.

What the patient does or does not say or do in the therapeutic situation is affected by the patient's perceptions of the analyst, perceptions rooted both in the patient's experience of earlier relationships and in what the analyst does. As mirroring and holding help a patient develop a sense of stability, security, and integration, the patient may become increasingly able to tolerate moments in which the analyst is not experienced as a reflection of the self. The individuality of the analyst will be better tolerated and not reacted to as a disruptive, negligent, or hostile intrusion. In fact, the perception of the analyst's individuality may serve to help the patient experience the self as bounded, given definition, meaning and value. Over time, a distressed patient may become able to tolerate increasing evidence of the analyst's separateness, making it possible for the analyst to function in the traditional capacity of providing interpretations of the patient's unconscious functioning.

Mrs. O

Mrs. O, an 81-year-old widow, was a resident of the nursing home for several years. She had no surviving close family members but was visited monthly by a niece. Mrs. O had a severe case of chronic obstructive pulmonary disease. Her illness had progressed to where her breathing was so impaired that her death seemed likely to occur within months.

Mrs. O was described by staff as a difficult person. She typically berated anyone who entered her room. In addition to her loud insults, she was very demanding, rarely making a request, but, rather, stating what she wanted done, how she wanted it done, and that she wanted it done immediately. Several staff members stated that there was a marked increase in Mrs. O's difficult behavior over recent weeks. They were feeling burnt out in dealing with her, so psychological consultation was requested.

When I first visited Mrs. O in her room, she was curt and dismissive, as staff members had described she would be. For example, when I introduced myself as a psychologist, she said, "I don't need a psychologist. If I need anything I'll call for a real doctor." However, as I tried to mirror her experience, she went on to describe how her day-to-day existence had become focused more and more on her loss of ability, personal effectiveness, or power. Mrs. O described her experience of being increasingly dependent as being "at the mercy" of others who assumed the right to intrude upon her most personal moments and functions without showing the respect of even the smallest reciprocity in their dealings with her. Her experience was that there was no give-and-take to provide evidence that she mattered, that she, as an individual, existed. She had increasingly relied on treating others in "the only way they understand", with insults and anger – the only way that got responses to her. Any responses that she could elicit, she explained, prevented her from "giving up, just rolling over and dying."

From our first meeting, Mrs. O had many questions. They ranged from demographic types like how old I was, where I went to school, whether I was married, etc., to how I felt about situations, things, people, her. My attempts to not answer, but to explore their meaning with her, only led to her angrily withdrawing, becoming impatiently dismissive and sarcastic. For example, early in our work together, Mrs. O asked what it was like for me to spend time with someone who was so clearly dying when just about everyone else did whatever they could to avoid her. I did not answer, but asked her what she thought it was like for me. In response, she silently shook her head and turned away. "I'm tired now, *Doctor*," Mrs. O said. "Turn on the TV (the remote control was out of her reach) and tell the nurse I want to talk to her."

I said, "When I didn't answer your question, it was like I pushed you away. Now you're pushing me away."

Without any apparent reaction to what I said, Mrs. O continued, "I think the news will be on soon."

Trying to restate the message of her behavior, I said, "You're really leaving me behind."

Mrs. O replied by saying, "I think you'd better go now, Doctor," not sounding quite as impatient or sarcastic as she had.

My response was, "It hurts when you're pushed away or left, as though what you're saying doesn't matter, as though you don't matter."

Mrs. O asked, "Are you speaking for yourself?"

"I think I'm speaking for both of us," I answered.

With that, Mrs. O's demeanor shifted. She paused. Looking at me, she smiled and said, "There's hope for you yet." She went on to say she appreciated that I responded to her, that I let her know how I felt. She continued by talking about how she was not dead yet, that there was still a "her" to be responded to.

Mrs. O apparently was sensitive to the experience of being pushed away, of being left, sensitive to evidence that she was being held at an emotional distance. It seemed that when she had this kind of experience, she tended to identify with what she saw as the hostile, withholding, other person whom she experienced as an aggressor who expressed aggression through neglect.

Identifying in this way, she was able to avoid being helplessly abandoned. She took the powerful, not the powerless position. Mrs. O appeared to project the unwanted experience of being powerless, unwanted, neglected, even disdained, into the other person. Unfortunately, this approach seemed more likely to push others farther away, leaving her without a more integrating experience of relatedness based less on splitting and projective identification. Once I acknowledged my inner experience of the pain of being pushed away and left, and how that pain seemed like her own, Mrs. O's attempts to be rid of me during this session ended. In fact, as similar episodes of mutuality occurred, Mrs. O's rudeness, demandingness, and insults notably declined. Initially, her apparently strong hunger for such reciprocal exchanges seemed indicated by her frequent initiation of these interactions. These types of interactions gradually decreased during our work.

Mrs. O's declining physical condition and increasing nearness to death were considerable insults to her sense of power, her sense of being capable. What facilitated improvement in her psychological and behavioral functioning was her experience of impacting another person in a way that allowed her to feel connected. She seemed to need others to be responsive to her reaching out to them, to have them tolerate her wanting to know them, to have them contain whatever reactions they had that would motivate them to avoid connection with her. Mrs. O's experience of the interpersonal environment appeared crucial to her optimal psychological and behavioral functioning. In the end, her psychological functioning was significantly influenced not only by her increasingly impaired health, but also by the meaning her existence, even her dying, had for her, meaning greatly influenced by her experience of herself in relation to others.

Conclusion

This chapter has focused on the utility of the psychoanalytic concepts of mirroring, holding environment, and mutuality in establishing and maintaining a therapeutic relationship in work with terminally ill, nursing home residents. The principal aim in the therapeutic approach described is that the relationship be one which the patient can experience as emotionally attuned, empathic. This aim may largely be achieved through the analyst's mirroring the patient's experience. In other instances, it can be furthered through self-disclosure on the part of the analyst.

For a terminally ill patient, having one's thoughts or emotions reflected back or reacted to by another person, or feeling those thoughts or emotions are acknowledged and tolerated by another can provide a sense not just of reassurance, but of still having existence, even as that existence is coming to an end. The subjective experience of being understood, grasped, or held in this way – until the point of accepting letting go and of being let go has been reached – may have a profound, positive effect in easing life's final, major transition, from life to death.

References

Aron, L. (1996) *A Meeting of Minds: Mutuality in Psychoanalysis*. Hillsdale, NJ: Analytic Press.

Beebe, B. and Lachman, F. (1988) Mother–infant mutual influence and the precursors of psychic structure. In A. Goldberg (ed.) *Frontiers in Self Psychology*, Volume 3, pp. 3–25. Hillsdale, NJ: Analytic Press.

Blanck, G. and Blanck, R. (1986) *Beyond Ego Psychology*. New York: Columbia University Press.

Bouklous, G. (1997) *Psychotherapy with the Elderly*. Northvale, NJ: Jason Aronson.

Bowlby, J. (1969) *Attachment and Loss: Volume 1, Attachment*. New York: Basic Books.

Bromberg, P. (1993) Shadow and substance. *Psychoanalytic Psychology*, 10(2): 147–168.

Ehrenberg, D. (1992) *The Intimate Edge*. New York: Norton.

Feil, N. (1993) *The Validation Breakthrough*. Baltimore, MD: Health Professions Press.

Ferenczi, S. (1988) *The Clinical Diary of Sandor Ferenczi*. Cambridge, MA: Harvard University Press.

Freud, S. (1920) *Beyond the Pleasure Principle. Standard Edition*, 18: 3–64. London: Hogarth Press, 1955.

Hirsch, I. (1994) Countertransference love and theoretical model. *Psychoanalytic Dialogues*, 4: 171–192.

Jacobson, E. (1971) *Depression*. New York: International Universities Press.

Klein, M. (1957) *Envy and Gratitude and Other Works: 1946–63*. New York: Delacorte.

Kohut, H. (1971) *The Analysis of the Self*. New York: International Universities Press.

Mahler, M., Pine, F. and Bergman, A. (1975) *The Psychological Birth of the Human Infant*. New York: Basic Books.

Mitchell, S. (1988) *Relational Concepts in Psychoanalysis*. Cambridge, MA: Harvard University Press.

Mitchell, S. and Black, M. (1995) *Freud and Beyond: A History of Modern Psychoanalytic Thought*. New York: Basic Books.

Muslin, H.L. (1992) *The Psychotherapy of the Elderly Self*. New York: Brunner/ Mazel.

Slochower, J.A. (1996) *Holding and Psychoanalysis: A Relational Perspective*. Hillsdale, NJ: Analytic Press.

Stern, D. (1985) *The Interpersonal World of the Infant*. New York: Basic Books.

Stolorow, R. and Lachman, F. (1984–1985) Transference: the future of an illusion. *Annual of Psychoanalysis*, Volumes 12–13, pp. 19–37. New York: International Universities Press.

Strachey, J. (1934) The nature of the therapeutic action of psychoanalysis. In M. Bergman and F. Hartman (eds) *The Evolution of Psychoanalytic Technique*, pp. 331–360. New York: Basic Books.

Winnicott, D.W. (1963) Psychiatric disorders in terms of infantile maturational processes. In D.W. Winnicott, *The Maturational Processes and the Facilitating Environment*, pp. 230–241. New York: International Universities Press.

Chapter 18

Love and death

Affect sharing in the treatment of the dying

Bruce Herzog

Years ago I saw two people in my practice who were dying and desperate to talk to someone. I initially had no idea of what to do with either of them, which was for the best, because as I searched in earnest for what was needed, I eventually found myself being directed by them towards a particular therapeutic event. What they seemed to require of me had to do with their wish to express something very important to them, and to know that I had understood them deeply enough to have felt what they had felt; to know that their affective experience had been *shared* by me. I like to refer to this clinical phenomenon as *affect sharing*, where a therapist both experiences and communicates about a mutual affect state occurring within the analytic dyad.

Affect sharing is very closely related to the topic of empathy. This particular function of an empathic connection keeps coming up over and over again in my practice, and in these two cases of people nearing the end of their lives, it was quite prominent. My interest is in a specific empathic function within the analytic dyad, where the patient attempts to communicate a feeling state in such a way that it reverberates within the therapist. As a result, the therapist may sense he or she is feeling what the patient feels. When this happens, the therapist's communication to the patient that the affective experience has been shared can have a profound therapeutic impact.

Affect sharing from birth to death

My thinking about the sharing of affect began during one of my first experiences of a successful termination of treatment with a woman who told me:

> I felt as if I'd gone back to my past, relived the scenes of my life, and that I wasn't alone anymore; that we were there together. When I knew that *you could feel how it felt to me*, then I knew that things had really happened . . . I don't feel as alone as I used to.
>
> (Herzog, 1998, p. 181)

It was then I realized that the ability to have your affective experience felt by another was a vital part of the therapeutic endeavour, an essential component of healthy development and something we continue to search for as adults.

That may sound like I'm overstating the case, but I'd like to go even further. I suspect that the sharing of affect is a central relational experience; important enough that if there is too little of it in our early life we may become severely depressed, and could be at risk of physical illness or even death.

Consider René Spitz's (1945, 1946) observation that infants who have had minimal human contact have a shockingly high mortality rate despite superior hygiene and care. Spitz elegantly demonstrated something that good psychoanalysts and parents have always intuitively known: children need to be held and played with; if not, they simply fail to thrive. It's a human need that is difficult to quantify and in fact may be beyond the reach of scientific measurement, but it is there all the same.

Spitz's children demonstrated to us the importance of the need to touch and be touched; but integral to the experience of mutual touching is the responsiveness of the other, and I believe that this responsiveness is necessary for the touch to be beneficial. Touching alone is not sufficient; there also needs to be a communication that the pleasure of the touch has been genuinely shared. To support this idea, I'd ask you to consider the simple act of hand holding. The offering of one's hand to someone we love carries with it the hope that the other hand will squeeze back, which can lead us to an experience of elation and wellbeing. When the other hand is limp and unresponsive, we can feel jilted, hurt and even damaged. Either eventuality involves the same two hands having contact, but the pleasure of touching just doesn't cut the mustard if there is no pleasure being experienced by the other party involved. Touching is more than just the action of skin, flesh and bones. Fundamental to someone's pleasure in touching is the experience of the other's resonating with the same pleasure.

The knowledge that a mutual affective experience has occurred is fundamental in affect sharing, and this sharing can come about through many means other than physical contact. The use of descriptive language is a very effective way to share affect, being the most common method used by our patients in their analyses.

Years ago the need for companionship and intimacy was acknowledged as a primary motivator of human behavior by Ian Suttie (1935), who understood and emphasized its importance. I believe that the basic motivation behind the need for companionship involves the universal human requirement to share one's experience and its associated affect with another. The notion of affect sharing narrows down the companionship experience to one of its primary elements: We need to know that others are feeling what we feel. If this were not the case, then much of what we search for in our relationships would be unnecessary. For example, without the motivation to share affective experience, there would be little need to have sexual relations, since masturbation is a much more efficient and considerably less troublesome method of drive discharge. Further, we would have no need to talk about a good book we just read, share something delicious we have on our plate, or dialogue with like-minded professionals at conferences.

In the analytic endeavour, a patient may attempt to create an atmosphere within the analytic couple through the presentation of a detailed and evocative narrative, which allows the therapist to share in that patient's affect state. This is one of the forms of affect sharing that is often manifested in the therapeutic environment which I have called *descriptive sharing*. *Active sharing* is another form, which refers to patient initiated efforts at engaging in a mutual activity with the therapist; what some might call an enactment. In both forms of affect sharing a patient strives for the sensation that what he or she has felt, has been felt by another. When a patient initiates either of these forms of affect sharing, the therapist's subsequent communication that he can understand and feel someone's affect state functions to provide credible reassurance that the patient is not alone.

Loneliness is a frightening and tragic part of the process of dying for many. When we are sought out by people who know they are dying, there may be a pressing need to assuage their sense of isolation. In the two cases I will be presenting, I believe that these people urgently wanted to have their affective experience shared by another so that they would know that they were not dying alone. Both patients were driven to seek help because of their need to have someone hear their story and feel an authentic affective connection with them.

Case 1

Getting called onto the ward at the Mount Sinai Hospital was never a favorite activity of mine when I worked there as a resident. I much preferred seeing my outpatients in psychotherapy. The ward consultations, instructive as they were in understanding the patient within a certain staff dynamic, were usually not of much interest to me – especially in this case, where I was asked to see a terminal cancer patient who had become psychotic on her morphine drip. "It's a no-brainer," I was reassured by the nurse in charge. "Just an order for Haldol and you're out of here."

Arriving at the bedside of the patient in question, I had a few surprises in store. She was a lovely West Indian woman who was only in her early thirties, diagnosed as being in the terminal phase of ovarian cancer. She had that look of desperation that tends to repulse people; her arms reached forward towards anyone that passed, her eyes widened when she found someone willing to return her gaze. In addition, her heavy accent combined with the slurring of speech that her medication caused made it hard for people to comprehend what she was saying. This was a profoundly tragic picture, compounded by the fact that all of her family was in the West Indies, and that she was dying alone in a hospital where people were actively keeping their distance from her.

Early on in my only meeting with her, she directed our interview to what the staff had felt were morphine-induced hallucinations: "The sand is black you know." I had worked for a few months in a medical ward on a Caribbean island just two years before, which helped me in understanding both her accent and what she was trying to talk about. The island where I had worked was famous for its volcanic black sand beaches. I commented: "Yes, black sand is quite something isn't it? Where are you from?" She became animated, and said "You know black sand beaches? I play there all the time as a child." We determined that where she was born and where I had worked were sister islands, and that she had been longing to share the beauty of her childhood surroundings with someone before she died in the desolate, sterile atmosphere of an unfamiliar hospital. The staff had interpreted her urgent requests to talk of the blackness of sand as a bizarre rant, and her slurred speech hadn't helped her cause any.

My arrival on the scene resulted in a change in her demeanour almost immediately. She calmed down when she sensed I was going to be hanging around for a while, and that I was interested in what she had to say. Her previously escalating agitation appeared to have been driven by a need to have a particular kind of human contact before she died, and she lost no time in doing what she needed once she had found a willing accomplice in me. She took my hand warmly, and didn't let go as she tearfully and gratefully told me of her earlier memories as a child in St. Lucia, where she ran free on black sand beaches chasing the crabs into their holes; joyful on the rare occasion when one was caught, so that she and her friends could relish the sadistic pleasure of roasting it over a fire. Hearing her story moved me deeply, provoking in me nostalgic images of the West Indies when I worked there; recalling my own delight in watching children chase crabs on the beaches. It also brought back memories of the more carefree times of my own childhood. The contrast between the image she was presenting of a beautiful, joyful existence and the reality of her wasting away in this desolate place was remarkable.

Listening to someone's story like this seems to be quite an obvious thing to do, but it's not as effortless as it sounds. Aside from the fact that I had rarely seen a consultant hold a patient's hand before (why should that have been so uncommon?), and was allowing myself to explore new territory as a therapist, the experience of listening to the joys of her childhood was very painful for me. It was a poignant reminder of how life's cruelties can attack anyone at random – the tragedy of a young, beautiful, energetic human being forced to watch herself deteriorate and die alone in a strange country. Taking in her story was hard for me to bear, so I certainly could understand her medical staff's inclination to adjust her morphine drip and diagnose her questionable utterances as drug-induced psychotic ravings. But she was neither raving nor psychotic. She was simply struggling to share her happy memories which functioned as an anchor to help her get through the overwhelming despair she was experiencing. The need for her to share these memories as well as the tragedy of her circumstance was her way of assuring herself that she was not dying alone. To be in a hospital, surrounded by people taking care of her illness, did not provide her respite from her sense of aloneness, because what was needed was an experience of her knowing that she mattered to someone in this strange place. She needed to tell me her story, so that I could experience with her the beauty of her early life and thus could also truly know the tragedy of her impending, senseless death.

As she became assured that she was heard, and that I was reverberating with her affective experience of happy memory and present tragedy, she became quiet and self-composed, eventually becoming sleepy and told me she was ready to have a rest (apparently for the first time in forty-eight hours). When I left, she had nodded off to sleep, and I made a mental note to myself to see if rummaging through a few drawers that evening could produce one of the vials of black sand I had brought back from the Caribbean with me, so that I might bring it in the next day to show her. A few hours later I called to inquire about her, and was told that without waking up she had died.

Case 2

Years ago, I decided to look for a piano teacher in my neighborhood, and was lucky to find someone who lived quite close to me. Oddly enough, I'd never seen her around before, not in the shops, or on the street, or puttering around in her garden. She was rarely seen because she rarely left her house, and if she had, she would have been hard to miss. Weighing in at well over 350 pounds, I'd estimate, she was a "shut-in" who was likely ashamed to be seen in public.

Those pudgy fingers of hers worked like magic on the keyboard though. A skillful musician she certainly was, but she was also occasionally ironhanded as my teacher. She was often impatient with my aggressive touch on the keyboard – "You're a musician, you should know better than to poke and hammer at the keys, the sound has to be pressed and coaxed out of a piano" – but I learned a lot at her side, even if I was often quite uncomfortable. And there were several reasons to be uncomfortable, aside from her musical admonishments. First, there was the smell of her house. Although I prided myself in my younger years for being able to walk straight from the anatomy lab to the lunchroom and eat a hearty meal with the smell of formalin still on my hands (yes, I scrubbed; but I could never get the aroma to completely wash out until the next day), the smell of stale sweat could be quite over-whelming in a house where a body hasn't been regularly washed and the windows not opened for years. To add to my discomfort, there was the bulk of her; no matter where she sat in order to see what was going on at the piano, there was a lot of her, and her mass could be distracting. This was especially a problem when she tried to demonstrate something at the keyboard. I often couldn't move away fast enough to prevent some body part of hers touching me, and I could not and would not want to identify just which part of her brushed against me on such occasions. What I did begin to identify was the fact that some of that accidental touching was not unpleasant for her. It was hard for me to imagine her as a sexual creature, but apparently she was.

The piano lessons ended when I achieved the level I needed for my composition studies, and we terminated our work. As she didn't get around much, I didn't see her until a few years afterwards when she called me and asked to see me as her therapist. During our first consultation, she had a very interesting story to tell.

In addition to her piano teaching, she had been supplementing her income by tutoring highschool students. One particular student of hers was in an alternative school program and had so improved with her help that it was arranged for her to teach him for several hours every day. Eventually this student spent more and more time being tutored and that much less time at school; so he decided to study exclusively with her. She agreed, and his family was happy to have her on board as his private instructor, since he was doing very well academically for the first time in his life. However, if this boy's family thought that the fat lady would be sexually aloof with their son, they were mistaken. She and her student began to have an intimate relationship. What's more, since her sexual activities necessitated her taking off her clothes, her young boyfriend was eventually able to examine parts of her skin that she had been unable to see before. His exploration of her body turned up a very unusual mole. By the time she presented herself to a doctor, the tumour, a melanoma, had already metastasized extensively, and was now untreatable. She needed to talk to someone.

She needed to tell me that she liked men and sex, but her first serious relationship with a man had ended unhappily many years before, at a time when she was much slimmer – only a few pounds overweight. Her boyfriend at the time made a request of her that would change the course of her life. He asked her to lose ten pounds, and she was devastated. By this one question, he had shifted her sense of him as someone she could trust to love her and accept her for what she truly had to offer, to someone who would impose his self-centred agenda on her when it suited him. This was a repetition of how she felt in her relationship with her father, who adored her, but was also highly critical of her academic and piano work. She had had much experience defying and silencing her father by practicing poorly when she felt he was getting on her back. She responded to the boyfriend in kind, aggressively defying him by gaining weight. When he eventually gave up on her and left her, she was despondent. She ate and ate following that, and gained and gained. Vowing never to bother with men again, she had no difficulty warding off advances by shutting herself in and maintaining a weight where she lost all of her attractive physical features behind pounds of flesh. She fantasized frequently about being in love, but the distressing reality she faced every day caused her to drown her sorrows in large quantities of comfort food.

When love finally came to her in the guise of this young student, who admired her and took an active interest in getting to know her, she felt like a teenager again – heady with infatuation. She began to lose weight, replacing her compulsive eating with the sexual pleasures she'd been denying herself for years. Even though her boyfriend was fifteen years her junior, the two of them felt that they could make things work and they began living together. Shortly after that, he discovered the tumour on her back.

She told me: "There's something terribly ironic about this. I thought that I could protect myself by avoiding men, but it turns out that the love of a man could have saved me." There was little doubt that if she had been able to be more open about her body, the tumour could have been treated at an earlier stage, when it was entirely curable. Instead, the last time I saw her was when she came to me feeling pleased that she had ruptured a cyst on her neck, expelling a large quantity of dark, fetid fluid. "It feels much better, so that's a good thing, right?" It was all I could do not to gasp. She missed her session the following week, and when I called to find out how she was doing, I was told she had died.

Her telling of this sad story powerfully conveyed the tragedy of her choice to withdraw from her sexuality and the company of men. She had never resolved the problem of mistrusting men, which had originated with the knowledge that her father could never be satisfied with her. At the first taste of a boyfriend expressing dissatisfaction with her, she decided that the experiment with trying to be close to a man was over, and she withdrew into her own reclusive world where her trusted piano, food and books were always available when she needed them. I can assure you that as her psycho-analyst, she did not leave my care without adequately exploring the connec-tions between relationships past and present, but I know that's not what she primarily came for.

I believe that the clue to what motivated her to come see me can be seen every time I now walk by her house, and sigh. Even years after her death, I know that she would still be alive if she only had the ability to shrug off the insult of her first serious relationship and search for the love she needed. In that way she wouldn't have had to hide her sexuality behind layers of fat and loose clothing, and the tumour could have been discovered when it was easily curable through a minor surgical procedure. I miss her when I go past her house and think what a waste it was to lose this musical and passionate woman. It's at those times I think I know what she had come for: she had come to tell me her story in a way evocative enough that I would feel deeply and genuinely what she had felt about her situation. She knew that I had reverberated with her affective experience when we laughed gently together at the ironies in her life or were tearful together within her despair. In this way her truth could be told: that it was tragic for a girl who only wanted to be loved for herself, to shut down her own life and eventually lose it because she had given up hope of ever getting what she needed.

Nearing her death, she came to see me searching for some genuine acknowledgment that her fear of attachment and resulting avoidance of men had tragically destroyed her life, and that the kind of love that could have saved her had come too late. I am convinced that my knowing this and communicating it to her allowed her to feel less isolated in her death.

Discussion

At first glance the psychoanalytic treatment of the dying may seem to be a futile endeavour, but if therapists allow themselves to be informed and directed by what their patients want to do, it can result in the discovery of valid treatment approaches that can significantly change the ordeal of dying alone. Such a position is in harmony with *specificity theory* (Bacal and Herzog, 2003) where the requirements of the patient and the capacity of the therapist determine the optimal response of the therapist. This kind of intuitive approach improves the flexibility of the therapist who, not being constrained by any predetermined technical position, can engage in therapeutic actions that can be highly spontaneous, making use of the therapist's interpersonal strengths to make powerful, beneficial interventions.

It's important to note that sometimes only someone's analyst is privileged in having the necessary information to be able to effectively reverberate with that person's experience. In effect, our mandate positions us to do this, and mostly we *do* do it when we allow ourselves. I would suggest when we feel a powerful empathic connection to a patient, that this is a natural response to that patient's efforts, often through a compelling narrative, to elicit an empathic reaction in the therapist. What I am suggesting further is that we let our patients know when we have shared in their affective experience, to offset their feelings of isolation and loneliness. It is only when they realize that what they feel is felt by others, too, that they truly know they are not alone.

My apologies to those who might feel that the concept of affect sharing is embarrassingly sentimental. Actually, sometimes I might even be tempted to concur with you. However, I must emphasize that many of our patients search for these sharing experiences in the treatment setting, a phenomenon which can be activated simply by the presence of the therapist, whether he or she is comfortable with it or not.

The necessity of contact with others, by either physical touch or sharing feeling states, is something that we all need and cannot do without. Just as we know it is as basic a necessity for infants as is food, shelter and adequate hygiene, there is no reason to think that the need for this form of human attachment is any less necessary for adults. Thus, when we sense that someone is struggling to communicate an affective experience, we must consider the need for affect sharing, and on the occasion that we feel we are reverberating with a patient's feeling state, we might try telling the patient that it has occurred. This is just as applicable to the living as it is to the dying.

Conclusion

Affect sharing is a specific event that can occur within the analytic dyad, where the patient attempts to communicate a feeling state in such a way that it reverberates within the therapist, and the therapist suspects that he or she is feeling what the patient feels. When this happens, the therapist's communication to the patient that the patient's affect state has been felt may have a profound impact. I hope I've been able to demonstrate that when we are confronted with patients who are terminally ill, the ability of the therapist to share in their affective experience is essential. It can be the principal element in converting a tragic and lonely process of dying into one that is considerably more comforting and humane.

References

Bacal, H.A. and Herzog, B. (2003) Specificity theory and optimal responsiveness: an outline. *Psychoanalytic Psychology*, 20: 635–648.

Herzog, B. (1998) Optimal responsiveness and the experience of sharing. In H. Bacal (ed.) *Optimal Responsiveness: How Therapists Heal their Patients*, pp. 175–190. Northvale, NJ: Jason Aronson.

Spitz, R. (1945) Hospitalism: an inquiry into the genesis of psychiatric conditions in early childhood. *The Psychoanalytic Study of the Child*, 1: 53–74.

—— (1946) Hospitalism: a follow-up report on investigation described in volume I, 1945. *The Psychoanalytic Study of the Child*, 2: 113–117.

Suttie, I.D. (1935) *The Origins of Love and Hate*. London: Kegan Paul, Trench, Trubner.

Part VII

Insights from (and to) literature

Chapter 19

Lifetime and deathtime

Reflections on Joyce's *Finnegans Wake* and Beckett's *How It Is*

Olga Cox Cameron

This chapter will discuss the Heideggerian notion of *Zukunft* (time which is yet to come, which Heidegger sees as the home territory of human existence) in terms of Lacan's, and indeed Freud's, designation of anticipation as the temporal dimension of human subjectivity. I show the subversions and reversals of this time factor both in Joyce's great, last novel, *Finnegans Wake* (1939), the dream of Finn McCool, asleep beside the river Liffey, which has always fascinated psychoanalysis, and in the last prose work to which Beckett accorded the title "novel," *How It Is* (1964), with its punning, French name, *Comment c'est*/commencer, suggesting both stasis and inception. What I hope to engage is a particular relation to time as it appears, not in the entire work of Joyce and Beckett, but in these two last novels. What they have in common is a very particular relation to that dimension of time that we call futurity. In *Finnegans Wake* and *How It Is*, the future does not exist.

What happens to time if futurity is abolished? The philosopher Emmanuel Lévinas says of the future tense that it is the essence of all temporality. In *Grammars of Creation*, George Steiner (2001) forcefully suggests that the grammatical forms of futurity, which include subjunctive and optative modes, have been indispensable to both the survival and the evolution of human beings, confronted as we are "by the scandal, by the incomprehensibility of individual death" (p. 7). "Shall," "will" and "if," which, as Steiner (2001) says, circle in intricate fields of semantic force around a hidden nucleus of potentiality, are the passwords to hope (p. 7). More somberly, and indeed with definite elegiac overtones, the remarkable Canadian writer, Carol Shields, called her last novel *Unless* (2002), noting in its final chapter the bizarre leverage possessed by this small conjugation and sometimes adverb, a leverage which can prise open closed clumps of fact and, like certain other tiny chips of grammar such as "otherwise" and "else," can hold open the interstices of possibility.

Hope and fear, Steiner (2001) suggests, are supreme fictions empowered by syntax, as indivisible from each other as they are from grammar (p. 7). Could Lacan's notoriously lapidary definition of the unconscious as structured like a language expand this statement for psychoanalysis? Psychoanalytic theory is certainly not unaware that futurity cannot be thought of as something extrinsic to the psyche, but is in fact intrinsic to its functioning. This is easily seen in the writings of Lacan, but is also visible in a less systematic manner, in many scattered references throughout Freud's work.

From 1936 onward, Lacan inserted the concept of the Mirror phase into the theory of human subjectivity. During this phase, which occurs between the ages of 6 and 18 months, the baby whose sense of her own body is discontinuous and fragmentary, sees in the mirror an image of wholeness which is wholly anticipatory. In his later work, Lacan (1962) revisits and enormously complexifies the theorization of this first identificatory phase which is the birth of the imaginary, but continues to specify that its temporal dimension is a very particular type of futurity, that of the future anterior. In the seminar on Identification, he puts it in these terms:

> The imaginary subject anticipates the one he designates ego. It is the very one no doubt that the I of the discourse supports in its function as shifter. The literal I in the discourse is no doubt nothing other than the very subject who is speaking, but the one whom the subject designates here as his ideal support is in advance, in a future anterior, the one that he imagines will have spoken: "he will have spoken," at the very basis of the phantasy there is even a "he will have wanted."
>
> (Lacan, 1962, p. 5)

Normally we are unaware of the degree to which this future anterior underpins classical fiction. As literary theorists like to point out, the detective story, in which, classically, the detective begins at the point of the accomplished crime and meticulously pores over the preceding events in order to expose their meanings and, by the same token, the solution to the mystery, is the archetype of all story. The reader enters a series of happenings, set in a temporal sequence which is not simply a present which is already past, but one which takes all its colour, consistency and meaning from a future which precedes it, and which by virtue of this hidden reversal, sets in motion the entire teleological impetus of the story. In the classic novel, this hidden reversal functions as a starting-point, propelling formlessness into narrative.

Freud is less specific than Lacan on the temporal dimension of subjectivity. Nonetheless, in his 1914 paper "On narcissism," when he describes the coming into being of the ego as a moment correlative with the division of the subject, he too suggests almost as a throwaway remark in a small footnote that this is the point where the subject enters temporality as such: "I should like to add, merely by way of suggestion, that the process of the development and strengthening of this watching institution might contain within it the genesis of (subjective memory) and of the time factor" (1914, p. 96). Freud does not elaborate on what exactly he means by the time factor here. However, time as futurity constitutes a crucial element in his theorization of the Oedipus complex whose essence is that the subject must somehow cut loose from the first and immemorial loves of early childhood and seek fulfillment in a trajectory fuelled by this loss, impelled out and forward toward what T.S. Eliot has called "the unknown remembered gate" (1968, p. 59). The Ego Ideal, the more or less completed identity that represents the outcome of the Oedipus complex, is characterized as comprising both prohibition and promise. Prohibition of incest and promise of future fulfilment: promise of a desiring identity whose vital temporal dimension will be, as Lacan was later to point out, in the future anterior.

This narrative historical time into which we are inserted as desiring beings is, of course, only one form of time. It is this kind of time which is completely absent in different ways in *Finnegans Wake* and in *How It Is*. The American critic, Hugh Kenner (1962, p. 69), suggested that Ireland, as a colonized country on the edge of Europe, never absorbed the humanist world view which created very specific depths and shadows in our perception of space and time via perspectivism in painting and novelistic narrative time in literature.

Time does not pass in *Finnegans Wake*. In the text itself, Joyce describes his work as "1001 stories all told of the same" (p. 5). The structure of the novel is meant to be cyclical, borrowed from the eighteenth-century philosopher, Giambattisto Vico. For Vico, historical time was spiral, comprising three successive ages, the divine, the heroic and the human, followed each time by a ricorso, a return to the beginning. This structure is, however, not always discernible, though it does give the prepared reader a tenuous foothold in the text, as does also the faintly etched day's journey into night of the Chapelizod publican and his family. What the immersed reader actually encounters is a teeming overflow of riddles, puzzles, accusations, exculpations and innuendoes incorporating an enormous range of cultural, historical and linguistic reference, but circling around a relatively small number of half-told stories. In the text itself, Joyce, no doubt with sly intent, calls this process "cycloannalism" (p. 254). So, for example, there are hundreds of hostile encounters between two brothers who sometimes are named as Shem the Penman and Shaun the Post, but more often are either mythically amplified or farcically whittled down and can be: Jacob and Esau, St. Patrick and the Pope, the Ondt and the Gracehoper, Burrous and Caseus (Butter and Cheese) or the Mooksie and the Gripes. Similarly, there are more than two hundred references to another non-story about an incident in the Phoenix Park involving exhibitionism. Three men and two women appear to have been implicated but there is no clear access to the unfacts, as Joyce would call them, since they can be abridged to mere exclamation ("o foenix culprit") or merged into visual symbol, such as the Dublin coat of arms which depicts three flaming castles and two women with their skirts slightly raised. As the stories merge, so do the personages. One critic has put the question succinctly: "Who is who when everybody is somebody else?"

This circularity of content is doubled by circularity of form where the opening phrase, "riverrun past Eve and Adam's, from swerve of shore to bend of bay" winds the "meanderthalltale" (p. 19) toward an eventual end which will reach back towards this beginning via the most connective word in the language, "the," which, in turn, is appended to the most desolate and nostalgic of rhythms: "A way a lone a last a loved a long the." At both macro and micro levels, the entire novel is a pun on the city's name "Dubbelin." Locally, on a given page, this creates a kind of effervescence since puns, parody and rhythm push proliferating meanings through every phrase. Observers of our climate may enjoy the hurried flight of the pirate queen, Grace O'Malley, "into the shandy westerness where she rain, rain, rain." Those who visit our pubs at sundown know all about "the twattering of bards." Visitors will appreciate the transformation of Ariel's song into the anthem of the shopaholic: "Where the bus stops there shop I." The cumulative effect, however, is one of claustration, unease and the kind of stasis peculiar to nightmare where all forward momentum is blocked by a kind of churning pullulation and every attempt at exit becomes a running on the spot.

In a completely different way, all of Beckett's fiction is characterized by this absence of futurity. The novel under consideration here, *How It Is*, is written in three untitled sections. We gather from the text that these refer to "before Pim," "with Pim" and "after Pim." An obvious teleological structure appears to be in place, but only the hyper-vigilant reader, attendant to little else, will manage to inhabit this structure. The short, repeating prose stanzas are completely without punctuation. No sentence begins, no sentence ends. The syntactical structure is held together by the rhythms of the speaking voice, but only just. The ordinary supports of narrative, time, place and person have all but vanished. The opening stanza does not really begin anything since it is also a constantly occurring refrain: "How it is I quote before Pim with Pim after Pim how it is / three parts I say it as I hear it" (p. 7).

Beckett's previous novel, *The Unnamable* (1958), had opened with the questions "Where now? Who now? When now?" interrogating the basic categories of space, time and subjectivity. In *How It Is*, space, time and subjectivity are in a state of anguished dissolution. The voice speaks of "great tracts of time," with markers of identity, such as memory, images or wishes, all reduced to attributes which are or are not assigned to the speaker by some outside force in "this present formulation." For example:

> The wish for something else no that doesn't seem have been given to me this time the image of other things with me there in the mud the dark the sack within reach no that doesn't have been put in my life this time.
> (Beckett, 1964, p. 12)

Furthermore, the voice does not own what it utters. "I say it as I hear it" is a recurring refrain. In this wasteland of gasped, unfinished phrases and half-lit, unspecified space, one burningly intense memory, which is perhaps not a memory at all, but stronger than memory, surges up:

> next another image yet another so soon again the third perhaps they'll soon cease it's all of me and my mother's face I see it from below it's like nothing I ever saw
>
> we are on a veranda smothered in verbena the scented sun dapples on the red tiles yes I assure you
>
> the huge head hatted with birds and flowers and bowed down over my curls the eyes burn with severe love I offer her mine pale upcast to the sky whence cometh our help and which I know perhaps even then will pass away
>
> in a word bolt upright on a cushion on my knees whelmed in a nightshirt I pray according to her instructions
>
> that's not all she closes her eyes and drones a snatch of the so-called Apostle's Creed I steal a look at her lips
>
> she stops her eyes burn on me again I cast up mine in haste and repeat awry
>
> the air thrills with the hum of insects
>
> that's all it goes out like a lamp blown out.
>
> (Beckett, 1964, pp. 16–17)

This vignette is altogether remarkable in the text as a whole. From a temporal point of view, it is extraordinary in that Beckett has changed the narrative time without changing the tense. Like the rest of the novel, this little scene is in the present tense, but while everywhere else in the novel this tense is expanded into grey tracklessness, here it contracts into vivid specificity. Color, texture, sound, scent underpin the immediacy of this small scene. The speaker owns what he speaks, he does not quote and, most crucially, the scene ends. It is brought to a conclusion. Throughout the rest of the novel, no affirmation is allowed to stand, being either immediately negated or buried in panic with the single other exception of the ending:

> So things may change no answer end no answer I may choke no answer sully the mud no more no answer the dark no answer trouble the peace no more no answer the silence no answer die no answer DIE screams I MAY DIE screams I Shall DIE screams good
>
> good good end at last of part three and last that's how it was end of quotation after Pim how it is.
>
> (Beckett, 1964, p. 160)

As with *Finnegans Wake*, time does not pass, but weighs massively and oppressively. What the reader experiences is a trackless present, or rather a present crisscrossed with countless tracks that run only into and across each other. Time is a kind of seething stasis instead of a movement through the vicissitudes of the known into the variousness of the unknown, a movement ordinarily safeguarded by certain parameters of stability and identity.

In his 1919 paper on "The Uncanny," Freud spoke of how intolerable it is for us to have this teleological, temporal dimension blocked. He recounts an anecdote from his travels to illustrate his meaning. One afternoon he strayed inadvertently into the red light district of a foreign city and immediately endeavoured, apparently with a degree of haste and anxiety, to exit to a more salubrious quarter. Each foray, however, resulted in his once again finding himself back in the exact same location, filled with the "sense of helplessness sometimes experienced in dreams" (p. 237). This unvarying recurrence of the same suspends temporal flow, gluing the hapless tourist to the spot. He goes on to connect this to disturbances of doubling (or "Dubbelin," as Joyce would have it) which, in turn, he connects to intimations of death. This doubling (of action or of identity) which blocks futurity, this constantly being brought up against the impossibility of the new, the closed door of the "always already," familiar to psychotic experience, but not in itself psychotic, is a doubling which Freud describes as "the ghastly harbinger of death" (p. 235). What is abolished, in Freud's words, is something essential to our identity: "all those unfulfilled but possible futures to which we cling in phantasy, all those strivings of the ego which adverse circumstances have crushed and all suppressed acts of volition which nourish in us the illusion of free will" (p. 236).

A couple of years later, in *Beyond the Pleasure Principle*, Freud (1920) turned his attention to the boundless present of trauma, marked by what he calls "subjective ailment" (p. 12) where the repetition compulsion can function in the absence of the protective buffer which is the ego. Events recur with an eerie accuracy that seems to hold subjective intentionality in thrall and render it inoperative. What is pre-empted by this inexorable pattern is the possibility of the different, and the expansiveness of real futurity. The die is already cast. In this work, Freud opines rather hesitantly that time as we know it is perhaps a protective device, and then apologises for not taking this thought any further:

> Our abstract idea of time seems to be wholly derived from the method of working of the system Pcpt.-Cs. and to correspond to a perception on its own part of that method of working. This mode of functioning may perhaps constitute another way of providing against stimuli. I know that these remarks must sound very obscure, but I must limit myself to these hints.

> (Freud, 1920, p. 28)

The stasis of trauma, of psychosis and of death exists behind and outside of this protective layer. It cannot always be corralled into the forward flow of the great myths of recuperation which sustain so much of human endeavor. In Trinity College, the ninth-century Book of Kells, in a reprise of Horace, speaks inspiringly across the centuries of its task as that of "turning darkness into light." However, because death and pain exist, there are darknesses that remain dark, there is time which does not pass. Joyce and Beckett, in their different ways, open out this strange time for us. It is one of the signatures of our humanity to acknowledge it, along with the helplessness to which it can consign us.

References

Beckett, S. (1958) *The Unnamable*. New York: Grove Press.

—— (1964) *How It Is*. London: Calder, 1996.

Eliot, T.S. (1968) Little Gidding V. In T.S. Eliot, *Four Quartets*. London: Faber & Faber.

Freud, S. (1914) On narcissism: an introduction. *Standard Edition*, 14: 67–102. London: Hogarth Press, 1955.

—— (1919) The Uncanny. *Standard Edition*, 17: 217–252. London: Hogarth Press, 1955.

—— (1920) *Beyond the Pleasure Principle*. *Standard Edition*, 18: 3–64. London: Hogarth Press, 1955.

Joyce, J. (1939) *Finnegans Wake*. London: Faber & Faber, 1975.

Kenner, H. (1962) *Beckett: A Critical Study*. London: Calder.

Lacan, J. (1962) L'identification, unpublished seminar. Trans. C. Gallagher. St. Vincent's University Hospital, Dublin 4.

—— (1966) *Ecrits*. Paris: Seuil.

Shields, C. (2002) *Unless*. London: Fourth Estate.

Steiner, G. (2001) *Grammars of Creation*. New Haven, CT: Yale University Press.

Chapter 20

Acceptance of mortality through aesthetic experience with nature

Yuko Katsuta

In this chapter, I am going to focus on an ancient Japanese story. Though not a legend per se, it was written more than a thousand years ago. I will try to use it to stimulate my imagination and understanding regarding how death and separation appear in the Japanese ethos. It is not my purpose to infer some essential element of Japanese culture from examining only one story. That sort of generalization regarding a specific culture is always a huge trap. This chapter, essentially, presents the process of my personal quest to understand how we can accept life and death. I create my own view on this universal issue employing this Japanese story as a vehicle.

The title of the story is "Princess Kaguya" which, literally, means "Shining Princess." This story is very popular and is read by almost all Japanese children. During the past ten centuries, it has been transformed into several versions, so that it is virtually impossible to detect its original form. I am going to relate the most popular version because tracing the original or historical text is not relevant here.

Story line of "Princess Kaguya"

Long ago, an old man who made his living by collecting bamboo happened to find a beautiful baby in a bamboo forest. She had been placed in the empty space inside a stalk of bamboo. He and his wife named her Kaguya. Because they knew that this baby was not an ordinary human and they believed that she must be a transformed goddess, they raised her in secrecy, not exposing her to the outside world. From the day they took her in, the old couple lived in peace. Merely looking at Kaguya erased their worries. Kaguya grew up unusually rapidly to become a surprisingly beautiful young lady. Rumors about her beauty eventually spread, and many men asked the old man to let them look at her. He rejected each request, one after another.

The old man did, however, become anxious about Kaguya's future. One day, he confronted her and told her that she must obey the rules of humanity to live in this human world. One of these rules was to get married and have a

family. Her blunt response was, "Why do I have to do it? I don't want to."
Sensing his disappointment, she acquiesced, with one condition. She would
marry only the man who could fulfill her unusual requests.

Several men accepted the challenge. They were asked to give her things
that were actually impossible to obtain. She asked, for example, for a piece
of jewellery from around the neck of a dragon, or a particular shell found
in the body of a swallow, or a branch of a particular tree which has a gold
trunk and silver roots, or a stone bowl for Buddha in India. Some of the
men seriously tried to get these things; others employed a cheating trick to
create these things artificially. It was no surprise that no one could bring the
real objects. Some men ruined their social and personal lives by trying.
Others died suffering from the aftermath of the trial. Princess Kaguya was
relieved knowing she didn't have to get married.

Finally the rumor of her beauty reached the palace and the emperor
asked to see her. She declined, even though it was the emperor himself.
Eventually, she did agree to receive his poems, and so the emperor and
Princess Kaguya began to exchange poetry.

When spring came, she became pensive, weepingly looking upon the
moon. She told the worried old couple that she would have to go back to
the moon, from where she had originally come. She had committed a sin,
and so had had to leave the moon for a while. Now she was allowed to go
back. While she didn't want to go back because of her great attachment to
them and to the earth, she knew she could not resist her destiny. She could
do nothing to oppose the order of the moon. Emissaries would come for
her the night of the harvest moon.

During the night of the full moon in autumn, the emperor sent his
soldiers to fight against the emissaries. The couple kept her concealed in the
locked space deep within their house. These human efforts turned out to be
useless. The soldiers' spirit to fight failed in the face of these emissaries who
came down to the earth; the door to the locked space unlocked magically;
the couple could do nothing to keep her.

She left behind a bottle of potion for the emperor. With this potion, one
could have eternal life. After leaving it, she put on a robe from the moon,
which erased every single memory of her sojourn on the earth. Her pain of
separation was gone. However, everybody else was left with great pain. The
emperor ordered his servant to burn the potion upon the highest mountain.
It was burnt at Mount Fuji (literally, "Immortal Mountain"). Since that
time smoke and fumes have poured from its top.

Why does this particular example of separation resonate so deeply across
the years? This story can be read not only as a lyric tale, but also, if we take
in its latent content and symbolic metaphors, as a sublimated form of
dealing with death. With this fundamental reading in mind, I am going to
look into three significant dynamisms in this story. One is Princess Kaguya,
who is an idealized, alien object, ultimately lost. The second is the emperor,

who represents a human, and is the only person to take action in dealing with the psychic pain of separation. The third is Nature, represented by Mount Fuji. These three can be represented along a vertical line: Super-nature,[1] Nature, and Humanness. I will discuss how this linear structure reflects a Japanese attitude towards mortality.

Western versus Japanese *Weltanschauung*

Before discussing each component, it is worthwhile to examine the quality of separation in this story. We first see a separation between two distinct realms: the non-human and the purely human. This separation turns up in many Japanese folktales and legends. A non-human figure comes down to the earth transformed into a human female figure. A man is attracted to her. They live together for a while. At the end, she has to be transformed back into her original form and go back to her original world. The bond between them is inevitably cut by their respective destinies. The world to which each belongs is different, and this difference is too distinct and deep to overcome. Having no way to struggle with the alien Super-nature, the man has to give up his attachment and endure the pain of separation. It implies that the power of Super-nature is beyond human speculation and comprehension. Human will to change one's destiny is abolished in the face of Super-nature.

As Kawai (1989), a Japanese Jungian psychologist, notes this pattern contrasts diametrically with many Western tales. In Japanese folklore, plants or animals appear in the form of humans. By contrast, in the Western pattern, some magical power transforms a human into an animal who, in the end, is able to resume human form. The human fights against the evil magical power in order to get his/her own original form or that of his/her beloved. Typically these Western tales end with marriage as a conclusive union between the man and the woman. In contrast, Japanese tales, as "Princess Kaguya" shows, propose no union, but a deep chasm.

According to Plato's *Symposium*, Eros is the force innate in humans which "calls back the halves of our original nature together; it tries to make one out of two and heal the wound of human nature" (Plato, 1997, p. 474).[2] "Eros is the name for our pursuit of wholeness, for our desire to be complete" (p. 476). God divided humans into halves as punishment for their audacious attempt to ascend to heaven. Here we can see a Western triangle consisting of God, man, and woman that stems from Greek philosophy. We find in "Princess Kaguya" not a triangle, but a vertical line between Super-nature, the Human, and Nature. I will elaborate upon the meaning of this Japanese system later. Here, it is sufficient to say that union is not a theme in the Japanese system, because there is no lost unity from the outset. After all, these disparate entities reside in different spheres. The man is destined to be stuck on earth while the woman returns to the unknown sphere. Destined also is pain upon separation.

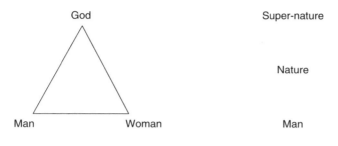

| Western triangle composed of man and woman | Japanese vertical line composed of Super-nature, Nature, and Human |

To illustrate the difference between the Western *Weltanschauung* and that of the Japanese, I will describe a Western version of an alien story. In Steven Spielberg's film, *E.T.* (1982), a child finds a lost alien, and they develop a strong bond. We can see a process of merging in the development of this bond (e.g., the boy gets drunk at school when E.T. consumes alcohol at home by mistake) which is ruptured by separation at the end of the film. At its climax, we see a trace of individuation in the human boy who has surmounted his pain of separation. Spielberg depicted the idea that human strength and love can overcome separateness without surrendering to destiny. The children challenge and push the limits of human capacity to make transcendence possible. E.T. tells the boy at their separation that E.T. will live in the mind of the boy forever. Through the course of interaction between the two, E.T. begins to reside in the boy's mind. The experiences with E.T. are internalized to become a part of the boy.

In my view, this is a beautiful story of developmental process. But it is a story between human beings, not truly between human and alien. E.T. as alien is assumed to react as a human does. Although E.T.'s appearance is weird, his mental and psychological make-up is fundamentally human. Remarkably, E.T. can even speak human language! In this optimistic view, there is no hidden or forbidden territory in the alien. Facing the alien, the human succeeds in integrating the alien who becomes more human. In short, the human wins over the alien. *E.T.* proposes the Western pattern: the human develops and gets vitalized by encounter with alien experience; the boundary between the human and the alien exists to be overcome. In addition, it must be noted, there is an underlining shadow of the parents in *E.T.* The mother is somehow unable to hold the boy, and one man plays a fatherly role, aiding the boy's development. In this vein, *E.T.* could be viewed as a story of becoming an individual, separated from the parents. E.T. represents the new experience as a gate toward society outside of the family. The new existence (E.T.) appears in the boy's life to be discovered and known.

The princess (Super-nature)

Unlike E.T., Princess Kaguya is detached from the beginning. She does not try to develop any emotional bond with humans. Because her separateness is a given, her ultimate separation is not separation in a strict sense: there is no truly intimate contact or interaction prior to the separation. Even with the old couple who raised her, she distantly withholds for years the hidden truth of her birth. She remains ever hidden, not to be exposed to reality. It is very difficult for people even to see her. Being human, people are eager to have a look at her and are preoccupied with fantasies of what she is like. They do whatever she commands to keep her. They are vulnerable and at her mercy. She destroys them emotionally, physically, and socially. Surprisingly, no man gets enraged at her harsh treatment! Everybody yearns for her. Even the majestic power of the emperor cannot uncover her. She remains invisible until the very end when she leaves for the moon. Although she expresses her pain at leaving the old couple, she herself makes no move to challenge her destiny. In this respect, she and humans are in the same position. Knowing they cannot challenge the will of Super-nature, they surrender to it. Kaguya leaves, forever obliterating every memory of the earth.

In my view, this is one of the most significant parts of the story, and the cruellest part. Remembering is left to the people as a task. The princess leaves for a world where there is no time dimension. Remembering requires a dimension of time. Only humans can remember. The people left behind are tormented helplessly by remembering her. In spite of her agony, we know that she will be free from it once she puts on the robe from the moon. It is cruel to know our beloved one forgets us; it is emotionally equivalent to being killed. We are not allowed even to live in her mind. Only humans mourn and must endure the pain of losing the princess. They remember her, knowing that they have been extinguished from her mind. Oblivion is such cruel treatment. Princess Kaguya can escape from the pain of oblivion. This, again, presents a striking contrast to *E.T.*, in which both participants keep living in each other's minds, and suffering can be shared. In "Princess Kaguya," we cannot expect this kind of mutuality. For this reason, I compare this separation to an ultimate loss, namely death. Human destiny is to face the loss of Princess Kaguya, to face their own psychic death, and to mourn the loss of her as well as themselves. These destinies cannot be challenged. In short, the human has to surrender to the will of Super-nature. This surrendering itself represents human destiny, though everything about its will is totally unknown to the human. Humans are precluded from knowing Super-nature. Enlightenment is not pursued. Humans stay in the darkness, ignorant of Super-nature.

After the presentation of the original form of this chapter, some colleagues asked if Japanese children, especially girls, tend to identify themselves with Princess Kaguya. The answer is no. Who can identify with a woman who is forced to separate from caring people? Children are attracted to her beauty and lyrical storytelling, but they do not want to be like her. They want to be like Cinderella or Snow White, who can marry a prince at the end. However, I know a Japanese person who wanted to be like Princess Kaguya. This man, who was in his late seventies, said, "When I die, I want to leave this life like Princess Kaguya while many people miss me." It is intriguing that impending death made him identify himself with a beautiful young lady. Perhaps he wished to achieve a form of immortality by living on in the minds of others and felt, in order to achieve it, he needed to transform concrete death into a purified drama of separation.

As I depicted, transcendent love is not the theme of "Princess Kaguya." Love, as one of the most basic human attributes, is dismissed in "Princess Kaguya." Love, as one of the strongest interpersonal powers to make us alive, has no voice here. Love, as a vigorous link with others, is overshadowed by the stern fact of death. We could say that Princess Kaguya is purely narcissistic: people are attracted to her on the basis of their own narcissistic choice; they suffer from melancholia as the outcome. In line with this assumption, we could say that the emperor's hidden aggression against her is expressed metaphorically by burning her gift. Although I do not dismiss these hypotheses, I read it differently. When we read Greek mythology, for instance, we usually do not analyze each character as if that character were a person, even though gods and goddesses are personified. Since I regard the "Princess Kaguya" tale as mythological, it is misleading to see the protagonists simply as people.

In my view, Princess Kaguya, deprived of any realistic female features, represents pure ideation. The moon itself has a strong character to make us ponder. It brings illumination to the darkness. It symbolizes the mysterious, the unknown, and untouchable beauty. Death is one of the most hidden territories beyond human control. It cannot be experienced while we are alive, yet its image haunts us, and we cannot be free from it. Freedom from death happens only when we actually die. However, I do not mean the moon represents death. Rather the moon is considered to be beyond the dichotomy of life and death. Not only death but also birth is an unfathomable mystery. The moon symbolizes death and rebirth, appearance and disappearance, going and coming. Above all, with its infinite, cyclic repetition, it tells time and gives a frame to time, the beginning and end of our experience. The finite lies within the infinite. The infinite conceives the finite. Life conceives death. And vice versa. This is beyond a simple dichotomy. The system of the moon remains unknown to the human. What we can know is that we are given a frame of time: the beginning and the end, namely life with its death.

Princess Kaguya comes from the moon. She is like a shining reflection of the moon on the water at night. We cannot touch it, or as soon as we try, it disappears in a whirl of water. The Princess is the shadow of death cast on the human. She so allures the human with her beauty as to swallow life. This allure can be fatal, but at the same time it gives a vital force to life. Life and death are intrinsically interwoven. Kaguya is found in the empty space inside the bamboo that, because of its rapid growth, is associated with the life force. Intriguingly, the shadow of death lies in an empty air pocket inside the living force. Death and its shadow lurk in the midst of life. She personifies the permeability between life and death. Because of her beauty and her attraction to the human, human attributes are enhanced: aspiration, greed, tenderness, grief, joy, and pain. All of the actions which people in the story take demonstrate the range of emotions. The princess extracts them via the fierce separation. As the humans die in Kaguya's mind, they experience painful reactions and despair.

The emperor (Humanity)

Consider a second component of the vertical line structure: humanness. The emperor plays a very distinct role. He renounces Kaguya's gift, the potion of eternal life. That he burns it says a life without her means nothing. By his action, he accepts mortal life. He could have attained immortality. He could have ascended to Super-nature. But he chose to be human with an act of will. Because of will, he is destined to die, but only so can he live as a human. His will is not used to make him free from destiny, but to transform his pain. He decides to stay with his memory about the princess. However, when he has deep pain, he turns toward Mount Fuji. He chooses the highest mountain, because he wishes the fumes could reach the moon. He wants to let the princess know his grief and pain. His action makes his pain everlasting, beyond his life. It is he who makes the humans' personal pain eternal. We, as descendants in the twenty-first century, are reminded of his pain when we see Mount Fuji. His grief lasts forever, making us remember Princess Kaguya. The process of remembering is to be passed across time. He chooses a mortal life, but wishes some immortality of his psychic experience, and moves toward Nature with this wish. Or perhaps he does not know whether he has a wish of immortality. He simply turns to Nature with his pain. I view this human act as similar to praying. To pray is a kind of meditation in which humans give themselves up and surrender to something beyond their power. Some pray with wishes; others with no particular wish. In either case, they give themselves over to a higher power. In the case of the emperor, it is not God, but Nature to which he prays. The emperor does not intend to make an eternal expression of his pain in the form of producing the fumes forever. The outcome of his act does not result from his intention. It is Nature that responds to his prayer by changing the mountain into a volcano.

Ghent (1990) distinguishes surrender from submission, defining submission as a miscarriage or perversion of surrender. He conceives that our wish to surrender derives from a "force" to growth and indicates our needs to be known, recognized, and penetrated.

> My hunch is that there is something like a universal need, wish or longing for what I am calling surrender and that it assumes many forms. In some societies there are culturally sanctioned occasions for its realization in the form of ecstatic rituals and healing trances.
>
> (Ghent, 1990, p. 218)

The act of the emperor towards Nature resonates with Ghent's definition of surrender. That might explain why the final resolution of the story has appealed to so many Japanese for over a thousand years. The dynamic interaction between the emperor and Mount Fuji gratifies our need to surrender.

Nature

The third component, Nature, appears in the act of the emperor. He joins his psychic pain with the mountain that is transformed into a vital force of Nature, a volcano. His emotion is not aggression in a narrow sense. Of course, his act of burning, and the transformation of mountain into volcano, easily remind us of aggression associated with fire and eruption. Indeed, Mount Fuji has erupted many times in the past to sweep away many lives. Mount Fuji as volcano can be lethal. Interestingly, Japanese readers react to the eruption in "Princess Kaguya" with little anger or resentment. We feel sad, but not angry. Is this denial of aggression? It is hard to imagine so. Elsewhere Japanese art eloquently describes aggression and resentment. The Japanese seem to have their own way of dealing with anger, and it would be worthwhile to investigate its nature. It is, however, beyond the scope of this chapter. Here, suffice it to say that we can hardly see a sign of overt aggression in "Princess Kaguya." Deprivation of an idealized beauty brings about strong pain without provoking anger.

This lost aspiration leaves amorphous affects, from which aggression could be generated. The emperor, however, renders his formless affects to Nature, and Nature creates a volcano and fumes. We do not see any transmutative process in his individual psyche, not to mention a process of reflection with words (though he made a poem before burning the potion). Nature functions as a bridge between the known human sphere and the unknown sphere of Super-nature. Nature processes only if humans call upon Nature. Humans are not supposed to elaborate or work through their suffering. What is required is calling upon Nature, and praying to it. Calling upon Nature is the same as praying. The notion of God does not exist. Nature replaces God. This version of "God" does not reign over the human. It listens to human prayer, grief, and pain. It gives back a shape of this indescribable experience. The emperor casts his feelings on Mount Fuji, and his affects are given a tangible shape. The important issue is that this shape must be created aesthetically. Nature manifests this aesthetic process. A visual image of a sovereign mountain and its vigorous fumes is an important product in this story.

All through Japanese literature, Nature embodies feelings. Not only feelings about Super-nature, but also any kind of feelings – from romantic relationships to small wonder in daily chores – take shape in Nature. In Japan, Nature is not overwhelmingly grand, but tender and exquisite enough to make us feel close to it. Its delicacy matches our subtle feelings. Japan is – or at least, was – rich in fine Nature. Unlike China, we do not have vast plains or gigantic chains of mountains. Among these fine natural assets, Mount Fuji is exceptionally grand in our view. Not only is it grand, but also it is holy and sacred. It is no wonder the author of "Princess Kaguya" calls upon Mount Fuji in facing the issue of death.

It is universal to associate Nature with the mother. It is intriguing to speculate that the emperor moves to the mother after feeling devastated by the other woman. He goes back to Nature when he faces death. Klein wrote (1940), "The poet tells us that 'Nature mourns with the mourner'" (p. 359). In this context, she regards Nature as the internal good mother. She wrote, "In the mourner's situation, the feelings of his internalized objects are also sorrowful. In his mind, they share his grief, in the same way as actual kind parents would" (p. 359). What we see in the emperor's action is exactly what Klein noted. But Nature goes beyond sharing his grief. As I noted above, it gives him back a transformed shape of it.

It is a shallow perspective to regard Japan as a male-dominated society. Japan is deeply mother-centered (not female-centered). I assume this is one reason why Christianity has not been deeply rooted in Japan. There seems to be a strong barrier against paternal structures in the core of Japanese culture. Even with regard to Confucianism, despite its great influence on the Japanese social system, its man-oriented quality could not shake the maternal bedrock of Japanese mentality. The bond between mother and child forms a basic thread as the ground as opposed to the patriarchal system as the figure. We cannot comprehend the intricacy of Japanese culture without grasping this double system.

Nonetheless, the maternal theme is completely absent in "Princess Kaguya." The princess is stripped of any maternal element, and the old wife is largely eclipsed by her husband. Instead, the mother appears in a form of Nature to hold human pain. It might be said that the author placed two facets of ideal female imagos, represented by Super-nature (Princess

Kaguya) and Nature. The man is subordinated to them. Given this context, marriage could not be expected.

Resignation, Buddhism, and immortality in psychoanalysis

I would like to explore the linkage between this priority of aesthetics and quiet resignation in the face of mortality. We cannot ignore the deep influence of Buddhism, whose discipline is detachment from desire. Although this subject was not discussed in this chapter, I would like to emphasize that "real" resignation in a tradition of Buddhism must not be a passive psychic attitude.

The issue of mortality and the human acceptance of it have been elaborated by many analysts. Here, I would like to refer to Kohut in particular. Regarding the acceptance of transience (mortality), Kohut (1966) wrote that, "Man's capacity to acknowledge the finiteness of his existence and to act in accordance with this painful discovery may well be his greatest achievement" (p. 454). He regards this achievement as "a shift of the narcissistic cathexes from the self to a concept of participation in a supraindividual and timeless existence" (p. 456). Kohut believes that this achievement "does not present a picture of grandiosity and elation but that of a quiet inner triumph with an admixture of undenied melancholy" (p. 458). This achievement

> must also be regarded as genetically predetermined by the child's primary identity with the mother. In contrast to the oceanic feeling, however, which is experienced passively, the genuine shift of the cathexes toward a cosmic narcissism is the enduring, creative result of the steadfast activities of an autonomous ego, and only very few are able to attain it.
>
> (Kohut, 1966, p. 456)

Kohut's description, in my view, strongly resonates with the Buddhist version of enlightenment. However, I do not see in "Princess Kaguya" any flavour of his "cosmic narcissism" as a transcendent achievement. What we find is not a resolute quietness but an ephemeral beauty. The Japanese seem to have a great preference for ephemera. Japan has modified and created her own Buddhism in which resignation is blended with aesthetic appreciation of ephemera. Aesthetics superimpose religion and ethics in Japan. As Kohut (1966) wrote, very few people can achieve the active acceptance of mortality without producing destructive outcomes. For the majority, it is impossible. Introducing Nature as a maternal saviour and creating an aesthetic bond with it might be one way for the Japanese to ease the pain of mortality.

Summary

To summarize my perception, or shall I say, my fantasy about life and death in the Japanese ethos, first we pose a stern line between two spheres: one is the known, and the other is the unknown. Death belongs to the unknown. We do not dare to challenge its territory. We let it be what it is, and it lets us be who we are. Nonetheless, we notice this boundary is actually very fuzzy. Life and death are interwoven in a very subtle way, and we tend to appreciate this ambiguity. We even think it savage and uncultivated to force a distinction between the two. Demarcation of the two would bring about enlightenment, and would reduce the fear of death by enlarging the territory of life as we can see in modern medical development. "Princess Kaguya" chooses ambiguity rather than enlightenment.

The princess represents the shadow of the unknown (death) cast on the known, namely the human. She mediates between the two disparate realms. Aesthetic interaction with Nature serves to hold the ambiguity of the boundary. In Japan, we are fond of depending on aesthetics as a value system rather than ethics or morals when we contemplate how to live and how to die.

The Japanese, like many cultures in history, require Nature as a medium to relate with and ultimately accept Super-nature, which can be equivalent to destiny, mortality, and the unknown. Nature is visible, audible, and tactile with its smell and taste. This concreteness contrasts with the abstraction exemplified by God. Nature enables us to communicate with it through our five senses, and to contain and mirror our thoughts and affects. This link between Nature and human is associated with a libidinal bond between the mother and the child. We need to surrender to Nature, but not to Super-nature. Nature is supposed to protect us from invisible, harsh Super-nature. A mother-centered Japanese society resonates with this expected function of Nature. Aestheticizing Nature strengthens the bond between Nature (mother) and us (child), engendering our need to surrender to it.

Perpetual supplication to Nature and incessant need to aestheticize it may, however, be attempts to appease Nature in order to not evoke its dark side. Chains of volcanoes traverse Japan. Beneath the surface of aesthetically gratifying Nature, there is an uncouth, underground world that would destroy everything ruthlessly and bring relentless chaos. In this vein, aesthetically channelling despair may cover and obscure raw feelings such as resentment and anger. The Japanese have traditionally gravitated to the aesthetic experience with Nature in the face of mortality, and it seems to have worked. However, we destroyed Nature so devastatingly that we are now exposed to Super-nature with no medium. With little to soothe us in the natural realm, we live in a society where rage emerges in cathartic, criminal, and perverse acts of violence. How does this rage relate to the dread of mortality, the universal substratum of human beings? Without a natural and aesthetic creation of volcanic eruption, how would the emperor deal with his amorphous feelings toward Super-nature? I will have to depart from the aesthetic story of Princess Kaguya to explore the dark side of the moon, our own social and psychological tectonics of destruction. Meanwhile, I look upon the moon, imagining what Princess Kaguya was like.

Acknowledgments

After the original version of this chapter was presented at the Second Joint International Conference of Psychoanalytic Societies in Dublin, another version was published in Katsuta (2003, 2004). It is published here by kind permission of Jerry Piven, and will reappear in the second edition of his *Eroticisms: Love, Sex, and Perversion* (Psychosozial-Verlag).

Notes

1 I invented the word, Super-nature, eluding a connotation of Supernatural. What I mean is a frame or structure beyond natural phenomena and ultimately unknown to the human. It does not have to be mystic or enigmatic.
2 Here I use "Eros" instead of "Love," though the translation of the original Greek *Eros* is love.

References

Ghent, E. (1990) Masochism, submission, surrender. In S.A. Mitchel and L. Aron (eds) *Relational Psychoanalysis: The Emergence of a Tradition*, pp. 211–242, Hillsdale, NJ: Analytic Press, 1999.
Katsuta, Y. (2003) Love, separation, and death in a Japanese myth. In J.S. Piven (ed.) *Eroticisms: Love, Sex, and Perversion*, pp. 242–257. Lincoln, NE: iUniverse.
—— (2004) Love, separation, and death in a Japanese myth. In J.S. Piven (ed.) *The Psychology of Death in Fantasy and History*, pp. 203–218. Westport, CT: Praeger.
Kawai, H. (1989) *Sei to Shi no Setten (Interface between Life and Death)*. Tokyo: Iwanami.
Klein, M. (1940) Mourning and its relation to manic-depressive states. In *Love, Guilt, and Reparation and Other Works 1921–1945: The Writings of Melanie Klein, Volume 1*, pp. 344–369. New York: Free Press, 1984.
Kohut, H. (1966) *The Search for the Self*. New York: International Universities Press.
Plato (1997) *Symposium*. Trans. A. Nehamas and P. Woodruff. In *Plato: Complete Works*, pp. 457–505. Indianapolis, IN: Hackett.

Part VIII

Termination

Chapter 21

The long good-bye

Omnipotence, pathological mourning and the patient who cannot terminate

Rita V. Frankiel

Contemporary writings on termination make careful distinctions between two types of patient. One is capable of understanding that the analytic transference (the transference neurosis) is a kind of living or reliving in the analytic relationship. This type undergoes intense experiences that allow for significant insight, and the termination process often poses no serious technical problems. The other type is incapable of making that leap of imagination and/or understanding because of incapacity or defensive blocks (Novick, 1982; Blum, 1989). Because they insist that the psychoanalytic hours are *life itself* and that the analyst is a real (libidinal) object, the task of initiating and/or completing a termination process is often prolonged and problematical. Many of these treatments appear to be among those that end in stalemate (Glover, 1955). In this chapter, I will describe the ending of one potentially interminable analysis in order to contribute something to the deeper understanding of termination through the study of individual cases.

Overview

The patient is one of those who form a morbid attachment to a cruel, abusive, possessive object. I came to see this morbid attachment as a form of pathological mourning. Although this attachment is commonly a consequence of the loss of a loved one, it can also develop in response to extreme deprivation or abuse based on parental inaccessibility, seduction, narcissism or heartlessness. Shengold (1989) has called such parents "soul murderers." Their children often have had no way of learning to contain or discharge the overwhelming affects aroused by their suffering. Frequently, their unrelenting attachments to their abusive and depriving parents exist not only in psychic reality but in overt reality as well. Such adhesiveness indicates that psychic change, which always involves a rearrangement of relations to internal objects, has become charged with an enhanced sense of peril. Healthy change and productive assertiveness are felt to be dangerous because they signify a break with the tie to the abusive other in the inner world. Suffering perpetuates the familiar relation to the abuser. Health breaks that disturbed relationship and leaves the patient feeling all alone.

A closer look reveals the following: in the face of overpowering object hunger, excitement, rage and terror, and without reliable objects to contain and give meaning to their experiences, children often fashion a fortress of impenetrable narcissistic invulnerability. They then manifest omnipotent defenses against recognizing or resolving their attachments. In the transference, their struggle against knowing and then resolving the relationship with the analyst sometimes takes the form of unwavering insistence that a special fantasy wish be granted. If that wish is frustrated, these patients may insist that the analysis is either unfinished or a failure. They engage in prolonged efforts to delay termination. How can they feel that their analytic gains have been sufficient if they have not gained the prize they crave? For my patient, that prize was the penis. Using clinical process material, I shall illustrate and explore these obstacles and difficulties in the patient's termination phase.

Omnipotence

Many of these patients create inner worlds designed to contain their overwhelming affects by means of identifications with idealized or bizarre versions of parental imagoes. Because for them, the outside world cannot be relied on to provide containment, their attachment to these images or to internal representations of their own minds, becomes the basis of their own containment and salvation (Corrigan and Gordon, 1995). The result is an almost impenetrable narcissistic organization (Rosenfeld, 1972; Joseph, 1982, 1983; Steiner, 1994).

Patients who have been raised in emotional deprivation, either because of object loss without suitable replacement or because their objects are unable to interact in containing and nourishing ways, make pathological turns toward their inner worlds. They use their imaginations to supplement the abuse and/or emptiness of their object lives in external reality. If they are gifted, they can create family romances that are elaborate and vivid. It has been observed both clinically and in more controlled studies (Eisenstadt, 1978; Eisenstadt et al., 1989; Pollock, 1989) that, as a group, writers, artists, and political visionaries have more frequently suffered early object loss than an unselected population. It has been speculated that the experience of loss can foster in the gifted the capacity to live productively in imagination. Shengold (1989) demonstrated the existence of certain repetitive themes in the work of Dickens, Kipling, and Orwell, namely retellings of childhood experiences of abuse, neglect, and overstimulation and efforts to hold the abusing adults up to scrutiny, blame and perhaps ridicule. In this, there is an effort to turn passively endured abuse into active criticism of the adult abuser. I found the same in the lyrics and libretti of W.S. Gilbert (Frankiel, 1985).

> My patient was this kind of person. In the initial phase of her treatment, she conducted her own analysis at night, thinking thoughts at home alone that she could not articulate when she was with me. She feared that if she were to associate freely I, like her mother, would label her mad. She reviewed her days in detail (including her analytic hours) in order to take elaborate precautions against expressing in action what she feared was her "mad core." She was trying to use me as the supervisor of her self-analysis. Other meanings that emerged in the analysis were the need for obsessional control. At first, control helped avoid loss of her inner substance in free associations; later she developed a fear of vomiting or diarrhea while on the couch so severe she sometimes had to interrupt her hours to use the toilet. Further elaborations centered on the wish to bind me to her in a state of frustrated rage and helplessness, as she was bound to her mother.

One basic task in ameliorating pathological mourning in the case of object loss is to bring into full consciousness hatred and ambivalence directed toward the lost object. This change facilitates a representation of the lost one that is real, lasting, with relatively full acknowledgment that he or she is gone forever. For the patient whose sense of psychic integration is compromised by such a recognition, implying as it does separation from fantasy objects that provide protection, this change amounts to a psychic death sentence. Weakened by separation from omnipotent protectors, they may fear that they will be overrun by their enemies and stronger psychic predators.

To schematically summarize the psychoanalytic view of mourning: it consists of gradual decathexis of elements of the relationship with the lost one combined with owning the full range of affects toward that person and, finally, identification. Freud was not satisfied that decathexis fully accounted for the terrible pain of mourning. Melanie Klein (1940) added to our understanding by proposing that in mourning after a death, the mourner must go through several painful stages before he or she can repair the inner world damaged by the loss and before the sense of being related to a whole, good internal object can again be experienced. In parallel with mourning after a death, when a patient is leaving the analyst and the analysis, he or she must feel in possession of an internal image of a "good enough" analyst – one who is neither idealized nor deprecated but is an internally represented, realistically seen whole object, an object that has both good and bad aspects but remains worthy of love. The patient will identify with the analyst at least to the extent of providing the template for continuing self-analysis.

Patients for whom early losses, cruelties, or inaccessibilities have been insufficiently resolved remain vulnerable to various pathological reactions to feeling abandoned or left: rage, detachment, defensive clinging, self-reproach, and denial that the object is permanently lost. An *incomplete separation* shields a patient from the full impact of an acknowledged loss. Patients who keep coming back at periodic intervals are sometimes described as those who "can't separate" from their analysts. I believe that this group includes many patients who have not brought out the full force of their anger at their lost cruel or unavailable objects. In their treatment they fear killing the present, loved, needed and hated transference object and so must return to be sure that the analyst is alive and well and has not been eliminated by their fantasies. Whenever we tend to excuse this incompleteness or overlook it, we find ourselves with an analysis verging on the interminable.

Steiner (1990) interrelates omnipotence, projective identification and the need to flee the painful stimulation toward mourning. A healthy projective process is flexible and reversible; constructive projective identification is the basis for empathy and compassion. One result of facing the ending of a constructive relationship is that each partner not only feels sad but also takes back into himself or herself some of what has been projected into the valued other. For this to happen, the patient must be able to tolerate twoness and not insist on omnipotently powerful oneness.

In primitive forms of mental illness (for example, pathological narcissism) intolerable parts of the self are evacuated into the person's object. Thus the person can rid him- or herself of hatred and envy, projecting them into the object. Persons who feel that their inner world is poisonous and destructive often project their goodness and creativity into others, for preservation and safekeeping. These processes are not conscious. These, too, must be reinternalized for mourning to be worked through.

My patient, who had been conducting her own analysis at night, wanting to use me as the supervisor of it, was working on an organizational project during a much later phase of her treatment. I discovered one day that secretly she had been keeping fresh versions of the back-up disc for her project in a storage closet in the vestibule of my office suite. The closet is considered by me and by most visitors to be private territory, although it is not locked. My patient disclosed a well-rationalized justification for this enactment. The closet was the only safe place she could think of. No place was as safe as mine. Keeping the disc in my closet allowed her to relax in the face of fears that her work would be filched and destroyed. On another level, this event developed further the theme of coercion: the patient often used silence and withholding of associations as part of her bid for power in our relationship. She feared being violated by my need to know her inner world. Once she even dreamed of surveying the content of my brain and eating what she pleased of my inner substance with a spoon. She wished to own my wisdom, but in a destructive way that terrified her. To have me, she could only imagine coercing or destroying me. There was no benign way for us to be interconnected. At first, the fact that she had inserted her disc into my empty space had no conscious sexual significance to her.

To be able to recover projected parts of the self, the person must first face the fact that he or she is different from that object. As soon as differences are acknowledged, point by point, he or she is in the process of relinquishing omnipotent control over the object. Steiner (1990) argues that this cannot take place if the person cannot mourn. In other words, in order to be able to relinquish omnipotent control over the object, the possibility of separation or loss must be accepted. The fantasy of being identical with the object is a fantasy of mastery and control, whether this is seen to emanate from the object or from oneself. In order to mourn, what must be faced is the difference between what belongs to the object and what belongs to the self, that is, what the object provides that one does not possess by oneself. It is necessary to reverse the earlier trend that aimed at possessing the object and all its valued attributes and denying the reality of separateness. This step will prove to be especially daunting to patients who must prove themselves and their object beyond the reach of illness and death.

Thus far I have been describing the desperation of patients facing the necessity of separating from their objects, yet feeling unable to allow the destabilization to take place. They live with the terror that if anything changes, and they move away from their sense of being the same as their objects, the disasters of death and loss will occur to either one of them or both.

My patient's fantasy of identity with her objects was so compelling to the patient that when her mother developed a senile dementia, the patient was convinced that she too was losing her capacity to think, plan and remember. Her refusal to tolerate the idea that their fates were different led repeatedly to our working on the way this fixation blocked any development of relatedness to other objects in her life, including me. Progress took place with what felt like the rate of growth of a stone. When the patient, who was homosexual, discovered that I was married, she was enraged and inconsolable. The sense of violation of our union by a phallic male led her to feel defeated and enraged. She was forced to notice that I had a life she did not know about, and this humiliated her and sent her into a massive withdrawal. She rapidly gained twenty pounds, bitterly trying to compensate herself for what she had lost, and barely communicated with me for many months.

No two patients or treatments are in all ways alike and, perforce, no two terminations will ever be the same. Once termination is mentioned seriously and patients begin to press in earnest for gratification of one or more unconscious or preconscious transference fantasies, the analyst has to face whatever guilty feeling he or she may be prone to; it may be guilt over not having done enough, or done well enough, or whatever else reinforces fantasies of incompleteness and inferiority in doing one's work.

Also to be noted is the fact that the most significant fantasy about the analysis being incomplete may not necessarily be one that has been worked on or even mentioned before. In apparently interminable analyses, patients try to stay on in a clinging and perhaps superstitious way; they continue to find crises that they are certain justify postponing a definitive parting. We have all seen negative therapeutic reactions as another way of trying to stay on.

Undertaking the treatment of such a person exposes the analyst to extreme feelings of uselessness. Finding a way to reach into such impenetrable narcissistic fortresses requires that we tolerate extreme feelings of isolation, failure and helplessness that these patients need us to experience and help them tolerate. An essential task of the analyst, especially with a more disturbed person, is to contain projected destructive fragments, and hold them until the patient is relieved of anxiety by the analyst's registering them and giving them new and tolerable meaning. "The patient is dependent on the availability of the analyst to act as the container and bring the projected parts and fragments of the self together and give them meaning" (Steiner, 1994, p. 60). This corresponds to the first phase of the depressive position, where what is essential is the continuing presence of the containing person. At this point, the *fear* of the loss of the object is primary and omnipotent control fantasies are the common mode of desperate interaction.

In the second stage of separation, the *experience* of the loss of the containing person is worked through. It is in this context that parts of the self that have been projected into the object are reinternalized or internalized in a stable way for the first time. These aspects of my patient's development in analysis will be described later in my presentation.

Case report

The woman who started out wanting me to be the supervisor of her self-analysis and who, much later, kept the back-up disc for her project in my coat closet, was a gifted, unusually intelligent, middle-aged woman. I was her fourth analyst. When we began our work, she complained of severe inhibition in achieving further success and creativity at work, as well as an inability to leave a destructive, sadomasochistic, homosexual relationship. Her relationships tended quickly to turn exploitative, and she felt she was often sitting on a volcano of inexpressible rage. She had been actively homosexual since adolescence.

Sexual exploitation and exploration began when she was 8. She had vivid memories of her experiences with her brother. These interactions usually culminated with my patient taking her brother's penis in her mouth. A view of herself as the abused, enraged, coerced, and unexcited participant pervaded her memories.

In the analysis, she was a silent patient – passive and intellectualized when she spoke at all. At first it seemed that she was enacting a nanny transference in which the analyst and the analysis replayed her extremely traumatic toilet training, begun before she was 1 year old. She held in what she had to give, and passively challenged me to force it out of her. But this was only the first level. She seemed to be in what, with John Steiner (1994), we would call a psychic retreat. She had a profound sleep disorder. She was staying up most of the night absorbed in two tasks: first, as I have already described, reviewing every event and interaction and thought of the day in order to inspect it for signs of madness; second, carrying on a self-analysis that was replete with free associations that she attempted to observe, analyze and interpret. In this we can see her effort to create an omnipotent oneness. There were not to be two roles, patient and analyst; she would be both. Later work on her need to control me completely emerged in fantasies and dreams. Clearly, she was manifesting a desperate, omnipotent and perhaps paranoid solution to major difficulties with forming a relationship with her analyst.

She dreamed repetitively of needing to relieve herself but finding every toilet she could get to polluted, filthy, and awash with excrement. It was important to find a way to show her that she also *needed* to have bad toilets so that she could justify holding things in. Of interest in this regard is that, in adolescence, she had practiced retaining urine with a masturbatory fantasy of total control.

The patient had been abused sexually not only by her brother but also, it seemed, by another relative as well, and she had been abused psychically by her mother. According to the patient's report, her mother had missed no opportunity to undermine and humiliate her. The patient was gifted in several artistic modalities, and her mother had been callous and careless to the point of complete irresponsibility with notes, drawings, and a set of letters that could have been the basis of a book.

Fifteen years after she began analysis with me, her father had died, the mother had advanced senile dementia, and my patient was a senior vice-president of her consulting organization. She was also the author of several as yet unpublished books in her area of expertise. She was sought after as a consultant for matters both large and small. She was, however, still in a desperate struggle to emerge from her omnipotent retreat, her seemingly unresolvable, hostile symbiosis with her mother, and her sometimes seemingly unendurable, frustrating relationship with me.

The process material that follows illustrates her adhesiveness to her objects and her obstacle to termination. I will sample her four times a week analysis in two phases. In the first, the patient had begun to talk about terminating, but no date had yet been set. We had spent much time in the analysis on the theme of her wish to have me all to herself, insisting that she and I commit to being lovers at the end of the analysis. Anything less would mean to her that I had contempt for her homosexuality. Among her themes along these lines was the idea that the reason that her life has gone as it has is because her brother got the penis, and because she doesn't have one, she will never get anything she really wants. Her acknowledged wish was that the analysis transform her anatomy; she was able to recognize that she had come for a penis. For long periods, her insistence on this was unrelenting.

A mid-week hour:

The patient enters looking more dressed up than usual. She lies down on the couch and, after a longish pause, begins, saying:

Pt: I am sad, desperate, in an unending struggle inside myself to be first – not second, not third. It is the only way to find love, to wrest love from someone who doesn't want to give it. Who feels you aren't good enough.

A: One part of you is an implacable withholding mother, persecuting the other part, that is desperate for love.

Pt: I don't understand. I feel if I give up the struggle with her it is the end of life. Just thinking about giving up on it makes me feel as if I am gasping for air . . . I don't know where you fit in all this but I came away with a very strong wish that my mother would say what she should have said when I was a child and was terrified of the doctor giving me a shot – soothing things like, "It's OK. It might hurt for a minute but it will be OK after a while." Even though I feel that if I separate from her, whatever that means, I will have no reason to live anymore, and I could fly apart.

A: You want me to say, "Not to worry" – when simultaneously you feel the mortar that holds your bricks together is this single-minded focus on her and getting recognition from her.

Pt: I am an animal in a trap. In my mind, like in the pictures, the animal sometimes chews a leg off to get free. Why don't I? I see two parts in conflict, in balance . . . but why don't I do something? (long silence)

A: Lately we have seen that addiction plays a part here. You are addicted to the trap.

Pt: My mother is the arch pusher of all time. She fosters that, and she and I are addicted to that addiction. I turn you into a persecutory figure in order to replicate that. In the past things that made me feel persecuted were the necessary forms of the treatment: Your not answering questions, not giving me information . . . my not having access to your mental processes and feelings, specifically about me. I live so much in the future: things will be better, things will be different. It is my habit to live in the near future: the pursuit of love, a fantasy of paradise over the next hill, paradise to be reached if only I can hang on and make myself more lovable.

We can see in the material thus far, the patient's tenacious grip on the bad object and her need to turn me into such an object in the transference. Most striking, however, is her full and responsible awareness of what is going on. Also, she was no longer making me the only responsible person in the room.
In this same hour, I announced a vacation. She was shocked and enraged . . .

Pt: (bitterly) Hair of the dog that bit me. The passion and life force my work represents so easily collapses into despair. Sometimes it makes me feel alive to be in a state of intense longing, but marred with broken-heartedness, suicidal feelings. If you were to ask what the analysis has done for me, on top of the list is saving my life. Now when I have suicidal feelings, it is just for part of a day. In the past, I was crushed by them, like Styron's descriptions of such hopelessness and fatigue at trying to go on. One of the things I am terrified of now is falling back into it. To revisit that material is terrifying. I have this fear of falling back into it. I don't think that's realistic at all. It is just the fear of going back into desperate territory. I was feeling a lot of that when I was involved with A (a former lover). I was with her, we loved each other but it did not stop the depression. My relation with her was a replay of the hair of the dog that bit me (referring here to her competition with her brother and with father for mother's love and approval).

A: Her husband and son were your rivals: here there is the vacation imminent and you have feelings about my husband that you do not mention.

Pt: It is a cycle, an addiction. On the other side is Death.

A: I think that what you fear on the other side is life.

Pt: Why would I be afraid of that? It is separateness that is my terror now.

In the next segment, we were closer to the ending of the analysis. The terror of separation had abated and it was possible to consider termination without total dread. In fact, she was engaged in an exciting project that gave her hope for a brighter future. A termination date was set; she would stop at the start of the new year. Since returning after the summer break, she had been as she was at the beginning of the analysis, silent and withholding. I had tried to take up her silence with her. One day she opened her hour by saying she is aware that she has ended the analysis in her mind in some way. She felt that she was without me, that when she came into the room, she was alone. I was not with her any more. Then she told me about an opera she had seen the night before, *Alice* (about Alice Liddell and Charles Dodgson, that is, Lewis Carroll and *Alice's Adventures in Wonderland*.)

Pt: In one scene, the girl is dressed in red velvet, and she is describing in double entendre terms the experience of being photographed as a young child, in very sexual terms. It is a sexual abuse, the whole set is red, deep deep red. It is blood, deep red, the inside of the body.

But very much a subtle set of allusions, what was done is alluded to and hard to get clear about, and what is more clear is how doubt-filled the incident becomes as one tries to recapture it.

A: Not unlike what we found when we tried to know what had happened to you (referring to her feeling that her father or grandfather had abused her).

Pt: I feel so alone now. I am overcome with feeling but I have no name for it, no way of capturing it in words, no way out of the alone state (a long silence).

A: When early things happen, excitement, overwhelming states, the little one needs a partner to make it make sense, by feeling alongside of the child and putting feelings into words.

Pt: When I was in elementary school, there was an Irish secretary, not the sort of person who could be counted on to understand or make sense of what I was feeling. When I was upset at school, when my stomach hurt, when I was feeling hopelessly alone, I used to go to her, but I never felt she really understood. I went to her but she wasn't right. I suppose I have to consider that I was doing something to not accept her comfort, but it doesn't feel that way to me. She was not right.

A: She may, indeed, have been a poor companion but you went to her, over and over. We should consider another hypothesis. Suppose that there were reasons not to feel really comforted by her, that in some way, you needed to feel she failed you. That it was more important to feel failed by her, than that she helped . . . (long silence).

Pt: When I was giving birth to Z, there was a nurse in the delivery room. I was in agony and she understood. She came to me and held my hand, and she said, "Why aren't you screaming?" I said, "I am, only it is all inside." All around me women were screaming for their mothers – that was the last person who could have comforted me. The nurse knew what I was feeling and she let me know: it was real comfort and support. Why can't I feel that here, now? (long pause). I am remembering another scene from the opera. He is photographing Alice, he is inside the still camera, covered by a huge black cloth, the lens keeps growing and growing and it begins to push into her body . . .

A: What does it make you think of?

Pt: It is a penis, of course, pressing into her. Taking her picture, violating her at the same time.

A: If I comfort you and you acknowledge it, I have the hard-on. Perhaps by being inconsolable, uncomforted, you keep the hard-on for yourself.

In this way, my patient had come full circle, bringing the phallic contest that she always lost in childhood into interaction with her unending grief over the penis she imagined she had and lost through some catastrophic castration that left her forever outside the world of success, love, and comfort. In a major sense, her analysis was a search for the lost object – her penis. Dream after dream of elusive jewels, almost found, always lost in the end, showed us how agonizing her deprivation was. In the transference, she returned over and over to her despair over my refusal to give her the fantasy penis she attributed to me. Ultimately, she needed to fuse with me to omnipotently control me, make me her container, and gain my phallus by refusing to fully feel she had my availability and attention as an analyst, not a lover. So both omnipotence and pathological mourning over her "incomplete anatomy" had joined together to make her unable to leave me.

Finally, she could acknowledge the contest she was staging between us. Then she was able to terminate.

References

Blum, H. (1989) The concept of termination and the evolution of psychoanalytic thought. *Journal of the American Psychoanalytic Association*, 37: 275–295.

Corrigan, E. and Gordon, P. (1995) *The Mind Object*. Northvale, NJ: Jason Aronson.

Eisenstadt, M. (1978) Parental loss and genius. *American Psychologist*, 33: 211–223.

Eisenstadt, M., Haynal, A., Rectchnick, P. and De Senarclens, P. (1989) *Parental Loss and Achievement*. Madison, CT: International Universities Press.

Frankiel, R. (1985) The stolen child: a fantasy, a wish, a source of counter-transference. *International Review of Psycho-Analysis*, 12: 417–430.

Glover, E. (1955) *Technique of Psychoanalysis*. New York: International Universities Press.

Joseph, B. (1982) Addiction to near death. *International Journal of Psychoanalysis*, 63: 449–456.

—— (1983) On understanding and not understanding: some technical issues. *International Journal of Psychoanalysis*, 64: 291–298.

Klein, M. (1940) Mourning and its relation to manic-depressive states. *International Journal of Psychoanalysis*, 21: 125–157.

Novick, J. (1982) Termination: themes and issues. *Psychoanalytic Inquiry*, 2: 329–365.

Pollock, G. (1989) *The Mourning-Liberation Process*. Madison, CT: International Universities Press.

Rosenfeld, H. (1972) A clinical approach to the psychoanalytic theory of the life and death instinct: an investigation of the aggressive aspects of narcissis. *International Journal of Psychoanalysis*, 52: 169–178.

Shengold, L. (1989) *Soul Murder*. New Haven, CT: Yale University Press.

Spillius, E.B. and Feldman, M. (eds) (1989) *Psychic Equilibrium and Psychic Change: Selected Papers of Betty Joseph*. London: Tavistock/Routledge.

Steiner, J. (1990) Pathological organizations as obstacles to mourning: the role of unbearable guilt. *International Journal of Psychoanalysis*, 17: 227–237.

—— (1994) *Psychic Retreats: Pathological Organizations in Psychotic, Neurotic, and Borderline Patients*. New York: Routledge.

Chapter 22

On the death of Stephen Mitchell
An analysand's remembrance

Rebecca C. Curtis

We will die if we do not create gods; we will die if we do not kill them.
(Mahmoud Darwish, Adonis, from *The Pages of Day and Night.*
English translation copyright © 1994 by Samuel Hizo. Reprinted
by permission of Northwestern University Press.)

The death of those with whom we are close is always difficult. It can be especially so when there is not an opportunity to mourn the death with others. Although family members, friends, and colleagues spoke at Stephen Mitchell's funeral and at the memorial service, no patients to my knowledge did.[1] My memory of Steve as my analyst may be not only interesting, but also useful to others who knew Steve as teacher, supervisor, or reading group leader, but did not have or take the opportunity to voice their feelings. Because he made such revolutionary changes in psychoanalytic theory, it also seems important to have some record of the way he actually worked.

I adored Stephen Mitchell with his keen intelligence, charisma, and powerful, poetic style of speaking and writing. Steve had made contemporary psychoanalysis palatable for me. Sullivan had done this for me previously. As I told Steve, he had some of the same sort of creativity and courage as the founders of the White Institute. Few others alive had a similar brilliance and passion for the work. Steve seemed to have views different from mine about certain subjects, however, and I wanted to be exposed to his viewpoint. Perhaps I didn't know enough. After all, I had never been in psychoanalysis. I was eager to have my beliefs disconfirmed. Or so I thought.

Early one morning in my analysis, before I began training at the White Institute, thinking about getting closer and closer to Steve, I expressed my concern that if Steve were to die – I was thinking in our old age when I no longer had any contact with him – I would not know about his death or his funeral. (I did not know about White's policy of phoning patients, as well as colleagues at the Institute. The Institute suggests that two colleagues know where to find a list of patients to be telephoned in case of the analyst's death or severe illness.) Steve simply took my fear as a wish for his death. This interpretation was not some Freudian relic, of course, or out of line, considering that I had earlier dreamed that I had sent the Mafia to kill him. I had been more focused on understanding that dream as killing off what Steve symbolized to me – true faith in psychoanalysis – or the negative aspects of myself I projected onto Steve. I still did not like that I could feel so close to someone, yet be excluded from the mourning of friends, family, and colleagues in a way I would be for no one else I would ever know. Steve did not tell me about White's policy, but focused only on my death wish.

Some years later, Steve mentioned that I had seemed annoyed at him when I had seen him jogging earlier that morning, as I often did. I told Steve that I was concerned about his health because his face was so flushed. Steve said something to the effect that I was wishing for his death. I told him that if I looked annoyed, I wasn't feeling that way – I was feeling frightened. Besides, I myself was running up the hill as he was running down. I was not feeling annoyed at Steve at the time, to the contrary. My father had died unexpectedly of a heart attack and he had never even looked flushed.

I adored Steve. I think that the intensity of my feelings can only be communicated in poetry. Excerpts from something I wrote toward the beginning of my analysis will give you a feel for my admiration of him. This was read in something of a tongue-in-cheek, teasing manner:

    In the Shadow of Daedalus Soaring

The tide was near the turn
And the day was on the wane,
When I sighted again in the far-off sky
That hawk-like figure flying
Above the sea, arms outstretched,
Gliding on the winds of his own creation –
Eclipsing the remaining light of the sun in the
    heavens,
There – the artist who has forged anew in his workshop
Out of the muddy quagmire of earth and water and
    teeming larval life
From whence we come
The new impalpable, imperishable being I am
    seeing now.

I have spoken to you for many years in the dark
    recesses of my mind
But did not know you could take on the form of another
    being

Who could hear my dreams
And, knowing well the perils of life's illusions,
Not tell me they would lead
To fiery consummation in the sun's blazing inferno
Or asphyxiated stupor in the ocean's watery grave.
Now, on the shore of this small island, dear Daedalus,
With liberty's torch, tablet, and broken chain only a
    boat ride away,
I, your shadow, look up
And, seeing you soaring there,
Know you're not an illusory vision only I can see
But, an animated artisan
Amusing earth's agnostics with your death-defying
    antics.

I was a difficult patient. When I entered analysis, things were going better for me than they had gone previously in my life or would go since. I wanted to obtain education in psychoanalysis and a personal analysis was one of the requirements. It seemed reasonable to me that I would need to experience something myself if I wanted to practice it. I told Steve that I wanted to become more creative and improve my relations with my husband and colleagues.

I got bored talking about the same things each session. Perhaps boredom was a defense against anxiety, but I soon realized I didn't want to change much. I was afraid of boring Steve and of his throwing me out. I had heard through the grapevine of someone he had thrown out and imagined it must be because she was boring. As I began to feel freed up, I would compose poems each morning jogging before my session. Together with my dreams, this would give me something new to talk about so I wouldn't bore Steve. Also, I found lying down that I remembered poems I didn't know any other time. There was something about being in Steve's presence that made me feel poetic. I hoped he liked poetry and assumed he probably did, but he never said he liked any of my poems. Here is something I came back with after a session in which Steve referred to his "crack-pot" theories:

Armchair Alchemy and Abstinence

When I awake on Friday morning
The armchair philosopher –
That modern-day scientist of the soul –
Is already sitting
At his workshop's drawing board,
Glasses on, tea cup steaming –
With planes, compasses, and straight edges waiting,

And Anthanor, his pot-belly oven,
Close by, heating the room
While he begins to tinker with a wingless flying
    machine –
Fitting together those fragments of facts and
    fantasies
Of human experience
Which are his stock and trade.
I, unseen within his walls,
Have been silently watching his secrets through the
    ages.
Now I beckon him toward me,
Urging him to touch this ivory tower's secrets.
Glimpsing a spot of dirt on the wall,
He begins to rub,
And slowly, the glimmer of an image of fingers and
    palm appears.
Then, more clearly,
Until, at last, a bas-relief hand grabs his tool,
And begins to chisel away vigorously at its wall
    itself.
A body emerges,
But, unable to attempt the impossible,
The eyes, still blind,
Await for life to be breathed
Into the unmoving limbs and lungs –
"Just one kiss,"
The Hermione-like statue begs.

No Magritte, this frumpy-vested feminist
Will no Galatea conceive.
Instead, he reaches for his elixirs
And, turning to his Anthanor,
Begins his own special brewing of organic-mental
    chemistry –
The analysis of elements,
The dissolution of the inferior –
Calcination, distillation,
Conjunction, coincidentia oppositorium,
Sublimation, and congelation –
Until, like Zephyr's fertile wind,
The vapors leaking out of his cracked pots
Quicken her nostrils
And her winged psyche quivers through that unseen door

Between idea and invention,
Between fantasy and flesh –
Through that mysterious opening of the human spirit
Between imperceptible passion and perceptible being
We call creation.

The armchair alchemist,
Still sitting by his Anthanor,
Feels the vehement forward rush of air-borne victory,
Pursing and moistening his lips,
He notices that his wall is in need of repair
And that his shutter has blown open.
Do I miss you?
Absence, felt strongly as presence,
Unveils substance,
And forever intertwined,
Space and form, both visible and invisible,
Become our essence;
Background becomes foreground
As we take brief glances
Through time's dark glass
Of existence conscious and unconscious
Till what is missed
In morning's mist
Emerges face to face.

I was inspired to write this poem by what I experienced as Steve's very classical style of working with me. He actually spoke quite infrequently, compared to what I expected from his writing. It felt to me like neglect or absence at times.

I also made up poems that I wanted Steve to write to me:

Desire

One day Intense Desire walked into my office.
She said she wanted to change my name.
She said she wanted to fly.
She said she wanted to read all of my books.
She said she wanted to know all about me.
She said she wanted my penis.
I told her no.
She said she would kill her.
I told her no.
She said she would kill Desire.

I told her no.
She cried.
Then she told me she would desire everything
And content herself with very little.
But have whatever fantasies she wanted.

Steve was very helpful in my relationship with my mother. I went from disdain to truly liking and admiring her before her death. This was attributable largely to Steve's feminism, I think. I realized that my father's subtle disdain for my mother and that of other men toward her served the purpose of preserving male superiority. My mother would express her often deviant opinion in a room full of men and they would think she was crazy. I, too, thought she must be. Steve told me that his uncle, who had emigrated from Russia, would say disdainfully, when his aunt spoke, "Who is that speaking?" meaning that women shouldn't speak at all. I began to realize that what my mother said was often quite intelligent, but different. I began to feel proud of her for speaking up in a room full of men and I began to identify with her, undoubtedly to many of my own colleagues' dismay. Steve's help with my relationship with my mother is something for which I'll feel eternally grateful. Overall I gained a great deal from my analysis with Steve. He was always engaging and I was always excited about going to my sessions.

Major points of controversy, however, had to do with Steve's beliefs about transference and psychoanalysis – beliefs that feelings I had for others were about him, that feelings that I had toward him were really toward others, and in psychoanalysis as the best form of therapy to the exclusion of all other forms of healing and psychotherapy. For example, Steve told me that he believed psychoanalysis was the best form of therapy for all psychological problems. Confronting him with the evidence regarding the superior effectiveness of behavior therapy for phobias conditioned by traumatic experiences without any particular meaning was fruitless. I fought with him "to the death," so to speak, about these issues and feel better prepared as a consequence to argue my own positions publicly.

In my subsequent therapy, I never said much about Steve or my analysis with him. On December 21, however, before I learned of his death, I told my therapist about the dream I had that led Steve to agree with my concerns that he was no longer being helpful to me. In the dream, I was an agent of the Central Intelligence Agency. Steve and I were in a hotel room and I had a gun in my pocket. Steve had done something wrong and I knew about it. I had this dream after seeing a film in which a naive, Midwestern type in the CIA ended up exposing the President and the head of the CIA for collusion with drug traffickers in Columbia. The dream was perhaps especially upsetting to Steve because I had discussed earlier in the analysis a dream about another Steve who was the most ethical person I knew. That dream I did think applied directly to Steve, my analyst, as well. Steve, to his credit, thought it was not appropriate for me to keep seeing him, given that I clearly was not finding him helpful. This did not end our analytic relationship, immediately, however. I was also writing an article he had requested for *Psychoanalytic Dialogues* and was also in his class.

After telling my current therapist about this that morning, I learned in the afternoon of Steve's death that morning. I had no one other than my therapist, my husband, and a few friends I could discuss my feelings with. I was not a close friend or relative, and if Steve had ever felt at all close to me, for obvious reasons, he hadn't told anyone.

All of us whose analyst has died have a story to tell. I know of little writing about this topic in the psychoanalytic literature. The literature I found that does exist, with one exception, is about the analyst or therapist telling patients about having a life-threatening illness (Kaplan, 1986; Firestein, 1992; Feinsilver, 1998). I think it would be useful for us to be able to speak more publicly about these feelings. A meeting of patients of a therapist who had died was suggested in an article in the *International Journal of Group Psychotherapy* (Rauch, 1998) and carried out. I spoke at my father's funeral and at my mother's and found it very helpful in the grieving process. I think that my comments here are helping me mourn the loss of someone as important to my psychological life as my own family members.

Somehow, the plan to speak on this topic at the Dublin conference on "Deaths and Endings: Finality, Transformations and New Beginnings" gave me a strength I didn't have before. When I wrote the abstract for the conference, I commented on how many people become more creative after losing a parent, but that had not happened to me. Somehow, mourning this loss and publicly acknowledging what Steve meant to me has now led to new creativity in living and in my professional life. The fervor with which Steve promoted psychoanalysis as the best way of understanding people and the best form of healing for everyone was too limited for me. Yet, somehow, in mourning this loss and publicly acknowledging what Steve meant to me, I have come to terms better with my need to kill what he symbolized for me and to create my own gods personally and professionally, in the tradition of Winnicott, Loewald, and the poets. Steve was a good model for such destructive creativeness.

During my analysis I saw Magritte's painting entitled *Heraclitus' Bridge*, a painting of an optical illusion where a white cloud creates the illusion that the bridge is incomplete and suspended in mid-air. Steve had two paintings of bridges in his office – a symbol of the connections made in psychoanalysis. At the exhibit, I purchased a book in which Foucault (1982) describes the world of the heteroclite – a world of disorder in which a large number of possible orders glitter separately. This concept seemed to symbolize the way I placed Steve's ideas side by side with mine in my mind.

In closing, I include what I wrote about Steve and I dancing across that seemingly incomplete bridge in Magritte's painting, across that river that remains the same while the individual elements change, and about the forces in the universe larger than the dancers and the dancing. This poem was written to Steve as my invisible dance partner. It conveys the sense of energy Steve imparts still, even though unseen:

Heraclitus and Heteroclitics

I hold your hand by the river,
With the bridge half-covered by a cloud –
Its reflection still seen in full.
From close by – yet far away –
Sensing the inner rhythms of existence,
My toes begin to tingle.

An invisible connection
Propels me –
Not illusion,
But a bond known only
By the way, all in white,
I dance with a dark force unperceived
In the blackness almost total
Except for my white dress and pearls.
Illuminated, I twirl and whirl,
And rise and float in the night.
Held firmly, an unseen mover turns me –
His presence only inferred
From my twists and leaps and spirals.

The Lord of the Dance watches,
And then strides forward on the bridge
Till he steps into that realm where one steps not
    twice,
But witnesses forever
The gay movements
All 'round from within.
We hear him laugh as he swims –
That master of pions playing in perceptual motion
Of life ordered and disordered,
Of patterns known,
But courses uncertain
In the eclipse of the night.

So tickle these,
These ivory keys,
With the fingers of our soul
Till others join the dancing –
Till toes and tutus twinkle,
And all of those
From paradise banned
See the heavenly protons prancing.
So tickle these,
These ivory keys,
On the soundboard of the sky.
Then take my hand and spin me.
Lift my waist high off the ground
And show the world my sparkle.

Rock with me
And roll with me
And waltz me over the bridge.
Pull me close and push me away
Throw me up and fling me –
Till collapsing, no breath left –
I step on the river glistening,
And laugh as the Lord laughed last.

So tickle these,
These ivory keys,
As the stars light up the sky,
And hear the laugh
As we cross the bridge –
"The Lord of the Dance am I."

Acknowledgments

An earlier version of this chapter was presented at the Second Joint International Conference of Psychoanalytic Societies, Trinity College, Dublin, July 26–28, 2002. The quotation from Adonis, *The Pages of Day and Night*, is reprinted by permission of Northwestern University Press. English translation copyright © 1994 by Samuel Hizo.

Note

1 Stephen Mitchell, PhD, training analyst and member of the faculty at William Alanson White Institute, New York, and New York University, was one of the founders of relational psychoanalysis and editor of *Psychoanalytic Dialogues*, as well as author of many books and articles.

References

Adonis (Darwish, Mahmoud) (1994) *The Pages of Day and Night.* Trans. S. Hazo. Chicago, IL: Marlboro Press/Northwestern University Press.

Feinsilver, D.B. (1998) The therapist as a person facing death: the hardest of external realities and therapeutic action. *International Journal of Psychoanalysis*, 79: 1131–1150.

Firestein, S. (1992) Death of the analyst: termination, interruption, what? In H.J. Schwartz and A-L. Silver (eds) *Illness in the Analyst*, pp. 333–340. Madison, CT: International Universities Press.

Foucault, M. (1982) *This is Not a Pipe.* Berkeley, CA: University of California Press.

Kaplan, A.H. (1986) The dying psychotherapist. *American Journal of Psychiatry*, 143: 561–572.

Rauch, E.H. (1998) A one-session memorial group following the death of a therapist. *International Journal of Group Psychotherapy*, 48: 99–104.

Chapter 23

On sudden endings and self-imposed silences

Ionas Sapountzis

I can still hear him, ten years later, walking in. I can still hear, ten years later, the total stillness in the hallway broken by the electronic "ting" of the elevator, an unmistakable sign that the door is about to open. I can still hear the hydraulic sound of the elevator doors opening up, pausing for a second or two and then closing, and I can still hear his hurried, awkward footsteps and his almost breathless voice as he was reading with increasing excitement the room numbers posted on the doors along the hallway: "five" step, step, "seven" step, step, "nine" step, step, "eleven" step, step, "fifteen" (there was no "thirteen") step, step, and then with an audible relief and relish "seven-teeeeeen" and then, a pause.

Slowly, the dysmorphic, oversized head of a 13-year-old boy would come into view, first the hair, then the forehead, then one eye, as if playing peek-a-boo with me. Then a smiling, utterly pleased face would appear at an angle and stay there, greeting me with such incredulous glee that made me feel like the most desired person on Earth. "Hi, Ionath," he would say haltingly and then, with a surprised exclamation after another pause that seemed to suggest excitement and incredulity: "You are here!"

I was there, at four o'clock every Friday afternoon, room seventeen in the basement of the university-based counseling center, sitting in the leather armchair next to the desk on which our usual tools were stacked: crayons, papers, one or two board games, various types of markers and little else. No clay, no construction materials, no toys – his stubbed, undeveloped fingers prevented him from manipulating them without feeling defeated. Ten years ago I was there, in room seventeen, waiting for Patrick. Every Friday after-noon around four o'clock, I would watch as the rest of him would slowly emerge from behind the wall, dressed in oversized Bermuda shorts, or jeans, and undersized, ill-fitting, poorly matched T-shirts or sweatshirts. I could see how uncertain he felt at exposing his disproportionate torso, his small legs, his short arms with the stubbed fingers. I would notice the awkward, somewhat out of balance, gait of a very conscious, 13-year-old boy whose deformed toes prevented him from having a steady gait, from establishing a secure footing in this world.

He would take his seat next to me, ready for our session that typically consisted of many drawings and squiggles and every now and then playing a board game, preferably the "thorry game." A voracious "drawer," he used the markers to draw pictures where everything was the opposite. The sea was brown, the earth was blue; the tree trunks were green, the leaves were brown; the apples on the tree were . . . "What is the opposite of red, Ionath?" before settling for a greenish-black. There was no "code," no set pair of opposites with the exception of the sun, which had to be black; the clouds which had to be blue; and the sky which had to be white. There were no people in his drawings because they had no color so no one could see them. No, they were not invisible, he explained, just people could not see them. One could hear them, though, if one would listen carefully, he reassured me, and maybe, just maybe, one could imagine them if he or she wanted to.

He would often ask for the "thilly thquiggle game" and he kept producing drawings that were not what they seemed to be: an airplane that was a submarine; a house that was a car; a face that was a foot. He drew a hippo with a thin nose, an elephant without a trunk, a shark that smiled. He kept on drawing, clutching the pencils and markers awkwardly with his stumped fingers, session after session. He kept on drawing the opposite, what could not be seen, unperturbed by the implausibility of his themes. In fact, he seemed to relish the opportunity to claim the opposite, to insist that the unexpected and unlikely could also exist if he wanted to. "Right Ionath?" my jovial iconoclast who expressed his defiance with colors and unrealistic images would ask, and then, with a wink, he would invite me to give him the next squiggly line.

He liked to ask me again and again, for my age as he was drawing. How old was I? How old would I be when he is 20, 30, 40, 50? He was asking, I felt, for some permanence, for a sense of continuity, and I took these questions as an acknowledgment that he valued our time together and he wanted to preserve it until he was 30, 40, 50.

I saw Patrick for several months. He would never talk about the here and now, the daily and the conventional. A boy who was very present in the room, eager to come, sorry to go, would never talk about school, friends, home, movies, games, favorite toys or TV shows and books. It was as if his life outside of the therapy room had no significance whatsoever, offered no promise at all. His life, it seems, had been a progression of relinquishments, a series of letting go of expectations and demands. School, friends, family, early adolescent aspirations offered no solace to him. Their deliberate omissions underscored the constant threat of humiliation that he experienced, and his sense of feeling incomplete and dysmorphic. He had withdrawn into a world where the opposite served not only as a means of expressing his defiance of conventional wisdom and aesthetics, but also as a potential space where he sought to create a playful moment and to assert himself in the nonexistent, in the never to be.

Why was his preventable calcium imbalance, a condition that affected his bone structure and resulted in a very irregular growth with some limbs being overgrown and others becoming atrophied, not detected until he was 2 years old, until the damage was irreversible and dramatic? Why were his current defeat and discomfort, and his benign and understandable rebelliousness not "seen" by his parents, as a touching and innocuous attempt to bypass the present and to deflect any attention from his deficits? Why were his poor handwriting and poor school grades emphasized as the only reasons why Patrick had been brought for treatment? Why was he seen by his parents as a lazy, unmotivated boy, and not as the depressed, resigned soul that he was?

I certainly felt a profound sense of sadness for this mother who, though she never expressed it, must have been ravaged with guilt. I certainly felt sorry for this mother who must have felt that she had contributed, directly or indirectly, knowingly or unknowingly, to Patrick's condition. She was destined to feel her sense of rage, guilt and despair more acutely as Patrick would grow older, as his physical deformities would become more pronounced and visible, more interfering. I felt sorry for how impotent and helpless this mother must have felt. She, like Patrick, could not discuss, nor contemplate, what had happened. She impressed me as a tragic mother who was raising a child whose intactness was terminated, in part, by what she felt was her neglect, during the first two years of his life. My sympathy for her, my reluctance to confront her, was undoubtedly strengthened by my antipathy towards the father, who had left the house several years ago, refused to pay for Patrick's expenses, and blamed her for his son's academic and social difficulties.

Patrick kept drawing his silly drawings that didn't seem silly to me or to him. Gradually, his drawings progressed from colorful expressions of his defiance, to somehow conveying how incomplete and outcast he felt, like the drawing of the half and half boy, half sad and rageful, half happy and merry. He drew amorphous, shapeless creatures like an amoeba, a sitting caterpillar with no feelers, a vase-face, a three-eared mouse, a jelly fish, a thick belly dinosaur, a bird with no feathers which he titled as "me," a shoe with a huge bow tie, and later, much later, a tree with bloodstained apples. He was drawing his life, his sense of lacking, of incompleteness, his sense of feeling deformed and castrated in the world.

Our sessions ended abruptly. I was waiting for him, same place, same room, same time. I heard the "ting" of the elevator door, the swish sound of the doors opening, then a pair of footsteps, hurried, determined, unmistakably different: there was no breathless reading of the door numbers, no sense of excitement and anticipation. His mother appeared at the doorstep. I could hear Patrick shuffling his feet behind the door, invisible from me, as his mother announced that she and her husband had gotten back together, that their reunion should help Patrick. They had decided to try for another child and her husband did not want to waste any money. They had to think of college after all. Without a pause or any trace of regret, she added that they had decided that this was the last session and that we should "wrap things up." There was no warning, no discussion, no consideration of what the sessions meant for Patrick, what Patrick wanted.

I was too stunned to express my incredulity as loudly as I would have liked. I became aware of trying to suppress my rage out of fear that I would become too inappropriate, that I would appear too wounded, too needy and vulnerable. I was also aware of how miniscule and invisible Patrick had become, shuffling his feet outside the door, smiling an empty smile at the opposite wall, unable to utter a word, to make any statement, to make any demand. What else could he have said? How could a troubled, depressed, utterly defeated 13-year-old boy find the words to confront his parents for their violent assault? He played the Sorry game again and again and smiled sadly when I remarked how sorry we both were. He reassured me, before leaving, that he would come back when he reached my age, when he would be 35 and I would be 58. "Right Ionath?"

What had happened? What happened? Why the violent ending? Why did it have to end in such a way that everyone involved and everything that was shared, became so denied and dismissed? Money was certainly not the issue. Nor homework, unless one wanted to forge it into an issue. One can, of course, point out that despite Patrick's eagerness to come for his sessions, there were no "breakthroughs," no carryover to school or home. But what was expected from a boy like Patrick? What did his parents expect? What was the reason why he was brought to therapy?

One can point to the parents' guilt and rage, their need to deny their reality. One can also point to their rageful hopelessness, their bitterness and need to disengage, to pull the plug so to speak, to end any illusionary expectations that they knew would never undo the damage that had taken place, would never restore Patrick to what he could have been. It was a way, perhaps, of saying that they could do nothing, that the "experts" could do nothing, a way of projecting the blame and their sense of impotence.

From a certain point of view, the abrupt ending spoke less of how "selfish" or "injured" his parents were, how inconsiderate they were in their desperation and knee-jerk resignation, and more of how much what I had to offer, what psychotherapy could offer, was of little solace to their pain, to their sense that his condition was irreversible, to their worry about what lay ahead. They had never accepted the loss, and words could never undo, or redo, what was done. Perhaps the mother understood, in an unconscious way, that the "homework" reason for referral was not a reason at all, just an illusionary hold onto some sense of normalcy that her child would never achieve. If Patrick were an A student, then one at least could find solace and reassurance in his academic achievements. Perhaps he could be a scholar, a scientist, Stephen Hawking, someone and something that would deflect the impact of his deformities, that would compensate for what he was not, and was not going to be. But Patrick offered no such reassurances. In his play and narrative, in his associations and drawings, he was always playing the themes of defeat and resignation, his sense of being different, incomplete, even repulsive. Sadly, in different ways, Patrick and his parents had all accepted that there was no hope, that what the future would offer was a constant reminder of how things went awfully awry, ten years ago, how much the past stunted the present and his future.

The violent ending left no room for further exploration of these thoughts and obliterated my efforts to establish contact, to understand. It was a denial, a violent dismissal of all that had transpired between me and Patrick. But for me, this was more than a denial. It was an assault on everything I believed and had tried to do, and made a mockery of my efforts, of what I valued and sought to become in my work. Worst, it rekindled countless times when I felt that the only option I had when faced with the fragility of my own parents who, just like Patrick's, could be not only irrational and overpowering, but also completely overwhelmed by their own inadequacies and defeats, was to deny my embarrassment, to numb my mind and soften my objections. Wasn't this what Patrick did in the hallway? Just like Patrick, who tried to soften the impact of his mother's destructiveness by regressing and avoiding making any demands, I would try to lighten my parents' load by becoming a self-less son, by silencing my reactions and by pretending that what they did, did not matter much. What else could I have done? What else could Patrick have done? A part of me regrets not asking Patrick's parents whether they felt embarrassed by their son's appearance, whether their discomfort and need to deny left him with no other option but to be childish, to deny himself. I certainly now regret not insisting to leave "things unwrapped," to not have a final session, to not participate in conveying the impression of a "tidy" end. But I could not even contemplate these questions and ideas then. I was still very much a self-less son, quick at repressing my reactions, at banishing any "improper" and "disrespectful" objections, at bailing parents out.

"Stations are all alike," remarks Italo Calvino (1979, p. 11) in his book, *If On a Winter's Night a Traveler*. Beneath their blurry or neon lights, their garbled, mechanized noise, their modern, colonial or dilapidated appearance and the constant shuffle of passengers coming and going, all railway stations are alike with the sense of departure that lingers long after a train has pulled out, and with the sense of the sudden arrival of a train that was not expected, its existence not known. All stations are filled with the same feeling of transience, whether one is arriving or departing, and the departures that linger long after the trains have disappeared carry within the expectation of a new arrival and of a new departure. Endings, like all departures, whether sudden or planned, smooth or abrupt, sad or happy, leave us with the poignant aftertaste of what was and is not anymore, what might have been but was never realized.

One could perhaps claim that one reason for the abrupt ending was that Patrick's parents were never committed to the treatment, never came to accept its necessity. Or, perhaps, that I was not a mature, confident therapist, that I was too timid and perhaps overwhelmed as a beginning psychotherapist to confront the parents. I certainly was. But what I regret most is how silent I became, how much I ended up not confronting the parents, and how in doing that I ended up silencing myself and contributing to the silence that characterized this family. Perhaps, there is a line between being tactful and silent, between letting go and insisting on not letting go, between confronting and allowing the irrational to be. But there was no fine line in this case, no room for tactful silence. One can argue that even if there was some room, it could not undo my sense of being nullified and dismissed.

Years later, I felt the same silence with Denise, a 10-year-old girl who reminded me so much of my daughter. I felt the same need to silence myself in order to not expose her father in front of her.

Denise was a girl whose exaggerated fears over perfectly logical and rather safe events that she could not control, like thunderstorms, a house alarm going off, the electrical power going off, and riding in an elevator, created a lot of commotion in her family, a family that was used to rationalizing fears away. She was the bold soul who dared to be afraid, who was not afraid to be afraid, in a house where everyone was terrified of being afraid and vulnerable, in a house where everyone acted like everything could be solved, smoothed over, and dealt with rationally. She was the lonely soul who insisted on expressing her fears, challenging the rationality that felt forced and contrived, challenging, in a sense, the family to visit their sense of failure and inadequacy, their sense of confusion and anger that they brushed aside with their perfectionism and manic reassurances.

The sessions went well, and unlike Patrick's case, there were many moments where the family felt touched and pleased to be involved in the experience. The mother cried for the sense of impotence and fear she felt when Denise was young, for not having protected her daughter from many early separations that were painfully mishandled, for all the missed moments with her daughter. The father did not report any regrets, but tried clumsily, yet touchingly, to be more engaged with his children, to lighten things up. During one thunderstorm, clad in his pajamas, he went out in the backyard under the pouring rain to dance – a stocky, stiff man who had never danced in his life – trying to prove to Denise that there was nothing to be afraid of.

But the success was moderate. Denise's symptoms did subside, the parents did notice a change and emphasis began to shift from Denise's fears, to the family's avoidance. But these changes and the many touching moments that were experienced in the room were not enough to offset their fears of being exposed, their discomfort with the uncertain. The sessions ended, conveniently as the school year ended, but I felt that the family's fragility, their fear of contemplating and tolerating the opposite, even Denise's anger, which fueled her anxiety, all these elements were only partially addressed. The father's panicky righteousness, the younger sister's flight to excellence, the mother's passivity and depression despite her professional successes, and Denise's conviction of her own badness, these systems were pretty much left intact. The sessions ended just as Denise was starting to express how rageful she felt – "like a caged animal," as she put it – over her parents' rigidity and shortcomings.

I did not know her final session would be her last until after it ended. In it, she insisted on playing hide and seek, a very difficult game to play in my small office that was awash with the light of a bright June afternoon, a very difficult game to play unless one is determined. She relished finding hiding spots in my room, hiding again and again, even though she knew perfectly well that she literally could not hide. She seemed to enjoy creating hiding places in a room that did not offer any, and seemed to also like being found.

We had agreed to meet for one more individual session and a family session before the family's vacation, and then for two more sessions after the break to sum up our work and determine whether to continue treatment in the following year. But as the father explained in the hallway, there was a confusion with their vacation schedule, and they had to leave the next week. They had no time to bring her for the next session. Instead, they would call me afterwards to schedule any additional sessions. But there was an unmistakable feel in the tone of his voice that gave me the impression that he could not wait to get out, to end the sessions, to close the book. He was, after all, the one who had objected to therapy from the very beginning. Unlike Patrick, who kept shuffling his feet and avoiding looking at his mother or me, Denise

stood there watching her father intensely, knowing very well – I feel in
retrospect – that despite the courtesies and reassurances, the family was not
going to follow up after they returned from their vacation.

Just like with Patrick's mother, I silenced my annoyance, fearful of
exposing the father in front of his daughter, fearful of making a scene and
acting "selfish." I had a lifelong training after all. Instead, I expressed my
understanding and ignored the voice inside me. I realize now that in not
expressing my annoyance and objections, in not listening to my unconscious, in allowing the father's polite explanations to exist, in not insisting
on scheduling follow up sessions, I had become as fearful and caged as
Denise had. Why did I allow this? Why did I allow my work, my presence,
my efforts to be nullified? Why did I allow this dissociated attack on linking
to exist? Why did I allow myself to be rendered immaterial and irrelevant,
as I had done so many times in my life when I felt coerced by the other's
fragility and intimidated by my own reactions? Who was I protecting
really? Was I protecting the father's narcissism and fragility? Was I protecting Denise from witnessing her father being exposed? Or was I protecting myself from my own persecutory demons and my internal objects?
Wasn't I, in suppressing my reactions and silencing my intuition out of fear
that I would be too destructive and selfish, acting like Denise? Wasn't I, in
identifying with Denise, also abandoning Denise?

I remember feeling that there was much more to the couple – as is always
the case. I was aware of several ghosts in the room that I kept at bay: the
mother's unhappiness, as evidenced in the dark circles underneath her eyes;
her sense of dissatisfaction; the father's rigidity and stiffness that obliterated
ambivalences and thwarted any exploration. I was aware of the father's
fragility underneath his rigidity, his tendency to feel easily threatened and
exposed. Both parents impressed me as damaged and fearful, and I, just like
I did with Patrick's parents, just like I did with my parents – my mother
after all had dark circles underneath her eyes too, and my father was also
very dismissive of anything that did not conform with his narrow view of
reality – did not argue, did not make what I was conditioned to regard as a
"selfish" statement. Wasn't my annoyance and rage, delayed until after
they left, my ex-post facto annoyance and rage so to speak, my self-
silencing, a "deja-vu all over again" experience, as Yogi Berra would have
remarked had he been my supervisor? And aren't the abrupt terminations
that are painful to me, if I look closely at what happened, variations of my
own painful theme, that of being rendered self-silent, fearful of my own
reactions, paralyzed by the toxic presence of a badness that I would so
readily introject?

There have been other abrupt endings that, despite their abruptness, do
not leave me as regretful. With every sudden ending, however, there is

always the feeling of sadness, sadness for the abrupt departure, for the ending of a relationship, for the denial that this act conveys. To some extent, all sudden endings deny the hopefulness that was present at the beginning of the treatment. I always regret the waste, the obliviousness at how wasteful clients' and parents' reactions can be, how obliterating and mutilating patients can be with their lives, how much they keep creating and re-creating the brokenness that has marked their lives, their broken relationships and experiences. These endings leave me wondering how futile words and deeds can be, a futility that I have been trying to offset all my life. Isn't that, after all, the task of psychoanalysis, the reason I, we, chose this profession?

But with Patrick and Denise it was how their terminations were staged that was particularly painful for me, that paralyzed me, and made me feel that any strong reaction of mine would be too destructive. I did not want to expose the parents in front of their children. In retrospect, it seems to me that I was reacting to their aloneness, to the orphan feeling that these kids experienced when faced with their parents' irrationality. I was identifying with the pain of witnessing the parents' fragility, a fragility I have been so familiar with, and yet I never fully understood until much later.

Didn't I, after all, at the age of 15, as I witnessed my father making a fool of himself on a beach on the island of Corfu, feel the need to protect my father, to protect myself, by starting a conversation with some bewildered and visibly offended tourists, informing them, as my father strolled away oblivious to the effects of his behavior, that my father had suffered under the dictatorship that had just ended in Greece, and that this was his first month as a free man, after a seven-year-long exile? Didn't I lie to lighten up, to deflect, what I was witnessing, and could not tolerate, and then conveniently forgot about this incident until now? Didn't I lie to protect my father, who always impressed me as a very lonely and troubled soul who could not tolerate any discourse? Didn't I lie to hide my embarrassment, to create another version of my father, that of a hero, to reverse what I was witnessing? Didn't I feel annoyed, embarrassed and betrayed by my father's shortcomings, a vortex of emotions not unlike the emotions Denise and Patrick experienced towards their parents, and didn't I also become protective of him, like so many children do, in order to preserve my links, in order to deny what I could not contemplate?

"How old were you when your brother died?" I ask, I finally ask, my father on the eve of his departure from his last visit to the United States. "What did he die from, what did you feel, do?" I insist to know, as I probe finally, at the age of 41, my father on and on, not satisfied with his flat, vague responses, his deadening enumeration of chronologies that were conveniently devoid of affect and personal meaning.

I knew that my father's 11-year-old brother (what was his name?) died from some kind of heart complication when my father was in his early adolescence. But I did not know, knew not to know, that once a week, every Sunday for a month and a half, my 13-year-old father and his mother made on foot the five-mile trip to the Children's Hospital of Athens, the Department for the Destitute, to see Riris, his brother, who had undergone an experimental procedure to correct his vocal cords. I can almost see my father, a silent confused boy, probably dressed in his only good clothes, and I can imagine his mother, a depressed refugee from the catastrophic war in Asia Minor, two refugees walking in silence through the streets of a city where they felt scorned and not wanted. Where was his father? What was my father thinking during the long walk? Was it during the summer or winter? Once a week they make the five-mile trip on foot to save the ridiculously cheap (but for them prohibitively expensive) fare of the filthy, dilapidated buses, only to be told at the gate of the hospital by the dismissive guard that Riris was in the intensive unit and they could not see him. Every Sunday they walk back without seeing him, with more questions than before, holding the small packages with some food and clean clothes for Riris. What were they thinking? What did they say? What was this walk like?

I can see my father standing there in his awkward preadolescence stance, in his well-polished, second-hand shoes, quietly watching, afraid to ask, afraid to notice, already establishing what I would later experience again and again in him, a background presence (Grotstein, 2000) of not asking, not observing, not seeking to understand, a mode of being and relating that followed him his entire life, and framed my relationship with him. I can visualize his mother, a young woman already marked at the age of 35 with a multitude of violent losses, feeling as an outcast, treated with suspicion and disdain, she who spoke four languages proficiently and was raised with aspirations and expectations that came to a sudden, crushing end. I can visualize the guard at the gate, cruel, dismissive and illiterate, full of a disproportionately inflated sense of self-importance that his uniform lent to him, telling them on their sixth (or maybe seventh?) trip, that Riris Sapountzis died four days earlier and was buried at the cemetery for the destitute, without ever having been visited or comforted by his parents.

What did they do? Think? How did they walk the five miles back? What did they do with the small packages of clean clothes and the homemade food? I am not asking any of these questions. I am too stunned, like my father must have been then, too stunned, like I felt with Patrick and Denise some sixty years later, too overwhelmed by the violence of the story, by the image of a boy, who at the time was not much older than my son is now, and a year younger than my daughter is today, dying alone in the hospital, without seeing his mother or anyone else, for a month and a half. Where was his father? Where was Riris buried? Where was that cemetery? What did they think? Do? What does a mother do when she learns that her little boy who could hardly speak, whom she had not seen for a month and a half, has just died, all alone?

I did not ask any such questions. Instead, I asked my father when did his father die? I knew that he died when my father was in his early adolescence, but I didn't know when. I was surprised, no stunned, to hear that he died six months after his son died. I was stunned to realize that throughout the years no connection was ever made between the death of his brother and the sudden breakdown and eventual death of his father. In a monotonous, flat voice, as if reading a passage from a book he was not interested in, my father reports that two months after his brother died, he and his mother woke up in the middle of the night in the little kitchen room where they all slept to the sight and sound of his father standing up naked on the edge of his bed, screaming with a contorted face, as he kept pointing to a spot on the ceiling, a spot that for him was filled by the sight of the Virgin Mary. He kept becoming louder and more incoherent, as he kept calling her in his incomprehensible speech, until the other tenants who lived in the other rooms intervened and the police came and tied him up, and took him to the psychiatric asylum thirty-five miles out of Athens.

They visit him once a month, my father and his mother, taking two or three or four dilapidated buses, trying the entire month to save for the fare, walking through the yard, he a frightened boy who never asked any questions, and a mother who had just lost a child, coming to see a man who once spoke fluently five languages and was now incoherent and kept mumbling with a contorted face, again and again, that his mouth hurt. That's all my father remembers sixty years later from the last time he saw his father. The dirty clothes, the unkempt appearance, the twisted mouth and the incomprehensible speech of a broken man whose gums were swollen and bleeding, and he could not look at him, hated looking at him, felt embarrassed by the state he was in. His father died several months later from unknown causes. They found out after his death, I never asked from whom and how, that at night, for many nights, his father was pinned down by several wardens and had his gold teeth ripped out from his mouth with pliers. As my father pauses and becomes silent, he does not display any emotion. He just keeps staring in space with a familiar, vacant expression.

Sixty-three years after my father's father was dying at the most wretched place in Athens, the infamous "looney-bin" at Daphni, his mouth swollen and his gums bleeding and infected without anyone doing or saying anything, my own father is dying at the most exclusive hospital in Athens, the "Therapeutirion Ygeia," in one of the three exclusive suites on the seventeenth floor which, like the Counseling Center at the university where I saw Patrick, had also excised the number thirteen from the building. There was no thirteenth floor, and no rooms that ended in thirteen. He is dying surrounded by all the amenities and privacies of a financially successful man, quite a contrast from his early years of poverty yet, still, very much a destitute refugee. He is dying alone, just like his brother and his father did, not in an asylum but in a luxurious suite, three rooms, two bathrooms and a foyer, unaware of what is happening, convinced that he only has a tropical virus, pinned down not by the physical grip of the wardens but by the grip of powerful tranquilizers – the modern suppression tools – which, as I learned after his death by one of the nurses, were given to him for weeks to make sure he would not be awake and lucid during the day while his assets were extracted, not by illiterate wardens with dirty pliers, but by his wife and an assortment of others, through an array of forged documents, false deeds, fake testimonies, threats and bribery. He has been denied treatment, his illness kept secret from him and me, until I find him, too weak and sick, without any assets, without even a single ID in his possession, unaware and cut off from any access to the outside world. I find him swollen and jaundiced, a shocking shadow of the imposing man he once was. His belated, partial realization of what is happening to him, what they were scheming against him, plunges him not in a fit of rage, as I for a moment had hoped, but in silence, the familiar passive silence that comes from the loss of words, from the inability to face the unthinkable. His loss of words is that of a man who is defeated, who has lost any spark inside him, who realizes, days before he dies, what a sham everything around him was.

I am not 10 years old any more, nor 15, nor 20, but 40, 41 to be precise, the father of two kids with whom I have tried to not be silent any more, and finally I refuse to be silenced, to be intimidated by the crooks who pray for and prey upon his death, despite their threats and accusations. I insist on being there. I sit next to him, listening to his heavy breathing, listening and responding to anything he might say or ask, trying to catch any flicker of a response, of this lonely, confused and resigned man whose dissatisfaction in life I did not understand until the very end, who inspired me to start this journey, to search for answers and for an understanding that he never dared to seek himself.

He wakes up, one of the few times he is lucid for a minute or two and tells me of a dream he had, a dream in which the voice of a woman was singing the French song, "Le Petit Matelot," a song his mother often sang to him as she put him and his brother to sleep, before disaster struck, before she herself suffered a breakdown.

He wakes up again with the memory of a boat, a boat at night that looks like the boat he, his brother and his parents found themselves on after his father lost his job and they had to head back to Athens. I have the image of him, he must have been 7 then, as old as my son is now, surrounded by a father in a state of defeat and despair, by a mother resigned in her depression, cuddled up for warmth next to his 5-year-old brother who could not speak, a destitute family again, refugees again, spending the winter night on the filthy deck surrounded by their few belongings, heading back penniless to Athens, to a future of misery and despair.

My father dies, slowly, quietly, and I am filled with a sense of waste at the silence that characterized our relationship, the fear of words, my fear of disturbing him, of making him see what was happening all around him. "Did you really protect him?" my wife asked me before I left for Greece to find out what was happening to him. Did I really "protect" him with my "tactful" silence, my inability to face the unpleasant, to utter the words, feeling pity and sadness for him? The answer, of course, is "No."

For a moment, I want a second chance, but like the nameless attorney in Camus' (1957) book, *The Fall*, I realize that, "thank God," it is too late for a second chance. Too late yes, one may say, but "thank God"? Well, thank God because I was not his father after all, could not undo what was done to him, could never, as a child, break the silence and loneliness that characterized our family when I was growing up. And Denise and Patrick? Thank God too? Maybe not. But the issue with Patrick and Denise, just like with my father, was not the sudden ending and my silent reaction, but the muffled beginning, the timid process, the fear that wove the background of our relationship, the waste that marked their relationships and was re-enacted in our relationship. If every ending implies a beginning, then the issue is not how silent and silenced I felt at the end, but how silent I was rendered right from the beginning, how quick I was to let go of myself and my presence, a silence and self-relinquishment that I have vowed not to repeat again. Psychotherapy is a process of elucidating omissions, noted Levenson (1995), and I did not have the presence of mind, the strength, to ask Patrick's parents what did they think of their son, who did they think he was, what according to them, were his struggles and fears? I never thought of asking Denise's parents what did they make of their daughter feeling like "a caged animal," why did the mother have dark circles underneath her eyes, and why did the father seem so frightened? I did not have the courage to emphatically congratulate Denise in the family sessions for her courage to be fearful, and to ask, to insist on asking why were the parents so afraid of their fears, that they had to deny them so categorically? It seems, in retrospect, that the regrets I had at the sudden and painful endings of their treatment were not due solely to the assault and narcissistic injury that I experienced, but also to the brokenness and waste that was re-created, to the reawakening of encapsulated experiences in my life that I had not been able to successfully integrate, to adequately mourn and thus, to overcome.

But there is hope, plenty of hope, not in an omnipotent remaking, but in the realizations that every ending has the potential of evoking in us. Patrick has promised to come back, and he might one day, as so many of our former patients do, as long as we stay around, because all the abrupt endings in the world cannot take away the fact that for several months we had a mutually playful and creative exchange, where each one felt wanted and eager to be in each other's company. I look at his drawings and I see that despite his stumped fingers, he was willing to paint, to express himself with colors, and I hope that one day, maybe it has already happened, he will start again expressing his life with colors, finding in the colors and in the rhythms of his brush a meaning and a glimpse of life that seems to escape from so many in this world.

Denise is an adolescent now, and I am sure she will slowly find the voice to express what she could not express before. Her parting game of hide and seek was a revelation and a statement, not only of our relationship and of her desire to be found, but also of how playful, articulate and engaging she could be in expressing herself. I hope that she still has fears, fears that she is not afraid to have, even irrational fears, and I hope that as she grows older she will realize that her irrational fears can be very rational indeed, especially if she allows the rage she has inside her to be experienced.

As for my father, there is the peace that I experienced after his death, the satisfaction and relief that I was present for him at the end of his life in a way I had never been before, the satisfaction that despite everything, we found a way to be in the company of each other at the end. In a sense, he is more peacefully present in my life now than he was when he was alive, for he was a maddeningly disappointing and disengaged man. My relief is also mixed with an achingly painful awareness of how much was wasted, how many moments we wasted, choosing instead to remain silent and to walk away, out of our inability to contain our fears. My relief and regret is also mixed with a deep sense of indebtedness, because he was also a decent man who, despite his limitations, has enabled me to live a decent life, and inspired me to become a writer. He, after all, always wanted to be a writer but never dared to become one, leaving himself forever dissatisfied despite his considerable business successes. I find a peaceful solace in the thought that before he died, he remembered his mother holding him as a little boy in her lap and putting him to sleep to the sound of "Le Petit Matelot." I find solace that his mother's voice came back, one last time, as he was going to sleep, and that for a brief moment, when he woke up, he smiled at the memory. He smiled again three or four days before he died, a day or two after he woke up with the sound of his mother singing to him. He smiled his last smile when he woke up and saw my daughter and held her hand and whispered to her, "ilie mou, ilie mou," which in Greek means, "my sun, my sun," and then wished her in a barely audible voice to be happy in her life, "nase eftichismeni ilie mou." I find solace that in the presence of my daughter, who is my sun after all, he was able to find a ray of sun before darkness claimed him.

I find some peacefulness that finally, at the age of forty-two, I was able to demand and claim, to insist on being present and alive. I find some solace that he died not alone as his father, his brother and later, his mother did, but in my company, that I was there to comfort him, to listen to the agony of his breathing as he faded away. I find some satisfaction that finally, after forty-some years, I have ceased being a Telemachus, waiting for a distant, self-preoccupied and troubled father figure to rescue me. I have ceased being a silent observer who loses his voice and presence of mind when faced with a silence that is expected and imposed on the Patricks and Denises I work with, a silence that I know very well and I cannot tolerate anymore.

I find solace that as a father myself, I have tried hard not to make my children feel burdened and silenced by my shortcomings, not to make them feel responsible for my failures and protective of my brittleness. Isn't this, after all, the silent promise I made many years ago over my daughter's crib, and later over my son's, and keep making to this day, as I tiptoe every night into their room before I go to bed, listen to their breathing, straighten their blankets and adjust the room temperature, the promise that I would not fail them? That I would not render them silent, that I would not embarrass them, that I would not make them deny themselves in order to protect me.

"In faraway and not traveled lands I now walk," wrote Elytis (1959). In this line from his poem, *Axion Esti*, one can locate a lot about our work with our patients, our own development, our willingness to search for answers, to give voice to the voiceless, to try not to silence the unpleasant, but instead, to seek to know. Aren't all psychoanalysts travelers in faraway and not traveled lands, searching for answers and meanings that create new images, new vistas? Aren't all psychoanalysts seekers of answers that enable them to become more present and aware in their lives and relationships?

How else can one work with patients like Denise and Patrick? How else can one work with their parents without feeling intimidated or paranoid, without becoming manicky, rigid or formulaic, without being rendered silent and avoidant? One has to be willing to search for the fears that generate other fears, the silences in one's history that impose other silences, the absence and the dissociated experiences that generate other absences and empty encounters, and leave one in a perpetual state of dissatisfaction and alienation.

There is a vast difference between the silence that denies and reduces, and the silence that enriches, the silence of the passive, resigned soul and the silence of the listener, the dreamer. One does not have to be noisy or wordy to offset the silence. One simply has to refuse the self-silencing that is imposed on him or her, however wordy or silent he chooses to be, as he or she continues to travel through life.

Postscript

When I presented this paper at the Second Joint International Conference in Dublin, my daughter was in the audience, a shy 12-year-old girl amidst thirty or forty adults who, I felt, was quite nervous at the sight of her father speaking in front of all these grownups and sought cover by drawing busily on the legal pad I had given her. We had spent the days prior to the conference driving around Ireland, talking, enjoying the country and each other's company. She did not explicitly know what the paper was about, but she had sensed that I wanted her to listen to the story of my father and how much his acknowledgment of her meant to me. The paper, I felt, was partly a tribute to my father and partly a tribute to my daughter for the emotions she stirred in him, a rather difficult and withdrawn man with whom I could get comfortable only toward the very end of his life. It was my story of course, my story as a child and now as a father.

I could not see my daughter's expression during the panel presentation, and she did not say much at the end, which, as I have come to know by now, is a typical reaction of hers when something has moved her. Later that night, as she handed me the pad, I noticed her drawings reflected our journey of the past ten days; a meticulous drawing of a horse and a scene from Ireland were followed by the drawing of a large bright sun, the size of almost the entire paper, that was turning into (or was being superimposed by) a full moon, and last, a large flower with a smaller identical one next to it and, on the other side of the paper, the outline of an empty one, one that had faded away and had lost its definition. The last two drawings took me by complete surprise. They seemed such a direct reference to the themes and metaphors of the paper, so articulate and evocative, that I found (like her) little to say. It became clear to me that she had listened, and that the paper had stirred in her the urge to express through her drawings the gratitude and sadness, the presence and absence that the memory of my father and his parting words evoked in her. Although she did not inquire any further, she had understood how much she had mattered to my father, and that is a memory I like her to have for the rest of her life. Not only for my father's memory and for her own experience of having mattered so much to someone, but also for my own need to come to terms with my father's loss.

References

Calvino, I. (1979) *If On a Winter's Night a Traveler*. New York: Harcourt Brace Jovanovich.

Camus, A. (1957) *The Fall*. New York: Vintage Books, Random House.

Elytis, O. (1959) *Axion Esti*. Athens: Icarus Press.

Grotstein, J.S. (2000) *Who is the Dreamer Who Dreams the Dream? A Study of Psychic Presences*. Hillsdale, NJ: Analytic Press.

Levenson, E.A. (1995) A monopedal presentation of interpersonal psychoanalysis. *The Review of Interpersonal Psychoanalysis*, 1(1): 1–4.

Part IX

Conclusion

Chapter 24

The transformative potential in the working through of deaths and endings

Lori C. Bohm

As this volume on deaths and endings draws to a close, let us take a moment to reflect upon the themes that reverberate in these pages. Many of the authors delved deep within themselves, sharing moving encounters with loss that have been the basis for personal transformation, albeit painfully won. Through work with patients both young and old, victims of public and private traumas, and through the analysis of literature, public memorials, and religious rituals the authors have presented a richly textured, contemporary psychoanalytic understanding of the significance and growth potential of working through the many losses of life. These diverse encounters with deaths and endings remind us of the essential nature of our bonds with others.

The psychoanalysts in these chapters suggest that the field has moved from Freud's original ideas about the role of detachment of libido from the lost object as crucial for successful mourning (Freud, 1917) to an emphasis on the continuation of feelings of attachment, but with the need to reconfigure internal object relationships as part of the mourning process. In so doing, not only are we able to repair the disruption to the inner self-object relationship caused by the loss (Gaines, 1997), but also we have the opportunity for further growth, as the loss is faced with all of its attendant ambivalences. As Slochower (Chapter 6 in this volume) notes, "The mourner's continued attachment to the deceased is not a pathological phenomenon but an integrative one."

Similar ideas about what is crucial for successful development through the life cycle have recently emerged from the work of developmentally oriented psychoanalysts. For example, an article on contemporary psychoanalytic ideas about the mother–daughter relationship notes that:

> The normal developmental thrust is not so much toward a kind of separation from mother that Freud was expecting to see as it is toward autonomy with connectedness. The connected feeling is not regressive; it is essential to . . . the feeling of mastery that supports autonomy.
>
> (Bernstein, 2004, p. 608)

Contemporary work on male identity development also repudiates earlier assertions that disidentification with mother is a cornerstone of healthy masculine gender identity development (Greenson, 1968). It favors instead a model emphasizing the importance of the young boy's continuing connection with his mother and her concomitant affirmation of his maleness (Fast, 1999; Diamond, 2005). If repeatedly reworking the relationships between oneself and one's most significant objects is crucial for healthy development, is it surprising then that reworking and reintegrating the representations of these relationships would be essential to growth following their loss?

Thinking about deaths and endings from the perspectives developed in these chapters, I am reminded of an essay by Thomas Ogden (2001) entitled "Borges and the art of mourning." In it, Ogden traces the life of Jorge Luis Borges, the illustrious Argentine poet. Borges' life was permeated by loss and by the sense of impending loss, as he was aware of having a genetic disorder that ultimately led to blindness in both his father and grandmother. After losing his beloved father, Borges suffered an accident that almost took his life. Later, he too became blind. This last loss was particularly significant because Borges handwrote his poetry in tiny, barely legible script, revising it multiple times in order to achieve the desired result. Thus, losing his eyesight meant losing his familiar way of expressing himself. He had to find a new way of continuing his craft and, indeed, of continuing to experience himself as himself. In the essay, Ogden reviews an elegy that Borges wrote for himself, entitled "Borges and I," in which he mourns the loss of his familiar self, and struggles to find a way to meaningfully continue to be Borges.

> An elegy, if it is to succeed as "Borges and I" succeeds, must capture in itself not the voice that has been lost, but a voice brought to life by the experience of mourning. The new voice cannot replace the old ones and does not attempt to do so; no voice, no person, no aspect of one's life can replace another. But there can be a sense that the new voice has somehow been there all along in the old ones – as a child is somehow an immanence in his ancestors, and is brought to life both through their lives and through their deaths.
>
> (Ogden, 2001, p. 152)

The "new voice," reflected in the title of this book as "transformations" and "new beginnings," comes about, our authors say, not by disengaging, decathecting entirely from the lost object, but by taking in and remaining connected to the lost object, making room for that relationship in one's internal life in an ongoing, though modified, way.

Complications in deaths and endings

In addition to offering wisdom about the keys to the successful handling of deaths and endings, some of the chapters describe impediments to that process. In each case, the possibility of creating or reorganizing an internal object relationship in order to permit full mourning is hampered. Aragno (Chapter 2) emphasizes the importance of symbolization as the prime mechanism for successful mourning, but in some situations, symbolization is difficult, if not impossible, to achieve. O'Loughlin (Chapter 7) reminds us that significant losses that occur before language develops and are thus presymbolic may be close to impossible to meaningfully mourn and integrate, leaving the person suffering the loss with feelings of ineffable, primitive dread and emptiness. Similarly, as Lobban (Chapter 9) and Weber (Chapter 10) note, receiving confusing, confounding messages from parents about a loss (e.g., that the child needs to be cheerful and not sad following the loss of a parent, or that the parent "lost" in a divorce situation is doing evil things) can profoundly interfere with the child's ability to develop. Growing up with a seriously depressed mother (the "dead mother" of André Green, (1986) and of the patient described by White in Chapter 5) or being prevented from acknowledging and processing the losses that come with being adopted (detailed by Kirschner in Chapter 11) may also have dire consequences when not therapeutically addressed.

In a different situation, when a young child loses a parent without ever really knowing him or her, such as in wartime, the bereaved may become a "perennial mourner" (Volkan, Chapter 3 in this volume). The loss is not worked through; the identification with the dead parent and the reconfiguring of an internal object relationship cannot occur. Instead, the individual may use external "linking objects," momentos, to cling to in the absence of first-hand knowledge of the deceased parent. In some cases, the mourner is able to use the concrete object (a photograph, a letter, a dog tag, etc.) to "modify their fantasized father representations, [making] such representations more realistic" (Volkan, p. 53), thus enabling the mourner to fully and productively mourn the loss and move on.

The significance of the termination phase of psychoanalysis

In psychoanalysis, the termination phase theoretically offers a unique opportunity for the working through of the loss of the significant analytic relationship, with its inevitable reverberations with other losses that have occurred outside of the consulting room. The chapters in this book focused on aberrations in termination, on patients who cannot terminate (as in Frankiel's case report in Chapter 21) or on therapies abruptly terminated (movingly described by Sapountzis in Chapter 23). But termination, like other endings, also has transformative potential. Loewald (1988) observed "that under the realistic pressure of the termination phase oedipal and earlier separation-individuation problems become more vivid and in a new way available . . . for mastery" (p. 162). In fact, termination may serve as a time to deal with a range of issues beyond separation problems that have not been fully reachable earlier, with a freshness and urgency brought about by being on the cusp of ending. For example, patients plagued with shame about needing and depending upon the analyst, who may have spent much of the treatment in self-sufficient denial of that dependency, will have to face these feelings of need during the termination phase. If the patient is able to weather the experience without precipitously or prematurely ending the treatment, the self-defeating belief that his or her needs are burdensome, greedy or destructive to those he or she needs may be transformed (Bohm, 2002). This is only one example among many of a situation where new growth may take place, even as the relationship is ending.

It is our hope that just as the creativity of this book's authors has been inspired by some of the more painfully moving experiences of their lives, the volume itself will inspire the reader to find new and transformative meanings in the deaths and endings they experience and bear witness to in the lives of their patients. We are all indelibly shaped by the people who have touched our lives. By reworking through symbolization these significant relationships, now lost, we may continue to develop and to provide opportunities for growth to our patients.

References

Bernstein, P. (2004) Mothers and daughters from today's psychoanalytic perspective. *Psychoanalytic Inquiry*, 24(5): 601–628.

Bohm, L. (2002) Shame about need and desire and the termination process. Paper presented at the Second Joint International Conference, Deaths and Endings: Finality, Transformations and New Beginnings. Dublin, Ireland, July 26–28.

Diamond, M.J. (2005) Boys to men: a contemporary perspective on masculinity through the life cycle. Presented at the Institute for Psychoanalytic Training and Research (IPTAR) Scientific Meeting, May 20.

Fast, I. (1999) Aspects of core gender identity. *Psychoanalytic Dialogues*, 9(5): 633–661.

Freud, S. (1917) Mourning and melancholia. *Standard Edition*, 14: 237–258. London: Hogarth Press, 1957.

Gaines, R. (1997) Detachment and continuity. *Contemporary Psychoanalysis*, 33: 549–570.

Green, A. (1986) The dead mother. In A. Green, *On Private Madness*, pp. 142–173. New York: International Universities Press.

Greenson, R.R. (1968) Dis-identifying from the mother: its special importance for the boy. *International Journal of Psychoanalysis*, 49: 370–373.

Loewald, H.W. (1988) Termination analyzable and unanalyzable. *Psychoanalytic Study of the Child*, 43: 155–166.

Ogden, T.H. (2001) Borges and the art of mourning. In T.H. Ogden, *Conversations at the Frontier of Dreaming*, pp. 115–152. Northvale, NJ: Jason Aronson.

Index